Theatre History Studies

2018 VOLUME 37

Edited by

SARA FREEMAN

PUBLISHED BY THE MID-AMERICA THEATRE CONFERENCE
AND THE UNIVERSITY OF ALABAMA PRESS

Manufactured in the United States of America

Template Design: Todd Lape / Lape Designs
Production by Publications Unit, Department of English, Illinois State University
Director: Steve Halle
Production Intern: Megan Donnan

Essays appearing in this journal are abstracted and indexed in
Historical Abstracts and *America: History and Life*

MEMBER
CELJ
Council of Editors of Learned Journals

Cover Art
Crowd to hear suffragettes, Oct. 28, 1908; courtesy of the Library of Congress, Prints and Photographs Division.

Cover Design
Todd Lape / Lape Designs

Please note: there was no issue published in 2013.

Theatre History Studies is an official journal of the Mid-America Theatre Conference, Inc. (MATC). The conference is dedicated to the growth and improvement of all forms of theatre throughout a twelve-state region that includes the states of Illinois, Iowa, Nebraska, Kansas, Missouri, Minnesota, North Dakota, South Dakota, and Wisconsin. Its purposes are to unite people and organizations within this region and elsewhere who have an interest in theatre and to promote the growth and development of all forms of theatre.

Theatre History Studies is devoted to research in all areas of theatre studies. Manuscripts should be prepared in conformity with the guidelines established in the *Chicago Manual of Style* and e-mailed to Sara Freeman at sfreeman@pugetsound.edu. Consulting editors read the manuscripts, a process that takes approximately four months. The journal does not normally accept studies of dramatic literature unless there is a focus on actual production and performance. Authors whose manuscripts are accepted must provide the editor with an electronic file, using Microsoft Word. Illustrations are welcomed and should conform with the instructions listed on the style guide on the website: http://matc.us/theatre-history-studies-4/theatre-history-studies-the-matc-journal.

This publication is issued annually by the Mid-America Theatre Conference and The University of Alabama Press.

Subscription rates for 2018 are $25 for individuals, $35 for institutions, and an additional $10.00 for foreign delivery. Subscription orders and changes of address should be directed to Allie Harper, The University of Alabama Press, Box 870380, Tuscaloosa, AL 35487 (205-348-1564, phone; 205-348-9201, fax).

Any single current-year issue or back issue is $34.95 each if ordered through the Chicago Distribution Center. (Please note: there was no issue published in 2013.)

Theatre History Studies is indexed in *Humanities Index, Humanities Abstracts, Book Review Index, MLA International Bibliography, International Bibliography of Theatre & Dance, Arts & Humanities Citation Index, IBZ International Bibliography of Periodical Literature*, and *IBR International Bibliography of Book Reviews*, the database of *International Index to the Performing Arts*. Full texts of essays appear in the databases of both *Humanities Abstracts Full Text* and *SIRS*. The journal has published its own index, *The Twenty Year Index, 1981–2000*. It is available for $10 for individuals and $15 for libraries from Sara Freeman, Associate Professor, Theatre Arts CMB 1084, University of Puget Sound, 1500 N. Warner St., Tacoma, WA 98416; (253) 879-2438.

CONTENTS

CONTENTS

CONTENTS

CONTENTS

ILLUSTRATIONS

Introduction

—SARA FREEMAN

In the field of theatre studies since 2016, many academic conferences have posted calls for scholars to look to theatre's past, present, and future in terms of protest, revolution, difference, discomfort, and otherness in theatre practices. Since the 2016 US presidential election, politics have been prodigious and unstable in ways that can only be explained by comparison to the build-ups to large cataclysms of centuries past. Where does theatre fit in these cycles? After a generation of political theatre seeming like a term of nostalgia, a concept of interest only to scholars and the people who were there in the 1930s or 1968, the timing of a special section focused on "Rousing Experiences: Theatre, Politics, and Change" seems even more apt than it did when Brian E. G. Cook and I began planning it. Cook's introduction to the special section details the patterns and disjunctions among the curated articles, which discuss work by artists such as Brett Bailey, Walid Raad, Rabih Mroué, Culture Clash, and Dario Fo and Franca Rame, as well as modes of performance employed in Mussolini's Italy, as a part of Israeli community and social movements, in the Anglo-American women's suffrage movement, and in pageants created by the African American community during the George Washington Bicentennial in 1932. As Cook points out, the eight articles included now address a very different world, one shaped by the Brexit vote in the United Kingdom and the election of Donald Trump as president of the United States, a world in the midst of a nuclear escalation between the United States and North Korea, an intensification of the renewed civil rights protests spurred by the Black Lives Matter movement, and crumbling senses of community and identity worldwide. Cook tracks the very theatricality of the outrages that populate news reports daily alongside case studies of theatrical events that roused different spectators and communities.

In this light, Noe Montez's Schanke Award–winning essay from the Mid-America Theatre Conference, in part 3, registers a powerful critique of a now bygone era, one that makes me wish we were still calling a system to account for not living up to its reasonably noble ideals rather than watching the gleeful violation of those ideals daily. Montez's analysis of Kristofer Diaz's play *The Elaborate Entrance of Chad Deity* names the unjust economic and social ideologies underpinning the Obama era that were not dislodged despite many hopes and efforts to do so, a failure Diaz theatricalizes in a story set in the world of the World Wrestling Entertainment empire, which happens to be one of the arenas where Donald Trump performed as a showman before his election.

In truth, the articles in this issue suggest to me that it is a very strange moment to be a theatre historian. Our sense of vindication about the centrality of performance analysis to understanding contemporary culture is fully consolidated. But equally urgent is the question of what we do when we engage the past. Historians are adept at understanding that appeals to past golden ages are mythmaking; there's no "great again" to get to, in America or otherwise. Past performances and performers also negotiated crucibles of political and social pressure, and their lives and creations reflect the interplay of technology, ideology, and theatrical reinvention. The four leading essays in this issue each revisit an artist, text, or event as part of prying open political and historiographical nuances, shifting the angle of vision on Meyerhold's politics, the role of props as avatars of science in English restoration theatre, true-crime melodramas, and visible onstage violence in ancient Greek theatre.

Stefan Aquilina's recovery of Meyerhold's complex significations of political resistance comes from reading the Russian director's techniques through the lens of Henri Lefebvre's theories about everyday life. Here, habits of the body and attitudes toward the regimentation of behavior matter a great deal to the political meaning of Meyerhold's productions. By contrast, Vivian Appler considers inanimate bodies—that is, props—as she investigates how Aphra Behn's farce *The Emperor of the Moon* synthesizes, critiques, and lampoons seventeenth-century scientific knowledge. Appler uses Bruno Latour's actor-network theory as a frame to help situate Behn as a significant female voice in Restoration science culture.

Kristi Good exhumes the documents of the real-life 1902 scandal around the Biddle brothers, who escaped from a Pennsylvania jail with the help of Kate Soffel, the warden's wife. Good tracks how contemporary newspaper reports crafted and reinforced turn-of-the-century expectations about ideal womanhood and feminine passivity. She then aligns that insight with the two plays created about Soffel's story, both early examples of the types of strategies now regularly employed on "reality" television.

Peter A. Campbell takes up the question of realistic staging in relation to ancient Greek tragedy, providing a dramaturgical and historiographical exegesis of scholarly commentaries about stage directions that may be nonexistent in the original, renderings of which always reflect the historian's and translator's assumptions and embellishments. He reopens the case of how the suicide of Sophocles's Ajax came to be understood as the exception to the rule that Attic theatre did not show violence and evaluates different solutions for creating the stage moment, all the while arguing that artists and historians remake the archive every time we attempt to reconstruct what the Greeks would have done with Ajax's suicide.

Theatre is an apparatus for seeing and knowing the world. It is also a way of refiguring memory and understanding and therefore remaking the world. The histories in this volume deal with the aesthetic and political valences of that double movement. This is some solid history in a time when nothing feels solid.

Part I

STUDIES IN THEATRE HISTORY

Meyerhold and the Revolution

A Reading through Henri Lefebvre's Theories on "Everyday Life"

—STEFAN AQUILINA

In the memoirs of his work with Vsevolod Meyerhold, the actor Mikhail Sadovsky wrote how the director "aimed at wrenching the spectator out of the familiarity of everyday existence, attempted to rip off his comfortable house slippers."[1] Ilya Ehrenburg, one of Meyerhold's literary collaborators, writes similarly: "Meyerhold hated stale water, yawning emptiness: he often resorted to masks precisely because he was terrified by them—and what he found terrifying in them was not some mystical fear of nonbeing, but the petrified vulgarity of everyday life."[2] Signaled in these quotations is "everyday life," a critical area of knowledge that steadily gained importance throughout the twentieth century. Within pertinent critical discourses, everyday life is now treated not as a trivial and undistinguishable domain, what "we routinely consider unremarkable and thus take for granted," but as "the basis of meaningful experience."[3] In this understanding of the everyday, daily activities such as walking, eating, and communicating become imbued with a sense of purpose that belies their repetitive and undistinguishable status. A crucial figure within these debates was Henri Lefebvre (1901–91), and the aim of this essay is to apply his theories to an evaluation of Meyerhold's place within the political and theatrical scenarios that developed in the first years after the 1917 October Revolution in Russia. This essay draws together for the first time the work of these two personalities, arguing that a Lefebvrian framework makes visible the tension between Meyerhold's support and critique of the emerging political status quo. It also repositions his aesthetic techniques and Biomechanical system as sites of body-based resistance.

The reading of Meyerhold's theatre through Lefebvre's theories qualifies this essay as an example of what Jackie Bratton refers to as "theorized theatre history," that is, an application of critical theory as a historiographical tool to challenge, partner, and ultimately interpret the historical content.[4] Theoretical framing within historical studies has recently given rise to some constructive debate. For example, Thomas Postlewait is wary of historical studies that are, to his mind, excessively rooted in theory, which becomes an all-too-restrictive channel that binds rather than informs: "There are…scholars who champion a reigning idea, derived from this or that theory. All events are illustrations of the theory, which defines the contexts and controls the interpretation."[5] Jim Davis, on the other hand, argues that theory is so ingrained in contemporary scholarship that it simply cannot be ignored; consequently, it is "far better to acknowledge the ideas that are influencing one's own opinions…than to assume naively that one is untouched by theoretical positions."[6]

This essay keeps an over-rigorous application of theory in check by identifying both congruencies and conflicts between Lefebvre and Meyerhold. In other words, Meyerhold's work will not always fit neatly within Lefebvre's theories, as the emphasis here will be less on establishing links between the two and more on contributing another layer to our understanding of the Russian director's work. In Lefebvre's theories, everyday life is a complex rather than straightforward phenomenon because it embraces "a wide range of tensions of contradictions."[7] A similarly complex picture of Meyerhold's encounter with the revolution will emerge here, wherein certain actions of his will be seen as directly supporting the new regime even as others already contained the seeds of confrontation and resistance. This clarification of Meyerhold's complex rather than straightforward placement within the embryonic Bolshevik state is the first result of applying Lefebvre's theories. It will be supported by several sources by Meyerhold that are unavailable in English translations. The English-speaking world has been slow to add to Eduard Braun's *Meyerhold on Theatre* collection, which remains the most popular source of Meyerhold's texts and therefore deserved a recent reissue. Though traversing the director's whole career, *Meyerhold on Theatre* collects only some thirty texts, speeches, and rehearsal transcripts, a fraction compared to, for example, the four-volume collection edited in French by Beatrice Picon-Vallin.[8] The Italian translations of Meyerhold's texts are also numerous, and it is those that I will use in my exposition.[9] I use these sources because they allow me to draw from an academic tradition that has been strongly invested in the heritage not only of Meyerhold but also of other Russian practitioners and theorists like Konstantin Stanislavsky, Yevgeny Vakhtangov, and Platon Kerzhentsev. This goes back a significant number of decades, and in many cases Italian translations of key Russian texts have preceded English versions.[10] Eugenio Barba, for example, dates Meyerhold's entry into Italian theatre culture to the early 1960s and hints that the Russian director's rehabilitation was never reverential but rich in critical analysis:

> Stalin had died in 1953. Three years later [the] so-called 'destalinization' began, and again it was permitted to write about Meyerhold. After a few more years the first important translations appeared. In Italy, at the end of 1962, Editori Riuniti—which was connected to the Communist Party—had published *La rivoluzione teatrale* (*The Theatrical Revolution*), a selection of Meyerhold's writings. A new cliché was created among theatre people which added a third element to the current schematic antagonism between Stanislavsky and Brecht. People said: 'Stanislavsky is bourgeois theatre; Meyerhold is the revolutionary.' But every time those who had worked with them spoke of them, these clichés crumbled, as did those based on the opposition of Stanislavsky and Brecht.[11]

Reading these sources through Lefebvre's theories allows me a "point of view," a focus on selected moments through which to compose one picture from what Postlewait refers to, when discussing historical reconstruction, as the "plurality of interpretations."[12] In a way, it is surprising that the two have not, to my knowledge, been brought together before, as they have enough recurrent concerns to warrant significant juxtaposed study. For example, Meyerhold's criticism of Soviet bureaucracy in his staging of Vladimir Mayakovsky's *The Bathhouse* (1930) chimes strongly with Lefebvre's own reading of bureaucracy as a phenomenon that uses blind systemization to curtail the creative potential and specificity of everyday life. Bureaucracy, Lefebvre argued, "regulates the relationship between the individual and society, and between the individual and the self."[13] Both were also interested in the human body. For Lefebvre, the human body is a "focal point of resistance" against a routinized everyday life, "because it has an organic vitality that cannot be easily suppressed."[14] Meyerhold, for his part, relied heavily on an aesthetic that was rooted in the actor's physicality. He also developed Biomechanics to prepare the actor for this physical role. The ensuing discussion will apply Lefebvre's discourse on the "appropriation/reappropriation of the body" to Biomechanics. I will show that whereas Meyerhold's prerevolutionary experiments put the actor's body on a dramaturgical pedestal vis-à-vis the other sign-carriers on the stage (a practice that renders the body into an act of appropriation), Biomechanics "reappropriated" the actor's body to elevate it into a seat of political resistance. This political reading of Biomechanics is the second contribution of applying the Lefebvrian framework.

Lefebvre-Meyerhold: Theoretical/Practical Conflicts

In evaluating the creative potential of the human body, Lefebvre shows a preoccupation with the status of the body as a fragmented and therefore trivialized phenomenon. He argued that fragmentation, including that of the body, is a characteristic feature of modernity: "That we are dealing with finiteness, with parts and subdivisions, with component elements, and with each part's uniqueness and origins (its 'etymology')—of this there can be no doubt."[15] Fragmentation is the result of an overt use of language as a means of communication, to the detriment of more immediate and physical modes of expression. According to Lefebvre, the precise alignment of separate body parts to particular tasks (e.g., sexual excitation to the genitals, visual stimulation to the eyes) fuels the "decomposition of the body into localized functions and its abandonment as a totality...so that the phallus, the eyes, and so on, became so many dissociated elements."[16] Interestingly, Lefebvre regards Taylorism, the industrial management of workflow by breaking up tasks, as a practice that fragments the body, which contrasts with the reading given by Meyerhold, who adopts Taylorism as a paradigm for the actor's efficiency: "Taylorism...reduced the body as a whole to a small number of motions subjected to strictly controlled linear determinations. A division of labor so extreme, whereby specialization extends to individual gestures, has undoubtedly had as much influence as linguistic discourse on the breaking down of the body into a mere collection of unconnected parts."[17]

The fragmentation that Lefebvre identified as a negative practice played a different role in Meyerhold's vision. It is given a positive reading, as seen in certain formulations given to the actor's work. This Meyerhold contrasted to the symbiotic—but for him, one-dimensional—relationship between the actor and the character that Stanislavsky's system professed to nourish. For example, in one lecture he asserted that "the first principle of biomechanics is the following: the body is a machine, the actor is a mechanic."[18] Here Meyerhold implied a heuristic separation between the actor and "his body" that allows the performer to stand back and analyze his opus. Moreover, in various lectures on Biomechanics delivered between 1921 and 1922, Meyerhold often discussed in isolation different body parts (such as the hands, eyes, face, trunk, and feet) to underline their respective acting potential.[19] What is however important to stress is that for Meyerhold fragmentation was not an end in itself but a means to work on the body in view of rendering it organic, that is, of treating the body, by both the actor and the spectator, as a unity and a whole: "The mechanics of one's body need to be studied in depth so as to understand with precision the interrelationships and function of each part. Every movement, even that of a little finger, must resonate immediately in all parts of the body: the movement of every part of the body reorganizes the interconnected relationships between the various parts."[20] Fragmentation thus becomes not a demoting condition, as it is in Lefebvre's theories, but a practical tool for stimulating networks of energy within the actor's body.

Implied in Lefebvre's criticism of fragmentation is his resistance to what Kirsten Simonsen refers to as "systemization and foundationalism."[21] Meyerhold's formulations on the work of the actor in the first postrevolutionary years took another direction. Those years saw Meyerhold attempting the systemization of the actor's work in the most precise and clear terms possible. A case in point is his use of commedia dell'arte types to create physical and dramatic templates for "set roles of the actor's art."[22] For example, the Hero needed to be male and of greater-than-average height, with long legs, a strong voice, and expressive hands and wrists. His dramatic function was that of "overcoming tragic obstacles on the plane of pathos."[23] Meyerhold's desire for the systemization of the actor's work is also seen in the often-quoted N = A1 + A2 formula, described in one lecture as the "formula which is necessary for acting."[24] Most gratifying must have also been how Biomechanics developed during the mid-twenties as a training approach and language that was shared by many professional and amateur theatres.[25]

When read from a Lefebvrian point of view, Meyerhold's formulations in the 1920s therefore served as "homogenizing abstractions."[26] In other words, Meyerhold sought to bring together the various strands that constituted theatre and acting in view of engendering uniformity and, consequently, control. This made Meyerhold a microreflection of the macro sociopolitical context. From as early as the first years of the 1920s, the Bolsheviks had trumpeted the revolution's success in eradicating all class hierarchies. Supposedly, no class was considered superior, as everyone was given the collective tag of "comrade." Several decrees were issued to formalize this, including an abolishment of private land ownership and the tsarist system of ranks.[27] The 1918 constitution of the Russian Soviet Federative Socialist Republic made all land and the corresponding means of production "the property of the entire people."[28] On paper at least, this must have created what Maxim Gorky called "a universal brotherhood," a utopian society wherein all commodities would be equally shared and consumed.[29] A formal bureaucracy was also set up. It was described by Vladimir Lenin as "the painstaking establishment of accounting and control,... [with] the strictest organization," which, while giving rise to endless tirades from its users over qualms of inefficiency, made the systemization and formalization of everyday transactions ever more possible.[30] Therefore, strategic regulation and control marked

Bolshevik processes to rebuild the country, to which Meyerhold contributed by systemizing the work of the actor. In this way, he was supportive of the regime in power, and he propagated this image by joining the party itself and taking the various national posts offered.

There have been readings of Meyerhold's early support of the Bolshevik Party as opportunistic, and a focus on his immediate reactions to the revolution and civil war easily confirms this, particularly when contrasted to the more silent and static reactions seen in such cases as Stanislavsky.[31] However, a look at a 1909 essay titled "Theatre and Society" shows that Meyerhold's appeal for systematization and even homogeneity in the theatre was more than a ruse to garner support from the new powers. It was not quickly formulated in reaction to the dominant political ideologies of the time but rather was a matter of principle that he had been articulating for some years.

In "Theatre and Society," Meyerhold presented the relationship between theatre and revolution in terms that would become perfectly at home after 1917. Theatre serves the revolution in moments "when a nation is intent in reorganizing its own existence," a formulation that was a staple in postrevolutionary propaganda.[32] Meyerhold's thinking in this essay presaged future political and artistic discourses: for example, he anticipated the repertoire problem that would characterize postrevolutionary theatre. The early years of the twentieth century had failed to create a tradition of political playwriting, which in retrospect one could see leading to the repertoire problem of the 1920s.[33] In a typically uncompromising voice that gave the whole essay a polemic tone, Meyerhold asserted that the repertoire problem resulted from the use of theatre to entertain and distract, which led playwrights to "[lose] any interest in theatrical action and [fall] into a psychologically oriented theatre, which offered no way out."[34] This sentiment was shared by Kerzhentsev, an early theorist on proletarian culture and Meyerhold's open opponent, who in his review of the postrevolutionary arena also traced theatre's decline in the audience's unquenchable desire for amusement.[35] Meyerhold's pre-1917 words on the reportorial issue became a reality in the early postrevolutionary years, which may have contributed to the favorable position in which he found himself.

Meyerhold located the playwright's apathy in the lost tug-of-war with the bourgeois public. Whereas Meyerhold had previously supported the spectator's creative role in performance, in this essay he offered an alternative reading by criticizing that spectator whose whims hindered theatrical developments.[36] Had this tug-of-war been resolved to the playwright's advantage, a "national theatre" would have been created, a theatre that would have educated the masses in and through culturally elevated productions.[37] Meyerhold criticized how theatre practice became fragmented to cater to different audiences such as the workers, the intelligentsia, and the well-to-do. All homogeneity was lost and, consequently, "the auditorium of the modern theatre is not unified.... Unless we are mistaken, the time will finally come when the theatre will cease to be fragmented and become again one. Our hope is that a future unified theatre is emerging from the present theatre-making trends. It is only this hope that makes work in the theatre worth doing."[38] In this prerevolutionary essay, Meyerhold is therefore unequivocal in his support of a theatre that unites the people under one banner. He must have read the Bolshevik call for a life that was both "collective and public" as an opportunity to concretely fulfill this prerevolutionary dream for such a unified and unifying theatre.[39] His 1909 statements for a homogenous theatre therefore mirrored the Bolshevik Party's drive to create a "homogenous" society, showing that any accusations against Meyerhold on grounds of opportunism need to be balanced by the understanding that the two initially shared a common vision of the future.

Lefebvre-Meyerhold: Theoretical/Practical Congruencies

Thus far, my juxtaposition between Lefebvre and Meyerhold has proceeded through several contrasting views on the nature of the human body. These views support Meyerhold's early image as a party adherent. However, the conclusion that Meyerhold supported the emerging status quo is problematized once certain congruencies with Lefebvre's theories are identified. Meyerhold's criticism of the party is usually traced to later years, and I have already referenced his 1930 staging of *The Bathhouse* as a criticism of Soviet bureaucracy. Braun also refers to the instance when Igor Ilinsky, one of Meyerhold's main actors, was directed to push a gun at the feet of Lazar Kaganovich, a Politburo member who led a party delegation during a private run-through in 1932 to evaluate Meyerhold's work on Nikolai Erdman's *The Suicide*. This action was seen as an invitation to Kaganovich to "help himself" to the gun and live up to his ruthless reputation—an all-too-clear provocation that accelerated Meyerhold's eventual demise.[40] While the deterioration of Meyerhold's relationship with the party was clear from the late 1920s onward—Joseph Stalin had in February 1929 asserted that, though "unquestionably connected to our Soviet state," Meyerhold's practice contained ample "negative features (posing, affectations, sudden and harmful leaps from living life toward the 'classical' past)" that needed strong "criticism"—an application of Lefebvre's theories will extend this time frame to include the early 1920s.[41]

A congruency between Lefebvre and Meyerhold is evident in Lefebvre's reading of "the communal body" and Meyerhold's practice of engendering in performance a close relationship between the actor and the spectator. Lefebvre wrote how the human body becomes a locus of resistance because of the communal networks that it nourishes with other entities. One manifests communal needs and desires through the body, such as what Michael Gardiner describes as "a longing for communal solidarity, of intense collective experience and action, and of the need for physical proximity and intimacy with concrete others."[42] The search for "communal solidarity," "intense collective experience," and "the need for physical proximity" between the actor and the spectator runs through Meyerhold's career, a concern that he also articulates as follows:

> What is particular to the actor's work—what differentiates him from the playwright, director, and other artists—is that the creative process occurs in front of the spectators' eyes. The actor finds himself in a sort of interdependence with the spectator. The latter assumes the position of a living resonance box, ready to react to every skilled demonstration from the actor. The actor follows with his fine hearing the resonance box that is the public, and reacts instantaneously, through improvisation, to all emerging needs. Through a series of signals (sounds, movements, coughs, laughter), the actor needs to locate with certainty the spectator's attitude towards the performance.[43]

Meyerhold's theatre was immediately communal because both actors and spectators were directly aware of each other, with the latter never made to forget that they were in a theatre watching a performance and not a slice of life. Meyerhold, therefore, "offer[ed]...a vision of community," which concretizes Lefebvre's eventual suggestion that the human body be applied as a seat to create meaningful relationships in everyday life.[44]

The congruency between Lefebvre and Meyerhold is also seen in their shared uneasiness with the use of textual canons as a regulatory strategy. Lefebvre argued that authoritarian regimes make use of linguistic codifications and literary canons to regulate consciousness. Interestingly, he uses theatre's physical rather than literary dimension as an example to drive his point home: "Among non-verbal signifying sets must be included music, painting, sculpture, architecture, and certainly theatre, which in addition to a text or pretext embraces gesture, masks, costume, a stage, a mise-en-scène—in short, a space.... To underestimate, ignore and diminish space amounts to the overestimation of texts, written matter, and writing systems, along with the readable and visible, to the point of assigning to these *a monopoly on intelligibility*."[45] The use of texts as a "monopoly on intelligibility" was evident in postrevolutionary Russia, even if its roots can be traced to at least the nineteenth century. Stephen Lovell argues that in the 1800s Russia had a much smaller literature public than did Western countries, a fact that did not stop print culture from acquiring "a significant role in nation-building and political debate," first within the intelligentsia and then, by the turn of the twentieth century, among the educated urban strata.[46]

During Bolshevik rule, the writing, publishing, and dissemination of a written declaration or document meant that the words had been scrutinized by an overbearing censorship and were, therefore, to be considered "true." This process is made clear by Katerina Clark and Evgeniĭ Dobrenko. Their scholarship describes how the Bolshevik Party acquired power not through a democratic process but through an armed insurrection, and how the use of texts became an essential factor in legitimizing such an action: "The regime's claims to legitimacy were largely grounded in a claim to cherishing and realizing more closely than might any rival the principles of the belief system—a secondary justificatory line of argument being improvements in the national economy and the material well-being of the citizens as indicators that they were progressing along the 'road to Communism.' As a consequence, written texts assumed enormous importance in the political life of the country. In the Soviet Union writing had such an authoritative status because it was felt it would establish the truth of the order to be found in Bolshevik experience. Writing was a means for promulgating the Party's ultimate authorship of Soviet reality."[47] One must keep in mind that, given the widespread illiteracy at the time, this inclination toward written texts was a marginalizing and elitist activity in itself. Very few people had access to and an understanding of these written texts, even when they were published in such regular newspapers as *Pravda*.

In contrast, Meyerhold based his theatre practice on the actor's body as an embodiment of theatre meaning; see, for example, how in *The Magnanimous Cuckold* he suggested the presence of a garden in how an actor handled a single flower.[48] Such physicality made his approaches, in theory at least, much more inclusive. The more physical training and production methods that Meyerhold used (before and) after the revolution conflicted with the Bolsheviks' textual strategy, and it is this conflict that marks Meyerhold's ambivalent status within the early years of Soviet rule. That Meyerhold conflicted with his surrounding postrevolutionary context on claims of physicality might appear a strange statement to make, particularly when one considers that physical dexterity was considered a hallmark of "Soviet man," or what Leon Trotsky called an "improved edition of mankind."[49] Toby Clark writes that even though the formulations on the "new man" were "generally conceived as an all-round development of mental and physical capacities, in the early Soviet period there was a particular preoccupation with the physical aspect, and the human body became a principal site for utopian speculations."[50] One such capacity was an immediate reactivity to any stimuli coming from the outer world.[51] Meyerhold's Biomechanics fit well within that discourse. For example, in a sociopolitical context that was constantly in flux, Meyerhold demanded that the actor "train his material (the body), so that it is capable of executing instantaneously those tasks which are dictated."[52] Other qualities included freedom from clumsiness, efficiency, and productiveness, and Meyerhold's preoccupation in these years with these same qualities heightens his consonance with the times. In this way, one can say that Meyerhold's work further contributed to the government's rebuilding process. However, discord rather than consonance emerges once theory is turned to practice and Meyerhold's physical models manifested on the stage, when his bodily based theatricalizations were fused to playtexts.

The playtexts that Meyerhold worked with after the October Revolution fall in two categories. On the one hand, he had to deal with contemporary works, which, with a few notable exceptions, he considered weak. Mikhail Podgaetsky's *D.E. (Give Us Europe)* (1924) and Aleksei Faiko's *Bubus the Teacher* (1925) fall in this category. On the other hand, he often tackled classics like Alexander Ostrovsky's *The Forest* (1924) and Nikolai Gogol's *The Government Inspector*, with which he scored some of his major successes. Meyerhold understood that both modern and classic texts needed to be "upgraded" or made relevant to a new epoch, and he searched for his solutions in a densely theatrical mise-en-scène that called on the actor's skilled use of his own physical apparatus. Examples of such physical practices abound in Braun's survey on Meyerhold, but I will refer again to a primary source that is unavailable in English translation.[53] This source relates to *D.E.* (*Give Us Europe*), which Meyerhold conceived as a platform for heightening the actors' skill in physical transformation: "In this production we have given each actor more than one role to interpret. We did this not because the Theatre has fewer actors than the number of roles but because our aim in this production is the principle of transformation. Transformation in the theatre has seldom been used before: for the first time, we make use of it in large quantities. The director usually resorted to transformation to diminish the number of interpreters. Moreover, he often sought to hide this practice from the audience. On the contrary, we inform the spectator of this practice from the posters. We invite the spectator to come and watch the actor's talent in his skilled transformations."[54]

The emphasis on the physical aspect of performance rather than on the preexisting text—which, one must remember, Meyerhold was criticized for "mutilating"—conflicted with the party's linguistic and textual means of expression.

In other words, the party's emphasis on the fixity of texts made Meyerhold's emphasis on the actor's body an act of resistance, one that was critical of the forces in power not through direct claims from the stage but through the practices adopted to create theatre. This critique is evident, for example, in how Meyerhold treated and transformed the "Return to Ostrovsky" theatrical program. Anatoly Lunacharsky, the first commissar of enlightenment, had formulated this program in 1923, and Ostrovsky's realistic tendencies, described as "a living mirror of surrounding reality," became a model for Soviet theatremakers.[55] Lunacharsky believed in the value of classic Russian and foreign drama, which he defended against the more extreme voices who after the revolution had demanded the obliteration of all prerevolutionary theatre from the scene.[56] He also valued professional expertise and did not believe that the amateur theatre staged by the proletariat could ever conceivably replace professional theatre. His approach to prerevolutionary drama was based on a process of displacement, rehabilitation, and assimilation, and Ostrovsky's critical disposition toward, rather than blind reproduction of, social realities proved a valuable model. Meyerhold responded to this "Return to Ostrovsky" policy by staging *The Forest* in 1924, though he made sure that this return was as forward-looking as possible. Thus, he divided the acts and scenes into a series of manageable episodes and used theatrical montage and character types to create "a totally unexpected 'return to Ostrovsky.'"[57]

Biomechanics as a Reappropriation Technique

In his analysis of the body as a seat of political resistance, Lefebvre distinguishes between appropriation and reappropriation techniques. The distinction between these techniques is helpful in evaluating Meyerhold's work, particularly in delineating how his experiments in Biomechanics differ from his earlier approaches. I will discuss appropriation techniques first. These techniques appropriate the human body by focusing on the body's external appearance and by proposing alternative shapes and routines that are uncharacteristic of how a human body is deployed in everyday life, for example, in how a person walks, sits, carries objects, holds himself or herself, and so on. Techniques of appropriation, therefore, treat the body as a one-dimensional phenomenon, a criticism that Eugenio Barba leveled at the military training that he experienced as a young man. It is worth developing a reference to Barba here, not only because the Italian has been vocal about Meyerhold's impact on his work, even referring to him as one of his theatrical grandfathers, but also because his theories help us clarify the difference between appropriation and reappropriation techniques.[58] Military training as understood by Barba reads as an example of appropriation technique, because the routines and drills practiced led to "a part of myself [being] cut off." The exercises "obliged us mechanically to carry out martial ceremonies which engaged only the body.... The highest value was placed on appearances."[59] It is this emphasis on physical appearance, detached from other human faculties, that best defines appropriation techniques.

Barba's criticism of appropriation techniques is echoed by Lefebvre, whose predilection is for the "reappropriation of the body." Reappropriation techniques are for Lefebvre different from simple appropriation acts: "Dominated by overpowering forces, including a variety of brutal techniques and an extreme emphasis on visualisation, the body fragments, abdicates responsibility for itself, in a word disappropriates itself. Body cultures and body techniques have been developed, in antiquity and since, which truly appropriate the body. Sports and gymnastics as we know them, however, to say nothing of the passive exposure of the body to the sun, are little more than parodies or simulations of a genuine 'physical culture.' Any revolutionary 'project' today, whether utopian or realistic, must, if it is to avoid hopeless banality, make the reappropriation of the body, in association with the reappropriation of space, into a negotiable part of its agenda."[60] Whereas *appropriation* techniques tend to place the body in a prominent position vis-à-vis other phenomena (such as language), *reappropriation* techniques seek to elaborate and transform the human body. This contrast between heightening the visibility of the body and its overall transformation permeates Meyerhold's physical experiments. The following distinction from Gardiner will help clarify this point: "Whereas for Foucault the body is best understood as an 'empty signifier' that can be reconstructed ad infinitum through the operation of external discourses of power, according to Lefebvre et al. the body manifests sensuous, inarticulate desires and impulses that cannot be fully colonized by rationalized systems."[61] In the reference to Foucault are indications of Meyerhold's early symbolist approach of using the human body as a signifier of his directorial dramaturgies. The Meyerhold of the symbolist years can be seen taking the "empty" vessel of the actor's body—what he believed to be a consequence of naturalism—and "filling it" with his own meanings and vision of the world and humanity. Braun describes this approach as one that used "expressive dance-like movements and...expressive poses," which lent a marked pictorial dimension to productions like *Sister Beatrice* (1906).[62] Although Meyerhold was critical of how naturalism had neutered the actor, this "empty" body was contingent on Meyerhold's more directorial temperament, in that it was more easily molded into the forms needed.[63] The second part of the quote highlights a practice that not only heightens the expressive potential of the actor's body but also works on it by infusing it with an energy that Barba coined as "extra-daily."[64] Barba's extra-daily energy is nourished through sustained processes of training and composition, and Meyerhold offered an early model of this when he argued that "all the movements of the actor...need constant and rigorous organization....Biomechanics does not tolerate anything to be accidental; everything needs to be carried out knowingly, through calculation."[65] It is the explicit and conscious process to transform and, in a Lefebvrian sense, "elaborate" the everyday body by infusing it with a reach and potential beyond what is exhibited in daily life that elevates Biomechanics into a technique of reappropriation.[66]

The word "appropriation" has connotations of procuring and taking for one's use, especially illegally and "typically without the owner's permission."[67] A hierarchical arrangement is implied in the attachment of this "illegal" tag to acts of appropriation: an entity appropriates a phenomenon to react to the force that is both in a higher hierarchical position and in possession of that phenomenon. In this way, an act of resistance is nourished that elevates an appropriation act and transforms it into a technique of reappropriation. It is interesting to point out that even Barba's attitude toward military training was elevated into an act of resistance and, consequently, a technique of reappropriation. This was possible through an inner-outer distinction that Barba called into play: although he appeared to be submitting to his superior's orders, internally he "cursed or silently mouthed obscenities, concealing anger or scorn behind the impassive façade of standing to attention."[68] The prefix "re" in "reappropriation" emphasizes that one is taking back a phenomenon that was previously owned. This chimes with early twentieth-century theatre, which actively reappropriates performance from an overdependence on the dramatic text. Antonin Artaud's Theatre of Cruelty encapsulates this thinking: "Instead of harking back to texts regarded as sacred and definitive, we must first break theatre's subjugation to the text and rediscover the idea of a kind of unique language somewhere in between gesture and thought."[69] This was done to give the actor's body the creative agency that it possessed in commedia dell'arte, medieval theatre, and Asian genres, a reappropriation to which Meyerhold contributed, both with his prerevolutionary studio experimentation and, though masked in a more scientific language, with Biomechanics.

Two aspects qualify Biomechanics as a reappropriation technique. First, the use of the actor's physicality as the main generator of performance material elevated the Biomechanical body into a force of resistance against the Bolshevik Party's textually oriented modes of systemization. Second, Biomechanics' emphasis on the actor's body did not, however, neglect its "inner" psychological dimension. Contrary to what appropriation techniques do, Biomechanics did not simplify the actor's body by ascribing it only an "outer" level. According to Meyerhold, the actor's body comprises different but interrelated levels, such as the physical, psychological, acrobatic, pedagogical, and so on. This multiplicity of levels is evident in Meyerhold's lecture "Ideology and Technology in the Theatre" (1933). I would like to quote from this lecture at some length, because this previously untranslated section brings together the various levels that Meyerhold deems to constitute the actor's work:

> We say that the actors need to be agile, precise in their movements, and athletic. They have to possess acrobatic skills. Moreover, we also say that the actor has to understand that his work is in a predetermined space and that consequently he needs to have architectural knowledge of this space. All this was misunderstood. Acrobatics, clowning, and grotesque processes have not been understood correctly and a hellish confusion has emerged. Subsequently, it is believed that the "To be or not to be?" monologue has to be performed in the following manner: once onstage, the actor performs a somersault, followed by part of the speech and a stretch at center-stage, after which the actor walks on all fours, like a bear. Finally, he stands up and continues to act. Or when we say that the actor must be a skilled juggler, what is understood is that virtuoso tricks are to be performed by the actor when playing in any modern piece, whatever this piece might be; remove from your pockets some balls and recite a monologue while juggling them. We suggest various things because they carry a pedagogical function, which is to perfect the actor's work. For example, the muscles of the hands need to be developed. In view of this, we make the actor practice the skills of the juggler, about which we are misunderstood and the opposite is carried out.
>
> The major mistakes in this field were made by TRAM, whose actors do not pronounce a single word without accompanying it with a series of acrobatics. And all this is treated as a series of tricks taught by Meyerhold's school. If we showed our laboratory work, you would realize that we never suggested anything of this sort. On the other hand, when creating the role and the mise-en-scène, we give every single movement a motivation that is linked to both the general conception of the production and the psychology of the role. . . .
>
> A recurrent point of discussion is what constitutes the actor's skill. The answer is not clear at all. We are here concerned with excitability (what was previously referred to as temperament, the ability to transform oneself immediately, inventively, and with good taste etc.), then with a sense of moderation, and an awareness of the balance between understatement and exaggeration.[70]

In no way was Meyerhold trivializing the actor's body by attributing it a one-dimensional, purely physical nature. Contrary to his experiments in symbolism, which accentuated the actor's plasticity but lacked the training approaches that could elaborate the actor's physical presence, Meyerhold envisaged

Biomechanics as a pedagogical tool that could harness the actor's physical potential, in turn transforming the body into a locus that brings together the disparate elements of the actor's arsenal. Within a context that stressed the fixity of texts as a regulatory device, his emphasis on the actor's body became more than an aesthetic choice. He reacted against the regulatory hand of the party through the way that he did theatre, emphasizing the body over the text and, in doing so, transforming the body into an act of resistance.

Conclusion

Lefebvre's theories were aimed at eradicating the stupor of everyday life. Meyerhold's theatre, with its unexpected turns (see his understanding of the "Return to Ostrovsky" policy) and physical aesthetic, which "creat[ed] a picture of the incredible, and invit[ed] the spectator to solve the riddle of the inscrutable," partook in this endeavor.[71] The results generated by the application of Lefebvre's theories to Meyerhold's work can be summarized as follows. First, there is the question of Meyerhold's placement within the developing postrevolutionary world. Meyerhold was certainly not averse to contradictions, both in his life—Jonathan Pitches, for example, frames his reading of Meyerhold's biography as "a life of contradictions"[72]—and in his theatre practice, in which his favored, grotesque, approach was one that "synthesises opposites."[73] In Meyerhold, theatre practice intertwined with his everyday dealings across the wider sociopolitical context. Lefebvre's theories supported the reading that Meyerhold's reaction to the revolution and the coming to power of the Bolshevik Party was not a straightforward affair, as evidenced by the juxtaposition of moments of support with others of resistance. Second, there is the analysis given to Biomechanics as a technique of reappropriation. In this reading, Biomechanics emerges not only as a training approach that elaborates the actor's body but also as a conflicting element to the Bolshevik Party's more text-based inclinations. In contrasting Biomechanics to appropriation techniques and their emphasis on physical form and appearance, Meyerhold's training approaches become infused with several layers of work, only one of which is the physical aspect. He looked at the holistic formation of the actor, which, though rooted in body-based approaches, did not prescribe physicality as the result of the training.

Lefebvre shared important concerns with Meyerhold's theatre work, accentuating the relevance of the everyday framework to the study of the Russian director's work. He did much more than simply seize upon the currents of the time and shared with Lefebvre a desire to reveal what lay beneath everyday realities. The application of everyday life theories is certainly not to be restricted to Meyerhold's work, and I have elsewhere provided evidence of how our understanding of Stanislavsky and postrevolutionary amateur theatre is also enriched through this application.[74] Theoretical application allows us to look at historical material with a fresh pair of eyes and to draw connections and make interpretations that might have escaped us in the past.

Notes

1. Paul Schmidt, ed., *Meyerhold at Work* (New York: Applause Theatre, 1981), 47.
2. Ibid., 65.
3. David Chaney, *Cultural Change and Everyday Life* (New York: Palgrave, 2002), 10. Other sources that tackle everyday life as a field for critical discourse include: Michael Sheringham, *Everyday Life* (Oxford: Oxford University Press, 2009); Michael Gardiner, *Critiques of Everyday Life* (New York: Routledge, 2000); Ben Highmore, *Everyday Life and Cultural Theory* (London: Routledge, 2002).
4. Jacky Bratton, *New Readings in Theatre History* (Cambridge: Cambridge University Press, 2003), 4.
5. Thomas Postlewait, *The Cambridge Introduction to Theatre Historiography* (Cambridge: Cambridge University Press, 2009), 10.
6. Jim Davis, "Research Methods and Methodology," *Research Methods in Theatre and Performance*, eds. Baz Kershaw and Helen Nicholson (Edinburgh: Edinburgh University Press, 2011), 92.
7. Sheringham, *Everyday Life*, 155.
8. Beatrice Picon-Vallin, ed. and trans., *Meyerhold* (Paris: CNRS, 1990).
9. My research on Meyerhold has been significantly boosted by my proficiency in the Italian language, which is much more developed than my rudimentary knowledge of Russian. Italian sources of Meyerhold's texts (transcribed as Mejerchol'd) include: Giovanni Crino, ed. and trans., *La Rivoluzione Teatrale* [The theatrical revolution] (Roma: Editori Riuniti, 1975); Fausto Malcovati, ed. and trans., *L'Ottobre Teatrale* [The theatrical October] (Milano: Felrinelli Editore, 1977); Nikolaj Pesočinskij, ed., Maria Rosaria Fasanelli, trans., *L'Attore Biomeccanico* [The Biomechanical actor] (Milano: Ubulibri, 2002); Fausto Malcovati, ed., Silvana de Vidovich and Emanuela Guercetti, trans., *L'ultimo atto* [The last act] (Fireze: La Casa Usher, 2011). All translations from the Italian are mine.
10. Franco Ruffini, for example, details how the Italian 1960 court case in Bari questioned the reach of Elizabeth Reynolds's copyright claims on Stanislavsky's book. This court case was the result of the translations in Italian of *An Actor's Work on Himself*, from the Russian original, which was published in Italy as early as 1956. See Franco Ruffini, "Three Periods of Stanislavsky in Italy," ed. Jonathan Pitches and Stefan Aquilina, *Stanislavsky in the World: The System and Its Transformations across Continents* (London: Bloomsbury, 2017), 45–53. Another case in point is Vakhtangov, whose writings have been only recently translated into English. See Andrei Malaev-Babel, ed., *The Vakhtangov Sourcebook*

(London: Routledge, 2011). Italian translations of key Vakhtangov texts appear in Fausto Malcovati, ed., *Il Sistema e l'Eccezione* (Firenze: La Casa Usher, 1984).

11. Eugenio Barba, "Grandfathers, Orphans, and the Family Saga of European Theatre," *New Theatre Quarterly* 19, no. 2 (May 2003): 109.
12. Postlewait, *Theatre Historiography*, 6.
13. Henri Lefebvre, *Critique of Everyday Life*, vol. 2, trans. Gregory Elliot (London: Verso, 2008), 62.
14. Gardiner, *Critiques of Everyday Life*, 16.
15. Henri Lefebvre, *The Production of Space*, trans. Donald Nicholson-Smith (Oxford: Blackwell, 1991), 181.
16. Ibid., 204.
17. Ibid., 204.
18. Mejerchol'd, *L'Attore Biomeccanico*, 79.
19. Space does not allow for a discussion of each body part, but the following is an indicative quotation: "It is through the eyes that one distinguishes a good actor from a bad one: nobody can see the eyes of a bad actor. A good actor can fix his gaze on an object without getting tired. . . . A weak mouth and eyes mean that the actor is not controlling them adequately. The articulation of the eyes is more complex than that of the lips. The lips have a great residual experience (through 'constant chattering'). Constant training in order to acquire a broad range of tested movements is necessary." In Mejerchol'd, *L'Attore Biomeccanico*, 72.
20. Mejerchol'd, *L'Attore Biomeccanico*, 95.
21. Kirsten Simonsen, "Bodies, Sensations, Space and Time: The Contribution of Henri Lefebvre," *Geografika Annaler* 87, no. 1 (2005): 2.
22. Marjorie L. Hoover, *Meyerhold: The Art of Conscious Theatre* (Amherst: University of Massachusetts Press, 1974), 299–310.
23. Ibid., 299.
24. Mejerchol'd, *L'Ottobre Teatrale*, 64. Elsewhere, Meyerhold elaborates on this formulation as follows: "N=A1+A2 (where N = the actor; A1 = the artist who conceives the idea and issues the instructions necessary for its execution; A2 = the executant who executes the conception of A1)." In Edward Braun, ed. and trans., *Meyerhold on Theatre* (London: Methuen, 1969), 198.
25. Edward Braun, *Meyerhold: A Revolution in Theatre* (London: Methuen, 1995), 193; and Nikolai Gorchakov, *Theatre in Soviet Russia*, trans. E. Lehrman (New York: Columbia University Press, 1957), 208.
26. Gardiner, *Critiques of Everyday Life*, 96.
27. Mervyn Matthews, ed. and trans., *Soviet Government: A Selection of Official Documents on Internal Policies* (London: Jonathan Cape Ltd., 1974), 20–29.
28. Ibid., 38–40.
29. Maxim Gorky, *Untimely Thoughts*, trans. Herman Ermolaev (New Haven: Yale University Press, 1995), 8.
30. Vladimir Lenin, *Collected Works*, vol. 27, ed. Robert Daglish, trans. Clemens Dutt (Moscow: Progress, 1974), 297.
31. Alma Law and Mel Gordon, *Meyerhold, Eisenstein and Biomechanics: Actor Training in*

Revolutionary Russia (North Carolina: McFarland, 1996), 27. That Stanislavsky's reaction to the revolution was a static one is asserted in sources like Jean Benedetti, *Stanislavski: His Life and Art* (London: Methuen, 1999), 245–47, and is a position that I revaluate in the article "Stanislavski's Encounter with the Revolution," again by applying a Lefebvrian everyday life framework to a set of Stanislavsky's letters and speeches. In *Studies in Theatre and Performance* 32, no. 1 (2012): 79–91.

32. Mejerchol'd, *La Rivoluzione Teatrale*, 70.
33. Several factors explain the repertoire crisis that engulfed theatre in Russia after the revolution. These include the failed emergence of a playwright who could typify the times in the same way that Anton Chekhov had two decades before and the tendency to simplify the complexities of the revolution by using sharp but limiting character types. Censorship, and the frequent demands for cuts and revisions, would later also play a significant role. Further discussion on this repertoire crisis can be found in sources such as Konstantin Stanislavsky, *My Life in Art*, trans. Jean Benedetti (Oxon: Routledge, 2008), 336; Nina Gourfinkel, *Teatro Russo Contemporaneo*, trans. M. Turano (Roma: Bulzoni Editore, 1979), 103–6; and Platon Keržencev (Kerzhentsev), *Il Teatro Creativo*, trans. Eugenia Casini Ropa (Roma: Bulzoni Editori, 1979), 17–18.
34. Mejerchol'd, *La Rivoluzione Teatrale*, 71.
35. Keržencev, *Il Teatro Creativo*, 17–18. The agreements between Kerzhentsev and Meyerhold probably did not go any further, as Kerzhentsev will be remembered as the person who more than anyone else engineered the closure of Meyerhold's theatre, in January 1938. Still, Kerzhentsev's theories are worth knowing about, which is why I make this brief reference to him here. A member of the Bolshevik Party from 1904, Kerzhentsev went on to take several high-profile governmental positions after the October Revolution. These included deputy head of the Department for Propaganda and Chairman of the Committee for Artistic Affairs (1936–38). His contribution to early Soviet theatre were theoretical rather than practical, and his policies are summarized in the book *Tvorchesky Teatr* [The creative theatre]. This was a popular book and was reissued five times between 1918 and 1923; in it, Kerzhentsev argued that what reflected best the social forces stimulated by the revolution was a collective approach to production rooted in amateur rather than professional theatre. His theories can also be treated as an early articulation of what today we might refer to as devised performance, thus extending his relevance to contemporary theatre studies. See Stefan Aquilina, "Platon Kerzhentsev and his Theories on Collective Creation," *Journal of Dramatic Theory and Criticism* 28, no. 2 (2014): 29–48.
36. Braun, *Meyerhold on Theatre*, 25–27.
37. A further reference to a "national theatre" can be found in the article "For a New Russian Repertoire," where Meyerhold writes: "The absence of a national repertoire (only a truly Russian repertoire can forge the new Russian theatre) is the cause of the apathy of today's theatre." In *La Rivoluzione Teatrale*, 75.
38. Mejerchol'd, *La Rivoluzione Teatrale*, 73.
39. Christina Kiaer and Eric Naiman, eds., *Everyday Life in Early Soviet Russia: Taking the Revolution Inside* (Bloomington: Indiana University Press, 2006), 1.
40. Braun, *Meyerhold*, 271.
41. In Katerina Clark and Evgeniĭ Dobrenko, eds., *Soviet Culture and Power: A History in Documents* (New Haven: Yale University Press, 2007), 58–59.

42. Gardiner, *Critiques of Everyday Life*, 16.
43. Mejerchol'd, *L'Attore Biomeccanico*, 94.
44. Schmidt, *Meyerhold at Work*, xvii.
45. Lefebvre, *The Production of Space*, 62; emphasis mine.
46. Stephen Lovell, *The Russian Reading Revolution: Print Culture in the Soviet and Post-Soviet Era* (New York: Palgrave Macmillan, 2000), 10.
47. Clark and Dobrenko, *Soviet Culture and Power*, xii.
48. Gorchakov, *Theatre in Soviet Russia*, 200.
49. Jochen Hellbeck, *Revolution on My Mind* (Cambridge, MA: Harvard University Press, 2006), 5.
50. Toby Clark, "The 'New Man's' Body: A Motif in Early Soviet Culture," in *Art of the Soviets: Paintings, Sculpture and Architecture in a One-Party State, 1917–1992*, eds. Matthew Brown Cullerne and Brandon Taylor (Manchester, UK: Manchester University Press, 1993), 33–50.

    Soviet discourses about the body were, however, much more complex than this. They vacillated between two extreme poles, with Clark's reading of a utopian body, an "uber-body," being countered by an engagement with the body's most basic needs and requirements. The body in Soviet ideology, therefore, was a space where "utopian speculation" collided with the everyday realities of hygiene, bathing, eating, and clothing. The two poles, however, were united in their commitment to political regeneration: "The cleansed body was not just a building block of the socialist utopia; it became the material manifestation of the revolution's success. Since the state, the nation, and the family would all 'wither away,' it was the population whose transformation would signal the success of revolution. Thus, the rationalized Soviet body was more essential to the socialist utopia than even the state; the creation of the body Soviet was the creation of the socialist utopia." Tricia Starks, *The Body Soviet: Propaganda, Hygiene, and the Revolutionary State* (Madison: University of Wisconsin Press, 2008), 4.
51. Clark, "The 'New Man's' Body," 35.
52. Braun, *Meyerhold on Theatre*, 198.
53. See, for example, how in *The Magnanimous Cuckold* Ilinksy and Maria Babanova physicalized the relationship between their characters through a series of runs, jumps, and lifts (Braun, *Meyerhold*, 181), or how the relationship in *The Forest* between Aksyusha and Petya was theatricalized through a whirling dance in the air and over the audience. Braun, *Meyerhold on Theatre*, 210.
54. Mejerchol'd, *L'Ottobre Teatrale*, 204.
55. Rudnitsky, *Russian and Soviet Theatre*, 116.
56. Anatoly Lunacharsky, "Proletkult and Soviet Cultural Work," in *Proletarskaya Kultura* 7–8 (May 1919): 1–3.
57. Braun, *Meyerhold*, 205.
58. Barba, "Grandfathers, Orphans, and the Family Saga of European Theatre," 108–10.
59. Eugenio Barba, *The Paper Canoe*, trans. Richard Fowler (London: Routledge, 1995), 3.
60. Lefebvre, *The Production of Space*, 166–67; my emphasis.
61. Gardiner, *Critiques of Everyday Life*, 16.
62. Braun, *Meyerhold on Theatre*, 21.
63. Ibid., 24.
64. Barba, *The Paper Canoe*, 15–16.
65. Mejerchol'd, *L'Attore Biomeccanico*, 77–78.

66. The term "elaborated body" is used by Gardiner to discuss Lefebvre's vision of a transformed human body and the way it contrasts with its dormant, trivialized counterpart. See Gardiner, *Critiques of Everyday Life*, 96.
67. Angus Stevenson, ed., *Oxford Dictionary of English*, 3rd ed. (Oxford: Oxford University Press, 2010), 77.
68. Barba, *The Paper Canoe*, 3.
69. Antonin Artaud, *The Theatre of Cruelty*, trans. Viktor Conti (London: Calder, 1993), 68.
70. Mejerchol'd, *La Rivoluzione Teatrale*, 192–95.
71. Braun, *Meyerhold on Theatre*, 139.
72. Jonathan Pitches, *Vsevolod Meyerhold* (London: Routledge, 2003), 1–42.
73. Braun, *Meyerhold on Theatre*, 139.
74. See, among others, Stefan Aquilina, "Stanislavski and the Tactical Potential of Everyday Images," *Theatre Research International* 38, no. 3 (2013): 229–39; "Stanislavsky and the Impact of Studio Ethics on Everyday Life," *Theatre, Dance and Performance Training* 3, no. 3 (2012): 302–14; and "Communal Solidarity and Amateur Theatre in Post-Revolutionary Russia: Theoretical Approaches," in *Redefining Theatre Communities: International Perspectives in Community-Conscious Theatre-Making* (Intellect: Forthcoming).

"Shuffled Together under the Name of a Farce"

Finding Nature in Aphra Behn's *The Emperor of the Moon*

—VIVIAN APPLER

Was Aphra Behn (1640–1689) a scientist?[1] Probably not.[2]

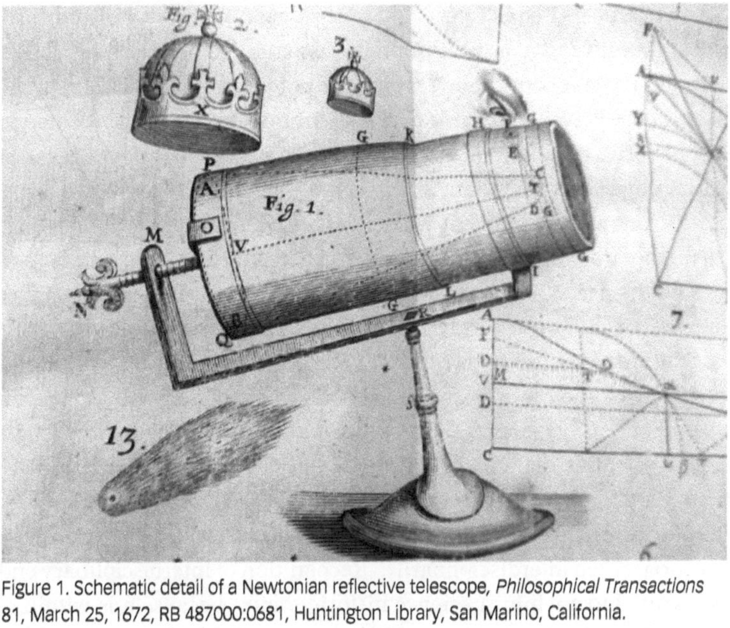

Figure 1. Schematic detail of a Newtonian reflective telescope, *Philosophical Transactions* 81, March 25, 1672, RB 487000:0681, Huntington Library, San Marino, California.

Could she have influenced the flow of thought about science despite her status as a disciplinary outsider? Perhaps. A focus on her late writing suggests an engagement with science concepts, objects, and philosophers that renders Behn at the very least a competent, critical, credible participant in the late seventeenth-century "new science" conversation, if not a natural philosopher in her own right.[3] Behn's late play, *The Emperor of the Moon* (1687), is emblematic of her interdisciplinary interests. A reexamination of the play's text and a historically informed imagination of its performances, considered along with Behn's other writing and translations of this period, indicates how Behn indeed contributed to late seventeenth-century cultural trends in science. *Emperor* holds an important place in late seventeenth-century theatre studies; it is the second-most performed of her works, after *The Rover*.[4] The play is prototypical of the English farce and pantomime entertainments that would sweep London's popular theatres over the course of the eighteenth century. Many scholars have addressed Behn's writing within the contexts of Restoration politics, protofeminism, and dramatic form. I suggest that *Emperor* is also an important mediator of interdisciplinary Restoration histories because of the questions Behn persistently raises about natural philosophy. Seen in this context, Aphra Behn, renowned as England's first uncloseted female playwright, should be recognized as a dynamic female contributor to the history of science.

In this article, Behn's late work is construed within a holistic historiographical narrative that, as philosopher of science Sandra Harding puts it, acknowledges the labors of "knowers who are not permitted to sit next to the scientist at their lab benches."[5] This feminist critique matters to performance and science histories because it articulates an early modern precedent for women's interdisciplinary participation in historically gender-exclusive science fields such as astronomy and physics while highlighting Behn's "pro-democratic" theatrical methods by which science was performed outside the domain of the laboratory.[6] Behn's participation in the popularization of science concepts through her late drama and prose may be understood as protofeminist for the increased access it afforded readers and audience members who were not working within the relatively closed ranks of the Royal Society, women as well as men. Behn's playful treatment of science concepts for mixed-gender audiences aligns her work with scientific material produced by early female practitioners of science such as Margaret Cavendish, Duchess of Newcastle (1623–1673), and Gabrielle Émilie le Tonnelier de Breteuil, Marquise du Châtelet (1706–1749), both of whom also worked interdisciplinarily.[7] Recognition of interdisciplinary endeavors is essential to a feminist science historiography, because it is within extra-laboratory domains that much work by women has historically been performed.

Bruno Latour's actor-network theory (ANT) aids in creating a critical shift in emphasis from political intrigue to science objects and ideas. Behn warrants an interdisciplinary reframing process in line with Latour's sociological science historiography because of her reliance upon the telescope (a science object) for storytelling purposes (figure 1). A science-oriented historiography of *Emperor of the Moon*, combined with an analysis of Behn's translator's preface to her translation of Bernard le Bouvier de Fontenelle's (1657–1757) *Entretiens sur la pluralité des mondes* (1686) (*A Discovery of New Worlds. From the French* [1688]), situates Aphra Behn as a significant female voice in Restoration science culture.[8]

Reshuffling Discipline: Aphra Behn and the "New Science"

Emperor of the Moon, an adaptation of Nolant de Fatouville's (d. 1715) *Arlequin, empereur dans la lune* (1684), is emblematic of the exchange of philosophical and theatrical ideas that transpired across the English Channel during the Age of Reason.[9] The English and French versions of this play feature telescopes and science themes that situate the story in a socio-scientific moment in European history at which point audiences eagerly responded to scientific ideas. The play's comedy is rooted in the commedia dell'arte; its stock characters and zany plot remain primary elements of Behn's Anglicized science farce.[10] In Behn's play, the *dottore* Baliardo is depicted as a harmless old man with a befuddling interest in the moon and its inhabitants. He is a self-identified Cabalist whose time is devoted to pursuing his interests in astronomy, astrology, and the occult.[11] Out of a concern for the *dottore*'s well-being (and a desire to marry) the *innamorati* (young lovers) devise a plot intended to shock Baliardo out of his irrational interest in unearthly things and shed his reliance upon the untrustworthy telescope. His concerned family members construct an elaborate practical joke to trick Baliardo into thinking that he really can observe moon-people through his telescope, only to shock him into a state of reality (in which his telescope has *not* enabled him to view and interact with moon creatures) during the play's final masque. Many of *Emperor*'s jokes deliver the moral that Reason must temper Sensation; if one succumbs to images transduced by such devices as the telescope, one runs the risk of taking false information for the truth.

Behn hones her science-targeted satire through the development of the commedia characters that appear in her adaptation of Fatouville's original. Behn's protofeminist dramaturgy expands the roles of the *innamorate*, Elaria (Baliardo's daughter) and Bellemante (his niece), so that these female characters become essential to the plot.[12] In *Emperor*, Scaramouch replaces Fatouville's

Pierrot as the doctor's assistant.[13] Harlequin's attempts to woo a witty female servant are consistent with the Continental original, though Behn changes the servant's name from Colombina to Mopsophil, the governess. Although Harlequin does engage in some elements of disguise toward the end of *Emperor*, a favorite conceit of the French audience, it is Charmante, Elaria's lover, who first appears in disguise as an ambassador from the moon to press the doctor for an introduction to Elaria on behalf of the fictional emperor of the moon. Where the French plot revolves around Harlequin's slapstick antics peppered with science-critical zings, Behn's action is consistently driven by the debate between Reason and the Senses; she closes the domestic situation with the philosophical moral that telescopes are not reasonable instruments for the exploration of outer space.

Of all the commedia stock that Behn borrows from Fatouville, none bears the brunt of her philosophical attack more than *dottore* Baliardo. In the very first scene of Behn's play, Baliardo's dreamy lunacy is introduced in a discussion between his servant and his daughter:

SCARAMOUCH: You must know, your Father, (my Master, the Doctor,) is a little Whimsical, Romantick or Don Quicksottish, or so,—
ELARIA: Or rather Mad.
SCARAMOUCH: That were uncivil to be supposed by me; but Lunatick we may call him without breaking the Decorum of good Manners; for he is always travelling to the Moon.
ELARIA: And so Religiously believes there is World there, that he discourses as gravely of the People, their Government, Institutions, Laws, Manners, Religion and Constitution, as if he had been bred a *Machiavel* there.[14]

As we shall see, Baliardo's "travels" to the moon are philosophical in nature and mediated by his garden telescope.[15] The dotty-yet-beloved professor is construed as unhealthily obsessed with outer-space and suffering from a misguided trust in scientific instruments to augment his visual sense. The telescope's magnifying technics work in tandem with the doctor's imagination in "The World of the Moon," a plot enacted by Charmante and his friend Cinthio (who happens to be courting Baliardo's niece, Bellemante), "wherein [Baliardo] shall be so impos'd on, as shall bring matters most magnificently about"; Baliardo will be cured of his lunatic malady.[16]

Behn's science farce represents a peculiar moment in the evolution of experimental laboratory practice because it demonstrates the subtle acceptance of telescope technology that emerged in England during the late seventeenth century. The Royal Society of London attained a Royal Charter in 1662, and developments in all aspects of experimental science, astronomy in particular, escalated across England and Europe. Notable advancements in telescope technology were accomplished by Sir Isaac Newton, who developed a telescope that worked by reflection, and Dutch scientist Christiaan Huygens (1629–1695), famous for the design of some of the century's longest and most powerful telescopes. Despite technological achievements, the practicality of knowledge gained through these new machines remained suspect in the European imaginary. The telescope had been a target of political satire almost since its invention, and Behn's mid-seventeenth-century peers Margaret Cavendish and Thomas Shadwell took stabs at the device in drama and prose. Cavendish derides the use-value of the telescope in *The Description of a New World, Called the Blazing-World* (1666) and *Observations upon Experimental Philosophy* (1666). Shadwell mocks the whole of the Royal Society in a comedy that turns upon the promise of a telescope in his play, *The Virtuoso* (1676). By the time *Emperor* premiered, the natural philosophy that embraced the telescope as a useful perceptual aid was being promoted by members of the Royal Society, but much of the British public (Behn included) remained skeptical about the trustworthiness of the device's capacity to transduce information about outer space to the earthbound observer. In the article "Retraining the Virtuoso's Gaze: Behn's *Emperor of the Moon*, the Royal Society, and the Spectacles of Science and Politics," enlightenment scholar Al Coppola suggests that *Emperor* is, "above all, an interrogation of improper spectating," in which Behn encourages a more critical audience to British politics through her satirical representation of the Royal Society.[17] Theatrical satire publicly criticized the elite, politically privileged group of people who claimed the unreasonable power to see the previously unseeable through a mastery of the telescope's lens technology. Unlike the works of Cavendish and Shadwell, Behn's *Emperor* does not reject the telescope outright. Rather, the manifestation of the telescope on the Dorset Garden stage in 1687 indicates a curiosity about this new machine that hooked popular audiences into participating in popular scientific debate via its socio-scientific satire.

For Behn to dramaturgically skewer the Royal Society's virtuosi, she must also have proven herself a scientific authority, a "knower" if not a natural philosopher like Newton. Newton's *Philosophi naturalis principia mathematica* (*Mathematical principles of natural philosophy*, commonly referred to as Newton's *Principia*) was published in the same year as *Emperor* premiered.[18] Literary historian Barbara Benedict outlines Behn's authoritative qualities as an editor and a translator according to the criteria that Behn and her peer John Dryden (1631–1700) identified as essential to the craft of credible poetry: Nature, Commitment, Art, Breeding, and Value.[19] Benedict states that the "importance [of these criteria] lies not in their originality, but in their deployment: Dryden and Behn use them not merely to assert their value as poets, but also to prove their value as editors."[20] These editorial criteria might also be used to situate Behn as a credible authority on natural science. Behn's fluency in the language of natural philosophy may be found in examples of "prefatory rhetoric," such as the dedication of *Emperor* and her translator's preface to *Discovery*, as well as in her own philosophical dramaturgy as expressed throughout *Emperor*.[21] While Behn's political commentary cannot be overlooked, neither should her participation in the circulation of science concepts during the latter half of the seventeenth century. Her status as a credible critic of natural philosophy becomes evident when attention shifts from her cutting political wit to the science objects and ideas that she deploys toward satirical ends.

While physical comedy and Dorset Garden's dazzling theatrical spectacle might have masked Behn's authorial engagement with the natural philosophical debates that waged across the English Channel, she intentionally directs the attention of Charles Somerset, Marquess of Worcester and her noble benefactor, toward the scientific nature of *Emperor of the Moon* in her dedication: "I am secure from this Censure, when your Lordship shall be its Judge, whose refin'd Sence and Delicacy of Judgment, will, thro all the humble Actions and trivialness of Business, find Nature there, and that diversion which was not meant for the Numbers, who comprehend nothing beyond the Show and Buffoonery."[22] *Emperor* was originally staged before a noble audience, but its production history suggests that the play's spectacle would have drawn popular crowds as well.[23] Although she might not have intended the science content for the "Numbers," that same general audience got an ample helping of it along with the play's bawdy jokes and commedia-esque physical humor, of which Behn was a British master. Despite the playwright's statement to the contrary, all audience members able to see the action would have engaged with the performance of science largely because of the physical humor in the central telescope scene.

Behn, nearing the end of her life, would likely have been involved in a parallel process of translating *Discovery* during *Emperor*'s production process.[24] *Emperor* can be read as a theatrical realization of the natural philosophy she publishes in the translator's preface. Behn's farcical treatment of telescope technology resonates with Fontenelle's subjunctive exploration of extraterrestrial life. *Entretiens* is an educational astronomy text intended to engage nonscientists, curious women in particular, as is implied through the book's conversations between Fontenelle's Philosopher and his hostess, La Marquise. Fontenelle structures his treatise as a dialogue through which he instructs his audience in such contemporary astronomy topics as the Copernican model of the universe (the idea that Earth and other planets revolve around the sun), the arrangement and qualities of planets and the "fixed stars," and tourbillions (a rotational theory of universal mechanics promoted by Descartes).[25] Fontenelle entertains his readers by lacing astronomy lessons with the imaginative, hypothetical provocation that the celestial objects discussed in the book might be inhabited by intelligent life. He expresses a philosophical curiosity about worlds that are unknowable due to their great distance from Earth: "If the Eye-sight were in perfection, you could as easily discern there were worlds in the Stars, as there are Stars.... We would gladly know more than we see, and there's the difficulty: for if we could see well and truly what we see, we should know enough; but we see most Objects quite otherwise than they are; so that the true Philosophers spend their time in not believing what they see, and in endeavouring to guess at the knowledge of what they see not."[26] He praises the telescope as a tool that improved human vision and thereby enabled advances in selenography (the mapping of the moon) made "by the Learned, who travel daily thither by the help of long Telescopes: They tell us, they have discover'd vast Countries, Seas, Lakes high Mountains, and deep Valleys."[27] In *Emperor*, Behn makes a comedically exaggerated leap in logic from the relatively small advances in the discernment of lunar topography to Baliardo's dramatized expectation that he will "snatch" a glimpse of "the Great Monarch of the upper world...into his Closet," through his backyard telescope.[28]

Behn's editorial preface provides philosophical credibility for her criticism of Fontenelle. Where Fontenelle lauds the telescope as a tool for human progress, Behn rejects the idea that telescopes could hold that much transductive power. Behn adheres to heliocentrism but expresses her disapproval of Fontenelle's over-reliance upon the telescope for astronomical observation. She grounds her translator's critique in Jesuit philosophy, personal experience, and an expression of Enlightenment reason:[29] "[Fontenelle] gives a magnificent *Idea* of the vastness of the Universe.... This he proves judiciously, by the Appearances and Distances of the Planets and fixed Stars; and if he had let alone his learned Men, Philosophical Transactions, and Telescopes in the Planet *Jupiter*, and his Inhabitants not only there, but in all the fixed Stars, and even in the *Milky Way*, and only stuck to the greatness of the Universe, he had deserved much more Praise."[30] As with *Emperor*'s assemblage of actors and objects, here Behn selects the telescope to stand alongside scientific texts and natural philosophers as objects equally worthy of ridicule.[31] Behn cites the contemporary natural philosophy of René Descartes and Jacques Rohault in defense of her few adjustments to Fontenelle's text.[32] Reason tempers the Senses: "I have laid the Scene at *Paris*, where the Original was writ.... I thought *Paris* and St. *Denis* fitter to be made use of as Examples, to compare the Earth and the Moon to, than

London and *Greenwich*; because *St. Denis* having several Steeples and Walls, is more like *Paris*, than *Greenwich* is to *London. Greenwich* has no Walls, and but one very low Steeple, not to be seen from the Monument without a Prospective Glass."[33] Without denying the telescope's capacity to augment human vision when restricted to earthbound observations, Behn maintains the reasonable natural philosophy that telescopes are fallible devices when applied to the study of the universe. She targets Fontenelle as her critical object in the translator's preface, but it is through *Emperor*'s socio-scientific satire that Behn shines as a skilled theatre artist and a credible critic of natural philosophy.

The theatre is a space where words can mean one thing while actions tell another story. Interdisciplinary scholar Barbara Dancygier notes that "communicative modalities do their job regardless of the context they are used in."[34] An embodied reimagining of *Emperor*'s early performances includes mechanical bodies, actors' bodies, and audience bodies in a meaning-making assemblage that reveals a participatory, collaborative capacity for engagement with science content in the play's production that is not necessarily apparent through the mode of script analysis alone. Linguistic interpretation leads to different conclusions than when *Emperor* is analyzed in terms of its material objects, regardless of the politically grounded, antimechanical circumstances of Behn's creative moment. When Coppola claims that "the chief spring of Baliardo's interest in the moon is political, not sexual, and certainly not what anyone, then or now, might call scientific," he emphasizes political context over issues surrounding sex and lumps the science in with political intrigue.[35] Coppola articulates a compelling argument regarding Behn's royalist sentiments in the context of the Exclusion Crisis, however, the science-popularizing potential of *Emperor* is nevertheless embedded in the narrative and may be discovered in scenes that feature telescopes onstage alongside human actors. Embodied readings of these scenes suggest that scientific and mechanical knowledge-production transpired in the environment of the Dorset Garden theatre. Behn asserted her science authority through knowledgeable manipulation of the telescope prop and its ensuing actions. A Latourian shuffle of physics concepts and objects brings the playwright's value as a knower-of-science into clear view.

Behn incorporated the relatively new technology of the telescope into her linguistic and embodied theatrical metaphors to discuss the social implications of the "new science." Latour suggests that the introduction of novel technologies historically catalyzes new understandings of the human condition: "A new vaccine is being marketed, a new job description is offered, a new political movement is being created, a new planetary system is discovered. . . . In each instance, we have to reshuffle our conceptions of what was associated together because the previous definition has been made somewhat irrelevant. We are no longer sure about what 'we' means; we seem to be bound by 'ties' that don't look like regular social ties."[36] Latour further claims that "it is an association between entities which are in no way recognizable as being social in the ordinary manner, *except* during the brief moment when they are reshuffled together."[37] Behn's theatre reassembles disciplinary distinctions when the telescope becomes the subject of productive curiosity for the attendant collective of the theatrical production. The performance becomes an experimental medium for an exploration of outer space, or it ironically rehearses that exploration through mechanically aided farce.

Behn deploys the telescope as a theatrical synecdoche, standing in as a target for her critique of seventeenth-century natural philosophy. Telescopes appear twice in Behn's *Emperor*: one large telescope constitutes the center of the action in act 1, scene 2, and two "Galilean" telescope props feature in the hands of historical scientist characters that cameo in the closing masque.[38] The theatricalized telescopes in *Emperor* metaphorically enact the function of observatory telescopes, causing distant objects and abstract ideas to appear in large, clear detail for the theatrical spectator.

So, what exactly do staged telescopes accomplish in Behn's socio-scientific shuffle?

- Telescopes capture the attention and curiosity of human agents, mediating ideas about astronomy in the domain of the theatre and creating science-arts mediators of attendant audience members.
- Telescope props represent their functional cousins in the domain of astronomy as objects of technological wonder. They are synecdoches of natural philosophy, standing in for the cultural science discourse of which they are a part.
- Behn's large staged telescope in particular may have performed in ways that conveyed an understanding of seventeenth-century lens technologies. I engage with this idea in a dramaturgical aside later in this essay.

Telescopes in the observatory capture stars, but telescopes onstage capture the attention of fictional characters and the imaginations of audience members who participate in the culturally productive performance of science. Behn's staged telescope of act 1, scene 2 captures not only stars but also human agents who participate in the arts-science network of astronomy.

Behn's large staged telescope was a culturally generative, socio-scientific mediator, "*an original event [that] creates what it translates as well as the entities between which it plays the mediating role*."[39] Latour expands upon an object's capacity to mediate culture within the structure of ANT: "If action is limited…

to what 'intentional,' 'meaningful' humans do, it is hard to see how a hammer, a basket...could act....By contrast, if we stick to our decision to start from the controversies about actors and agencies, then *any thing* that does modify a state of affairs by making a difference is an actor—or, if it has no figuration yet, an actant. Thus, the questions to ask about any agent are simply the following: Does it make a difference in the course of some other agent's action or not?"[40] Behn's telescope did not act of its own accord, but the playwright's choice to include it onstage invited knowledge generation and exchange among curious participants assembled to witness the theatrical science event. The telescopes called for in *Emperor* make a difference in plot development and audience engagement. Behn's theatrical telescopes mediated the playwright's understanding of technology, its relevance to astronomy praxis, and the audience's participation in the perpetuation of its cultural viability.

Telescopes allow those who gaze through them to see more of the world than the naked eye permits, and thus they hold the capacity to spark an emotional state of curiosity within the observing agent, who, when looking through the viewing lens, is suddenly able to discern distant objects in great detail. Behn's theatrical assemblage held the potential to transform an idly curious spectator into an active experimenter. Curiosity, according to certain lines of seventeenth-century protestant rhetoric, caused the fall of man from God's grace and therefore fell into a category of sinful human activity. Bacon and his philosophical descendants in the Royal Society found their way around this moral obstacle by distinguishing between two different types of curiosity: idle curiosity and productive curiosity. Early modern expert Joanna Picciotto argues that "well beyond the laboratory, the Baconian image of paradise as 'a place Consecrated for sober Discipline' inspired contemporaries to discover the subject of innocence in the laboring collective."[41] Through what otherwise may have been considered the idle pastime of theatre attendance, Behn's collective audience might have become productively curious about the novel science object despite its satirical situation onstage because of its mediating capacity. Picciotto clarifies the seventeenth-century positivist position regarding the culturally valuable work of the scientist: "The authority conferred by the spectatorial body to which [the lone investigator] stood in prosthetic relation was nobody's to claim. But if no individual was entitled to the state of total knowledge and power the experimentalist sought, humanity as a whole was."[42] Human vision may have been imperfect, but prosthetic perfection of vision, even for the solitary natural philosopher by means of helps such as telescopes and microscopes, held the possibility of bettering the condition of all humanity. The act of scientific observation enabled an authority of knowledge to transfer to and benefit the collective via the laboring individual. Behn transformed her audience into amateur natural philosophers by means of theatrical prosthetics as they observed the events that transpired around *Emperor's* actant telescopes.

A Latourian analysis would consider the hybrid body of the observer-and-telescope as well as the collective body of all spectators assembled in the theatre. Responding to the hybrid Baliardo-telescope body performing onstage, spectators—enmeshed as participant to the whole social, cognitive system *including the actions of staged science objects*—might have proceeded to get caught up in a state of productive curiosity that put "contemplation and delight at the heart of work and exercise."[43] Behn's telescopes entertained, but their entertainment value did not detract from their potential to affect curious audience members as parts of a whole cultural system that included science and art, objects and agents.

Aphra Behn's Very Large Telescope

Two narratives unfold in the performance of *Emperor of the Moon*: on one hand, the comedic banter tossed among characters as they mock seventeenth-century telescope technology and those who practice it and, on the other, the interactions among the science props, dramatic characters (embodied by human actors), and the audience. *Emperor's* knowledge-generative potential can be found when mechanical bodies are reassembled to share status as mediators with human actors. With embodied and textual theatrical narratives in mind, Behn's large telescope of act 1, scene 2 invites its audience to engage with questions about astronomy: How much detail *can* the century's long telescopes transduce compared to telescopes of the past? Are we just as well off sticking to naked-eye observation for fear of falling prey to pranks and mistakes due to lens distortion? Behn's theatrical satire allowed conflicting narratives—rejection of the telescope as scientific tool and subtle acceptance of the new technology as a part of the seventeenth-century sociocultural landscape—to coexist in the minds of participant audience members. Her jokes dismiss the "new science" machines as superfluous to unaided human vision, and *Emperor's* introductory telescope scene has, indeed, been analyzed solely for the bawdy banter among Baliardo, Scaramouche, and Charmante. However, if the scene's critique were to focus on the telescope as part of a whole astronomical knowledge-production assemblage, a story would surface in which all objects and intentional human agents are tied together in a knowledgeable demonstration of seventeenth-century astronomy concepts, technics, and techniques. The mechanical, performing body of Behn's very large telescope catalyzes a curious audience engagement with the very science concepts that the play's text rejects.

Behn's purpose in anglicizing Fatouville's *Empereur* is to demonstrate the imprecise nature of science instruments and therefore the illogic of putting stock in observations made through them. Behn acknowledges Fatouville's influence but downplays the similarities between the two plays in her dedication: "A very barren and thin hint of the Plot I had from the Italian, and which, even as it was, was acted in *France* eight odd times without intermission. 'Tis now much alter'd, and adapted to our English Theatre and Genius, who cannot find an Entertainment at so cheap a Rate as the French will, and who are content with almost any Incoherences, howsoever shuffled together under the Name of a Farce."[44] Cheap gags and Arlequin's acrobatics might be enough for French entertainment, but Behn's English science farce incorporates her own natural philosophy as well as Dorset Garden's special effects. While most of the play's spectacle is reserved for the final masque, Behn's very large telescope makes an impressive entrance in act 1, scene 2.

The scene is set in Baliardo's garden, a space that would have conceivably contained the doctor's large telescope. Behn's stage directions indicate the device's proportions and the assemblage of human bodies and scientific gadgets with which it should be performed: "*Enter Doctor, with all manner of Mathematical Instruments, hanging at his Girdle; Scaramouch bearing a Telescope twenty (or more) Foot long.*"[45] Behn is going for laughs at Baliardo's expense:

DOCTOR: Set down the Telescope.—Let me see, what Hour is it?
SCARAMOUCH: About six a Clock, Sir.
DOCTOR: Then 'tis about the Hour, that the great Monarch of the upper World enters into his Closet; Mount, mount, the Telescope.
SCARAMOUCH: What to do, Sir?[46]

A series of phallic jokes typical of commedia recur throughout the scene. The intricate network of European natural philosophical dialogue becomes evident when the presence of the telescope is considered on equal footing with the characters who mock it. The facile double entendre and easily understood stock characters recede, and Behn steps in as a participant in the cultural history of the long telescope.

Behn's "twenty (or more) Foot"-long telescope invites a comparison to its contemporaries in the domain of science, which would have caused the sizeable prop to appear laughably small. Two types of telescope technology were in use during the late seventeenth century: refractive and reflective. Refractive telescopes work by collecting light through lenses and thereby augmenting perception of size and detail of observational objects such as the moon, Jupiter's spot, or Saturn's rings. A reflective telescope collects light and improves the telescope's focus using mirrors as well as lenses, as illustrated in Newton's diagram, published in *Philosophical Transactions* in 1672 and shown in the schematic detail at the top of the article. Two continental astronomers, Johannes Hevelius (1611–1687), of the Polish-Lithuanian Commonwealth, and Christiaan Huygens, experimented with long refractive telescopes throughout the seventeenth century.[47] In 1673, Hevelius constructed the longest telescope of the century—a one-hundred-and-fifty-foot-long refractive telescope—and arranged its lenses, without a tube, along a wooden trough in the open air. Huygens also built a long, tubeless telescope, in 1686 (the year before Behn's *Emperor* premiered), but his was only one hundred and twenty-three feet long. These telescopes would scarcely have fit in the entirety of the Dorset Garden theatre lengthwise, let alone on its stage.[48] If the stage device were crafted according to Behn's specifications, the twenty-foot length would probably have taken up most of the width of the stage, a metaphoric statement regarding the extent to which the machine had come to occupy Baliardo's thoughts.

Behn borrowed the concept for the large telescope gag, along with much of the plot, from the *comédie italienne*. The French telescope should have been large, but the stage directions don't indicate how large.[49] Fatouville's stage directions are not as detailed as Behn's, but they do state clearly, "*Le Théâtre represente un Jardin, au fond duquel on voit une grande Lunette d'approche montée sur son pied.*"[50] The inspiration for Fatouville's "grande" telescope might be traced to Giovanni Domenico Cassini (1625–1712), an Italian astronomer who worked in France and is remembered for his discovery of the gaps between the rings of Saturn (now known as the Cassini division). Cassini moved to Paris in 1669, joined the Académie Royale des Sciences, and became somewhat of a professional nemesis to Huygens.[51] He made many discoveries with a seventeen-foot-long telescope, which meets the parameters described in Behn's stage directions.[52] Fatouville establishes a linguistic conceit early in *Empereur* to indicate *dottore* Baloardo's outsider, Italian, status.[53] Fatouville's Baloardo speaks a blend of French and Italian; in this early monologue, he begins speaking in French but slips quickly into Italian: "S'il y a des Crepescules dans la Lune, *bisogna ch'a vi sia una Generation, & una Corrution; e s'al ghè una corruption, & una generation, bisogna ch'a ve sasea dei Animali, e dei Vegetabili; e s'al ghe nasce dei animali, e dei vegetabili, ergo la Luna è un Mondo abitabile com'al nostro.*"[54] The *dottore*'s Italian, like his science, is often not quite correct.

In Behn's *Emperor*, Don Charmante jump-starts the "World of the Moon" plot with a telescope demonstration that reveals how easily the senses may be deceived by lens distortion. In the scene, Charmante, "*drest in a strange Fantastical Habit*," his disguise as an ambassador from the moon, greets Baliardo: "Hail from the great Caballa—of Eutopia."[55] Baliardo immediately welcomes Charmante, who proceeds to invite the *dottore* to gaze upon his fellow lunar citizens. The trick/demonstration scene commences with Charmante's instructions for Baliardo to position himself at the viewing end of the telescope, leaving Charmante to take an aside to the audience. Behn's stage directions specify:

> [*He [Baliardo] looks in the Telescope.*
> [*While he is looking, Charmante goes to the Door to Scaramouch, who waited on purpose without, and takes a Glass with a Picture of a Nymph on it, and a light behind it; that as he brings it, it shows to the Audience. Goes to the end of the Telescope.*[56]

Charmante asks if Baliardo has seen anything, and Baliardo gives a response typical of an amateur astronomer trying to get *something* to come into focus in the viewing lens; essentially, a hopeful, "maybe?" or, "Methinks I see a kind of Glorious Cloud drawn up—and now—'tis gone again."[57] Charmante appeals to Baliardo's spiritual side and instructs him to return to the viewing lens in an attitude of supplication. While Baliardo is occupied with his prayers, "*Charmante puts the Glass into the Mouth of the Telescope.*"[58] Baliardo looks into the viewing lens and finally sees a moon nymph (an illustration drawn on Charmante's trick lens), "a Beauty young and Angel like, leaning upon a Cloud," and he is assured of the telescope's extraordinary power to reveal the inhabitants of the moon to earthbound viewers.[59] Repetition is the key to comedy, so Charmante repeats the ritual: instructing Baliardo to pray, "*Char[mante] claps the Glass with the Emperour on it, [Baliardo] looks in and sees it.*"[60] This time, Baliardo sees Iredonozar, the emperor of the moon, "seeted on a Throne…most sad and pensive."[61] Now convinced of the emperor of the moon's existence, Baliardo is set upon a course of action that eventually leads to the wedding at the end of the comedy and his own cure of faith in the telescope.

Baliardo's misguided curiosity is made evident through the ease with which Charmante dupes the doctor into mistaking a sketch on a lens for life on another world. Behn's telescope prop, like the refractive telescopes that it represented, functioned via lens manipulation: the two trick lenses that Charmante intentionally shows the audience cause Baliardo to believe in lunar civilization. The material nature of the trick and the scientific context of the play inspire a science-historiographical dramaturgy that situates Behn's telescope among the lens-and-mirror technologies that populated domains of science and entertainment in the late seventeenth century. Such a dramaturgical proposal further enmeshes Behn herself in the natural philosophical cultural assemblage of her time.

Historiographical Shufflings: A Dramaturgical Aside

A present-day revival of Behn's *Emperor* might embed an elaborate theatrical trick within the play's mechanical scenery to enhance the social associations signaled by Behn's synecdochal stage telescope. When the large telescope prop is considered within the context of seventeenth-century advances in lens technology, it becomes plausible that it could be used to mask a magic lantern—an early image-projection device—that may deepen an audience's curiosity about seventeenth-century optics in general, if not astronomy per se. A production of *Emperor of the Moon* staged with such a socio-technological history in mind might draw attention to the science objects at the heart of the plot to emphasize the historical science context of the play's original production. Baliardo and the Royal Society would remain the butts of Behn's linguistic humor, but a staged trick would support Fontenelle's natural philosophy, rephrased by Coppola, that "the more one learns about how nature actually works, the greater one's capacity is to enjoy its wondrous show."[62] A magic lantern demonstration embedded within act 1, scene 2 would perform Behn's moral that information transduced by the telescope can easily be misinterpreted while theatrically instructing a live audience about seventeenth-century advances in optics. Using the same assemblage of materials necessary to construct a Newtonian reflective telescope—mirrors, lenses, and light—the telescope that appears in act 1, scene 2 might be designed as a functional magic lantern to ironically enhance Behn's antimechanical message in a dramaturgy conversant with late seventeenth-century innovations in optics. Such a demonstration would also align with the Jesuit philosophy that surfaces in Behn's translator's preface.

As magic lanterns gained popularity throughout Europe over the course of the seventeenth century, religious and philosophical authorities "reshuffled" long-standing attitudes about the truth of human existence in light of this new technical curiosity. The optics involved in projection technology mediated cultural knowledge in a way that we have already explored with the telescope's earlier emergence. Film historian Laurent Mannoni identifies Huygens, the astronomer, as having invented the magic lantern sometime during the early 1660s, and science historian Koen Vermeir identifies "the magic lantern [as] part of a Baroque culture which was fascinated by illusion."[63] Jesuit philosophy of the late seventeenth century was rooted in the pursuit of knowledge of God through sensory experiences, yet, "for the Jesuits, a stage play is not an illusionist entertainment but a place where truth is shown, where the invisible is made visible and explicit. They made a strict distinction between *imago* (true image) and *idola* (false images, showing something that is not there; an aberration or deformity)."[64] Secular, experiential knowledge, such as knowledge gained from theatre attendance, was inseparable from knowledge of the divine, and Jesuit plays reflected this notion. In this experiential vein, seventeenth-century German Jesuit scholar Athanasius Kircher (1602–1680) experimented with magic lantern demonstrations as expressions of the truth, specifically, the true nature of light. To incorporate a magic lantern demonstration into a scene in which Baliardo's family members are striving to dissuade him from falling prey to *idola*—by means of deliberately projecting false images that the audience could clearly view and understand—would cohere with the Jesuit worldview that Behn professes in the translator's preface. The images of aliens required for Behn's slides certainly fit the bill for seventeenth-century magic lantern demonstrations, which often projected frightening, and intentionally false, images of devils, monsters, and magical creatures.

Jane Spencer suggests that in the original performance of *Emperor*, Charmante's slide, backlit by a candle, would be seen more clearly when shown to the audience, and again if the telescope were pointed at the audience, but the image would remain as small as the telescope's far end.[65] A strict reading of Behn's text suggests that the images that Baliardo sees are only apparent to the audience on the slide and through Baliardo's verbal description of them. However, if the production of this scene were to replicate a magic lantern demonstration, then the audience would share Baliardo's sensual experience visually through projections (or theatrical illusions meant to represent projections) and aurally through Baliardo's exclamations. If a historically accurate magic lantern projection were the desired effect in a production of act 1, scene 2, then a rearrangement of Newton's refractor telescope components would be in order. Newton's telescope incorporated two convex lenses and a mirror, in addition to a viewing lens and the distant light emanated by the observational object. A candle replaces the celestial object as light source and a glass slide, with the projected image drawn upon it, replaces the viewing lens. Charmante's candlelit slide apparatus should be backed by a convex mirror, and a tube containing the necessary pair of convex lenses would be placed between the light and the slide to create the projection.

The whole thing would be inserted into Charmante's end of the telescope tube while Baliardo is praying. The telescope prop should be set downstage on the apron. From there, the telescope could be pointed upstage to achieve a clear projection onto a backdrop that might be viewed, if dimly, by the audience.

Of course, twenty-first-century projection technology could enhance the performance of this effect. It is important to this dramaturgical aside to understand that projections as scientific demonstrations and entertainments were part of the cultural landscape in which Behn devised her performance and could plausibly have played into a seventeenth-century imagining of this scene. Even in the seventeenth century, the successive images of moon-nymph and Iredonozar may have been tricked to appear upstage, by means of Dorset Garden's legendary special effects system, and thus have created an illusion of projection that the audience would have been able to see.[66] In either scenario, hypothetical or historical, the audience, while captivated by the theatrical spectacle, could also become enthralled in a mechanically performed dialogue shuffled among seventeenth-century lens technologies.

To stage *Emperor* so that it contains a magic lantern demonstration would complicate Behn's intent to admonish supposedly gullible believers in the knowledge-productive capacity of the telescope. Charmante's repeated demonstration would reinforce Behn's moral lesson that science machines intended to improve human vision cannot be trusted, because they are too easily manipulated, but it would also teach the audience about magic lantern technology in an amusing manner. The knowledge production performed by the telescope prop would not negate the antimechanical prejudice delivered by Behn's dialogue any more than Huygens's invention of the magic lantern (an entertainment) would have impeded his advancements in telescope technology. An intentionally transparent mechanical demonstration embedded within this scene could encourage audiences to see both sides of the seventeenth-century debate over applications and practicalities of technics involving light, mirrors, and lenses.

Mythologizing Galileo's *Perspicill*

Emperor's prop telescopes mediate a cultural discourse about natural philosophy in the space of Behn's theatrical laboratory because of their situation within a triangular relationship among natural philosophy and its practitioners, Dorset Garden's elaborate mechanics, and lens technologies used in telescopes.[67] A Latourian reading of mechanical and human bodies in Behn's *Emperor* reveals a narrative that does not reject science technologies out of hand but rather yields to an invested attention on behalf of the audience. This embodied narrative suggests that "the Numbers" in attendance at Behn's play were curious about the lens-based technologies at work in the telescope and, possibly, about other advances in physics and optics. The technology presented onstage in act 1, scene 2 is itself an acknowledgment of the *social* use-value of telescope technologies in 1687. The connection is subtle. If "telescope" is reshuffled—through its component assemblage of mirrors, lenses, and scientists who experimented with both types of machines—to become at once an instrument of entertainment and an instrument of astronomy, then lens-manipulative optics (magic lantern, microscopes, stotoscopes, etc.) become part of the "new science" culture performed at Dorset Garden.

Emperor is conspicuously absent of telescopes after act 1, scene 2 until the play's final masque, when Dorset Garden's stage becomes a metatheatrical telescope of sorts.[68] The spectacle at the end of the play captures the audience's attention (both the audience in the theatre and the attendant characters in the play) by bringing the moon itself into the theatre. This is the final step in the reeducation of *dottore* Baliardo; the masque reveals Charmante's elaborate trick, and Behn uses this scene to dissuade her audience of any delusion that the telescope can significantly improve upon naked-eye astronomical observations. The mechanical masque that closes *Emperor* would have been the kind of entertainment that Dorset Garden audiences expected in 1687, and Behn stages a final comment on natural philosophy by placing *perspicills* in the hands of historical astronomers Galileo Galilei and Johannes Kepler (1571–1630), who are lampooned as "Galileus" and "Keplair" in the scene. The masque's setting on Mount Parnassus effectively mythologizes the telescopes and astronomers of old that appear in the spectacle. Contrary to the play's persistent message that telescopes are useless in their application to astronomy, the embodied, mechanical performance nevertheless demonstrates the function of the telescope by bringing the staged moon into a closer, clearer perspective for the Dorset Garden audience.

Stage directions at the top of the scene indicate, "*The Gallery [should be] richly adorn'd with Scenes and Lights*."[69] Upon seeing the elaborately dressed stage, Baliardo struggles to contain his experience of wonder for fear of being thought a rube. He alternately expresses his excitement to his niece, his daughter, and the theatre audience: "Let not thy Female Ignorance Prophane the highest Mysteries of Natural Philosophy; To Fools it seems Inchantment—but I've a Sense can reach it,—sit and expect the Event.—Hark—I am amaz'd but must conceal my Wonder—the Joy of Fools—and appear wise in Gravity."[70] The irony of this statement would not be lost on the audience, as they would be eagerly awaiting Baliardo's final comeuppance after having witnessed the women repeatedly trick Baliardo throughout the play. Baliardo verbally checks himself for the sake of his appearance in front of the characters in the play, but his asides directly invite the audience to join in his thought process and share his emotional engagement with the anticipated spectacle.

The masque begins with the appearance of a succession of exotic characters that imagistically combine tropes of classicism, colonialism, orientalism, and the occult: "*The Scene in the Front draws off, and shews the Hill of Parnassus; a noble large Walk of Trees leading to it, with eight or ten Negroes upon Pedastals, rang'd on each side of the Walks. Next Keplair and Galileus descend on each side, opposite to each other, in Chariots, with Perspectives in their Hands, as viewing the Machine of the Zodiack. Soft Musick plays still.*"[71] Seventeenth-century masques were frequently populated by characters from myth, fantasy, and legend; Behn's placement of Galileo and Kepler in chariots that descend from the heavens, each with his own *perspicill*, conveys her skepticism about the telescope and its origins. This mythological context underscores the playwright's message that reliance on telescopes for generating knowledge about astronomy is akin to studying myth as history or asking an astrologer to read one's horoscope to know the future. The playwright acknowledges the historical fact of these scientists' existence, but their placement in a masque casts doubt on the cultural value of their scientific legacies. The craze for astronomy based on telescopic discovery was, according to reasonable critique, fantastical. The *perspicills*' presence onstage artifactually locates Galileo and Kepler on the opposite end of Behn's scientific and philosophical continuum. The natural philosophers' depiction as heralds to the arrival of the emperor of the moon diminishes their historic accomplishments in the advancement of astronomy.

But then, Dorset Garden's proscenium becomes telescope-like when the audience sees the moon grow ever larger as it descends.[72] The final spectacular metaphor is performed through the descent of the moon onto the stage so that the theatrical masque becomes the machine that captures the moon and brings it closer to the audience. After the masque's obligatory song and dance, the mechanical spectacle continues: "*The globe of the moon appears, first like a new moon; as it moves forward it increases, till it comes to the full. When it is descended, it opens, and shows the emperor and the prince. They come forth with all their train, the flutes playing a symphony before [the emperor], which prepares the song; which ended, the dancers mingle as before.*"[73] The emperor of the moon travels on the moon as a vehicle by which he might come to know more about the Earth. Once the Emperor arrives, he weds the lovers with the technical assistance of a Stentraphon, a device used to amplify the voice.[74] "Keplair" reveals the joke: in truth he is the Viceroy and, as a friend, he counsels Baliardo to give up his lunatic preoccupations: "It was not in the Power of Herbs or Minerals,/ Of Reason, common Sense, and right Religion,/ To draw you from an Error that unman'd you."[75] Baliardo is not castigated as a fraud but cured from the (natural) philosophical fog that has been clouding his Reason. Baliardo concedes that he now "see[s] ther's nothing in philosophy," but his sudden conversion to reasonable Enlightenment leaves one to wonder if it is all philosophy that Behn considers bunk or just natural philosophy based on experiential observation.[76]

The representational telescopes in *Emperor of the Moon* provide multiple points of entry by which curious audience members and readers might access science as a cultural practice. Although Behn mouths dissent through her characters' dialogue, her choice of telescope technology as an essential narrative artifact indicates that the process of accepting machines as a part of extended and enhanced human perception had begun on London's hybrid stages by the end of the seventeenth century. The play's production history and Behn's concurrent science-oriented publications suggest that women had also permeated the boundaries of experimental science. The interdisciplinary analysis of this play disrupts traditional, liberal narratives of scientific progress and proposes an early modern model of women's scientific authority. By reshuffling the disciplinary deck, Behn's late play places the trailblazing female playwright squarely in the company of other seventeenth-century scientists and philosophers who explored "new science" concepts in a variety of experimental spaces.

Notes

1. This article was researched, in part, thanks to a Dibner Fellowship in the History of Science and Technology at the Huntington Library in San Marino, California. Thanks also to the Articles-in-Progress session at the Mid-America Theatre Conference for valuable feedback.
2. The image of a telescope (figure 1) is taken from John Wallis, "An accompt of a new catadioptrical telescope invented by Mr. Newton, Fellow of the R. Society, and Professor of the Mathematiques in the University of Cambridge." Sir Isaac Newton (1643–1727) did not invent the telescope but adapted it during his lifetime. The telescope was first patented by Hans Lipperhey (1570–1619) in 1608. I have written elsewhere on the origins of the telescope and its early appearances on the English stage. See Vivian Appler, "Among Actions, Objects, and Ideas: The Telescope in Thomas Tomkis's *Albumazar*," *Comparative Drama* 50, no. 1 (Spring 2016).
3. The term "natural philosophy" was used well into the nineteenth century to describe disciplines such as astronomy that now would be subcategorized under the vast domain of "science." The study and practice of astrology and alchemy also fell under this heading,

an association that fueled much of the seventeenth-century criticism of the discipline. During the seventeenth century, the term "new science" came to be applied to scientific processes that prioritized individual experience and observation. Galileo Galilei (1564–1642) was a chief promotor of this method. Sir Francis Bacon (1561–1626) developed the experiential mode of natural philosophy in England. In 1660, London's Royal Society took up Bacon's standard and became the central institution for "new" scientific inquiry in England. L'Académie des Sciences was established in Paris in 1666 by Jean-Baptiste Colbert (1610–1683).

4. *Emperor* enjoyed most of its staged productions in London's theatres during the late seventeenth and early eighteenth centuries. Jane Spencer also makes this observation in her 1995 edition of the play: Aphra Behn, *The Rover, The Feigned Courtesans, The Lucky Chance, The Emperor of the Moon*, ed. Jane Spencer (Oxford: Clarendon, 1995). *The Stationers' Register* records that *Emperor* was licensed on April 6, 1687. *The London Stage: 1660–1800. Part 1: 1660–1700*, ed. William Van Lennep (Carbondale: Southern Illinois University Press, 1965), 356. After its premiere, in March 1687, at the Dorset Garden Theatre, *Emperor* had a lengthy history in repertory at Drury Lane, a brief revival during the last gasps of Dorset Garden in 1706, significant representation at Lincoln's Inn Fields, and a final run that alternated performances at Covent Garden and Drury Lane during December 1748. In 1699, a song by Daniel Purcell was added.
5. Sandra Harding, *Objectivity and Diversity: Another Logic of Scientific Research* (Chicago: University of Chicago Press, 2015), xi.
6. Ibid.
7. Cavendish was a prolific playwright and natural philosopher of the mid-seventeenth century who published two volumes of plays during her lifetime. Du Châtelet translated and amended Newton's *Principia* and anticipated Einstein's theory of special relativity.
8. Bernard le Fauvier de Fontenelle, *A Discovery of New Worlds. From the French. Made English by Mrs. A. Behn. To which is prefixed by a PREFACE by way of ESSAY on Translated PROSE: wherein the Arguments of Father Tacquet, and others, against the System of Copernicus (as to the Motion of the Earth) are likewise considered, and answered: Wholly New* (London: William Canning, 1688), RB 113394, Huntington Library, San Marino, CA. Fontenelle also wrote several plays, including *La Comète* (1681). In 1697, Fontenelle became the secretary of l'Académie des Sciences, and the academy was granted official recognition by Louis XIV in 1699. For more on Fontenelle and L'Academie des Sciences, see Schaffer, Simon, "Fontenelle's Newton and the Uses of Genius," *L'Esprit Créateur* 55, no. 2 (Summer 2015): 48–61, *Project Muse*, July 29, 2016.
9. *Arlequin, empereur dans la lune* premiered at *l'Hôtel de Bourgogne* in March 1684. The French scenes were published in Evaristo Gherardi, *Le théâtre Italien ou le recueil general de toutes les Comédies et Scènes françaises jouées par les Comédiens Italiens de Roi* (1697, 1741) (Genève: Slatkine Reprints, 1969). Joseph Haydn revived the story as the *drama giocoso, Il mondo della luna* (1777), which relied upon Carlo Goldoni's 1750 adaptation of Fatouville's original. See Michael Brago, "Haydn, Goldoni, and *Il Mondo Della Luna*," *Eighteenth-Century Studies* 17, no. 3 (Spring 1984): 308–32, *JSTOR*, July 9, 2014.
10. Spencer tracks Behn's changes to Fatouville's original.
11. Baliardo's interest in cabalism is Behn's thinly veiled critique of the Royal Society, which

some detractors claimed was interested only in esoteric information that lacked practical applications in the real world. While "Cabal" has a specific context within Judaism, seventeenth-century England underwent a fad for applying the term to all kinds of secular, secret organizations and practices, including the Royal Society.

12. These female characters are present but mostly silent in Fatouville's French scenes.
13. Pierrot appears as Pedro in Behn's play.
14. *Emperor*, act 1, scene 1.
15. Poetry, prose, and dreams—imaginative thought—was often referred to as travel.
16. *Emperor*, act 1, scene 1.
17. Al Coppola, "Retraining the Virtuoso's Gaze: Behn's 'Emperor of the Moon,' the Royal Society, and the Spectacles of Science and Politics," *Eighteenth-Century Studies* 41, no. 4 (Summer 2008): 481–506, *JSTOR*, February 16, 2014, 482.
18. Behn makes no direct reference to Newton, his publications, or his telescope in either the translator's preface or her dedication to *Emperor of the Moon*.
19. Barbara M. Benedict, "Editing as Art: Authenticity and Authority in the Miscellanies of Dryden and Behn," *Restoration Studies in English Literary Culture, 1660–1700* 35, no. 1 (Spring 2011): 21–38, *Project Muse*, July 20, 2017, 22–23.
20. Benedict, "Editing as Art," 23.
21. Benedict, "Editing as Art," 35.
22. Aphra Behn, dedication, *The Emperor of the Moon. A Farce. As it is Acted by Their Majesties Servants. At the Queens Theatre* (London: R. Holt, 1697), RB 1120066, Huntington Library, San Marino, California.
23. *Emperor* moved to Drury Lane after its first few performances. Dorset Garden fell into decline midway through the 1690s. Attempts at the theatre's revival were made in 1706 and 1707, and *Emperor* was one of the Drury Lane repertory shows produced during that short Dorset Garden resurgence before it was finally torn down in 1709.
24. Behn's other philosophical translation projects from this period include Fontenelle's *The history of oracles, and the cheats of the pagan priests in two parts* (1688) and Abraham Cowley's (1618–1667) philosophical nature poetry, *The third part of the works of Mr. Abraham Cowley being his Six books of plants never before printed in English* (1689). Behn translated the sixth book, on trees, from Latin. Cowley was a poet with interests in science. He published *A Proposition for the Advancement of Experimental Philosophy* in 1661.
25. "Fixed stars" was a term that had long been used to refer to celestial objects that were not observed to move in the night sky.
26. Fontenelle, *Discovery*, 8–9.
27. Ibid., 55. The moon's geographical features had begun to be cataloged as early as Galileo's observations in 1610.
28. *Emperor*, act 1, scene 2.
29. For a discussion of the protofeminist themes of Behn's translator's preface to *Emperor of the Moon*, see Susan Goodfellow's "'Masculine Strokes': Aphra Behn as Translator of 'A Discovery of New Worlds,'" *Albion: A Quarterly Journal Concerned with British Studies* 28, no. 2 (Summer 1996): 229–250, *JSTOR*, July 9, 2014. Behn's Jesuit-influenced biblical interpretation of the state of late seventeenth-century astronomy includes a lengthy scriptural defense of Copernicanism following Father Tacquit, a Jesuit. The two points to which Behn repeatedly returns are 1) that the Bible can be interpreted as supportive

of either Ptolemic or Copernican models of the universe and 2) that "the Bible was not to instruct Mankind in Astronomy, Geometry, or Chronology, but in the Law of God to lead us to Eternal life," a point to which Galileo also returned in his letters written in his own defense during his trial with the Roman Inquisition earlier in the seventeenth century.

30. Behn, preface, *Emperor of the Moon.*
31. *Philosophical Transactions* was the title of the Royal Society's first periodical publication.
32. "I have made bold to correct a Fault of the French Copy, as to the heighth of our Air or Sphere of Activity of the Earth, which the French Copy makes twenty or thirty Leagues, I call it two or three, because sure this was a Fault of the Printer, and not a mistake of the Author. For Monsieur DesCartes, and Monsieur Rohalt, both assert it to be but two or three Leagues" (preface).
33. Ibid. The term "prospective glass" could refer to many kinds of glass lens devices from the magnifying glass to the spyglass. In this context, she must mean "spyglass" (or, telescope), because a magnifying glass would not function to bring distant objects into clearer focus.
34. Barbara Dancygier, "Multimodality and Theatre: Material Objects, Bodies and Language," in *Theatre, Performance and Cognition: Languages, Bodies and Ecologies*, ed. Rhonda Blair and Amy Cook (London: Bloomsbury, 2016), 24.
35. Coppola, "Retraining the Virtuoso's Gaze," 493.
36. Bruno Latour, *Reassembling the Social: An Introduction to Actor-Network-Theory* (Oxford: Oxford University Press, 2005), *ProQuest ebrary*, July 24, 2015, 6.
37. Ibid., 65.
38. A spyglass telescope was commonly referred to as a "Galilean" tube.
39. Bruno Latour, *We Have Never Been Modern* (1991), trans. Catherine Porter (Cambridge, MA: Harvard University Press, 1993), 78. Italics original.
40. *Reassembling*, 71.
41. Joanna Picciotto, "Performing the Garden: The Experimentalist Eden and 'Paradise Lost,'" *ELH* 72, no. 1 (Spring 2005): 23–78, 36, *JSTOR*, July 13, 2015. She quotes John Salkeld's *Treatise of Paradise, and the Principall Contents Thereof* (1617) as evidence for idle curiosity as sinful: "God would not have men idle: not an ill item for our lazie gallants, who thinke their gentilitie to consist in idleness, and a point of honour to live of other mens labour: but even in this (I am of opinion) that God doth punish them, that they have more griefes, and more discontent in their idle pleasures, then others in their most wearisome toiles, and labours, which though it be a most voluntary bondage, yet is it likewise the most base, and cruell slaverie to the base appetites" (Salkeld in Picciotto, "Performing the Garden," 35).
42. Picciotto, "Performing the Garden," 32.
43. Ibid., 28.
44. Behn, dedication, *Emperor of the Moon.*
45. *Emperor*, act 1, scene 2.
46. Ibid.
47. Hevelius created the first topographical lunar map, *Selenographia* (1647), and Huygens described Saturn's rings; the Huygens Gap and Hygens Ringlet bear his name.
48. Mark A. Radice estimates Dorset Garden's stage to have been twenty-five to thirty feet wide and as much as fifty feet deep, including an apron of a generous twenty feet. The

entire building is estimated to have been between 140 and 147 feet long. See Mark A. Radice, "Theater Architecture at the Time of Purcell and Its Influence on His 'Dramatick Operas,'" *The Musical Quarterly* 74, no. 1 (1990): 98–130, *JSTOR*, January 26, 2015.

49. Gherardi's *Le Théâtre Italien* typically documents the text for the French scenes and omits much of the improvised *lazzi*. No description of the telescope is included in Gherardi's published text other than that the device should be "grande." Without any other indication in the extant French scenes, it is difficult to determine exactly what kind of telescope would have occupied the stage in Paris in 1684. Visual representations of the play depict detailed portraits of the characters and hint at the scenario but do not feature a telescope.
50. "The theatre shows a garden, at the bottom of which is mounted a large telescope." Translation mine.
51. For a detailed discussion of the seventeenth-century competition to make the best telescope, see Albert Van Helden, *Huygens's Ring, Cassini's Division, and Saturn's Children*, Dibner Library Lecture, October 27, 2004 (Washington, DC: Smithsonian Institution Libraries, 2006).
52. Cassini's telescope was a gift from another Italian telescope maker, Giuseppe Campani (1635–1715).
53. Fatouville's Bal*o*ardo becomes Bal*i*ardo in Behn's adaptation.
54. "If there are sunsets on the Moon, there must be procreation, and contamination; and if you have a contamination and procreation, there must be animals and vegetables; and if animals are born and also vegetables, then it must be stated that the Moon is a habitable World like ours." Gherardi, *Le Théâtre Italien*, 139. Translation mine. This scene also appears in John Rudlin, *Commedia dell'Arte: An Actor's Handbook* (London: Routledge, 1994), 137–38.
55. *Emperor*, act 1, scene 2.
56. Ibid. In the 1687 publication of *Emperor*, [...followed by italicized text is the original format in which stage directions appear.
57. Ibid.
58. Ibid.
59. Ibid.
60. Ibid.
61. Ibid.
62. Coppola, "Retraining the Virtuoso's Gaze," 485.
63. Koen Vermeir, "The Magic of the Magic Lantern (1660–1700): On Analogical Demonstration and the Visualization of the Invisible," *British Journal for the History of Science*, 38, no. 2 (June 2005): 127–59, *JSTOR*, July 11, 2014, 128. For a fascinating narrative of Huygens's personal struggle between antitheatrical prejudice and technological innovation, see Laurent Mannoni, *The Great Art of Light and Shadow: Archaeology of the Cinema*, trans. and ed. Richard Crangle (Exeter: University of Exeter Press, 2000).
64. Vermeir, "The Magic of the Magic Lantern (1660–1700)," 131.
65. Spencer includes her imagination of the scene in her notes to the play. She suggests, "The light, perhaps a candle, allows the picture to be shown to the audience before it is put into the telescope." She hypothesizes that "the telescope is probably pointed towards the audience." Spencer, ed., *The Rover, The Feigned Courtesans, The Lucky Chance, The Emperor of the Moon* notes, 383.
66. As with the precise measurements of the Dorset Garden stage, details regarding Dorset

Garden's stage machinery remain vague. Radice notes, "In the specific case of the Dorset Garden Theatre, we lack any concrete evidence verifying the use of a dispersed shutter system," though, based on his own analysis of Purcell's libretto to *The Fairy Queen*, he surmises that there would have been shutters (Radice, "Theater Architecture at the Time of Purcell and Its Influence on His 'Dramatick Operas,'" 119).

67. *Perspicill* was Galileo's original term for the telescope. In the final masque, the *perspicill* is also referred to as a "perspective," which is short for "perspective glass," another seventeenth-century synonym for "telescope."
68. There is a scene in the middle of the play in which a "prospective glasse" is used, but context suggests that the instrument in this instance is a magnifying glass, not a telescope.
69. *Emperor*, act 3, scene 3.
70. Ibid.
71. Ibid.
72. This action perhaps makes the moon more like a spaceship than the theatre like a telescope. It is likely that Dorset Garden's capacity for "much-loved flying machines" would have played a part in the staging of this masque (Radice, "Theater Architecture at the Time of Purcell and Its Influence on His 'Dramatick Operas,'" 129). Coppola, in "Retraining the Virtuoso's Gaze," makes a strong case for Behn's re-use of Dryden's *Albion and Albinus* masque machinery.
73. *Emperor*, act 3, scene 3.
74. The Royal Society experimented with the stentorophonic horn, tube, or trumpet during the seventeenth century. The "Newdigate newsletters" comments on March 16, 1687, "A Country man haveing invented a head & soe contrived it that whatever language or tune you speak in the Mouth of it it Repeated distinctly and Audibly." *London Stage*, 357. The instrument is also employed in *Emperor*'s prologue.
75. *Emperor*, act 3, scene 3.
76. Ibid.

Kate Soffel's Life of Crime

A Gendered Journey from Warden's Wife to Criminal Actress

—KRISTI GOOD

Many residents of Pittsburgh are well acquainted with the story of the "Biddle Boys," Edward and John (Ed and Jack), who escaped from the Allegheny County Jail in winter 1902, with the help of the warden's wife, Kate Soffel. Their escape from the city and the ensuing horse-drawn sleigh chase across the snowy roads of Butler County thrilled newspaper readers across the country. The final confrontation between law enforcement and the "desperadoes," as journalists characterized them, was a bloody shoot-out that left the Biddles and Soffel on the brink of death. Soffel survived, but the public's excitement about her role in these events waned much more quickly than did their enthusiasm for the event itself.

In *Medea's Daughters: Forming and Performing the Woman Who Kills*, Jennifer Jones posits, "Idealized 'woman' has traditionally been constructed as self-sacrificing, passive, and nurturing; therefore, when actual women become violent, some sense must be made of their actions if the myth of feminine passivity is to be maintained."[1] Jones cites as a major influence the work of Ann Jones, who, in her book *Women Who Kill*, analyzed how various historical murder trials have perpetuated the subordination of women. Jones builds on this feminist analysis by exploring the dramatic texts that spring from these criminal events and legal proceedings and argues that dramatic representations of female criminality serve as similar historical documentation to "contain and control cultural anxiety" regarding the abnormality of the criminal woman.[2]

The jailbreak itself was a public spectacle that held the interest of the American people from coast to coast, and a popular true-crime melodrama by Theodore Kremer quickly followed the newspaper headlines. *A Desperate Chance* detailed the sensational events of the Biddle jailbreak and debuted in the same year as the escape. Kremer's play functions as Jones suggests: a morality play that warns women of "the dangers of self-determination" and encourages them to "embrace their submissive status."[3] But Kremer wrote his play before Soffel served her jail time, and her determination to cultivate a public life for herself post incarceration was not consistent with the narrative of passive femininity that the media, the courts, and Kremer had constructed to assure society that this unnatural, criminal woman was no longer a moral threat. While *A Desperate Chance* played across the country for years following the crime, Soffel's attempt to reclaim her life through a career in the theatre was met with opposition, particularly in her home region. This article serves as an act of feminist reclamation by documenting Soffel's involvement with the Biddles as well as her attempt to reenter society, a period heretofore unexamined in her life, and intervenes in the current historical narrative by painting her as a model not of submissive femininity but of feminist subversion.

Peter Soffel and Kate Dietrich were married in the German Evangelical Protestant Church in Pittsburgh on December 9, 1886.[4] They started a family within the first years of marriage and had four children. Aside from her duties as a mother, Soffel regularly ministered to men incarcerated at the Allegheny County Jail, where her husband was the warden. This was how she came into contact with Ed and Jack Biddle in 1901, as they sat waiting for their execution dates.

The Biddles were sentenced to execution for fatally shooting a Mount Washington grocer named Thomas Kahney during a robbery in April 1901. Police profiled the Biddles and an accomplice named Walter Dorman, who were understood to be members of a group of robbers known as the Chloroform Gang. The day following the shooting in Mount Washington, police arrested Dorman and his common-law wife, Jennie Seebers, at their residence. At another house nearby, authorities arrested Jack Biddle on the ground floor before a shoot-out began upstairs. By the end of the skirmish, a police officer was killed, Ed Biddle was in custody but close to death, and a woman named Jessie Bodyne was arrested while trying to flee.[5]

The Biddles were the only two of the group to be sentenced to execution; Dorman turned state's evidence in return for a penitentiary sentence, and both Seebers and Bodyne were released after being charged with receiving stolen property.[6] Most accounts of Soffel's relationship with the Biddles suggest that Ed hypnotized her into helping them escape, but Soffel's confession shows a clear, reasoned approach to her involvement. She said, "I thought the purpose and cause was just and forced by a Christian spirit. Ed told me he was innocent and each day it impressed itself upon me. I made up my mind he should not suffer innocently and I planned to help the boys."[7] The topic of hypnosis, particularly when used by criminals to coerce innocent individuals to do their bidding, was popular at the time, but the Biddles' claim of innocence was not just a ploy directed at Soffel. Even on their deathbeds, with no hope of mesmerizing law enforcement, the brothers maintained their innocence. Ed claimed that Jennie Seebers was responsible for the Kahney murder, and Jack corroborated that while he was not present at the Kahney robbery, Ed and Dorman were there along with Seebers, who was dressed in men's clothing.[8] Without any additional evidence, this scenario seems plausible: Seebers could have been mistaken for a man during the robbery, and Dorman would have plenty of incentive to fabricate the Biddles' involvement to save his common-law wife and commute his sentence.

The Biddles broke out of the Allegheny County Jail on January 30, 1902, with the help of Soffel, who provided saws, revolvers, and disguises. Their flight through the Butler County countryside in a horse-drawn sleigh ended in a violent confrontation with law officials on February 1, leaving both the Biddles and Soffel wounded: Jack shot by the police, and Ed and Soffel suffering from self-inflicted wounds. Officials took them to the Butler County Jail, and Soffel was eventually removed to the local hospital, under guard, when it appeared that she would make a full recovery.

Within the sensational narrative the newspapers created during the escape and capture of the criminals, the depiction of Soffel remains focused on her perceived frailties as a woman. Alongside the suggestion that Soffel had been hypnotized by Ed Biddle and had no agency whatsoever in the decision to facilitate their escape, the newspapers gleefully reported the discovery of a letter in Soffel's possession that hinted she and Ed were having a romantic affair.[9] The media narrative then shifted to focus on Soffel as a cheating wife and delinquent mother who had abandoned her family, rather than solely as a criminal who had helped convicts escape from jail. The *Salt Lake Herald* reported the events following Warden Soffel's realization that his wife had played a part in the jailbreak. "Under the crushing grief of this discovery Mr. Soffel behaved in a most heroic manner. He at once made public the humiliating fact that he believed his wife to be responsible for the escape.... Warden Soffel's great mental suffering was visible to scores of persons who saw him, but he bore up manfully and attended to all the duties which the trying occasion imposed upon him."[10] Journalists depicted Warden Soffel as the victim-turned-hero, an individual who needed to regain his manhood after suffering humiliation at the hands of his wife.

Before the jailbreak, Warden Soffel had been warned very publicly that the burgeoning relationship between his wife and the Biddles was cause for concern. The *Herald* reported that a newspaper article two weeks before the jailbreak implied that Kate Soffel was "too much interested in the Biddles," but the Warden "served notice on every one of the jail employes [*sic*] that his wife was to do just as she pleased inside the jail."[11] The narrative proposes that Warden Soffel's humiliation stemmed from the fact that his wife managed to deceive him. The media undermined the Warden's masculinity by rendering him incapable of controlling his wife, rather than ineffectual at maintaining the security of his jail.

Officials incorrectly informed Warden Soffel on February 1 that his wife had died in the shoot-out in Butler County. The *Pittsburg Press*[12] recorded his reaction: "He fell into a chair, exclaiming: 'It is God's will! The poor, foolish woman! She has been punished.' Later he said: 'The woman has done wrong. Perhaps she has been punished by God. One thing that must be considered—she is the mother of my children. She will be brought to the house. She can do no further harm to mankind now. She will be laid to rest properly. She has done all the harm toward me she can, and I would far, far rather bring back her dead body to the home that she has wrecked than to have shame cast on the children by their mother's imprisonment, which might have occurred.'"[13] There are two types of punishment mentioned in this statement: lawful imprisonment and the reckoning of God. The warden references Soffel's actual crime of aiding and abetting criminals, as well as the perceived crime of neglecting her societal duty to husband and family. He suggests the latter is more deserving of the wrath of God, clearly stating that it is better that she is dead in the "home that she has wrecked" than casting shame on the family by serving a prison sentence. Unfortunately for the warden's pride, Soffel's suicide attempt was foiled by a stay in her corset, which prevented the bullet from causing its intended fatal damage. She went on to serve one year and seven months at the Western State Penitentiary for her role in the Biddles' escape.[14]

Until the capture of the fugitives, the excitement with which the public followed the case in the newspapers could only be estimated, but a physical manifestation soon made the scale of the fervor clear. Once authorities had captured the Biddles and Soffel, the public satisfied their curiosity by seeking out the captives in person. The *Philadelphia Inquirer* reported: "The excitement in the country is simply beyond description. Many people were so curious that they drove and rode to Butler last night.... Shortly after midnight they began to arrive and the crowd was augmented from that time on until 6 o'clock, when it was estimated that fully seven thousand persons were standing in front of the large oaken doors of the Butler County Jail. . . . The Butler county fair, which is always famous for the crowds it draws, was scarcely ever such a drawing card as the Butler county jail to-day."[15]

The article stated that the crowd had "no other excuse except that they were attracted to the black fame" of the criminals.[16] The *Inquirer* estimated that nearly two thousand people from the crowd—women especially—gained access to the building itself.

> While physicians were dressing the Biddles' wounds women were admitted to the cell rooms. Sympathy was expressed on all sides for the dying murderers. Some women were even so bold as to lay their hands on their foreheads, and few had any hesitancy in talking to Jack Biddle and expressing their sorrow for him. Girls, mothers and wives wept, and had it not been for the prompt action of the jail guards yesterday afternoon two women would have fainted. The men visitors cared but little as to the dying pair. They came in from every door and were readily admitted to the cells. While the doctors were applying bandages or placing fresh cotton on the wounds of the Biddles thousands of the morbid curiosity-stricken men looked on. Even while the Rev. Father Walsh was administering the last sacred rites of the Roman Catholic Church men and women were admitted.[17]

The *Inquirer* justified the overwhelming appearance of women by saying that many believed in the Biddles' innocence, but this claim of morality is overshadowed by the sheer indecency of putting two dying men on display for entertainment purposes. Even the intimate ministrations of a holy sacrament did not warrant privacy.

The impropriety did not end here, as people sought objects related to the Biddle death as they would buy trinkets at a performance. Individuals who were eager to have a physical remembrance of the occasion found what they craved in a ten-foot-square section of snow and gravel by the south corner of the jail. Officials had unloaded Soffel and the Biddles here the preceding evening, and the area was covered in "no less than a half gallon of the life's blood of the trio," reported the *Inquirer*.[18] Souvenir-hunters had picked the stones clean by morning, going "so far as to get stones, wash them in the blood-covered snow, in order to preserve them as souvenirs of the occasion."[19]

The Biddles both died on Saturday, February 1, and the officials exhibited the bodies in the hallway of the jail the following day. A "continuous stream" of people entered the jail for three hours to look at the bodies, and when the Biddles were removed to Pittsburgh the following day, a similar crowd waited at the train station for their arrival, where "there was a rough scramble to get to the platform of the depot, during which several were bruised by being crushed against the stairway."[20] The crowd followed the bodies to the morgue, but police prevented them from entering the building.

Given this spectacle, the popular playwright Theodore Kremer wasted no time in reaping the benefits of the Biddles' scintillating tale. He submitted his dramatization of the Biddles' escape, titled *A Desperate Chance*, to the Library of Congress for copyright on May 3, 1902, and it had begun playing in New York theatres by the fall. The melodrama's four acts chronicled the tale of the Biddles from the Kahney murder to their escape and eventual death in the Butler County Jail. The *Cambridge Chronicle* reported on the play before its Boston opening in 1902, writing, "While Mr. Kremer has followed as near as practicable the facts of the case, he has of course elaborated and added until he has evolved a story of intense heart interest that cannot fail to entertain all lovers of the drama."[21]

Kremer did, in fact, follow the details of the case very closely, even adding factual details like a play-by-play of the altercation between fugitives and guards during the jailbreak and the number of times each Biddle brother was shot during the standoff. Aside from a vague attempt to disguise the names of those involved, Kremer's deviation from the facts to create "heart interest" lies in details that few, if any, individuals could know: intimate dialogue between characters and the eventual outcome of the historical event. The thematic through line of the jailbreak plot concerns character Ed Ribble's hypnotic power over women. The now-common trope of a villain who uses hypnosis for personal gain was only in its infancy in 1902. George du Maurier's 1895 novel, *Trilby*, which psychologist Deirdre Barrett credits as "the most influential prototype" for this irresponsible depiction of hypnosis in popular culture, introduced the iconic character of Svengali, a mesmerist who seduces and exploits the beautiful woman Trilby.[22] Kremer's dialogue paints his female characters as distinctly frail and submissive, a move he ultimately employs to gain sympathy for the character Kate and her inability to resist Ed's persuasive powers.

In the first scene, Peter and Kate Loffler encounter Ed Ribble in Tom Kenny's store, where Ed and his brother, Jack, are engaging in reconnaissance. All the women in the store are mesmerized by Ed, commenting on his "wonderful eyes" and "fascinating glances."[23] Kate begins to swoon when Peter asks about Ed's taste in women and he boldly replies, "Oh, about the same as your own."[24] Peter is incensed and challenges Ed, who replies, "Oh, come Warden. I am not such a scarecrow as you intend to imply, whenever Ed Ribble makes up his mind to win and conquer a woman married or single he always succeeds. (*Folds arms looks passionately at Kate*)."[25] Before Peter can strike a blow, Kate calms him.

The end of the first act shows the confrontation between Kenny and the Ribbles during the robbery, and Ed shoots the grocer at point blank range, leaving no question for the remainder of the play that Ed is guilty. The second act takes place in the prison during visiting hours. Kate and Mrs. Pearce, a wealthy widow, stress their belief to the Warden that the Ribbles are innocent, even though a button from Ed's coat was found clutched in Kenny's hand. The Ribbles overhear and comment:

ED: (*Aside*) It's lucky that women have so little common sense!
JACK: (*Grinning*) Yes and such large charitable hearts! (*Snickers*)[26]

Kate is visibly agitated throughout the scene, and when Peter forces her to stay with the Ribbles and cast her "sunny smiles"[27] to cheer them up, the audience sees that she has been trying to deliver revolvers and a saw for their jailbreak. Kate bemoans, "Oh, Ed, it if were not for the thought that I am convinced of your innocence I would despise myself!" but Ed assures her that "every Christian woman will admire you for rescuing an innocent man from the gallows!"[28]

Kremer's bold assertion that Ed is, in fact, a murderer is underscored by Ed's violence and deceit throughout the play. Kate's willingness to believe him, as well as Kremer's depiction of women as ornaments who are valued for their "sunny smiles," casts her as a weak, gullible figure on whom hypnosis would be effective. Kremer shows throughout the scene that Kate's resolve to commit a crime wavers whenever she breaks contact with Ed. Barrett notes that power via eye contact is common in the "Svengali genre" because of its link to what animal behaviorists call the "copulatory gaze," or a practice of continuous eye contact that is certain to result in a violent or sexual act.[29] Kremer adds the following exchange, replete with melodramatic exclamations:

KATE: But remember, Ed, no violence!
ED: Don't you worry! You are the best and the bravest little woman in the world!
KATE: Oh, don't! Only Christian motives and the firm belief in your innocence prompt me to this desperate action!
ED: Don't say that, Kate! You love me! Look at me, and tell me that you love me. (*He looks fixedly at her.*)
KATE: (*Stares at him long, as if by an unseen power her hands leave her panting breast and steal up to his through bars. She utters as if in a trance.*) God help me, I DO love you![30]

Kremer's push toward the supernatural to show Ed's undeniable power is one of the devices he employs to build sympathy for Kate, rendering her a victim and blameless for having broken the social code of submissive femininity. Another such device is the introduction of the character Clara, Peter and Kate Loffler's only child.

From the first scene, Clara is a model of childlike innocence and wisdom. She gravitates to Jack Ribble, who Kremer paints as a softer, more compassionate figure than Ed, and comes to visit him in the prison after Kate's emotional scene. Clara brings Jack a piece of cake from her own meal. Peter asks her why she isn't bringing cake to Ed as well.

CLARA: Well I don't like him so much!
PETER: Indeed, why?
CLARA: His eyes—they look at you so—so—you know around the corners!!
PETER: (Laughing) Yes, but that's what all the ladies admire so much!
CLARA: Oh, well I suppose I'm no lady![31]

Kremer's depiction of childlike innocence is borne out in Clara's instinctual dislike of Ed, though this conceit suggests that once a female child reaches puberty, her innocence and good sense are compromised. Kremer implies that once a female body matures, her capacity for sexual desire strips her of her natural intelligence and she is fit only to satisfy a husband's sexual needs in the hopes of reproducing and becoming a mother.

These ideas are reinforced by the old guard, Biebrich, representing Kate Soffel's father, Conrad Dietrich, who was a guard at the Allegheny County Jail. Biebrich has noticed Kate's behavior with Ed and confronts her. He reminds her of her marriage vows and chastises her. "Do you comprehend that this unholy attachment will not only dishonor your husband, who trusts you, and disgrace your child, but also bring me, and the mother who bore you, to an early grave? Oh, Kate, dear forget that unnatural infatuation! Come back as you left us with a pure heart and unsullied! Ah, Kate don't waver! For God's sake don't hesitate! All our lives and happiness hang in the balance! Go back to the man who loves you! Back to the little one who honors you! (*Sobs violently*)"[32] This passage makes clear that Biebrich thinks only that Kate is in love with Ed, not that she is plotting a crime. It is her sexual desire that will be responsible for the utter ruin of her husband, child, and parents.

The final act takes place in the Butler County Jail, as Ed and Jack lie dying and Kate is wounded. Father Walsh assures Peter that Kate's suicide attempt was not successful, and she is pleading for forgiveness. Father Walsh counsels Peter, "Remember, my son, she is only a weak woman!"[33] But Peter is resolved that he will divorce Kate, and Biebrich assures everyone that divorce is a worse parting than death. Only Clara, robed in a white satin cloak, remains optimistic that her parents will make amends. A Detective Kindheart agrees with Clara and sympathizes with Kate. He says to Peter, "No one will blame her, sir. Ed Ribble's hypnotic power over women was a well-known fact. The public realizes this and will consider her a heroine."[34] Kremer uses Clara as a symbol of innocence and uses the aptly named Detective Kindheart to stress Kate's redeemable nature and Ed Ribble's insidious power. In his last moments, Ed acknowledges this as well and begs Kate for forgiveness, assuring her that her husband will take her back. Ed lives long enough to see Peter and Kate reunited by the hands of Clara, who pluckily delivers the final line of the play, "Ah, di'nt I tell you so!"[35]

Without knowing how things would fall for the real Peter and Kate Soffel, Kremer gave their characters a fairy-tale ending where the crime was forgiven and the social order was restored. Seen as a historical document, by Jones's definition, *A Desperate Chance* reinforces traditional gender roles through imagining a conclusion to the then unfinished story of Kate Soffel's life, a conclusion that, as Jones says, functions by "reassuring the patriarchy that women embrace their submissive status."[36] In reality, Peter Soffel—now resigned from his post as warden and serving the Pittsburg Carnegie & Western Railroad as a right-of-way man[37]—divorced Kate Soffel while she was incarcerated at Western State Penitentiary. In the libel suit, Mr. Soffel accused her of having an affair with Ed Biddle during the brief period between the jailbreak and their capture.[38] James and Theodosia Stevenson, the owners of the hotel in Mt. Chestnut where Kate Soffel and the Biddles rested during their flight, testified during an extensive line of questioning that the bed in the room Kate and Ed occupied for approximately an hour and a half appeared to have been slept in by two people.[39] The jury granted the divorce and gave custody of all four children to Peter Soffel.[40]

Kremer successfully capitalized on the true-crime genre, and the melodrama was still playing regularly across the country at the time of Soffel's release. In fact, the play was so popular that it was regularly performed up until 1908. But Kremer wasn't the only person inspired by the true story of the Biddles and Kate Soffel; a manager by the name of Louis Lesser visited Soffel toward the end of her incarceration to propose a new career as an actress. Perhaps Lesser imagined himself as theatre producer David Belasco and Soffel as Mrs. Leslie Carter, the famed socialite-turned-actress. Belasco's work with the New York School for Acting (NYSA), which he cofounded in 1885, focused on developing emotional range, especially in actresses. Kim Marra explains in *Strange Duets: Impresarios and Actresses in American Theatre, 1865–1914* that the NYSA's mission was "one of moral and social uplift with particular concern for the reputations of young women who sought a livelihood in the theatre."[41] The correlation between actresses and promiscuity was still strong in this era, Marra notes, due to persistent Victorian gynecological theories that connected elevated emotional states with overstimulated reproductive organs. Hence, an actress who was capable of giving a passionate performance could do so only because she was in a state of sexual arousal. An actress could legitimize her skill and repair her reputation, however, if it was understood that she was under the tutelage of a master such as Belasco and his colleagues. Marra comments on Belasco's "Svengali-like influence" over actresses such as Carter, who, though requiring extensive social rehabilitation after a very public and salacious divorce trial, went on to a theatrical career of great esteem.[42]

Regardless of whether Lesser had any concern for rehabilitating Soffel's reputation, he must have counted on her infamy to draw interest. An article in the *Saint Paul Globe* suggests as much with its headline "Mrs. Soffel to Act: Woman Who Helped Biddles Escape Goes on Stage." The article states that Soffel had been training for her stage career since her release from the penitentiary and that she would be joining a company to play the lead role in a play called *A Daring Woman* by Vic Calver, which the article assured readers had "nothing in it to recall the Biddle tragedy." The true content of the play is a mystery, as it appears the physical script no longer exists, but the article describes, "The scenes are laid in Montana and California, and Mrs. Soffel will appear in the character of Agnes Gray, a noble but misunderstood woman without a past."[43]

The play was slated to open in late January 1904 at the Colonial Theatre in Connellsville, some fifty miles east of Pittsburgh, but there was already trouble in the surrounding area. The managers of Gamble's Opera House in Monongahela, Pennsylvania, had refused to book the play, and while the play was slated to open in nearby Charleroi, there was a petition to have management cancel the performance.[44]

It is not clear who began the petition to stop the Charleroi performance, or why. Peter Oresick, an author and editor who dedicated much of his life to compiling a bibliography of books, films, and plays that showcase Pittsburgh, suggests that the content of Calver's play changed dramatically after the communities in Charleroi and Monongahela raised objections. The newspaper article describing these boycotts lists the play as *A Dangerous Woman*, which was the title under which it was billed in the December 1903 booking announcement in the *New York Clipper*.[45] All other newspaper articles list the play as *A Daring Woman*, and Oresick proposes that Calver altered the content and title due to this local backlash.[46] The *Globe*'s pointed disclaimer, that the play had "nothing in it to recall the Biddle tragedy," alludes to this possibility. Because the *Globe*'s brief description does not contain anything that appears objectionable by reasonable standards, Oresick's hypothesis seems likely; Calver eliminated the scandalous material from the script, while Soffel remained in the cast.

While the sources of the Charleroi and Monongahela unrest remain unclear, the major force behind the interruption of the opening night in Connellsville was the Women's Christian Temperance Union, which did not want Mrs. Soffel to appear. "The Connellsville W. C. T. U. was up in arms the moment the bills were posted, and immediately called a public meeting to enter a protest against Mrs. Soffel appearing upon the Connellsville stage. In the notices calling the meeting the W. C. T. U. says, 'A momentous question faces Connellsville. Will we put a premium on vileness and lawlessness?'"[47] The local burgess stated publicly that his "sympathies are wholly with the W. C. T. U.," but there was no legal way he could stop Soffel from performing without the possibility of being liable for thousands of dollars in damages, should Soffel decide to sue the borough.[48] However, they could take legal action if she actually set foot on the stage. Soffel's manager, Lesser, and the manager of the theatre, George Challis, were served with the following notice: "You are hereby notified that if you allow, permit, or are responsible for or concerned in the production of the play, 'A Daring Woman,' in which Mrs. Kate Soffel of Pittsburg appears or takes part, in any theatre in Fayette county, Pennsylvania, you will be prosecuted for committing a public act in violation of decency and morality."[49]

The company prepared for opening night, but Soffel never made it to the stage. A Detective McBeth arrested her in her dressing room before the curtain went up. Lesser and Challis demanded to see a warrant, which McBeth claimed to have but would not produce. Soffel was already in costume, and the stage manager held the curtain in the hopes that the show would go on. Lesser and Challis placed a call to the district attorney to dispute the premature arrest, but "after hours of argument," Soffel was not allowed to appear onstage, and the stage manager read her part.[50] The situation reached a wide audience, with New York City's *The Sun* reporting, "The audience clamored for the appearance of Mrs. Soffel. There was much disorder in the house as the result of her non-appearance."[51]

The jury found Soffel, Lesser, and Challis guilty of publicly violating decency and morality, despite their failure to actually break the law. While one newspaper defended Soffel by saying that she had already "paid the penalty of her crime," the opposition was successful.[52] Yes, Soffel had served her time for her role in the jailbreak, but had she made amends for the social crime of deviating from submissive femininity? Kremer's *A Desperate Chance*, when viewed as a historical document, reinforced Soffel's crime as an unnatural female act, one for which she had been legally convicted and served time. However, Soffel's physical presence in *A Daring Woman* undermined that lawful and social verdict by giving her the agency to remake and present herself not as a fallen woman but in the guise of her character Agnes Gray, "a noble but misunderstood woman without a past," and as a skilled artist intent on living her life as she pleased without regard for social expectation. Lesser was no Belasco, and Soffel's brief training as an actor was not enough to rehabilitate her feminine image. It appears that the prosecution's case against her performance cited an example of immorality other than the Biddle jailbreak; the district attorney requested Soffel's divorce proceedings to use as evidence against her.[53] In case her crime of aiding and abetting murderers was not enough to convince a jury that she was amoral or indecent, the district attorney hedged his bets by including her failure as a woman to remain faithful to her husband and children.

Soffel would ultimately face another injunction, instigated by the Washington Ministerial Association, which prevented her from performing anywhere in Washington County, Pennsylvania. She encountered a mixture of opposition and acceptance during the rest of her tour, which ended in May 1904. She retired to Pittsburgh, took up seamstress work, and died of typhoid fever on August 30, 1909.[54] Soffel has since been reduced to folklore in the city of Pittsburgh—a ghost haunting the second floor of her former-home-turned-restaurant—while the Biddle Brothers are commemorated more publicly, lending their surname to a street, a biking trail, an official government building, and a popular coffee shop, Biddle's Escape. Soffel and her unnatural crimes—more unnatural, it seems, than a pair of murderous brothers on death row—are virtually erased in the historical record to assuage cultural unease surrounding female criminality. Kremer capitalized on the major event of her life, writing one of the most lucrative plays of his career, while Soffel was legally and socially condemned for the role she played, both in real life and on the stage. This essay details for the first time Soffel's refusal to adhere to the submissive role society required of her following such a moral breach and reframes it as a radical act of feminist subversion.

Notes

1. Jennifer Jones, *Medea's Daughters: Forming and Performing the Woman Who Kills* (Columbus: Ohio State University Press, 2003), x.
2. Ibid., ix–x.

3. Ibid., xv, xii.
4. "United in Marriage," December 9, 1886, File 1996.0079, Detre Library & Archives, Senator John Heinz History Center, Pittsburgh, PA. Special thanks to archivist Sierra Green for making me aware of this collection.
5. James A. McKee, *20th Century History of Butler and Butler County, Pa. and Representative Citizens* (Chicago: Richmond Arnold Publishing Company, 1909), 123–24. Several articles from the time refer to the members of the Chloroform Gang by different names, and it is never clear as to which are legal names and which are aliases. Walter Dorman is also known as Robert Wilcox, and his common-law wife Jennie Seebers is alternately known as Jennie Wilcox. The Biddles went by the alias surname Wright, and several publications claimed that Jessie Bodyne (alternately Bodine), went by the alias Jessie Wright, because she was married to one of the Biddles, though which brother was never made clear.
6. "May Be the Biddles," *Evening Star* (Washington, DC), January 31, 1902.
7. "Mrs. Soffel Confessed Her Crimes," *Pittsburg Press*, February 1, 1902.
8. Ibid.
9. "Women Sympathized with Murderers," *Philadelphia Inquirer*, February 2, 1902.
10. "Warden Was Warned."
11. Ibid.
12. The city of Pittsburgh added the "h" to its spelling in 1911. In this essay, the earlier spelling without the "h" is used if the name is used in a proper title or if a publication from the time is quoted. The current spelling with the "h" is used all other times.
13. "Mrs. Soffel Confessed."
14. "Mrs. Kate Soffel Dead," *New York Times*, August 31, 1909.
15. "Women Sympathized."
16. Ibid.
17. Ibid.
18. Ibid.
19. Ibid.
20. McKee, 123–24; "Warden Was Warned."
21. "Theatres: Grand Opera House," *Cambridge (MA) Chronicle*, February 28, 1903.
22. Deirdre Barrett, "Hypnosis in Popular Media," *Hypnosis and Hypnotherapy* (Santa Barbara: Praeger 2010), 77.
23. Theodore Kremer, *A Desperate Chance*, unpublished manuscript, Library of Congress copyright entry, May 3, 1902, 9.
24. Ibid., 13.
25. Ibid., 14.
26. Ibid., 23.
27. Ibid., 24.
28. Ibid., 27, 28.
29. Barrett, "Hypnosis in Popular Media," 79.
30. Kremer, *A Desperate Chance*, 30.
31. Ibid., 40–41.
32. Ibid., 46.

33. Ibid., 72.
34. Ibid., 80.
35. Ibid., 90.
36. Jones, *Medea's Daughters*, xii.
37. "Peter Soffel Testimony," October 24, 1902, File 1996.0079, Detre Library & Archives. Senator John Heinz History Center, Pittsburgh.
38. "Peter K. Soffel vs. Kate Soffel, nee Kate Dietrich," August 1902, File 1996.0079, Detre Library & Archives, Senator John Heinz History Center, Pittsburgh.
39. "Stevenson Deposition," February 21, 1903, File 1996.0079, Detre Library & Archives, Senator John Heinz History Center, Pittsburgh, PA.
40. "Verdict," October 21, 1903, File 1996.0079, Detre Library & Archives, Senator John Heinz History Center, Pittsburgh, PA.
41. Kim Marra, *Strange Duets: Impresarios and Actresses in American Theatre, 1865–1914* (Iowa City: University of Iowa Press, 2006), 160.
42. Ibid., 178.
43. "Mrs. Soffel to Act: Woman Who Helped Biddles Escape Goes on Stage," *Saint Paul Globe*, January 19, 1904.
44. "Management Commended," *Daily Republican* (Monongahela, PA), January 20, 1904.
45. Ibid.
46. Peter Oresick, interview with Kristi Good, personal interview, Pittsburgh, February 18, 2015.
47. "Mrs. Soffel, 'Back up!'" *Daily Gazette and Bulletin* (Williamsport, PA), January 22, 1904.
48. "Soffel Show Legal," *Courier* (Connellsville, PA), January 22, 1904.
49. Ibid.
50. "Mrs. Soffel Bluffed by a Lot of Officers," *Mail* (Hagerstown, MD), January 29, 1904.
51. "Mrs. Soffel Didn't Act: Woman Who Helped the Biddles to Escape Arrested in Theatre," *Sun* (New York, NY), January 24, 1904.
52. "Mrs. Soffel, 'Back up!'"
53. "Alfred E. Jones to George M. Stosock, Esq.," March 6 or 16, 1904 (writing illegible), File 1996.0079, Detre Library & Archives, Senator John Heinz History Center, Pittsburgh, PA.
54. "Mrs. Kate Soffel Dead."

Staging Ajax's Suicide

A Historiography

—PETER A. CAMPBELL

When I was commissioned to write an adaptation of Sophocles's *Ajax* for a theatre festival in lower Manhattan in 2004, I immersed myself in the various translations and editions of the play, which of course included editorial notes and commentaries. These notes often emphasized the great poetry of Ajax's monologues and the unevenness of the play's structure. But every single one of them discussed at length the staging of Ajax's suicide. There are numerous ideas of how this scene was originally staged and of its significance to the logistics and aesthetics of Greek staging practice, dramaturgy, and reception. The suicide is considered important because it is one of the few moments in Athenian tragedy in which an act of violence may have been staged in view of the spectators. As a playwright and director, I was compelled by the challenges of staging that moment and looked to the editorial notes and commentaries for information and suggestions. As a theatre historian, I was also interested in exploring how the moment of Ajax's suicide came to be understood as such a compelling piece of theatrical history.

In reading the various versions of play, I was initially struck by the difficulty the writers had in describing the stage action at this key moment of the play. Sir Richard Jebb's translation, from 1893, has the most straightforward stage direction: "*Ajax falls on his sword*."[1] Jebb suggests that the action is visible but does not fully address the logistical concerns of the original staging, which begs a central question for a director and a theatre historian: *how* does the actor portraying Ajax fall on his sword? Since we may assume he doesn't actually fall on an actual sword, which would likely kill him, Jebb requires us to imagine the staging of this moment. In John Moore's popular and well-respected translation from 1957, Ajax "*falls on his sword and collapses behind the bushes.*"[2] If Ajax falls on his sword and then falls behind the bushes, the original question of *how* he falls on his sword remains, and more staging elements like "*the bushes*" are brought into play but not described. In Herbert Golder and Richard Pevear's Oxford University Press translation of 1999, "*The platform is wheeled back, disappearing into the grove as Aias speaks his last words.*"[3] Here it seems the act of suicide is not visible. But if there is a platform that moves backward, an *ekkyklêma*, does the action take place on the moving platform, before it leaves, or offstage, after the platform has left? The *ekkyklêma* also typically rolls in to reveal things, not out to hide them, leading to additional staging questions.[4] In Peter Meineck and Paul Woodruff's translation, published in 2007, the stage direction, similar to Golder and Pevear's, reads: "*The* ekkyklêma *withdraws through the* skene *door, and the door closes.*"[5] In an extended footnote, the translators explain the reasoning behind their stage directions: "Many commentators and a scholiast's note on a later manuscript of the play suggest that the suicide was staged in full view of the audience. We think Ajax's language of withdrawal from the light and discovery of his body at line 891 point to the exiting of the *ekkyklêma* here and not to a depiction of the act of suicide onstage. The myth of Ajax's death was well known to the audience...and Sophocles would increase suspense by not depicting this most private of acts."[6] Meineck and Woodruff make a set of choices based on their interpretations of the text as they read it and the historical staging and how they understand it. And they do not suggest that the suicide is visible. Their primary reasoning here is that the audience would already be familiar with the image and thus would not need to see it.

These stage directions illuminate the complicated nature of playtext and its relationship to staging and to theatrical history. They also reflect the scholarly commentaries that attempt to reconstruct the original staging of the scene in fifth-century Athens: as the analysis of ancient Greek staging became more and more significant as a viable and legitimate pursuit in the late part of the twentieth century, so too did the demand for more definitive staging ideas, especially for scenes like Ajax's suicide. This tension between staging, text, and history creates a concrete version of Michal Kobialka's idea that "history is never present to us in anything but a discursive form that obliterates material bodies in their nondiscursive practice."[7] The commentaries that speculate on the actual staging, and the stage directions in the published versions of the playtext, are trying to create a physical description of a historical performance. Instead, they make us keenly aware of the lack of that performance in the present, illustrating Kobialka's point and its echoes of Peggy Phelan's observation that it is impossible to write about any performance without re-marking it, changing it, in essential ways that reflect the context and historical placement of the analysis. The original staging of Ajax's suicide is an event in performance that changes as it is written about.[8]

I am going to treat the writing about the staging of Ajax's suicide as an archive that, as Rebecca Schneider suggests, "becomes a social performance space, a theatre of retroaction. The archive performs the institution of disappearance, with object remains as indices of disappearance and with performance as given to disappear."[9] Thus, I will be looking at various scholarly reconstructions as the "indices of disappearance" for the staging of Ajax's suicide, a performance that continually disappears, just as the protagonist, the actor playing Ajax, himself does in the play. However, even though the actor playing Ajax is potentially replaced onstage by a dummy, he may also live on by playing the role of Teucer. The fact that there would have been a maximum of three actors for the original production of *Ajax*, which is well established, means that the actor playing Ajax would have to come back as either Teucer or Agamemnon. As P. J. Finglass discusses in his comprehensive 2011 commentary on *Ajax*, the most likely role for the actor to return as is Teucer, primarily because the characters have a blood relationship. Other factors include the thematic connection of parallelism between Ajax and Teucer, but Finglass does not find that compelling because of its subjectivity. As an example, he points out that an "antithetical" relationship could also be argued by having the same actor play Ajax and Agamemnon.[10] Finglass concludes it is most likely that the actor playing Ajax returns as Teucer but, significantly, insists that the evidence is not definitive and we thus "must leave the question of part division open."[11] As with the performance itself, then, Ajax has possibly both disappeared and returned, in a slightly new and amended form but still engaged with the memory of the past and a movement toward the future. In a sense, Teucer represents here the contemporary, that which is commenting on the past; while the subject, in this case probably Ajax, is no longer with us, he is still memorialized and given his due, even though his values and ideologies have died with him.

The "probably" in both of these instances is essential and again suggests the problematics of the archive for any sort of reconstruction. The commentaries on historical performances always depend upon the perspective of the contemporary commentator. Commentators on Greek tragedy have privileged literary interpretations, because their primary concern has typically been the philology of the texts themselves: they are interested in establishing and explaining the sources and forms of the language of the texts, which for ancient tragedy has meant putting together manuscripts and discussing their provenances and relationships with the other texts. However, there is and has always been a desire to also describe or illuminate the aspects of staging that affect or can be gleaned from the text. This makes even the most philological commentary of ancient Greek tragedy a form of performance criticism, interested at some level not just in the language but also in the historical performance that the language inhabited. As Niall Slater explains, "All critics of drama rewrite the plays they study in process of criticizing them; performance criticism asks—no, demands—that we rewrite these plays in ways that will mean in real time, in real space, within a theatre."[12] In the commentaries, this usually entails some attempt at understanding the original contexts and potential meanings of the works being critiqued. While Slater admits that no "restaging of the plays become the definitive performance," he also suggests that there must be something like a definitive historical performance to serve as one "electrical pole": "those two performances, the original and the contemporary, are the electrical poles between which we must look for the spark," which for Slater is the way the works "mean."[13]

But is it even possible to conceive of a definitive historical performance for fifth-century Athenian tragedy? Historian and memoirist Rebecca Solnit, discussing the writing of history and the reasons behind human behaviors and events, suggests that our attempts at "filling in the blanks" take us further from "the truth" than admitting we do not and will never know: "Often enough, we don't know such things even when it comes to ourselves, let alone someone who perished in an epoch whose very textures and reflexes were unlike ours. Filling in the blanks replaces the truth that we don't entirely know with the false sense that we do. We know less when we erroneously think we know than when we recognize that we don't. Sometimes I think these pretenses at authoritative knowledge are failures of language: the language of bold assertion is simpler, less taxing, than the language of nuance and ambiguity and speculation."[14] While Slater and others believe that the representational quality of Greek tragedy allows us to surmise meanings, those suppositions are based in our own expectations, which have been formed by critics and commentators over the centuries and are thus, in Solnit's construction, the result of more than two millennia of filling in blanks that serve our own critical perspectives and almost certainly not those of the original texts and staging practices. Simon Goldhill's related idea that "We are always already in the frame" is a concept that is still controversial for classical philologists.[15] As recently as 1999, influential classicists like Hans Ulrich Gumbrecht have insisted that "commentary always provides supplementary knowledge and always fulfills an ancillary function in relation to interpretation."[16] The idea that commentary is not interpretation belies a belief in the authoritative nature of the text itself, giving it the quality of a "bold assertion," as Solnit might say, that simplifies its relationship to its historical context.

Melinda Powers analyzes a recent example that demonstrates the kinds of assertions that commentators make that reveal as much about their own culture as they do about the original culture of the ancient Athenian stage.[17] In discussing Richard Green's analysis of gesture, she points out that Green's use of the term *sōphrōn* to describe a controlled and "civilized" form of gesture in theatrical performance requires an anachronistic reading that depends on a modern and even Victorian definition of proper behavior. Green takes his idea of the term from Plato, who uses it to describe the behavior of Polemarchus: instead of hurrying to catch Socrates himself, Polemarchus sends his slave to run him down. However, the application of the term to theatrical gesture demands more than a sociological context. We cannot be certain about what Athenian theatrical gesture looked like, because we only have the still lifes of vase paintings and descriptions that use adjectives like Plato's and Green's. These give us a quality of gesture but not a quantifiable description that can be clearly communicated across time and space. Instead, Green's idea of gesture reflects his own ideas about what would have been considered appropriate, which is always already informed by what he *thinks* would be considered appropriate.

Goldhill's idea that interpretation is always present is common among scholars of performance, however. As Schneider discusses, referencing Richard Schechner, the idea that "all bodily practice is, like language itself, always already composed in repetition and repetition is, paradoxically, both the vehicle for sameness and the vehicle for difference or change"; this reinforces Goldhill's idea that the frame of the critic is always a reflection of the present, which is at the same time a reflection of the repetition of interpretations of the past. So, this "always already" is true not only of the contemporary but also of the many commentators of the past, each taking us further from that original performance and the bodies and negotiations of the original performance environment, even as they somehow reflect those histories in their contemporary iterations. In a sense then, in this analysis of the historical commentaries and how they have staged Ajax's death, "*againness* becomes the subject itself, both available to experience and to analysis."[18] While I analyze some proposed stagings and the reader will experience my interpretation of them, we will ultimately be exploring how interpretations make their way through history. The writing of history about performance necessitates a re-marking and replaces the disappearance of the performance with a new kind of performance, which is the writing itself.

The historical commentaries about the staging of Ajax's suicide begin with the ancient scholiast of Sophocles's *Ajax* text, about whom we know very little except that he was likely writing in the fourth century BCE, at least a hundred years after *Ajax* premiered (which was probably around 445 BCE) and after significant political, cultural, and social shifts in Greece. This scholiast notes at line 815 of *Ajax*, when the scene shifts from the camp to the beach, fifty lines before Ajax's final words: "The scene changes to a deserted place, where Ajax prepares the sword and delivers a speech before his death. For it would be ridiculous for him to enter and fall upon his sword without saying anything. Such scenes are infrequent among the older poets, for they are accustomed to report events through messengers. What is the explanation? In *Thracian Women* Aeschylus had already reported the death of Ajax through a messenger. And so perhaps wishing to innovate and not to follow in the footsteps of another, or rather wishing to astonish he placed the deed in full view. It is irreverent and unfair to randomly criticize one of the older poets."[19] The scholiast seems to regard Sophocles's attempt to stage the suicide as an innovation that was perhaps inappropriate, but he avoids judging it too harshly lest he seem improperly critical. As Falkner notes, "The commentator is caught between his sense of tragic propriety and his respect for the classics."[20] The scholiast's reverence, however, doesn't stop him from famously declaring elsewhere that Sophocles wrote an ineffective second half.[21] This more literary criticism, which claims that all that happens after Ajax's death is a petty argument over the burial between crass, unlikeable, and dishonorable characters, has historically dominated the discussion of the play. At the same time, it has put an enormous amount of pressure on the suicide scene, which becomes even more central as a climactic point when the second part of the play is dismissed. The suicide scene in *Ajax* pressures one of the more rigid perceived dramaturgical conventions of tragedy: the genre avoids actions of violence onstage, preferring to show the results of those actions. Sophocles's apparent decision to show Ajax committing suicide is questioned by the scholiast, but only after it is asserted that Ajax visibly "prepares the sword." It is the scholiast, not Sophocles's text, that indicates that Sophocles "placed the deed in full view." Already we see the scholiast as an interpreter, bringing his historical frame to the commentary. The rarity of the onstage action is noted and the explanation for why Sophocles did it is condescending and odd: maybe because he wanted to do something new or astonishing? The fifth century in Athens is an era in which innovation was not necessarily viewed positively. As Bernard Knox discusses at length in his essay on *Ajax*, neither the character of Ajax nor the Greek language was enamored of things that were new, as the Greek word *veos* (Nay-os) "had a collateral notion of *unexpected, strange, untoward, evil.*"[22] Scott Scullion, in his extensive 1994 commentary on the staging of the suicide, suggests that the visible staging of the act of suicide itself would have been an "unparalleled phenomenon" and argues against what Finglass calls "positing a singularity."[23] Scullion and Finglass agree that the visible suicide is unlikely not only because of the difficulty of innovation for the fifth-century stage but also because it may have been the only time an action like it happened. Scullion argues that the classical scholiast's claim has no evidentiary value, as the only production he would be referring to was contemporary to him and not to the original production approximately one hundred years earlier.[24] The comment itself offers no concrete or even textual evidence to establish that the suicide was in full view of the audience.

The scholiast reflects a literary reading of the play, interested primarily in the themes and events in the text but not focused on the logistics of their staging except as potential obstacles to understanding the literary text. In a self-fulfilling prophecy that Athenian drama was focused on the text and dialogue and not the spectacle or the stage action, reinforced by Aristotle and by most commentators since, the primary significance of the actions is found in their consequences, not in the spectators' potential viewing of the actions themselves. The idea, expressed by classicist P. E. Easterling and common among classical philologists and text-focused commentators, that "a brilliantly told (and mimed?) narrative might be more easily 'read' in a large open-air theatre than a piece of more realistic stage business" fits into this assumption that the literary "narrative" is a clearer route to meaning than a specific physical choreography[25]—which might be true if the spectators are expecting only a clear literary narrative and expecting a clear route to meaning. However, this neglects the possibility that the large space, which we know encapsulated groups of actors such as the choruses engaged in dancing and movement, might have been primed for large gestural or physical actions that perhaps do not fit into the "believable" aesthetic of a more modern realistic mode of representation and interpretation. Looking at other theatrical forms such as Kabuki or Kathakali provides clear examples of gestures and bodies generating quite clear meanings without being realistically representational. Easterling concludes that "the intricacy with which violent events are thus 'orchestrated' suggests that in avoiding direct presentation of the moment of killing or violent wounding the dramatists were making creative choices for positive reasons," which might include a focus on the causes and effects of violence and not their representation. Again, the bias for the literary and "realistic" is clear, taking its cue from Aristotle, who clearly saw spectacle as a potential distraction that could also open up the dramatist to criticism along representational or even religious lines.[26]

The changing interpretations of the purpose and cultural significance of the performance of tragedy have also affected the commentaries on it. Page duBois, for example, has argued convincingly that our contemporary understandings of tragedy have been thoroughly influenced by Aristotle's commentaries in the *Poetics*, which was written a century after *Oedipus Rex*, its exemplary tragic text, was first performed.[27] This lens profoundly affects the history of interpretation of the texts and their staging. As duBois argues, Aristotle's focus on the actions of the individual and on a "disciplining of the social body" makes tragedy a tool for "perform[ing] the role of fantasy, displacing the struggle over social power, which generates pity and fear, into the realm of art in order to maintain order."[28] Even though Aristotle, like the *Ajax* scholiast, was basing his own commentaries on revivals and corrupted texts from the fourth century, his influence on the interpretation of fifth-century tragedy has transformed the most basic ways that we consider and evaluate it. For duBois, this shift significantly changes the nature of what we think of when we think of tragedy, even though her perspective is obviously shaped by her ideology, which is also (already) in the frame: "While tragedy is a collective, poetic, ritual, and eminently democratic form, concerned with the social whole, with the dynamic interaction that is the city, the polis, Aristotle concerns himself with the management of individuals. His emphasis on the control of citizens reflects a wider social change, a move away from democracy in the fourth century."[29] This movement to a focus on the individual is just one example of the kinds of cultural and interpretive shifts that took place in the first hundred years or so after *Ajax* was first performed. Max Reinhardt's production of Hugo von Hofmannsthal's adaptation of Sophocles's *Electra* in 1903, especially the performance of the actor playing Electra, Gertrud Eysoldt, shocked audiences because of the way it demanded "a new vision of Greek culture" that was no longer "a model of one's own culture."[30] Through its graphic language and the visceral performance of Eysoldt, which Erica Fischer-Lichte argues represents a sacrifice of the actor's own body, the performance suggested not the "civilized" language and propriety of classical philological commentaries but an embodied and "primitive" exploration of ritual and violence that transgresses the boundaries of both "realistic" and "classical" performance.[31] It also suggests a different kind of interpretation of a classical text that focuses not on the Aristotelian aspects of plot, character, and language but on the embodiment and presence of the actor and spectators and their relationship to their physical reality.

Such experiments, however, are difficult to document in language and thus often get forgotten, neglected, or marginalized in the historical record. Instead, the scholarly focus has traditionally been on the text first and foremost. The text for Sophocles's *Ajax*, however, was certainly not the same as the text for the original performance of *Ajax*, which was probably a century before the earliest extant commentaries. The literary bias is clear even in the analyses of the historical fragments that we do have. For example, the assumption that the tragic poet's "authoritative" version existed but was just impossible to find plays out in the discourse about the corruption of texts, especially in the century after they had first been performed. Eric Csapo and William J. Slater argue that even the texts that have survived have been corrupted by performances and performers and their "interpolations" and tendencies "to magnify their roles and expand the crowd-pleasers."[32] In this reading, the actors only served to "interpolate" on the literary texts and were the most responsible for the fact that the texts were "corrupted" from the poet's originals. Because of this, "the correction of texts has been the aim of philologists since the time of Aristotle," when tragic texts and other available documents about the performance of tragedy did not include "music or even metrical arrangement."[33] Csapo and Slater claim that these texts "were made available primarily for the benefit of the reading public," not as texts for performance, and there is thus no "proof that any of the surviving stage directions are anything but additions by later scholars. Indeed there is a general dearth of interest in the realities of production, especially in the stage machinery.[34]

Again, the archive is affected by the literary bias almost immediately, as production notes or stage directions are not a part of the classical archive but later emendations. Even the scholiasts were not contemporaries of the original productions. They "often tended to be anachronistic on matters of staging,"[35] coming from the later Hellenistic period or even medieval Europe. In fact, even the most definitive modern versions of the plays are assemblages of fragments from different periods and places. As Finglass explains, the text that he puts together and is considered authoritative is an amalgamation of multiple sources. First, there are four ancient papyrus fragments, dating from the second century CE to the fifth or sixth century CE. These fragments together contain less than 100 lines of a text that is considered to have 1,420 lines in most modern editions. The remainder of the text is made up from dozens of medieval manuscripts from the mid-tenth century to the fifteenth century.[36] Thus the text itself has quite a distance from the original performance—the earliest parts of it are from about six hundred years after *Ajax* was first performed. The manuscripts lack stage directions, so ideas about staging were inevitably influenced by the commentators' own experiences of performances, which were most probably quite different from ancient Athenian tragic performance. Here we see two concurrent through lines that demonstrate, first, that the texts and the evidence of original performances were already historical, fragmentary, and corrupted within one hundred years of the original production and, second, that the actors, the ones who embodied the text in performance, were treated as corrupters of literary texts, not as authorities on their performance or its historical documentation. Both of these factors make the exploration of staging in fifth-century Athens particularly complex.

While it is reasonably not a focus of the more literary commentaries, those that focus on staging are still unable to come up with a definitive staging for the suicide. The reasons for this are mostly obvious—there are no stage directions in the manuscripts, few pictorial records of the actual productions, and very few ancient commentaries that focus on staging. Even the archaeological evidence that we have is disputed. And the suicide scene in *Ajax* would seem to depend upon some sort of stagecraft to be presented. Because the scene shifts to the barren beach and because Ajax discussed the sword planted in the ground near him at such length (at 815, 819, and 821), it is usually assumed that the act would take place there. There are also issues of height and perspective in the theatrical space, as "the steep rise of the auditorium in the theatre of Dionysus would have enabled a considerable portion of the audience to look over anything resembling a bush" or an actor trying to obscure the action of falling on the sword or the replacement of the body with a dummy.[37] We know that there are only three actors at this period of tragedy, so the "dead" body could not stay onstage. It is usually surmised, as mentioned earlier, that the actor playing Ajax comes back a scene later as Teucer, a supposition in Jebb's influential text from 1893 and since propagated in many commentaries.[38] If the actor playing Ajax falls (or, in some translations, leaps!) on his sword, how does this happen and how does he then get offstage to become Teucer?[39]

T. B. L. Webster took many cues from Jebb in his 1956 monograph *Greek Theatre Production*, which gave a state of the field of ideas about the staging of Greek tragedy in the middle of the twentieth century. Webster argued that the change into Ajax's final monologue would have entailed the moving downstage of the *ekkyklêma* through the open center stage doors, with a sword already placed in the *ekkyklêma* and a panel with bushes painted on it attached to the *ekkyklêma*. The suicide then, after Ajax's last line, would involve the actor portraying Ajax leaping onto the sword in a way that the bushes covered his body. This presents several staging problems. If the sword is visible, how does it become invisible for the actual action? There is no evidence of retractable blades for staging at this time, although this is partly because there is no expectation in the commentaries of any other circumstances that would demand them. As Finglass states, summarizing Scullion's 1994 commentary, "since classical drama has no need for them, producers would not have had them on hand."[40] The issue of spectator perspective limits the efficacy of this staging, as one sitting higher up in the *theatron* might very well be able to see over the screen.

There are also controversies about whether painted scenery was a part of fifth century scenography.[41] Current scholarship generally posits that there may have been scene painting but that it would likely have been for the *skene* and in place for the entire performance. There is no evidence of the stagecraft of adding or changing painted scenery, and in *Ajax* this is complicated by the fact that the change would have to happen such that it was visible to the audience, as there is no break in the play when Ajax moves to the grove for the suicide scene.[42] Webster's ideas come clearly from Jebb's commentaries and are an attempt to make the literary and archeological commentaries viable for staging; however, there is little historical evidence or precedent for the painted bush. Frankly, from a contemporary perspective it seems like a bad cliché of an amateur theatrical set, something perhaps the commentators experienced in an early twentieth-century secondary school production. It is not convincing as a piece of scenery for a twenty-thousand-seat theatre with raked spectator seating. And most scholars agree that the *skene* would not be something that was changed during the course of a performance, making it even more unlikely.[43]

Peter Arnott, leaning heavily for his arguments on the fourth century scholiast, notes in his influential 1962 monograph *Greek Scenic Conventions in the Fifth Century BC*: "The suicide scene in Ajax is an extraordinary adventure into realism, like nothing that had ever been attempted before and very little after it."[44] Arnott thus transforms the scholiast's speculations that Sophocles was attempting "to innovate" or possibly "to astonish" into the specific modern aesthetic principle of "realism." Arnott does not think that the scarcity of violent actions or death onstage was based in religious, moral, or even generic principles but was instead a matter of logistics. He points out that there are several onstage deaths in tragedy, Hippolytus perhaps most prominent.[45] The complexities of making such a scene convincing to an audience, given the stage technology and acting style, made it rare. Arnott rejects the entrance of the *ekkyklêma* to create the scene for Ajax's monologue and instead has the sword fixed on the *ekkyklêma* but leaves it in a visible position upstage of the open center stage doors. He notes that "there is no parallel in tragedy for the use of an ekkyklêma to withdraw a character from sight"—it is used to reveal things, not hide them.[46] The *ekkyklêma* is saved until later to reveal the dead body, which by that point is not played by the protagonist but has been replaced by a dummy. For Arnott, the moment of death remains out of sight, but the staging should come "as near to the death-blow without portraying it."[47] In his staging, Ajax plays the scene in front of the doorway and the doors close as he walks back to the sword. As

Arnott mentions, using one of the later scholiast's comments (from about 100 CE), the effects of this depend on the strength of actor to convince the spectators that he is about to fall on his sword: "We must surmise that he falls on his sword; and the actor must be someone powerful to lead the audience up to the revelation of Ajax as Timotheus of Zacynthus is said to have done. He led the audience on, and so inspired them with his acting that he was called 'cut-throat.'"[48] Arnott's interpretation incorporates both scholiasts' commentaries, as he focuses on the actor's ability to create the emotional buildup and certainty, a gesture toward the physical presence of an actor in a live performance. However, Arnott's definitions of emotional and physical presence reveal a modern, realistic aesthetic, or at least one that can only be traced to centuries after the original staging of the play. And he also reveals an uncertainty about the scholiast comments even as he uses them: he doesn't propose that the act of suicide is actually visible to the audience.

The *ekkyklêma* also provides the platform for the suicide in S. P. Mills's 1980 essay on the staging of Ajax's suicide. However, Mills proposes a solution that requires the actor playing Ajax to "go back [to the sword] and throw himself down in such a way that he seemed to be falling on the sword; in fact, he would only need to fall close in front of it, much as modern stage actors in dueling scenes learn to pass the foil between arm and side, away from the audience, to simulate a hit."[49] As it turns out, Mills is the only one of the major commentators who proposes "showing" the suicide onstage, despite the fact that Ajax's suicide has become known as an example of visible violence. For Mills, the spectacle is "exciting in its own right" and fulfilled the desire of Sophocles (according to the fourth century BCE scholiast's comment) to provide an innovative staging for the scene. Mills pursues this argument further, addressing not only the desire for innovation but also the ubiquity of the image of Ajax fallen on his sword, which can be seen in several extant vase and pitcher paintings and was most likely an easily recognizable image in the mid-fifth century BCE, something we saw referenced in Meineck and Woodruff's note on their stage directions.[50] For Mills, this suggests that a visible staging of the tableaux so well known from other visual media would have provided a "tableau in action" or an "animated painting" that "must surely have equaled anything an eagerly waiting audience could imagine."[51] This seems not only modern but also specifically melodramatic, with a surprise revelation and the staging of a famous tableau. Of course, the opposite argument can be made as well: that the ubiquity of the image made it unnecessary to stage.

Rush Rehm reflects a desire to read Greek tragedy through a structuralist scenography that creates a framework for interpretation based on spatial relationships. In *The Play of Space: Spatial Transformation in Greek Tragedy* (2002), Rehm rejects the painted scenery, but his staging does not offer a significantly different interpretation of the movements of Ajax from those of Webster or Jebb. His focus is also on the movement of the *ekkyklêma* as an indicator of the external and the internal, and he does not directly address how Ajax would throw himself on the sword fixed into the platform but focuses on how the space is set up by moving in the *ekkyklêma*.[52] The actor playing Ajax would be able to sneak off and be replaced when Tecmessa brings out a sheet in lines 915–16. Rehm also depends upon the supposition that Sophocles was looking for an innovative staging even as he recognizes that the spatial relationships that he identifies are common to other violent actions and especially to the revelations of bodies.

David Wiles, in his book *Tragedy in Athens*, also depends upon the *ekkyklêma* to create the scene and remove the body. For Wiles, as with Rehm, the function of the *ekkyklêma* is as much symbolic as it is logistical, as the structuralist binary of the seen and the unseen is also representative of other binary relationships (private/public, heroic/cowardly, male/female) and needs to be maintained for the Athenian spectators to generate the appropriate response. The movement of it back through the doors as Ajax finishes his speech and heads to the sword both expresses the intended action clearly and avoids what Wiles calls an "unprecedented visual killing."[53] It also provides a moment of stage technology and potential spectacle, almost a cinematic movement of the action that is inevitably about to occur as the platform moves upstage and Ajax approaches the sword.

Cynthia P. Gardiner's 1979 essay on the staging of the suicide scene proposes the simplest staging, as she claims it demands "no need to devise any realistic illusion" but fits within the conventions and technologies of the ancient Athenian stage.[54] Gardiner has Ajax come out from the doors, leaving one ajar but not fully open, and has him deliver the text to the audience and occasionally and appropriately gesture to behind the doors when referring to the sword. She argues that the language demands only that the sword is close, and not necessarily visible, and the focus on Ajax's language in the monologue, which clearly describes what Ajax is about to do and why, gives the audience all they need to understand the action that is about to occur.[55] After his last line, Ajax walks through the door, closing it behind him, as the chorus begins its lamentation. The body, a dummy, is revealed on the *ekkyklêma* when Tecmessa "discovers" it. This reading is closest as well to Scullion's, which is considered by Finglass and many others to be the most significant and comprehensive understanding of the staging of the modern era.[56]

Gardiner and Scullion avoid many of the difficult potentialities of the staging, mechanics, and space of the work and demonstrate how each of the commentators who insist on a visible suicide looks back, even if it is unknowingly or unwittingly, to that first commentary, that infamous scholiast of the fourth century BCE. The scholarly commentaries, of course, always involve interpretation, even though in the history of the commentaries "the 'I' of the commentator tends toward the mute."[57] The staging of Ajax's suicide, however, is a clear example where the commentator, the fourth-century scholiast, is not mute at all. He is instead a "single strong subject" whose voice has been "in fact often heard clearly."[58] As classical scholar Irene J. F. de Jong observes in her discussion of what she calls the "authoritative nature of classical scholarship," "once a scholar of note has stamped a word or passage as problematic, all later scholars feel obliged to respond."[59] Without the scholiast's mention of Sophocles's desire for innovation and astonishment, for example, there might never have been so much conjecture about the possible staging. Without such a suggestive commentary, we might have been satisfied with a literary or simple staging like Gardiner's. Because beyond that commentary, all that leads us to a more complicated staging are some textual ambiguities about the placement of the sword and a potential change of scene. Every other staging issue that arises comes from the scholiast's insistence in figuring out the logistics of a moment that was supposedly unlike the many that had preceded it.

This doesn't necessarily mean Gardiner is right, of course. Her choice is to not engage fully with the physical possibilities of the space, the confusing, paradoxical, contradictory, and uncertain archeological and physical evidence, and instead to focus on the reading of the text, which we know comes at least partly from more than two millennia of subsuming the physicality of theatrical history to the literary drama. Like Gardiner, Scullion's methodology reveals a strong bias for the literary and artifactual: "My arguments are based on the assumptions that a solution to the staging problem that does not involved unparalleled phenomena is preferable to one that does, and that the credibility of a proposal diminishes as its unparalleled elements multiply."[60] This method of writing history, by depending upon the relative concreteness of text and archaeology, also necessarily subjugates the possibility of the unique phenomena of bodies in space. In part *because* this kind of history does not find much useful evidence of physical staging, it brings us closest to Kobialka's obliteration of the physical bodies. This, ironically perhaps, also might make it the closest to the most useful version of history, as it allows for disappearance and thus for the recognition that the historical is a subjective, interpretive act. As Phelan argues, "It does no good, however, to simply refuse to write about performance because of this inescapable transformation. The challenge raised by the ontological claims of performance for writing is to re-mark again the performative possibilities of writing itself. The act of writing towards disappearance, rather than the act of writing toward preservation, must remember that the after-effect of disappearance is the experience of subjectivity itself."[61] In another twist, it is the writing of history, its performance by many in and as writing, that has made this Ajax scene very important, when perhaps during its own contemporary context it was not significantly different from others. The writing about it, as history and as performance, has most certainly transformed it, from whatever it might have been in ancient Athens to something that is almost always visibly staged.

Peter Sellars's infamous production of Robert Auletta's adaptation of the play, which was staged in Washington, DC, in 1986, had a staging of the suicide that blended a cinematic sensibility with some theatrical spectacle. Auletta's stage direction simply reads, "*Ajax throws himself upon his sword and dies.*"[62] Before Howie Seago, the actor playing Ajax, enters to begin his final speech, a messenger wearing US military camouflage and large angel wings holds the sword on the ground, pointed up, while singing the African American spiritual "Down by the Riverside." Athena is standing behind Ajax for the entire speech, which, as with all of Ajax's text in this production, is signed in American Sign Language by the deaf Seago and spoken by another actor amplified with a microphone. After Seago's final gesture and piece of text, the lighting changes from red to blue, and he falls to the floor next to the messenger and the sword. He is obscured by the shadows in the blue lighting. The messenger places the sword as if it has struck through Seago's body, embracing Seago on the ground while he screams. Seago then remains on the raked stage as a mixture of water and blood-colored liquid drips down toward the audience. The staging uses modern technology to obscure the action, but it is still basically visible onstage. There is no *ekkyklêma*, and Seago remains onstage for the rest of the performance; as there is no three-actor rule and Teucer and Agamemnon are played by different actors, there is no need to remove his body and replace it with a dummy. In much the same way, the actor playing Ajax in Sarah Benson's 2011 production at the American Repertory Theatre in Cambridge, Massachusetts, is described by *Boston Globe* reviewer Don Aucoin as spending the "second half of the play sprawled immobile on the stage."[63]

It is often difficult to discern these staging details from any of the published reviews or essays about this production, as they usually note that Ajax commits suicide without characterizing how. This is another function of the language of the time being accepted as a stand-in for a clear description of staging practice. The writing indicates that Ajax commits suicide onstage and visibly, but rarely how. In the modern and contemporary era, and from my own limited viewing experience, it is usually done as it was in Sellars's production of Auletta's adaptation: by obscuring the blade as the actor falls onto or in front of it. Most of the productions I have viewed are not fully convincing, however, as they cannot fulfill the demands of realism: it is clear that the actor falls in front of the blade, or that there is a retractable blade that then does not go through the body, as it does, for example, in the vase paintings of the fifth century BCE.[64] The preparation and action is usually visible, though, which is likely why there are many readers and audience members who assume the suicide of Ajax must have been visibly staged. This reflection of our expectations of theatrical representation, and especially the influence of stage realism, have brought us to expect to see the suicide of Ajax onstage. Only through a study of the practice and commentaries can we see that in Athens in the fifth century BCE, it almost certainly was not seen.

In my 2004 production, which had the actors costumed as American soldiers in contemporary Iraq, I ended up with Ajax finishing his final speech and walking upstage toward a folding chair painted in camouflage as the chorus covered him with a large red cloth. There was no sword or gun and no mimed action by the actor playing Ajax of falling on a sword. It was a big physical gesture, symbolic and not at all realistic in its representational practice. I did not try to emulate any of my readings of the stage directions of other translations or the commentaries. In fact, if anything, it was a reaction against the lack of imaginative potential I found in many of those stage directions and commentaries: they seemed to cling to staging techniques that I equated not with the grand gestures of a masked theatrical form in a twenty-thousand-seat amphitheater but with the everyday representational demands of modern realism. This is a reflection of their twentieth-century version of the scholiast's innovation, just as my staging was a reflection of my ideas of a large-scale masked performance. It was also, of course, visible to the audience. Even though I did not attempt a more realistic action, I still did not have the actor playing Ajax leave the stage. Instead, I tried to create an image that might speak not just to a modern psychological aesthetic but also to a symbolic and ritualistic gesture that might have larger connotations. Like duBois, I think Athenian tragedy was trying to engage its spectators not merely with the actions of individuals as representatives of the polis, and how these individuals are controlled, but also with the larger potential of democratic ideas about justice and power. So, the large red sheet, which looked like a flag, was both Ajax's blood and a political marker that is then negotiated and fought over in the second part of the play. We can see through tracking the commentaries of this scene how our own desire to create a history that gets close to what Robert Sarlós calls "the *dynamic sensory presence*" of performance necessitates the re-marking of the past through the eyes of the present.[65] In my production, I reflected my own view of the historical and its particular relevance (and irrelevance) to a staging that I thought created the kind of scene that would affect the spectators how I thought the scene should in the present.

When Schneider discusses the problems of the historical in the context of Civil War reenactments, she points out that the evident "problems of ambivalence, simultaneous temporal registers, anachronism, and the *everywhere* of error" were clear to most of the reenactors.[66] I suggest that, as theater historians and practitioners, we take a similar view: we are not attempting to reenact the original, which is an impossible task, but are instead recognizing the "everywhere of error" as a part of both the historical record and the contemporary practice, both of the writing of history and the performance of the theatrical work. This is not just a failure of the archive but a reimagining of it, according to more nuanced understandings of history and performance. We all know that performances of the past will never be re-created exactly as they were, as this is both a temporal and ontological impossibility. However, Schneider, following the work of Elizabeth Freeman, suggests: "The past can disrupt the present… but so too can the present disrupt the past…; neither are entirely 'over' nor discrete, but partially and porously persist. Something is different here than simply remembering, or a simple negotiation with 'a time gone by.' Thinking through 'mutually disruptive energy' implies that the bygone is not entirely gone by and the dead not completely disappeared or lost, but also, and perhaps more complexly, the living are not entirely (or not only) alive."[67]

Schneider is talking about the reenactment of historical events, but I think this applies as well to the consideration of a historical document such as a playtext, which in the case of *Ajax* is used to write a reenactment of a historical performance. A commentator like the fourth-century scholiast is not a performer like a Civil War reenactor, as he does not embody the historical attempt in the same way. However, his attempt to create a reembodiment through writing serves a similar function in that he has similar temporal and ontological separations from the historical event, yet is attempting, through using documentation, to create a reperformance. If we look at the attempts to determine the staging of Ajax's suicide in the commentaries as we might look at Civil War reenactments, embedded as they are with different sources and the influence of the commentator's contemporary aesthetics and ideologies, these writings about historical performances also contain the "*everywhere* of error," along with the potential for a "mutually disruptive energy": filled with history, and a desire for history, but imbued as well with the present and all that has come between the historical performance and the present. So, then, we look back to this scene from *Ajax* and hope it was something special, even as we recognize that it is only our own performance of history that makes that possible.

Notes

1. *Sophocles: The Ajax of Sophocles*, edited with introduction and notes by Sir Richard Jebb (Cambridge: Cambridge University Press, 1893), line 865.
2. *Ajax*, in *Sophocles II: Four Tragedies*, edited by David Grene and Richmond Lattimore (Chicago: University of Chicago Press, 1957), 39.
3. Herbert Golder and Richard Pevear, trans., *Aias* (Oxford: Oxford University Press, 1999), 57.
4. P. J. Finglass, *Sophocles: Ajax* (Cambridge: Cambridge University Press, 2011), 378–98: "But the ekkyklema is only used to reveal the interior of some kind of dwelling.... In tragedy a grove could not be treated as if it were a house."
5. *Sophocles: Four Tragedies* (Indianapolis: Hackett, 2007), 38.
6. Ibid.
7. Kobialka, "Theater/Performance Historiography: Politics, Ethics, and the Now," *Modern Language Quarterly* 70, no. 1 (March 2009): 21.
8. In *Unmarked: The Politics of Performance* (London: Routledge, 1993), Peggy Phelan posits: "To attempt to write about the undocumentable event of performance is to invoke the rules of the written document and thereby alter the event itself. Just as quantum physics discovered that macro-instruments cannot measure microscopic particles without transforming those particles, so too must performance critics realize that the labor to write about performance (and thus to 'preserve' it) is also a labor that fundamentally alters the event" (148).
9. Rebecca Schneider, *Performing Remains: Art and War in Times of Theatrical Reenactment* (London: Routledge, 2011), 104.
10. Finglass, *Sophocles*, 25.
11. Finglass, *Sophocles*, 24.
12. "From Ancient Performance to New Historicism," in *Intertextualität in der griechisch-römischen Komedie*, edited by Niall Slater and Bernard Zimmerman (Stuttgart: M & P, 1993), 11.
13. Ibid.
14. Rebecca Solnit, "Woolf's Darkness: Embracing the Inexplicable," in *Men Explain Things to Me* (Chicago: Haymarket Books, 2014), 88–89.
15. Simon Goldhill, "Reading Performance Criticism," *Greece & Rome* 36, no. 2 (October 1989): 176.
16. Gumbrecht, "Fill up Your Margins! About Commentary and *copia*," in *Commentaries—Kommentare*, edited by G. W. Most (Göttingen: Aporemata 4, 1999), 443.
17. *Athenian Tragedy in Performance: A Guide to Contemporary Studies and Historical Debates* (Iowa City: University of Iowa Press, 2014), 102–4.

18. Schneider, *Performing Remains*, 124.
19. Quoted in Thomas Falkner, "Scholars versus Actors: Text and Performance in the Greek Tragic Scholia" in *Greek and Roman Actors: Aspects of an Ancient Profession*, edited by P. E. Easterling and Edith Hall (Cambridge: Cambridge University Press, 2002), 354–55.
20. Falkner, "Scholars versus Actors," 355.
21. Jan Kott, in his essay "Ajax Thrice Deceived, or The Heroism of the Absurd," states: "Everyone, from the first scholiast to the writers of the last decade, has considered the second part of Ajax a bore, tasteless, or at any rate an artistic blunder." In *The Eating of the Gods: An Interpretation of Greek Tragedy*, trans. Boleslaw Taborksi and Edward J. Czerwinski (New York: Random House, 1973), 70. Kott disagrees and sees the second part as an innovation by Sophocles in representing the end of the heroic age.
22. "The *Ajax* of Sophocles," *Harvard Studies in Classical Philology* 65 (1961): 32.
23. Scott Scullion, *Three Studies in Athenian Dramaturgy* (Stuttgart: Teubner, 1994), 97; Finglass, *Sophocles*, 377.
24. As Scullion concludes: "In short, no scholion can safely be assumed to provide authoritative information on fifth-century staging" (105).
25. P. E. Easterling, "Form and Performance," in *The Cambridge Companion to Greek Tragedy* (Cambridge: Cambridge University Press, 1997), 154.
26. Ibid. Easterling also mentions the possibility that there was a religious prohibition on the enactment of violent actions as a part of the City Dionysia. This idea is basically rejected in Peter Arnott, *Greek Scenic Conventions in the Fifth Century BC* (Oxford: Clarendon Press, 1962), 135, where he uses several other onstage deaths to argue against a serious religious prohibition.
27. Page duBois, "Ancient Tragedy and the Metaphor of Katharis," *Theatre Journal* 54, no. 1 (March 2002): 19–24.
28. Ibid., 24.
29. Ibid., 23.
30. Erica Fischer-Lichte, *Theatre, Sacrifice, Ritual: Exploring Forms of Political Theatre* (Routledge: London, 2005), 3–4.
31. Ibid., 4.
32. Eric Csapo and William Slater, *The Context of Ancient Drama* (Ann Arbor: University of Michigan Press, 1995), 4.
33. Ibid., 19.
34. Ibid., 20.
35. Oliver Taplin, *The Stagecraft of Aeschylus: The Dramatic Use of Exits and Entrances in Greek Tragedy* (Oxford: Clarendon Press: 1990), 369.
36. Finglass, *Sophocles*, 59.
37. Cynthia Gardiner, "The Staging of the Death of Ajax," *The Classical Journal* 75, no. 1 (October-November 1979): 10.
38. Jebb lists Ajax and Teucer as being both "played by the Protagonist" in the Dramatis Personae. *Sophocles: The Ajax*, edited by Richard Jebb (London: Rivingtons, 1893), 29. Found online at https://archive.org/stream/ajaxeditedbyrcjeoosophuoft#page/n27/mode/2up.
39. S. P. Mills, "The Death of Ajax," *Classical Journal* 76, no. 2 (December 1980-January 1981): 129.

40. Finglass, *Sophocles*, 377.
41. Mills mentions Arnott's claim that "painted scenery did not exist in the fifth century" (11).
42. Finglass, *Sophocles*, 13–14. See also William Stanford's commentaries about the staging in his edition of *Sophocles Ajax* (Bristol: Bristol Classical Press, 1963), 165–66, 173–74. Stanford relies heavily on Webster, his contemporary, and the earlier Jebb commentaries but begins to acknowledge the difficulty of using textual interpretation for staging practice.
43. Scullion, *Three Studies in Athenian Dramaturgy* (109–116) details the history of this discussion.
44. Arnott, *Greek Scenic Conventions*, 114.
45. Ibid., 134.
46. Ibid., 132.
47. Ibid., 131.
48. Quoted in ibid., 133.
49. Mills, "The Death of Ajax," 131.
50. Previous and contemporary images of Ajax's suicide are summarized in Finglass, *Sophocles*, 28–31.
51. Ibid., 135.
52. *The Play of Space: Spatial Transformation in Greek Tragedy* (Princeton: Princeton University Press, 2002), 131–32.
53. David Wiles, *Tragedy in Athens: Performance Space and Theatrical Meaning* (Cambridge: Cambridge University Press, 1997), 164.
54. Gardiner, "The Staging of the Death of Ajax," 14.
55. Ibid., 8.
56. Finglass, *Sophocles*, 14.
57. Christina Shuttleworth Kraus, "Reading Commentaries/Commentaries as Reading," in *The Classical Commentary: Histories, Practices, Theory*, edited by Roy K. Gibson and Christina Shuttleworth Kraus (Leiden: Brill, 2002), 4.
58. Ibid., 5.
59. Irene J. F. de Jong, "A Narratological Commentary on the *Odyssey*," in *The Classical Commentary: Histories, Practices, Theory*, edited by Roy K. Gibson and Christina Shuttleworth Kraus (Leiden: Brill, 2002), 51.
60. Scullion, *Three Studies in Athenian Dramaturgy*, 96.
61. Phelan, *Unmarked*, 148.
62. *Ajax: Sophocles* (New York: Broadway Play Publishing, 2014), 29.
63. "ART's 'Ajax' runs afoul of its gimmicks," February 8, 2011.
64. Several of these productions are available for viewing online. See, for example, https://www.youtube.com/watch?v=KizZ9qwahn8, a production directed by Jeff S. Dailey at the American Theatre of Actors in New York City in 2011, and https://www.youtube.com/watch?v=Q2b_LWOZdNc, an outdoor staging at the University of Newcastle, Australia, in 1997.
65. Robert Sarlós, "Performance Reconstruction," in *Interpreting the Theatrical Past: Essays in the Historiography of Performance*, edited by Thomas Postlewait and Bruce A. McConachie (Iowa City: Iowa University Press, 1989), 198.
66. Schneider, *Performing Remains*, 8.
67. Ibid., 15.

Part II

ROUSING EXPERIENCES: THEATRE, POLITICS, AND CHANGE

Introduction to the Special Section

—BRIAN E. G. COOK

As I write this, the United States is undergoing a radical test of its democratic structures and the very notion of "truth" is increasingly questioned. The White House often functions more as a reality show catering to big personalities, ratings, and large crowds, and so I'm going to take the opportunity of this introduction on "rousing theatre" to attempt to read the political and cultural landscape in terms of performance as I saw it in fall 2017. Though Sara Freeman and I didn't know when we put out the call for papers that the mood in the United States would so profoundly change in the fall of 2016, global politics will likely influence the immediate understanding of this section, and for someone picking it up in twenty years, such reflection might be necessary to provide context. And, since each issue of *Theatre History Studies* has a long production time line, at least a year will have passed between the period when I wrote this introduction and the time you are reading it, so given the tremendous instability of the current US administration and the rapid apprehension of its every nuance by the national media, I expect the world you're currently experiencing to be different than mine.

Political events are riper for performative analysis than ever before. From my couch in July 2017, I witnessed the media's clamor over the "dramatic" vote of Republican Senator John McCain against the "skinny repeal" of the Affordable Care Act.[1] Earlier this week I lived through the fallout from and breathless media analysis of Anthony Scaramucci's phone call to *New Yorker* journalist Ryan Lizza, wherein, amid trying to get Lizza to identify a confidential source, the gregarious Scaramucci also claimed he had no interest in gaining publicity for himself, because, as he said so eloquently, "I'm not Steve Bannon, I'm not trying to suck my own cock."[2] Scaramucci was fired days later, and Bannon left the

White House in August 2017. I'm sure you and future-me will have lived through stories even more compelling as the Reality Star Presidency continues its bewildering quest for viewership and ratings.

For this special section, we called for papers that focused on "plays, productions, processes, and/or people which have been rousing: specifically, where theatre and politics have intersected to embolden, comfort, or incite artists or audiences, or which have piqued curiosity, exasperation, or anger," and we offered a definition of "rousing" that included "to startle out of inactivity." Like many of you, I teach about theatrical riots in my theatre history classes, and my students are often surprised by the importance placed upon what appeared onstage and bemused by the raucousness in the theatre and adjacent spaces during the Old Price, *Hernani*, or Astor Place Riots, having never encountered any such thing in their own lives as audience members. My students are also usually surprised by Piscator and Brecht's desire to use theatre to provoke an audience into action, because, for them, theatre has never had such impact.

Multiple events that have occurred over the past few months and others that will happen in the future are likely to shift their understanding, and I predict having very interesting conversations with my students about the modern impact of theatre. Though I'll dig into these more deeply later, the attendance of Vice President-elect Mike Pence at a performance of *Hamilton* in New York City in late 2016, performances of Robert Shenkkan's play *Building the Wall*, and the reaction to the New York Public Theatre's 2017 production of *Julius Caesar* with a distinctly Trump-like Caesar have all brought theatre into national headlines.[3] Beyond the theatre, *Saturday Night Live*'s continued lampooning of the Trump administration and its central figures have brought home the important role that cultural reflections of the political have come to play in our modern society. If nothing else, as *Vulture*'s Mark Harris writes, "In search of believable oracular leadership that politicians and pundits have failed to provide, it's tempting to turn to art."[4] Anecdotally, he appears to be right: *The West Wing* has become a rediscovered treasure for many of my binge-watching students, and I myself got through the immediate aftermath of the election by engrossing myself in Netflix's *The Crown*.

Harris describes the viewer's experience of 2017 pop culture as a "mix of intentional resonance and discovered resonance" and uses *SNL* as an example of the former and *Boss Baby* ("a malevolent toddler in a suit voiced by [Alec] Baldwin") of the latter, for, as Harris writes, the producers could not have foreseen the context of 2017 when they began work a year or more earlier. I find it nearly impossible to interact with culture and not connect it to our current political moment. When Netflix suggested that I screen *V for Vendetta* again, though the original graphic novel was written under Thatcherism and the film made following 9/11, I found a "discovered resonance" addressing Trumpism:

> And the truth is, there is something terribly wrong with this country, isn't there? Cruelty and injustice, intolerance and oppression. And where once you had the freedom to object, to think and speak as you saw fit, you now have censors and systems of surveillance coercing your conformity and soliciting your submission. How did this happen? Who's to blame? Well certainly there are those more responsible than others, and they will be held accountable, but again truth be told, if you're looking for the guilty, you need only look into a mirror. I know why you did it. I know you were afraid. Who wouldn't be? War, terror, disease. There were a myriad of problems which conspired to corrupt your reason and rob you of your common sense. Fear got the best of you, and in your panic you turned to the now high chancellor, Adam Sutler. He promised you order, he promised you peace, and all he demanded in return was your silent, obedient consent.[5]

When I attended the *NT Live* broadcast of *Angels in America* in the summer of 2017, I largely expected to encounter it as a period piece, but once again glaring connections between the artistic responses to 1980s neoconservatism and twenty-first-century Trumpism became apparent.[6] In one scene, Roy Cohn (Nathan Lane) attempts to recruit a reluctant Joe Pitt (Russell Tovey) to help him avoid disbarment by rationalizing his illegal activities: "The whole Establishment. Their little rules. Because I know no rules. Because I don't see the Law as a dead and arbitrary collection of antiquated dictums, thou shall, thou shalt not, because, because I know the Law, a pliable, breathing, sweating...organ.... This is gastric juices churning, this is enzymes and acids, this is intestinal is what this is, bowel movement and blood-red meat—this stinks, this is politics, Joe, the game of being alive. . . . I'm gonna be a goddam motherfucking legally licensed member of the bar lawyer, just like my daddy was, till my last bitter day on earth, Joseph, until the day I die."[7] Trump is more than a little like Cohn, and, in fact, since Cohn was Trump's lawyer in the 1980s prior to his death, it is likely that Trump picked up some pointers: be ruthless, never apologize, always believe that what you do is right, and fuck over everyone who disagrees.

Trump's election was and is being heralded by the reactionary, activist "alt-right" (typified by Fox News's Sean Hannity and various writers at Breitbart) as a landmark event that will remake America in a revolutionary way (not unlike the election of Ronald Reagan had been described). He's arguably one of the more "theatrical" (as in pejorative over-the-topness) presidents that the United States has ever seen. "I think he's great," said entertainer Jerry Lewis in 2015 when asked about then-candidate Donald Trump. "He's a showman and we've never had a showman in the president's chair."[8] Despite Reagan's acting fame or Teddy Roosevelt's magnetic personality, it is true that Trump is often discussed in terms of his showmanship. He himself is keenly aware of this, hence the many stories we have seen about his obsession with crowd size. His debut announcement at Trump Tower in New York City on June 16, 2015, was well attended but subsequently derided when it was revealed that many audience members were paid to attend. Trump's modern-day claques came from one of several companies that specialize in providing extra bodies for major events, and the *Atlantic*'s report on such practices highlights that it is often impossible to sort out when there is genuine enthusiasm for a candidate or event and when the enthusiasm has been enhanced monetarily.[9]

Perhaps the most noted example of Trump's crowd obsession was the flap over the comparison of his inauguration crowd with Barack Obama's in 2009. Or, indeed, any other inauguration, for then-Press Secretary Sean Spicer loudly proclaimed the 2017 crowd "the largest audience ever to witness an inauguration, period."[10] In response to most media outlets, which used photographs, DC Metro ridership figures, and even television viewing numbers to discount that claim, Trump kept insisting in public and via Twitter that the media was lying. Factcheck.org sorted the facts from the "alternative" ones: "Trump and Spicer argued that the media misrepresented the size of the crowd at the inauguration, and we don't find any evidence of that," writers Lori Robertson and Robert Farley summarized. "To the contrary, it was Trump and Spicer who provided false information to feed a false narrative about crowd size."[11]

Trump seems to have a pathological need for large crowds and good ratings, and he wants the media and his critics to know how many people want to hear what he has to say. "Thank you everybody, what a crowd!" he said when visiting Texas after Hurricane Harvey hit Houston. "What a turnout!"[12] (That he was two hundred miles away in Corpus Christi and not in the Houston area, where the hurricane had its impact, was apparently irrelevant to him.) Trump also ensures that all of his staff know that only a full house will do, and he derides the media when they don't show footage that "proves" the size of his crowds. However, when the proof shows a much smaller crowd, he says the media is lying.[13] Ratings are comparably important to crowd size: Trump announced the pardon of Arizona sheriff Joe Arpaio as Hurricane Harvey was about to make landfall in Texas, because, he said, "even though it was a Friday evening, I assumed the ratings would be far higher than they were normally."[14]

Ratings matter as a sign of audience approval, because part of Trump's self-mythologizing requires preserving the impression that he has been elected on a tide of popular sentiment. He's viciously claimed that the popular vote he lost by nearly 3 million was skewed by illegal votes.[15] Though the past eight months have demonstrated that he doesn't have the bully pulpit he believes he does, Trump wants to bend government to his will because the American people have supposedly placed him in power to revolutionize government, "drain the swamp," and "Make America Great Again." The idea of this so-called revolution is ridiculous from many angles, as is the notion that such revolutionary change is even possible. One of the many things that Trump doesn't understand is that, for better or worse, politics in a democracy is based upon consensus and compromise, especially when one does not have a clear popular mandate nor clearly articulated policy ideas. (Conservative British Prime Minister Theresa May learned just such a lesson in 2017.) Trump's heavy-handed tactics and lack of regard for facts or anything that is not self-aggrandizing is of course not designed to cater to the dwellers of Washington's "swamp," but that is the very reason he has largely been unsuccessful in convincing anyone in Washington to enact his initiatives, such as they are. If he truly had swept into office on an immense popular victory, perhaps he'd be more able to wield a heavy hand what for counts for his "legislative agenda," but this would be nearly unprecedented in presidential politics.[16] Trump's swamp-draining "strategy" that seems to have led so many into naively supporting him was always bound to fail.

The other aspect of Trump's self-mythology is his repeated insistence that his perspective on any issue is in tune with "many many" people, regardless of what little evidence might exist to support his claims. The nadir of this approach (though what actually qualifies as a "nadir" in Trump's America?) came with Trump's disastrous remarks after the events in Charlottesville, Virginia, August 11–12, 2017. On August 15, Donald Trump, president of the United States of America, stood center stage in front of the gold elevators of Trump Tower, pontificating about himself and singing his standard theme song about the press as "fake news." When he was pressed by journalists to defend his initial remarks on August 12 that laid equal blame for the violence on both white nationalists as well as those who were there to oppose them, he said that his initial statement was "correct," defended it as a "fine statement," and made no reference to the prepared (likely by an aide) remarks he had made on August 14, which did not refer to blame on both sides and which had been seen as a concession to the outrage generated by his original comments. Continuing to be pressed for an answer, he went on: "But you also had people that were very fine people, on both sides. You had people in that group—excuse me, excuse me—I saw the same pictures as you did. You had people in that group that were there to protest the taking down of, to them, a very, very important statue and the renaming of a park from Robert E. Lee to another name. . . . I'm not talking about the neo-Nazis and the white nationalists, because they should be condemned totally. But you had many people in that group other than neo-Nazis and white nationalists. OK? And the press has treated them absolutely unfairly."[17] Trump seems to expect that we set aside the semiotics of the moment when, on a lovely summer Friday evening, hundreds of (largely white and male) Americans marched through Charlottesville and into a park carrying flaming (tiki) torches. The throng upliftingly chanted things like "You will not replace us" and "Jews will not replace us," and, as they were confronted by a small band of students at the foot of Thomas Jefferson on the University of Virginia campus, "a brawl ensued. At least one person was led away in handcuffs by the police," according to the *New York Times*.[18] The next day, the planned "Unite the Right" rally was held, attended by white nationalists and members of the Ku Klux Klan (KKK), including David Duke, former KKK imperial wizard and Trump fanboy, who told the *Times* that their intent was "to fulfill the promises of Donald Trump" to "take our country back." The rally was opposed by protesters from many constituencies, and minor arguments and fisticuffs were reported throughout the day. Later in the day, a twenty-year-old Ohio man drove his car into a group of counterprotesters, wounding several and killing thirty-two-year-old Heather Heyer.[19]

The problem for Trump was that—for almost the first time—lawmakers of all political stripes condemned the violence in Charlottesville as well as Trump's response, which was seen to give safe harbor to white nationalists, who showed their appreciation to the president. It is hardly surprising that Trump should do so, for his famous "crowds" have often been seething with violent and racist sentiment. At the mere mention of Hillary Clinton's name, his crowds chant the refrain "Lock Her Up!" and when Trump mentions the supposed actions of undocumented immigrants, they encourage him to "Build the Wall!" So virulent and chilling were the crowds toward the press, often at Trump's bidding, of course, that many media outlets hired security for their reporters.

Many journalists and observers have likened the phenomenology of a Trump rally to the fascist spectacles of Nazi Germany and Mussolini's Italy, and the number of public staged readings of the play *It Can't Happen Here* rose dramatically in the months before November 2016. Sinclair Lewis's 1935 novel focuses on the rise of a fascist candidate who defeats Franklin D. Roosevelt to win the presidency, and the story was likely based upon the rise of populist Louisiana senator Huey P. Long. The 1936 stage adaptation received simultaneous productions as part of the Federal Theatre Project, one of many decisions that likely led to the FTP's defunding. In September 2016, Berkeley Rep produced a new adaptation of the novel by Tony Taccone and Bennett S. Cohen, and in honor of the simultaneous FTP opening of the play at twenty-one different theatres on October 24, 1936, Berkeley Rep coordinated a simultaneous reading of the new adaptation at theatres across the country. While there was no Trump lookalike onstage in the Rep's production, the reviewer for the *Mercury News*, tongue firmly in cheek, wrote that "somehow the time seems right for a new look at this old story."[20]

Julius Caesar

Stoop, Romans, stoop,
And let us bathe our hands in Caesar's blood
Up to the elbows, and besmear our swords:
Then walk we forth, even to the market-place,
And, waving our red weapons o'er our heads,
Let's all cry "Peace, freedom and liberty!"[21]

Of course, in no place was the resonance more intentional than in New York's Central Park, where in June 2017 the Public Theater produced Shakespeare's *Julius Caesar* directed by Oskar Eustis with Caesar in Trump-like drag, played by actor Gregg Henry. The production faced vitriol from right-wing news organizations like Breitbart before it had even opened. In the wake of the controversy, the National Endowment for the Arts distanced itself from the production, and major funders Bank of America and Delta Air Lines decided to take their money elsewhere after supposedly receiving phone calls from "thousands."[22] The original Breitbart story, which of course fanned the flames for Trumpists, makes clear that the writer had not seen the show and was relying upon an interview with an audience member done by the website Mediaite.[23] The Mediaite story identified the audience member as Laura Sheaffer, a sales manager with Salem Media, a Christian-oriented broadcasting group.[24] Neither Breitbart nor Mediaite seems to have sought comment from the Public Theatre for their articles, nor does it appear that the authors of those pieces witnessed the production itself. Neither article contains details of Shakespeare's play, including none of the consequences that the assassination has for the conspirators. Both articles specifically mention Kathy Griffin's severed Trump-head photo, an admittedly over-the-top and inappropriate move from the stand-up comedian.[25]

Amid the flap, Eustis blamed what he called the "right-wing hate machine" for incensing people. "Those thousands of people who are calling our corporate sponsors to complain about this—none of them have seen the show," he said.[26] This raises troubling questions about the makeup of the "audience" that was being roused: surely it should be essential for someone to actually experience the artwork they are critiquing? Indeed, what these "critics" are responding to is an idea, a thing that may or may not be like the art-thing they dislike. Was a Trump lookalike murdered in the Delacorte? Yes, but the murder happened within the context of a story being told. At all times the action is fiction and fantasy, because it happens in a play.

How can you hate what you haven't seen?[27] From Eustis's perspective, the objectors "are not interested in seeing the show. They haven't read *Julius Caesar*. They are being manipulated by *Fox & Friends* and other news sources, which are deliberately, for their own gain, trying to rile people up and turn them against an imagined enemy, which we are not."[28] Indeed, many who objected were so uninformed that they couldn't even identify the correct Shakespeare-producing company on which to vent their rage, with angry calls being received at theatres all over the country who just happened to be simultaneously producing *Julius Caesar*.[29] However, Eustis is on to a new tactic of Trump and his followers that is far more sinister: if you don't like what the media says about you, decry it as a product of the bias of those who are clearly against you and your beliefs and therefore "fake." The term "fake news" is now currency, but what it is exactly is far from clear; we know that Trump tweets to denounce the fakery of mainstream media sources like the *New York Times*, the *Washington Post*, NBC, CBS, and ABC, and then he retweets stories from Breitbart and Infowars and other sites that don't tend to subscribe to traditional journalistic practices. The major difference between real and fake for Trump is in who covers him better and with whom he agrees. The frightening impact is that reality-via-Breitbart is blurred: *Caesar* becomes a problem that typifies violence against the president as part of a left-wing conspiracy encompassing all traditional news outlets, but pay no attention to the lack of detail and facts in our own reporting. The same can be said for Trump's tweets and speeches.

We have had politicians bemoaning media coverage before, and the oft-vaunted "journalistic impartiality and objectivity" belies the fact that journalists are human beings who have opinions that shape how they think and report. What seems different now is that we're not getting "spin" in response to credible media stories using time-tested journalistic, fact-checking processes but instead diatribes of lies and easily disproven claims from Trump and his aides that are supposed to substitute for reality. As a BuzzFeed story notes, "Trump has bragged that he doesn't need the mainstream media to reach his supporters given his large audiences on social media," and so Trump herds his followers by decrying all other media as lies and declaring his Twitter as the one true place to get the real story.[30]

What is clear is the impact that such blurred reality can have, as those swayed by the rhetoric and who believe what they've read or seen online take action. As *Julius Caesar* actor Corey Stoll (Brutus) described in an editorial in *Vulture*, in addition to online and phoned objections, the production also had protesters in its audiences. Coming to protest *Julius Caesar* at the Delacorte Theatre required some dedication in preparing for the big moment. Tickets for Shakespeare in the Park are free, so while protesters didn't have to shell out any money to the Public, they did have to wait in line: tickets are given out only on the day of each show on a first-come, first-served basis. To protest inside the Delacorte, these people had to show up early in the morning to stand around in Central Park, likely for hours, among genuine Shakespeare fans and the newly curious, to ensure they got a seat. Once inside, the protesters employed a variety of tactics. As Stoll described it: "Our first protester hurled insults about us continuously from a legal, but still audible, distance for the first hour of our show," he wrote. "At curtain call, a man wearing an American-flag jacket who had politely sat through the play stood and unfurled a Trump 2020 flag. At first I flinched, thinking the worst, but he just stood there smiling proudly."[31] Even more disruptive activity would transpire in the audience. In a Facebook post, audience member Samantha Rehr described the events she witnessed on Friday, June 16, 2017, two days before the show closed:

> About thirty minutes in, Caesar is brutally stabbed to death over and over by the senators. It's really graphic and disturbing. Enter stage right from the audience a young woman dressed all in black yelling at the senators and the audience[,] "Stop violence against conservatives!" Slowly the crowd realizes she isn't an actor . . . , she's a real protestor. A man stands up in his seat and starts yelling at the crowd, and now the audience is booing and hissing and people are standing up out of their seats to yell at the protestors (someone near me yells, "I hope you didn't wait all morning for this!"), and the stage manager comes on the god mic to pause the show, and security come on stage to drag the woman off. The commotion settles, and the SM comes on again and announces, "actors, pick up from 'Liberty! Freedom!'" (that was literally the line) and the crowd goes wild. Standing ovation. The scene picks up and ends, and the real police, in full regalia with bullet proof vests, cross back into the theater in front of the stage as the senators exit the stage through the audience and have to weave around the police, as actors dressed as police in riot gear enter the stage (I can't even describe how wild this image was), and the scene shifts to Brutus's speech to the Romans, during which a dozen planted actors throughout the theater jump out of their seats and begin yelling at the stage, and audience members, now not knowing what to believe begin heckling the "protestors" again! Madness! Long live art imitating life imitating art imitating life.[32]

If you listen closely, Artaud's heart is singing.

In spite of that, the production has not roused the audience itself into any direct act, and, in fact, the production could be seen to be unsuccessful if solely viewed in terms of producing actions, since those undertaken by audience members ran counter to the production and the company that produced it. Can/does theatre intentionally incite opposition to itself? We obviously must move beyond the idea that an action in a theatre can/must/will incite an audience member to direct action, but what of the reverse? In the case of *Julius Caesar*, no one has explicitly said that they intended to provoke the Trump camp with the production; indeed, Eustis himself claimed, "I thought there might be some fuss. I did not see this." Eustis also downplayed the intent behind the production: "What we are doing is . . . [to] make the dramatic stakes as real and powerful for contemporary people as we can, in our time and our place."[33] (He also referenced a 2012 production at the Guthrie where Caesar was an analog for Barack Obama and there was no backlash and Delta did not pull its funding.) However, Caesar is a stand-in for audience members: as the Roman senators vent their rage and vengeance on a public figure whose actions are particularly loathsome to them, the audience can vicariously imagine the 2017 parallel in an act of Aristotelian purgation. It is this act on which the protesters are so focused; it is also the most misunderstood, for while those on the left understand the assassination to be in the context of the play, many on the political right, especially those who did not see the show, believe the action to be a real and treasonous threat (though similar "threats" arising from 2012's Obama-as-Caesar production did *not* rouse their ire). Stoll described limited applause at Caesar's stabbing at early performances, causing him to realize that "a nontrivial percentage of our liberal audience had fantasized about undemocratic regime change in Washington." However, as the aftermath of the assassination plays out, the audience (possibly) realized that "acted out to its logical conclusion, that fantasy was hideous, shameful, and self-defeating."[34]

Jacques Rancière has already warned of the problems in artists seeking to "educate" or "enlighten" or even "provoke" an audience. Of Brecht and Artaud, he wrote: "For one, [the audience member] must refine his gaze, while for the other, he must abdicate the very position of viewer."[35] In both cases, the audience member is subject to the needs of the artist: "Emancipation begins when we challenge the opposition between viewing and acting; when we understand that the self-evident facts that structure the relations between saying, seeing, and doing themselves belong to the structure of domination and subjection." Instead, says Rancière, "it is not the transmission of the artist's knowledge or inspiration to the spectator. It is the third thing that is owned by no one, whose meaning is owned by no one, but which subsists between them, excluding any uniform transmission, any identity of cause and effect." That "thing," the performance in this case, is a shared experience that contains possibility and options for both actor and audience. "The collective power shared by spectators does not stem from the fact that they are members of a collective body," Rancière wrote. "It is the power each of them has to translate what she perceives in her own way, to link it to the unique intellectual adventure that makes her similar to all the rest in as much as this adventure is not like any other."[36] Rancière's "emancipated spectator" provides a frame for viewing many of the articles in this special section.

In the first article in the section, Megan Lewis examines Brett Bailey's *Exhibit B*, which faced protests and the cancelation of its run at the Barbican in London in 2014. Lewis situates the controversy as due to misreadings of Bailey's intent and questions about who is allowed to examine and represent racial histories. *Exhibit B* was an installation in which audience members would encounter various scenes, the intent of which was to disturb by deliberately invoking uncomfortable yet likely forgotten instances of racial subjugation. For example, Lewis vividly recounts one scene that features a black woman naked from the waist up and shackled to a bed; the viewer is given a chair in which to look and observe the woman, prompting any number of responses from sadness to a desire to intervene. However, despite Bailey's intent and the willing collaboration of his actors, a preview article in the *Guardian* misunderstood and informed readers that Bailey was subjugating his black performers. This fired a wave of online protest—including a petition—even though none of the signers had seen *Exhibit B* itself and had seen only published images removed from their performative context. After a skirmish outside the Barbican, the theatre canceled the show.

Similar to the reaction to *Julius Caesar* at the Public, the outcry against *Exhibit B* was not based upon the work itself but rather upon what people projected onto it and how they translated it into their own lives. If Rancière is right and the artist and the audience engage over the translation of the thing which is between them, what does artistic intention matter? Indeed, Rancière might say that the result of the canceled installation is as admirable as if it had played to thousands. And, yet, those who did not see it could not do their own translation; in this case, the provocation came via the mediation of a review. As Lewis quotes J. S. Rafaeli: "You may have loved to see this piece and decided for yourself whether or not it was worthwhile. But now you can't because some people decided you weren't grown up enough to make up your own mind." Lewis's article raises the question of actors' agency and the assumption in this case that they had none. Not only was Bailey's intention not fulfilled, but neither was that of the actors.

The cases of *Julius Caesar* and *Exhibit B* foreground the goal of the special section, which is the exploration of what impact(s) theatre does have. As we spelled out in our call, "definitional debates about political theatre are less of concern than historical analysis of places and performances where change is visible in and through theatre." Lewis's paper and the seven that follow cover a wide range of times and places. Not all the papers focus on uplifting theatre, but they all do question whether theatre has efficacy in that time and that place. As *Caesar*'s Stoll said: "In this new world where art is willfully misinterpreted to score points and to distract, simply doing the work of an artist has become a political act. I'm thankful for all the beautiful defenses of our production written in the last few weeks. But the cliché is true: In politics, when you're explaining, you're losing. So if you're making art, by all means question yourself and allow yourself to be influenced by critics of good faith. But don't allow yourself to be gaslighted or sucked into a bad-faith argument. A play is not a tweet. It can't be compressed and embedded and it definitely can't be delivered apologetically. The very act of saying anything more nuanced than 'us good, them bad' is under attack, and I'm proud to stand with artists who do."[37]

I feel we need to explore that question now more than ever.

Theatre in Trying Times

Our intent with the special section became about exploring the impact of various theatrical acts. Shifting to the question of efficacy seemed important given the messiness of the term "political theatre," since at the current moment, all theatre seems to have strong political resonance. In a recent podcast, theatre scholar Dan Rebellato and right-wing critic Kate Maltby discuss "right-wing theatre," and Maltby says a key shift she's seen is how no one on either side seeks to reason or persuade. There's no attempt made to compromise nor to understand the opposing side, and in that, theatre is mirroring political reality.[38] Peter Marks in the *Washington Post*, writing about several theatrical responses to the Trump administration and its policies, noted, "Theater makers seem to be scurrying to take up rhetorical arms and secure a place in the vanguard of artistic resistance. In other words, the rush is on, to vent onstage about Trump." Marks profiled various examples, including *Julius Caesar*, of course, and also Robert Schenkkan's *Building the Wall*. Schenkkan wrote the play immediately after the election, and within months, had multiple theatres lined up to perform it.[39] The play is set in 2019 following in the wake of both Trump's impeachment and the implementation of "expedited removal" of immigrants in a massive "roundup." Rick, the former head of a detention center for deportees, is being interviewed in prison by Gloria, an African American academic looking to understand what led to Rick's imprisonment. Throughout their discussion, Schenkkan explores the rationale of people like Rick, whose enthusiasm for the man-who-would-be-president led to an almost-blind allegiance to any policy his administration put forward. In the wake of an unspecified event in Times Square, Rick becomes directly involved in the detention of millions of "illegals" after Trump declares martial law and the Republican-led Congress suspends the filibuster to enact draconian laws regulating immigration. As the numbers of detainees increase, prison space becomes increasingly limited as most countries begin to refuse to accept the deportees in an effort to get the United States to end its policies. Rick describes concentration camp–like conditions, where disease and malnutrition lead to widespread death and the need to begin cremating bodies en masse to deal with the "problem," and eventually the corporation running the prison and US government representatives decide to murder the detainees to solve the problem once and for all.

Schenkkan's play is clearly the nightmare vision that many Americans on the left envisioned given Trump's violent denunciations of illegal immigrants and the consequences of an entirely Republican-led government. As Rick sums up at the end:

> The President said he was going to build a wall, a beautiful wall, and he would make Mexico pay for it. And everybody laughed at that, all you smart people laughed at that because of course, it's absurd. You can't really build a wall that big and that high to keep people out if they really want to get in. And Mexico was never going to pay for any of that shit. But that's not what he meant. See. That was the revelation. It wasn't a real wall, a brick and mortar wall. That wasn't what he was talking about. What is a wall? It's a, a construct, a, a device, for keeping people out. What we built was so much more effective. It will keep people out for years because nobody will want to come here now.[40]

Eight months into the Trump presidency, thankfully dictatorship has been avoided largely due to presidential incompetence and the checks and balances built into the constitution to preserve democratic processes. However, Rick's final sentence about nobody wanting to come to the United States resonates with what has become the real problem of Trump's presidency: a decline of American prestige internationally, largely due to numerous poor interactions between Trump and other world leaders.[41] Schenkkan's play serves as a reminder of what could have been but also of what has had its impact blunted by what did not come to pass.

While there have been any number of theatrical, left-wing responses to Trump, we have not yet seen any significant attempts to bring the Trumpist agenda to the stage from a conservative perspective. This isn't really surprising, as rarely have there been examples of truly right-wing political theatre, largely for two reasons: first, because of how we have defined the baseline of theatre politically and, second, because many artists lean left. "I can not think of a single time when I have sat in a theatre," theatre critic Susannah Clapp told Jay Rayner in an extraordinary *Observer* article, "and been struck by the idea that what I'm watching is coming from the right."[42] Rebellato and Maltby circle around to the understanding that both sides can, and do, claim any piece of theatre, using Shakespeare as an example.[43] To be "conservative" in theatrical terms is to be traditional, to appear to be espousing cultural standards or replicating conventional societal expectations and norms (i.e., critiques of realism as upholding traditional values) and/or to be utilizing conventional Western narrative form. In Rayner's article, he interviews multiple people, none of whom can name a right-wing British play. "There is, however, plenty of conservative theatre—small-c—which suggests that the left-right categories are inadequate. Most romantic comedy is deeply conservative," he quotes former National Theatre director Nick Hytner as saying, "and is in effect propaganda for marriage and what we call family values. I'm not sure, though, that most theatre-goers would call it right-wing."

In the wider political sphere, of course, we have seen rightist revolution before, most clearly in Spain, Germany, and Italy prior to World War II, and indeed, Trump's alt-right "movement" has earned comparisons to those movements. Those movements tended to spark a return to producing classic texts, both because of nationalist glorification of great German literature of the past (especially Wagner) and because especially the Nazis decided contemporary plays focused on everyday issues were more difficult to control in terms of messaging.[44] In Italy, as Patricia Gaborik details in her article, theatre under fascism has falsely been seen to be governed solely by political motivation. As Gaborik says, historical "depictions [of theatre in Italy] are shaped more by assumptions about what fascism was—and was not—than by the research conducted." She broadens long-held genealogies of theatre in the fascist period, revealing that theatre under Mussolini was largely shaped by his own love of dramatic literature and theatre artists. Good art could be brought to the masses that wasn't steeped in fascist ideology, especially since such blatant messaging was rarely popular or effective. Well-produced theatre still served a propagandic purpose confirming the generosity of the government and its desire to entertain the people.

Gaborik attributes a lot of the historical misrepresentation of theatre under fascism to the depictions of Silvio D'Amico in his 1944 book *The Theatre Must Not Die*. D'Amico, director of the National Academy of Dramatic Arts, appears to have had a vested interest in maligning Mussolini's approach to theatre, especially in that it avoided funding smaller, artistic playhouses for the sake of large-scale spectacles. That did not mean, however, that government-funded theatre hadn't produced quality performances, despite what D'Amico would have his readers believe. Gaborik details the government funding of multiple large-scale, open-air shows that would tour the country, performing throughout the 1930s until the war made such gatherings too dangerous. The repertoire included both Italian and European classic plays and operas but also translations of American dramatists like Eugene O'Neill and Thornton Wilder. Gaborik writes that there is truth in the notion that very little theatre openly challenged the government and its authority, but censorship seems to mostly have focused on moral issues rather than on political ones. And, despite the government's desire to create national unity through the widespread adoption of the Italian language over regional dialects, a significant percent of the government-sponsored theatre tours performed in the vernacular. Gaborik reveals that, contrary to widespread belief, the Italian theatre under Mussolini was far more nuanced and remarkable than most have given it credit for.

This shouldn't be surprising. Censorship, whether under Soviet Communism or the British Lord Chamberlain, has rarely posed an overwhelming challenge to theatre artists. Indeed, theatre has often served an important counter-discursive function to censorship in many contexts. A new challenge, though, is posed by the overwhelming impact of the internet and social media, which as it proliferates seems like a space without censorship, capable of disseminating ideas outside of official channels. This mode of communication and connection does not function only to encourage democracy, however, as news accounts of Russian ad buys on Facebook and Twitter affirm. The overwhelming speed and quantity of internet and social media spaces challenges citizens and artist alike: how can one possibly "curate" their own experience on the internet effectively? The problem with social media and even Google is that what users encounter has already been "selected" by whatever algorithm Facebook or Google has used to give the content users "want" to see, supposedly based upon what they have previously engaged with. The internet is therefore not a truly democratic space, since it is actually never without moderation. The question now is, given the internet's overwhelming size and complexity, about regulation. Who regulates? What is the means by which the regulation is decided upon? Facebook banning photos of breastfeeding women seems clear evidence that their own regulation isn't always effective or in line with its users. Until regulation is in place, the challenge for consumers is to find a way to cut through all of the truly fake news and for news outlets to continue to deliver a high level of scrutiny.

What is theatre's role in this? Ilinca Todoruţ and Anthony Sorge's article on Lebanese artists Rabih Mroué and Walid Raad indicates that one way might be to embrace and reflect the chaos. Todoruţ and Sorge reveal that both artists, while working completely independent of one another (the latter's work is usually seen in art galleries, whereas Mroué employs the stage), nonetheless converse through their work on issues relevant to Lebanese audiences. Raad and Mroué represent a blurring of artificial boundaries between artistic disciplines and have both explored and critiqued the media landscape that surrounds their culture. A critic is a spectator, of course, a surrogate for the potential audience member, and both artists at times adopt a lecture-style performance mode, where the performer/presenter reflects critical authority, but re-used found media material undermines that authority. Todoruţ and Sorge examine performances that reveal hidden truths behind mediatized images, including *Three Posters* by Mroué, where using a hidden recording booth, the artist performs what seems to the audience to be a speech by a martyr in the midst of a 1980s battlefield, though the recording apparatus is soon revealed, undermining the original video. Then the real video of an authentic, well-known 1980s martyr speech is played unedited, with flubs and mistakes that never appear in the original. Raad's series based around the Atlas Group, a "fictitious research organization," publicly displays and presents both real and fictionalized archival material "to deconstruct and reflect on Lebanese history, trauma, and identity." This is especially important given the loss of both official and personal archives in the midst of the civil war, and the Atlas Group work recovers as much as it questions.

The work of Mroué and Raad explore and dismantle the binary between real and fake, especially where that boundary has been mediatized. Is this a counterargument for Rancière and his purely "democratic knowledge" argument, demonstrating that some sort of artistic expertise, knowledge, or skill is necessary? Both artists seem to be focused on giving the audience training in discernment, in critique, by showing them how to sift through competing, potentially specious claims. In her article in the special section, Shulamith Lev-Aladgem explores what she feels is a shift away from the "political" in both mainstream and community-based performances in Israel. As part of her analysis, Lev-Aladgem uses Rancière's notion of equality as the true "political" to ascertain the possibilities of this idea in practice: "His indication that theatre is 'effective in organizing a sensory space where plebeians happen to speak like patricians' is highly evocative if we ask ourselves how we might realize this maxim in practice, assigning new possibilities of politicalness for theatre, both mainstream and fringe." One demonstration of this is a moment in the performance *Sea Breeze*, where a Palestinian mother and daughter toss off convention and jump into the ocean with all their clothes on; the Israeli audience's shared joy and appreciation of this moment reveals "a brief moment of utter freedom and a microcosm of emancipation."

In a way, the shift Lev-Aladgem implies via Rancière is that rather than being historical (documenting experience), or even educational, theatre should be philosophical; in other words, instead of saying "here is what happened" or "isn't this thing horrifying," theatre should explore what might be possible. Lev-Aladgem mentions performers who use Augusto Boal's work, and this is perhaps a good model in that the spect-actor first reviews the history and then revises it. Her article, based on her expertise in making and analyzing community performance in Israel, highlights the shifts in the way we understand "political" in theatre spaces, and the following articles provide case studies that demonstrate this.

Theatre and Activism

The remaining four articles in the special section each attempt to use theatre to call attention to social issues: women's suffrage, the place of African Americans in American history, the Italian working class, and Latinx identity. In all cases, the impact of the performance isn't immediately clear, though most of the artists do intend for the audience to be impacted. Christine Woodworth's article on the 1910 performance of a suffrage matinee in New York City offers an early twentieth-century example of activists and artists bringing social issues directly into the theatre. The intersection of the suffragette movement and theatre was a move away from the typical parlor/closet drama that ran parallel with women's increased movement into the social sphere, both acting and enacting women's roles in public. The event also transcends the urban/rural divide, and Woodworth documents the connection between the rural upstate New York towns of Geneva and Seneca Falls and the broader suffragette movement. Not only did Geneva invite multiple speakers, including British suffragette leader Emmeline Pankhurst, but it also hosted theatrical performances of plays like *How the Vote Was Won* by Christopher St. John and Cicely Hamilton, which had appeared in the 1910 New York suffrage matinee. Woodworth's re-creation of that event demonstrates both the prominent performers and audience members it attracted but also the derisive way the press of the day covered it and events like it, preoccupied more with what the women were wearing than with what they were saying. "Fortunately, for the world's peace of mind," wrote one journalist in 1907, "most reforms are slow, very slow of consummation." Though the impact of the suffrage matinee isn't immediately clear, as we know, women's suffrage does become law in 1920.

Lurana Donnels O'Malley begins her article on a 1932 pageant play by making a parallel to Lin Manuel Miranda's *Hamilton: An American Musical* (2015). Hamilton's inclusion of actors of color playing major figures of the American Revolution including Alexander Hamilton and George Washington and its use of rap and R&B music has made it a cultural bellwether of the Obama era.[45] The show's success brought Vice President-elect Mike Pence to New York in the weeks after the 2016 election, an occasion *Hamilton* actor Brandon Victor Dixon did not let pass. After the curtain call, Dixon spoke from the stage, directly addressing Pence: "We, sir—we—are the diverse America who are alarmed and anxious that your new administration will not protect us, our planet, our children, our parents, or defend us and uphold our inalienable rights. We truly hope that this show has inspired you to uphold our American values and to work on behalf of all of us." Perhaps unsurprisingly, Trump himself took offense and tweeted that Pence was "harassed," that the statement was "rude," and that Dixon owed Pence an apology. Dixon tweeted in reply that "conversation is not harassment[,] sir" and that he appreciated Pence staying to listen.[46] By contrast, the visits of Hillary and Bill Clinton to the theatres of New York have been entirely different thing: "Mrs. Clinton is greeted as a vanquished hero—standing ovations, selfies, shouted adulation."[47]

O'Malley invokes *Hamilton* by way of introducing us to a prior portrayal of George Washington by an African American actor, in Mary Church Terrell's *Historical Pageant-Play Based on the Life of Phyllis Wheatley* (1932), produced as part of the bicentennial celebration of George Washington's birth. The play focused on the life of slave and published poet Phillis Wheatley, a contemporary of Washington and who once had a brief correspondence with the future first American president. Terrell's play was intended to address both the absent and negative portrayals of African Americans in other performances connected to the bicentennial as much as it was to highlight Wheatley as a figure of historical significance. Unlike *Hamilton*, the production encountered a number of problems, including a meddling white director who tinkered with Terrell's story line and characters. While most other bicentennial events happened at the Sylvan Theatre at the base of the Washington Monument, *Phyllis Wheatley* was moved twice, first to the five-thousand-seat Washington Auditorium and then to the auditorium of Armstrong Technical High School located in the northeast part of the District with only 1,100 seats. Given that only one performance was planned, the move greatly limited the impact of the production, and it was explained variously as due to the Depression and because it was believed that not enough people would come to fill the five thousand seats in Washington Auditorium. O'Malley points out that a twenty-one-year-old African American playing George Washington also could have played into the decision. Despite these limitations, the production played to a sold-out house and was generally acclaimed, albeit sometimes by white attendees who seemed shocked by the ability of a play about African Americans to be engaging. Once again, the production didn't produce immediate change, though perhaps the contemporary response to *Hamilton* indicates that the pageant had some genealogical impact.

Juliet Guzzetta's article explores the way that theatre participates in political dialogues by connecting the work of Dario Fo and Franca Rame with the recent Theatre of Narration (ToN) performance genre in Italy. The self-created and self-performed *teatro di narrazione* performers "re-visit historical events of national importance from local perspectives . . . [and] demonstrate the ways in which ordinary people have major influences on the legacies of the past," which links them to Fo and Rame (and echoes the solo presentation format of works by Mroué and Raad). Guzzetta is careful to also articulate the differences, including Fo's facility at physical performance, something most of the ToN writers do not emulate. She recounts several of Fo and Rame's most remarkable productions, including *Accidental Death of an Anarchist* (1970) and Rame's *The Rape* (1983) alongside examples of ToN, including the work of Laura Curino, which directly addresses Curino's inheritance from her predecessors. Curino "discusses the couple at the end of her play *Passione* and then quotes one of Rame's scenes from *Mistero buffo* by performing a large portion of it," and in so doing, Guzzetta reflects that Curino is also reclaiming Rame's contribution to Fo's legacy. While both Fo/Rame and ToN performances focus on politics, "the major difference is that Fo and Rame . . . invoked current events largely in order to strengthen an argument about contemporary politics, whereas the narrators contemplate the historicity of a particular event in order to understand the present more dynamically." This does not lessen the ToN productions' efficacy, but it does make it less definite.

In her article, Ashley E. Lucas looks at Culture Clash's *Chavez Ravine* (2003, revived 2015) as a multifaceted "combination of ethnography, history, fiction, and art." Though Culture Clash conducted historical research as they sought to depict the forced eviction of the Latinx and others living in LA's Chavez Ravine so that Dodger Stadium could be built, the production wasn't limited by its history. As Lucas shows, Culture Clash makes no pretense of being fair in its depiction; history hasn't previously been fair to Latinos, anyway. Both the actors and the audience become witnesses to historical events through the process of re-embodying. By conflating time and distance and placing historical figures alongside everyday Latinx people, the play gives voice to those who have not previously been heard. Where Mroué and Raad used fake documents as they reinstated lost histories, Culture Clash uses performative means to do the same thing. "General audiences, people with emotional or familial ties to Chavez Ravine, and even cultural historians might glean more from [assembled character] Señora Ruiz's life on stage than they would from reading/hearing all the research Culture Clash needed in order to construct her." Lucas questions whether the fictive, performative event is more effective/essential than historical research. How should we read this in light of Rancière's spectator *and* his learner? These four articles provide provocations to other theatre artists to think more broadly about what the audience might take away, and, despite Rancière's derision of the "community" within a theatrical performance, I think audiences do indeed have communal experiences. We perhaps cannot expect that everyone will "learn" the exact same thing, but the act of exchange can—and does—produce change. As *Julius Casear* audience member Samantha Rehr recalled: "After the stabbing, there's still an hour and a half left of the show, during which the conspirators suffer and die for their crime and Rome (or America) falls into civil war and chaos. It made me think actually about the risk of impeachment. We are so divided and so passionate and seemingly unchangeable, and that dystopia on stage might not be far off if we continue not to be able to sit down for a couple hours, even the horribly offensive detail thirty minutes in, and listen to one another."[48] Rehr's hope as she recounted her experience indicates that theatre can provide a space for possibility. We are in the midst of a major test of our institutional/constitutional structure due to many people's profound distrust of that structure. Theatre is as much an institution as any other. What we had initially been thinking about for this special section was an exploration of the efficacy of theatre, and in large measure we got it, though perhaps not entirely as we'd imagined. Given the historical range of subjects in this section, I'm left to wonder if, in this current political climate and in the midst of rising ticket prices and increased competition from people's couches, theatre artists have to live with two possibilities for building and developing audiences: spectacle and efficacy.

I'll set the former aside for now, given the focus of this section. Is "efficacy" a measure that rightly serves theatre? In her book on "participatory art," her blanket term for visual art that directly interacts or is even created by those who are viewing it (a practice she admits is akin to theatre and performance), Claire Bishop writes: "Rancière's point is important for drawing attention to the work of art as an intermediary object, a 'third term' to which both the artist and viewer can relate. Discussions of participatory art and its documentation tend to proceed with similar exclusions: without engaging with the 'aesthetic thing,' the work of art in all its singularity, everything remains contained and in its place—subordinated to a stark statistical affirmation of use-values, direct effects and a preoccupation with moral exemplarity. . . . Instead of extracting art from the 'useless' domain of the aesthetic to relocate it in praxis, the better examples of participatory art occupy an ambiguous territory between 'art becoming mere life or art becoming mere art.'"[49] As theatrical influence has waned over the course of the twentieth century, artists have been using theatre as a more limited and targeted tool to make the audience see/understand/recognize something and act. In addition to Rancière's critique that that maintains discordant binary positions, I've started thinking that there's also an ethical question about engaging audience: an artist wants to connect to a new audience, but that connection can be hampered by content. If artists believe it imperative and most ethical to make clear what a performance is about, then the audience may be self-selecting. And, as Harris writes in *Vulture*: "Critics and audiences alike can be suspicious of art that looks like it wants to have an effect. We like to be unsettled but we also want our politics to be confirmed; some of us disdain 'preaching to the choir' but like being in the choir; we want to discover resonance but prefer it to be well-enough concealed so that we can give ourselves credit for ferreting it out; we want artists to be clever but not to try to be clever."[50] The question "what will audiences come to the theatre for?" is maybe a trap, and I believe that Rancière gives us an escape. To presuppose that we can know what the audience is seeking is also to attempt to fulfill that through the theatrical product, thus replicating a hierarchy that many artists would want to disavow. The larger implication of embracing this is on the artist directly, for in emancipating the spectator, isn't Rancière also emancipating the artist?

In the spring of 2016, I directed *Stalking the Bogeyman*, a play adapted by David Holthouse and Markus Potter based on Holthouse's true-life account of childhood sexual abuse. The play is both an emotional journey and a cracking piece of suspense, as later in the play, the David character plots the murder of his childhood Bogeyman, just as Holthouse did in real life. After that is thwarted, the play ends with a public confrontation between the two men where words become as powerful as weaponry. Holthouse has said that he wrote his story to see if "the Mac [can be] mightier than the Glock."[51] The production opened at the University of Alaska Anchorage and subsequently toured to five other Alaskan cities: Palmer, Homer, Seward, Valdez, and Fairbanks. The aim of the production was to "turn up the volume" on the discussion about childhood sexual abuse—an epidemic problem in Alaska.[52] We sought partnerships with other departments on campus and with local service agencies to assist in this effort, and large grants were secured to pay for the tour.

In hindsight, I am of two minds about the project: one side of me is happy that the show was seen by hundreds of people and was very well received. The other side feels unfulfilled, not because the production didn't have a profound impact on childhood sexual abuse in Alaska, but rather because I don't know what impact it did have. I remember sitting with Holthouse as we were about to do a Q&A session at the Last Frontier Theatre Conference in Valdez, and both of us were anxiously looking forward to the project wrapping up. Our exhaustion came from two different places, and I admittedly can't imagine what it is like to have such a dark segment of your life writ large for your friends, your family, and perfect strangers to see. Mine was borne from a sense that the possibility that the production offered as we planned for it was gone; I knew what had happened and the limitations of our work was made abundantly clear. What we didn't factor in to our plans were any next steps, for the continuation of possibility through additional productions or conversations. I can say that in summer 2016 in Valdez, I was glad that we had not. I now feel emancipated from the continued responsibility of having to change people's minds; the production did what it did and stands as a thing that happened. Maybe there will be a direct follow-up by us, or maybe our work will inspire others to take up the challenge. I nonetheless feel hopeful, in spite of this potentially complicated genealogy.

David Greig wrote, "Theatre cannot change the world, but it can allow us a moment of liberated space in which to change ourselves."[53] If Rancière is right, that we as artists cannot and should not aim to inculcate ideas and actions in our audience, I don't think that means that there are no changes in ideas and actions resulting from a performance. The impact of something like *Stalking the Bogeyman* may not become clear for years, if ever. I did see a tremendous response from the audiences who saw it and stayed to talk about it, and I definitely saw the positive impact it had on the student-actors who were in it. By being too literal in talking about theatre's efficacy, I think we miss out on thinking about wide-ranging and genealogic change. We want to have an impact *now*, so that we know that there was one. I think we can do ourselves a favor in giving ourselves the benefit of the doubt.

Notes

1. Ed O'Keefe, "The Night John McCain Killed the GOP's Health-care Fight," *Washington Post*, July 28, 2017. McCain's vote, though the focus of so many stories, was perhaps only less significant than the votes of forty-six Democratic senators (the entire caucus), two other Republican Senators (Collins and Murkowski), and two Independent senators (Sanders and King, who caucus with the Democrats).
2. Ryan Lizza, "Anthony Scaramucci Called Me to Unload about White House Leakers, Reince Priebus, and Steve Bannon," *New Yorker*, July 27, 2017.
3. Christopher Mele and Patrick Healy, "'Hamilton' Had Some Unscripted Lines for Pence. Trump Wasn't Happy," *New York Times*, November 19, 2016.
4. Mark Harris, "We're Approaching a Major Turning Point in Trump-Era Pop Culture," *Vulture*, July 24, 2017. http://www.vulture.com/2017/07/were-approaching-a-turning-point-in-trump-era-pop-culture.html.
5. *V for Vendetta*, directed by James McTeigue (2005, Warner Bros., 2006), online via Netflix.
6. Produced by the National Theatre (UK) and broadcast globally by NT Live. Broadcasts July 20 and 27, 2017. Production ran in the Lyttleton Theatre, London, from May to August 2017.
7. Tony Kushner, *Angels in America: Millennium Approaches* (New York: Theatre Communications Group, 1993), 66–68.
8. EWTN, *World Over—2015-12-17—Jerry Lewis Exclusive with Raymond Arroyo*, video, 56:55, December 19, 2015, https://youtu.be/sGmyHivWyN8.
9. Dan Schneider, "The Business of Hiring a Fake Crowd for Political Campaigns," *Atlantic*, July 22, 2015.
10. Elle Hunt, "Trump's Inauguration Crowd: Sean Spicer's Claims Versus the Evidence," *Guardian* (London), January 22, 2017.
11. Lori Robertson and Robert Farley, "The Facts on Crowd Size," *FactCheck.org*, January 23, 2017, http://www.factcheck.org/2017/01/the-facts-on-crowd-size/.
12. Chris Riotta, "Trump Is Obsessed with the Size of Crowds, Hands and Now Hurricanes," *Newsweek*, September 6, 2017.
13. Jeremy Diamond, "Trump Fumes at Staff over Phoenix Rally Crowd Size," *CNN*, August 29, 2017, http://www.cnn.com/2017/08/29/politics/trump-phoenix-rally/index.html; and Sean Sullivan and Jenna Johnson, "Yes, Donald Trump's Crowds Are Big, but not Quite as 'Yuge' as He Often Claims," *Washington Post*, October 29, 2016.
14. Glenn Thrush and Julie Hirschfeld Davis, "Trump Eyed 'Far Higher' Ratings in Pardoning Joe Arpaio as Hurricane Hit," *New York Times*, August 28, 2017.
15. Trump, Donald J. Twitter Post. November 27, 2016, 11:30 a.m. https://twitter.com/realdonaldtrump/status/802972944532209664.
16. The largest popular mandate in terms of vote differential was that of Warren G. Harding in 1920, where he had a 26.2 percent margin of victory against his opponent James M. Cox. The most recent large mandate was that of Richard Nixon in 1972, where he had a 23.2 percent popular vote margin over George McGovern, but he had a slightly higher overall percentage of votes than Harding (60.7 percent vs. 60.3 percent) and an overwhelming majority of electoral votes (521 of the 538; McGovern won only Massachusetts

and the District of Columbia). I can't let it pass that even after these overwhelming election victories both Harding and Nixon remained in office only for just over half of their elected terms. Harding died on August 2, 1923, after presiding over what is generally considered one of the more scandal-plagued administrations, and Nixon resigned on August 9, 1974, as he faced impeachment over Watergate. Data from *American Presidency Project*. http://www.presidency.ucsb.edu.

17. CNN, "READ: President Trump's Q-and-A at Trump Tower," *CNN.com*, August 16, 2017, http://www.cnn.com/2017/08/15/politics/read-president-trumps-q-and-a-at-trump-tower/index.html.
18. Hawes Spencer and Sheryl Gay Stolberg, "White Nationalists March on University of Virginia," *New York Times*, August 11, 2017.
19. Sheryl Gay Stolberg and Brian M. Rosenthal, "Man Charged after White Nationalist Rally in Charlottesville Ends in Deadly Violence," *New York Times*, August 12, 2017.
20. Sam Hurwitt, "Review: Fascism Comes to Berkeley in 'It Can't Happen Here,'" *Mercury News* (San Jose, CA), October 1, 2016.
21. William Shakespeare, *Julius Caesar*, in Massachusetts Institute of Technology: The Complete Works of William Shakespeare, http://shakespeare.mit.edu/julius_caesar/julius_caesar.3.1.html.
22. Michael Paulson, "Oskar Eustis on Trump, 'Julius Caesar' and the Politics of Theater," *New York Times*, June 13, 2017.
23. Daniel Nussbaum, "'Trump' Stabbed to Death in Central Park Performance of 'Julius Caesar,'" Breitbart, June 6, 2017, http://www.breitbart.com/big-hollywood/2017/06/06/trump-stabbed-death-central-park-performance-julius-caesar/.
24. Aiden McLaughlin, "Senators Stab Trump to Death in Central Park Performance of Shakespeare's Julius Caesar," Mediaite, June 6, 2017, https://www.mediaite.com/trump/senators-stab-trump-to-death-in-central-park-performance-of-shakespeares-julius-caesar/.
25. I should note that while Griffin received tremendous backlash, photographer Tyler Shields who took the photo and also distributed it on his social media largely escaped any blame.
26. Paulson, "Oskar Eustis on Trump," *New York Times*.
27. Editorial note from Sara Freeman: This question calls to mind the vigorous debate and outcry when in 1994 Arlene Croce published "Discussing the Undiscussable" about her refusal to review Bill T. Jones's *Still/Here*. Croce contended that Jones "put himself beyond the reach of criticism" on an aesthetic level by using terminally ill HIV/AIDS patients onstage. Jones's multimedia dance piece was about living and dying with HIV/AIDS (Jones is HIV positive and lost his partner to the disease); Croce declared that Jones had made a political statement and participated in "victim art," so she didn't have to see it to register her critique of the piece.
28. Paulson, "Oskar Eustis on Trump," *New York Times*.
29. Cleve R. Wootson Jr., "People Mad about the Trump-like 'Julius Caesar' Are Sending Death Threats to the Wrong Theatre," *Washington Post*, June 18, 2017.
30. Claudia Koerner, "Trump Has Launched a 'Real News' Program on His Facebook, Hosted by His Daughter-In-Law," *BuzzFeed*, August 2, 2017, https://www.buzzfeed.com/amphtml/claudiakoerner/trumps-daughter-in-law-hosting-real-news-videos-for-the.
31. Corey Stoll, "What It Was Like to Star in the Trump-themed *Julius Caesar*," *Vulture*,

June 23, 2017, http://www.vulture.com/2017/06/what-it-was-like-to-star-in-the-trump-themed-julius-caesar.html.

32. Samantha Rehr. Facebook post, June 16, 2017, 8:37 p.m., https://www.facebook.com/samantha.rehr/posts/10213072883274850.
33. Paulson, "Oskar Eustis on Trump," *New York Times.*
34. Stoll, "What It Was Like," *Vulture.*
35. Jacques Rancière, *The Emancipated Spectator*, trans. Gregory Elliott (Brooklyn: Verso, 2009), 4. Kindle.
36. Rancière, *Emancipated Spectator*, 12–16.
37. Stoll, "What It Was Like," *Vulture.*
38. Dan Rebellato, "Thatcher, Right-Wing Theatre, Interview with Paul Miller," *Stage Directions*, podcast audio, August 2017, http://www.danrebellato.co.uk/stage-directions/.
39. At the Region Seven American College Theatre Festival held in Denver, Colorado, in February 2017, Schenkkan said in a Q&A that he'd specifically ensured that the play would be made available to anyone, anywhere who wanted to perform it, as opposed to limiting the initial performances to major regional theatres.
40. Robert Schenkkan, *Building the Wall: The Play and Commentary* (New York: Arcade Publishing, 2017).
41. Isaac Stanley-Becker and Scott Clement, "Poll Shows US Tumbling in World's Regard Under Trump," *Washington Post*, June 26, 2017.
42. Jay Rayner, "Why Is Nobody Doing the Right Thing?" *Guardian* (London), November 11, 2007.
43. Rebellato, "Thatcher, etc.," podcast.
44. Gerwin Strobl, *The Swastika and The Stage: German Theatre and Society* (Cambridge: Cambridge University Press, 2008).
45. Is it too much to call it an "Obama-non?"
46. Mele and Healy, "Hamilton," *New York Times.*
47. Michael Paulson, "Hillary Clinton's in the House," *New York Times*, February 20, 2017.
48. Rehr, Facebook post.
49. Claire Bishop, *Artificial Hells: Participatory Art and The Politics of Spectatorship* (Brooklyn: Verso, 2012), 38. Kindle.
50. Harris, "Trump-Era Pop Culture," *Vulture.*
51. David Holthouse, "Outing the Bogeyman," *Anchorage Press*, June 19, 2015.
52. Sara Bernard, "Rape Culture in the Alaskan Wilderness," *Atlantic*, September 11, 2014, https://www.theatlantic.com/health/archive/2014/09/rape-culture-in-the-alaskan-wilderness/379976/.
53. David Greig, "Rough Theatre," in *Cool Britannia?: British Political Drama in the 1990s*, ed. Graham Saunders and Rebecca D'Monté (London: Palgrave, 2007), 220.

Until You See the Whites of Their Eyes

Brett Bailey's *Exhibit B* and the Consequences of Staging the Colonial Gaze

—MEGAN LEWIS

> In this world of unequal power, in which various hegemonic orders try to convince us that one nation, one race, one gender, one sexual preference, one religion, one ideology, one cultural framework is superior to all others, is it really defensible to insist that the arts should be unshackled from social agendas?
>
> BRETT BAILEY, 2014 WORLD THEATRE DAY MESSAGE

The title of this chapter draws upon a common military command used during the eighteenth century and made popular at the Battle of Bunker Hill during the American Revolution. Embedded in this adage are the dual notions of combat and proximity, of being close enough in war to know who one is shooting, as well as the suggestion of whiteness and sight, or white-sightedness. We are at a moment in history that demands that whiteness pay for its past and present sins. As a system of privilege based on fictional difference that often refuses to acknowledge its own construction, whiteness functions predominantly as an invisible, unmarked norm that has been naturalized as the default category of existence. This is particularly true in the global north, where to maintain its power, whiteness requires forgetting. Whiteness is a machine, what Melissa Steyn calls an "assemblage of practices and affective formations," and the machine is lubricated with "epistemologies of ignorance".[1] In other words, for whiteness to remain in power, we must forget that it is there, we must train ourselves not to see it, or to only see the world *whitely*. Theater—as a space and a practice—can be one way of engaging and examining whiteness critically and working through "how we look at art artifacts" as Mike Sell suggests.[2] But what happens when a white artist—and a white South African man at that—attempts to address the sins of the past in contemporary Europe? South African theatre-maker Brett Bailey did exactly that with his performance installation *Exhibit B*, which is aimed at interrogating empire and addressing the European legacy of whiteness and its relationship with Africa.[3] *Exhibit B* is Bailey's multiyear performance installation,[4] framed as an ethnographic exhibition, that explores the racist (il)logic and violence of the colonial era and particularly the European framing of the Other. What did Bailey ask us to see in *Exhibit B*, when he invited us to "have a good look at difference?" Who were included in that assumed "us"? And what were the protesters who shut down his show in Fall 2014 at the Barbican in London seeing differently, not seeing, or only willing to see?

The story of how this work of art—aimed at exposing racism in the European past and present—ended up being censored raises several important questions and provocations within our post- and neocolonial condition about agency, definitions of activism, and racially charged performance. And it registers the potentials and pitfalls of representation, questions of freedom of expression and censorship, and the stakes and politics of social media and journalism in the 24-hour news machine. The dueling claims over this controversial work register the racialized tensions that continue to haunt Europe and Africa, particularly, and our larger world in general.

So much attention has been paid to the protests of *Exhibit B* that the performances themselves have been lost in the fray. A quick internet search of Bailey's name brings up the *Exhibit B* controversy immediately, and this digital record has become the central story and assumed final truth about the piece.[5] This provocative piece of work demands deeper analysis, and thus, in the first half of this essay, I position *Exhibit B* within the trajectory of Bailey's twenty-year body of work and map the installation in some detail to explore what Bailey means by "having a good look at difference." In my analysis, I suggest that *Exhibit B* is an artistic intervention that dredges up painful scenarios of the colonial past to shed light on contemporary racism and xenophobia and to underscore the difficulty and necessity of the act of witnessing another person's humanity in a world divided by racial fictions. In the second half, I investigate the ways *Exhibit B* tested the limits of racially charged artistic expression in contemporary Europe through the protests waged against it by Sara Myers and other activists and its ultimate censorship at the Barbican in the fall of 2014. I explore what this performance offers to conversations around the stakes of representation: who has the right, and the responsibility, to represent? on behalf of whom? and who is addressed, or omitted, in such representations? And I map how whiteness haunts *Exhibit B* and its creator and question if, and how, white artists—and whiteness itself—can ever defy their own hegemony.

"Having a Good Look at Difference"

Exhibit B is structured as an ethnological cabinet of curiosities, looking backward to the practice of human displays in the nineteenth century, when African bodies were framed by their European exhibitors as strange, unfamiliar, and exotic and were imagined as dehumanized objects to be gazed upon with wonder, disgust, lust, and scientific curiosity. These historic scenarios and practices, which Bernth Lindfors[6] terms "ethnological show business," included: the Khoisan woman Sara Baartman from South Africa, billed as the "Hottentot Venus," who was paraded through salons and displayed as the "missing link" in the evolutionary chain between human beings and apes in London and Paris in the early nineteenth century. A *village nègre*, an African village of four hundred people, was installed at the 1889 Parisian World's Fair for Europeans to gaze upon. In 1904, at the Louisiana Purchase Exposition in St. Louis, Missouri, a *kraal* composed of South Africans from varying ethnic affiliations, but blanketed with the title "*Kaffirs*,"[7] was on display as Boer War generals reenacted battles on horseback and in ox wagons. And in 1906, Mbuti pygmy, Ota Benga, from the Kasai River, Congo Free State, was displayed at the Bronx Zoo in a cage in the Monkey House with Dohong the orangutan and an African grey parrot, a staging choice that positions him within social Darwinism and its associated discourses of racial difference.[8] The practice of human zoos—and the systems of representation they engendered and leveraged—was imbricated in a larger colonial discourse that justified the subjugation of Africans, the plunder of the continent's resources, and the superiority of European (white) privilege.

So what occurs when the relationship of spectator and spectacle is itself made strange in the twenty-first century, asking audience members to examine the white-sightedness of privilege and oppression and to "take a good look at difference," as *Exhibit B* does? "The dim chambers of our collective imagination," writes Bailey, "are haunted by twisted representations of racial Otherness: the violent, sexualized barbarian; the scientific curiosity; the submissive victim; the Master's property. These silent stereotypes continue to energize degrading, dehumanizing systems such as Apartheid, the one that I grew up in."[9] *Exhibit B* is an exploration of the racist systems of representation that undergirded colonialism in Africa, but Bailey says its focus is on the increasingly xenophobic and racist policies of the European Union toward African immigrants today. Such policies "evolved from the scientifically legitimized and state-sanctioned racism of the late 19th century," Bailey says. "[They] do not exist in historical isolation." Bailey describes *Exhibit B* as "a series of installations, featuring performers who identify themselves as black [who] present a catalogue of the atrocities that were committed—and concealed—by European powers in Africa in the name of 'civilization.' It commemorates the men and women whose dignity was stripped away in this process."[10]

Brett Bailey has been making iconoclastic theatre in South Africa since 1996.[11] He is known for his large-scale Dionysian installations involving sensory immersion, spectacle, ritual, and trance that the late John Matshikiza described as a kind of "collective possession, dancing on the edge of a reckless madness, but finally opening a door to the possibility of a kind of collective catharsis."[12] Daniel Larlham describes the conventions of these large-scale performances as "site-specific stagings using semicircular hay-bale seating; burning herbs and lighted torches that create an atmosphere of multisensory stimulation; song, dance, and percussion overlaying and driving the play's action; actors whose faces and seminaked bodies are often smeared with gray-white pigment (sparking associations with Xhosa initiates, European mimes, and the stone visages of Eastern statuary)."[13] In his evolution as an artist, recently Bailey has tightened the scale of his work, creating more Apollonian performance installations that facilitate an encounter between a single audience member and the performance she or he experiences. Bailey's earlier work emphasized theatre as a communal space in which he attempted to create crossings of the old borders of the apartheid era that still haunted the South African socialscape after the 1994 transition to democracy and to engage diverse audiences together in rituals of community that allowed them to see, hear, and relate to one another. But since then, Bailey has shifted away from collective Dionysian events to audiences of one. For Jacques Rancière, the collective power of theatre lies not in its collection of multiple bodies that become a unified whole but rather in the individualized responses, experiences, and translations that audience members discover in the work. He emphasizes the spectator's agency in his or her "power to translate in their own way what they are looking at."[14]

The shift in Bailey's work from large communal ritual to intimate audiences of one happened in 2009 with *Terminal*. The performance, which I saw at the National Arts Festival in Grahamstown that July, took place nightly in and around the abandoned train terminal and its tracks at the edge of the city of Grahamstown, the ruins of the desecrated 1820s settlers[15] cemetery, and the township of Joza, where the majority of the town's black and brown South Africans reside. According to Bailey, "The Grahamstown Railway Terminal was built in 1878 on this boundary line between Us and Them. It sits directly below the Settler cemetery—an inter-zone between Here and There. The last train pulled out of the station in February 2009, and the empty platforms of this dead end, like the vandalized graves nearby, are haunted by memories trapped in airless limbo."[16]

Audiences of thirty-five people at a time were admitted to the waiting room of the old terminal building, where we waited to be randomly called, one by one, to begin our journeys. As we waited, we read the following admonishment, printed on a large placard in the waiting room: "Somehow, in the popular consciousness of white South Africa, the 1820 Settlers—imported from Britain to provide a colonizing buffer between the amaXhosa and the Cape Colony—have managed to retain a butter-wouldn't-melt-in-the-mouth innocence. As if they were any less rapacious, opportunistic, violent and bigoted than the other 'civilizers' that have used blades, bibles and brute arrogance to shatter the despised societies and cultures of indigenes, to annex their land, and to enrich themselves off the fragments. As if they had little to do with the history that has fouled up our country."[17] My English surname suddenly felt like a burning brand on my identity. Upon being called up and entering the dark train platform, I felt disoriented as my eyes adjusted to the darkness; my vision was immediately engaged as part of the performance. I also felt somewhat uneasy, as I did not know what to expect and was left all alone to experience an event in the darkness of an abandoned part of town that as a (white) (South African-American) (woman) I would never visit alone, especially at night. Then, suddenly I felt a small, cold, rough hand sliding into mine, its little fingers gently grasping my much bigger hand and I turned to discover a small boy, dressed in tatty clothes and a sweater with holes in it, putting his finger to his lips to remind me to remain silent.

In the hands of this small guide, I journeyed "across the tracks," and out of my literal and figurative comfort zones, to parts of Grahamstown I had never before encountered. Along the journey, I witnessed a series of Bailey's signature tableaux: scenarios of complex and troubling racial and sexual dynamics and provocative visions of South African politics, often set into corners of the train station and on the tracks themselves, behind security gates, and beside gravestones in the cemetery. In one scenario, a woman dressed in the standard maid's uniform so ubiquitous across South Africa, with pantyhose over her face that both blurred her identity and was suggestive of some type of criminality, stood at an ironing board deliberately burning a starched white shirt. In another, a pile of newspapers and other rubbish came to life as the little boy guided me across the train tracks, revealing the discarded human beings who occupy the outskirts and fringes of this colonial city of white privilege. On a gravestone in the cemetery, I saw an old black man cradle an old white man, rocking him as if he were a baby. And in a gutted old building, a man dressed in British colonial military uniform sat gloating over the collapsed body of a black worker, electrical wires dangling from the wall above him.

My guide and I never exchanged a single word; our hands became our system of communication. He would squeeze or pull my hand, advertently, to show me the direction we should walk. When I was startled by an image, I squeezed his hand and we made eye contact. At the end of the event, my guide disappeared into the night as silently and suddenly as he had emerged on the train platform at the start of the performance. I was stunned and felt abandoned, and I sat on the front steps of the train terminal and wept. I wept for the loss of this little anonymous child's company, wanting—as a mother and as an audience participant—to thank him and acknowledge his individual humanity. I wept because the images I had seen brought up all manner of shame I carry as a white South African born under apartheid. I wept cathartically, releasing the tension in my body that came from being out in the cold and darkness on unsure footing in frightening places. And I wept in gratitude for having experienced this work, for being moved as a spectator—physically, emotionally, intellectually—to consider the history, dynamics, hierarchies, and inequities of the town of Grahamstown, a microcosm of the larger South African social field. I became, in Rancière's terms, an emancipated spectator, a spectator who "makes his poem with the poem that is performed in front of him. She participates in the performance if she is able to tell her own story about the story which is in front of her."[18]

Bailey carefully selected the site for *Terminal*—the abandoned Grahamstown train station that marks the dividing line between the town's black and white residents—as he did for each new iteration of *Exhibit B*. Bailey's sites augment the meaning of the piece and simultaneously abolish the traditional relationship, or sight lines, between the space of the performers (stage) and the place of the audience (auditorium). Daniel Sack, in his *Howlround* review of *Exhibit B* at Avignon, describes how the space of the Église des Célestins, "a church without an altar, just the skeleton of faith," added to his experience of the installation. *Exhibit B*, he writes, "forces us to come face to face with the history not only of specific events and genocides, but of spaces and institutions, traditions of representations. By presenting the piece in a church, Bailey prompts an elegiac response while at the same time requiring our recognition of the fact that the imposition of a Western system of belief is inevitably intertwined with the crimes committed against these people in that distant colony."[19] In addition to the church Sack describes, the school in which I first saw *Exhibit A* in Grahamstown, the Playfair Library in Edinburgh, and the countless other spaces *Exhibit B* has performed in are all institutions of Western culture and hegemony that frame and speak to the performance. At the Playfair Library Hall in Edinburgh, for example, each scenario was framed within an alcove presided over by white marble busts of figures like Charles Darwin, David Hume, Alexander Graham Bell, Arthur Conan Doyle, and William Wordsworth. The busts cast their lifeless, marble gaze over the scene, and whiteness ghosted through the space. Their lifeless yet ubiquitous gaze spoke to the white-sightedness of many Europeans, whose culture and identity are built on colonialism and who are shielded by their privilege to not have to see racism in its current incarnations. Simultaneously, the whites of their marble eyes "busted through" consciousness, making Europe's racialized history explicit for contemporary audiences and allowing the flawed representational practices of the past to shed light on continued racist practices in the present.

I first saw *Exhibit A* in Grahamstown in July 2012 and then *Exhibit B* in 2014 in the Playfair Library Hall at the University of Edinburgh with my students. The conceit of the piece is to "gaze into the hidden Curiosity Cabinets of European racism"[20] and to connect past practices of human displays with today's increasingly xenophobic policies of the European Union toward African immigrants. Audience members are allowed into the space at staggered intervals, one at a time, and move from tableau to tableau at their own pace.[21] At the end of the exhibition space, audience members have a chance to reflect on the performance.[22] Several tableaux vivant depict and embody scenes that look backward in time to frame static ethnographic snapshots of the past, scenarios of colonial violence, genocide, and degradation. As the installation progresses, the scenarios become about contemporary segregation, deportations, and ongoing racism toward Africans in Europe. *Exhibit B* turns the tables on the historic power dynamics of (white) European spectators consuming (black and brown) African bodies as the live performers look back at the present audience (one person at a time) in a strategically unnerving gaze reversal.

Exploding the logic of the museum, audiences at *Exhibit B*, who are usually disciplined to visually consume inanimate objects and dioramas behind rope cordons or glass barriers are instead included as one of the media on the museum placard of each tableau. The fourth wall is eliminated and the diorama or curiosity cabinet comes to life, locking its gaze with you as its witness (figure 1). The power in this scenario is the live body, the living, breathing human being who makes constant eye contact with you. Bailey's singular direction to the actors is to never let the audience member out of their sight. Audiences are asked to gaze into the whites of the performers' eyes, and they, in turn, look back at the spectators with a powerful, unrelenting gaze.

It is in this exchange—uncomfortable, awkward, intimate, sometimes shame-etched—that the performance really takes place. A relationship between object and subject, between the actor representing a past scenario and that actor's present presence, between spectator and performer, is open for negotiation. The live bodies in this scenario are powerful agents in their own right, looking upon us as spectators and wielding their formidable gazes over us as their objects of visual pleasure and scrutiny. *Exhibit B* underscores the necessity—and the difficulty—of the act of witnessing another person's humanity. If we can look

© VALERIA ZALAQUETT

Figure 1. María Liliana Caicedo Valencia returns the gaze in *The Missing Link*. Photo credit: V. Zalaquett.

Figure 2. Danny Muboti in "Origin of the Species." Photo credit: Anke Schuettler.

at difference, really see one another, *Exhibit B* suggests, we can work toward dismantling systems of oppression and privilege.

The first thing I experienced as I entered the front door of the Gadra Matric School in Grahamstown was a hallway filled with taxidermied animals: rooibok and wildebeest heads mounted on the walls, a full-size warthog and a complete duiker on the floor level. Running the literal gauntlet of stuffed and displayed animal specimens, I turned to look through a doorway on my right and encountered a stunning tableau: a scene reminiscent of a colonial-era ethnographic postcard or cabinet of curiosities aptly titled "Origin of the Species" (figure 2). An African couple (Asanda Rilityana and Andrew Mugenyi) stood nearly naked within a frame of colonial memorabilia, including a caricatured blackface doll, nineteenth-century maps and travelogues, a baboon's skull, and several stuffed antelope heads. A museum placard and velvet rope cordoned off the "exhibit" from me as a spectator. The placard read: "Origin of the Species. Trophies Brought to Europe from the Congo Free State. Mixed media: maps, various trophies (antelope heads, 2 Pygmies, cultural artefacts), vitrines [glass display cases], anthropological paraphernalia, observer/s."[23]

Wearing headbands, wristbands, and anklets made of yellow measuring tape—and tagged, as objects in a museum might be, with specimen numbers—the living performers actively locked their gaze on each individual audience member who came into the room, watching us as much as they were being watched. In *looking backward* to frame familiar static snapshots of the past, *Exhibit A* (and later *Exhibit B*) turned the tables on the historic power dynamics of white European spectators consuming black African bodies by *looking back at* us as audience members. This reversal of the usual spectator-spectacle relationship was disarming. Brent Meersman, in his review of the Vienna performance, describes how "it detonates the status quo of passive African victim presented sympathetically to the liberal European patron of the arts."[24] Bailey's installation offered to potentially emancipated spectators what Rancière calls "the spectacle of something strange, unusual, which stands as an enigma and demands that [s/he] investigate the reason for that strangeness."[25]

Bailey says that he designed *Exhibit B* for "European audiences, to confront them with a history that they have hidden and forgotten."[26] He charged his performers with a powerful action as they enact their individual tableau: to never let the person watching them out of their sight. Thus, the audience (the "observer/s" in the list of media on the museum placard of each tableau) becomes the object of study. Whereas the traditional, gendered relationship of the gaze places the power in the (usually male) observer over (she) who is looked at, the live bodies in this scenario are powerful agents in their own right, looking upon us as spectators and wielding their formidable gazes over us as their objects of visual pleasure and scrutiny. Sack describes this dynamic as "the brilliance and the vertiginous terror of Bailey's piece. I find it impossible to turn away," he writes, "and yet absolutely pressing that I do so."[27]

I, too, found myself simultaneously unable to look, because the piece's dramaturgy required me (as a white South African) to gaze upon black bodies as a colonial consumer might. Simultaneously, I felt obligated to make eye contact with the actors before me, to acknowledge their humanity and presence in the space and perhaps also to absolve myself of the shame the piece triggered for me. As I gazed and looked, my (decidedly white) body registered a fraction of the exposure, dehumanization, and scrutiny that Baartman, Benga, and others might have felt in the nineteenth century. I become acutely aware of my race, of the burden of European history, and my accountability—as a person of European descent—for the ignominy of the practice of human displays. And, as I processed these emotional and intellectual reactions within my own body, I became aware of how this performance also invited me not just to "look at difference" as Bailey suggests but also to "perform" a negotiation between myself and the performers in each scene.

In the second room on the upper level of the installation, I encountered a black woman (Portia Memani), naked from the waist up, sitting with her back facing me on a wrought-iron bed. In a scene based on a photograph from the estate of Hermann Schlüter held by the Braunschweigisches Landesmuseum, Memani sat tied to a bedpost, a large iron shackle around her neck. On the bedspread was a musket. On the wall of this bedroom were more taxidermied animal heads, a mirror, and framed images of colonial era scenes of rows of shackled Africans. The placard for this installation read "A Place in the Sun. Quarters of An Officer of the German Colonial Forces, Windhoek, 1906."[28] A single chair was placed facing the installation for audience members to sit on and from which to gaze upon the scene.

Here, the negotiation between me as audience member and Memani as performer became more active. She refused her gaze to me as I watched her. She sat with her back turned to me; yet she could watch me in the mirror on the wall. When I shifted in my chair to seek out her image in the mirror, she retreated. Once I pulled back, she engaged me in the mirror once again. Playing a kind of provocative hide-and-seek, she seduced me with her eyes, inviting me to seek her out and follow her tantalizing game. Countering what film theorist Laura Mulvey reminds us is the gendered dynamic of the gaze, where women are positioned as the "bearer[s] of meaning, not [the] maker[s] of meaning,"[29] Memani held the power over this scene, she possessed agency, even if its content was about female exploitation.

Placed in the voyeur's seat, as if I were the German officer looking upon her naked flesh, I simultaneously attempted to apologize with my eyes for the horrors of the past and to communicate my empathy for her in this scene. The scene was clearly framed as one of sexual exploitation—marked by her nakedness, the bedroom setting, and the instruments of enslavement and violence that surround her. Bailey himself describes the opposing tensions inherent in the piece: "I wanted to create images where you are seduced by beauty—you want to look—but the content is so horrific you also don't want to look. You don't know where to look."[30] In my engagement with Memani, she taught me where to look, and I had to discover a way to look that moved us toward an unspoken understanding and helped us work through the deeply troubling power dynamics of this scenario. We negotiated the she-who-is-looked-at and I-the-one-looking gaze back and forth between us, in silence, with only our eyes. Rather than being a field in which a spectacle is on display for a viewer, the crux of the performance in *Exhibit B* was what occurred between us, in this negotiated dance we did with our eyes.

Thus, the dynamics of *Exhibit B* created a space of exchange, of dialogue (without words), of potential between spectator and performer. A mutually negotiated conversation about power, looking, racialized bodies, and spectatorship took place in silence. Sack describes the profound pull of the performance but also remarks on how its construction asked him to perform.[31] Such a possibility exists, as spectators may feel obligated to perform their remorse, sorrow, or shame, especially in the extreme intimacy of the space between themselves and one other human body—or, to perform in the presence of other audience members who they pass or encounter as they journey through the installation. I, too, became acutely aware of my own performance in the space. I found myself caught between the privacy of my tears (brought about by emotions of shame, profound sadness for the human condition, anger at the past, disgust at the continual exploitation of Africans in the present, awe at the beauty of the artists and artistry before me) and the desire to demonstrate remorse, to connect with the live human performers in the intimacy of the room with me. Following Rancière, the poem I wove with the poem of *Exhibit B* was a deeply personal one, woven from my own history as a white South African, a performance scholar concerned with unpacking whiteness, a postcolonial historian, a mother. And I imagine that every individual who experiences the piece weaves his or her own stories from and with it as well. Contrary to Guy Debord's formulation of spectacle, in which spectacle alienates the self, this performance asked me to confront myself and my own position, beliefs, and discomforts. Rather than alienate me from myself through a seductive or soporific display that rendered me passive, *Exhibit B* activated my vision and consciousness, asking me to reflect deeply and inwardly.

Indeed, Bailey intended the piece to provoke and his highly controlled structuring of it is designed to create a confrontation between bodies in the present around shameful issues of the past. He manipulates the encounter, setting up a dialectic in which spectator and performer come face-to-face with each other to negotiate painful realities of the past and present and in which, as Sack points out, "feeling could not sufficiently encompass what should be felt."[32] Bailey is also candid about his own sense of shame as a white South African, descended from colonials who most likely were slave owners and raised under apartheid. "I can't ignore that that's part of my cultural DNA," he says. Bailey also is clear that he did not make the work to shame people. "No, not at all," he says, "I made this work to excavate. . . . I wasn't out to deliberately create images of shame, except a lot of the stuff I came across shamed me and then I tried to find the images that articulated that."[33] His provocation—what he calls the theatrical "trick"—is the strategic reversal of the gaze, so that audiences see "reflected in the glasses of the display cases their own reality."[34]

From a scene of sexual consumption of black African women, the dramaturgy of *Exhibit A* in Grahamstown next shifted to a scene of scientific consumption of black African bodies. In two rooms, the Herero and Nama genocides were the historical contexts for the performance. The program described the experiences of indigenous people during the early twentieth century: "In the forced-labour camps set up after the war, rape and beatings were routine, and thousands more Herero and Nama died of disease, exposure, starvation and exhaustion. The attempted annihilation of these people is acknowledged as the first genocide of the 20th Century."[35] The beautiful harmonies of a chorus of voices drew me into a room that contained four white plinths lined up before a bank of windows. In "Dr. Fischer's Wunderkammer (Cabinet of Curiosities)," four Namibian singers (Avril Nuuyoma, Chris Nekongo, Marcellinus Swartbooi, and Melvin Du Pont) whose bodies were entirely contained by each plinth, save their heads which were painted shiny black, formed a chorus of disembodied faces. As replicas of historic images of Nama decapitations hung above them over the windows, the Namibian choir (who were trained by Swartbooi, a Windhoek-based composer) sang traditional songs of lamentation in Nama, Otjiherero, Oshiwambo, Tswana, and isiXhosa. The placard for this scenario referred to Dr. Fischer's experiments and how his practice of the theories of racial hygiene in German South West Africa "laid the ideological foundations for the justification of the Holocaust."[36] Bailey also reminded his audiences of the long legacy of European exportation and exploitation of African resources—natural, mineral, and human—telling us that "tens of thousands of skulls of the ancestors of the people of the free world are still held in the underground vaults of the museums and universities of their former colonial masters."[37]

Here, witnessing, and experiencing aurally, the four singing heads became an exercise in terrible beauty. The exquisite harmonies of the voices acted as a soothing balm, but one that never allowed for catharsis, for the ever-present archival photographs of decapitated Nama heads literally hung over the scene, their sunken, lifeless eyes a reminder of the human lives extinguished in the name of racist science. The strange enigma (Rancière) of this scenario lies in the tension between beauty and horror, between the exquisite sound of the choir's voices and the subject matter of the scene, between the disembodied heads of the actors (that are intact live bodies) and the dismembered heads of real bodies, real Nama people killed during the extinctions. And even when the aural promised to soothe, the visual remained searing and disquieting, as the live voices of the singers conjured up those no longer living.

In a second room, a woman (Siphokazi Matinyane) wearing a brown sheepskin cloak *kaross* and an ochre-colored headdress sat within a small enclosure demarcated by barbed wire. In her right hand, she held a human skull, in her left, a shard of pottery. Across the wire hung a German sign reading "*Achtung*!" and at her feet was a large cast-iron cooking pot. The placard for this room, "Civilizing the Natives: Domestic Scene (1905–1908)," read: "Women in the concentration camps of German South West Africa had to boil the decapitated heads of fellow prisoners and scrape them clean with shards of glass. The camps were set up following the extermination of tens of thousands of Hereros and Namas by German colonial forces. The skulls were exported to European research institutes, where they were measured and analysed to 'prove' the theories of European racial supremacy that legitimised colonial policies."[38] The combination of this terrible information and Matinyane's fierce stare, never letting go of her onlooker's gaze, made us as audience members look the past directly in the eye. Through her resolute, accusatory stare, her scenario in the installation shifted the stakes for African bodies beyond the humiliation of being put on display to the brutal violation and humiliation of those bodies.

In these two scenarios, *Exhibit B* examined the history of racism and the European empires built on the backs, and at the expense, of Africans. A profoundly moving, ethically savvy critique that used the power of live bodies within static frames, Bailey's installation questioned the inherited narratives and cultural stories (myths) reinforced for centuries by colonialism, those "sly bullies" as Naomi Iizuka reminds us, "constructed to persuade, to seduce, to silence the competition in the moment of the telling."[39]

Bailey's installation looks back to a time when "Europe's powers scrambled for African colonies, and her scientists formulated...pseudo-scientific racial theories"[40] to justify their exploits across the continent. And through the powerful presence of live performers, *Exhibit B* underscores how vital, yet difficult, it is to witness another person's humanity.

If, as Naomi Iizuka suggests, "making theatre is the act of remembering," then I argue that Bailey's intervention functions as an attempt at *righting* the wrongs of the past. His performance *rite*—a solemn communion between live performers and those who witness them—facilitates a remembering of the past (and a re-membering of the mainly anonymous African bodies displayed across the nineteenth century). Starting in Europe in 2010 and then "returning" to South Africa in 2012, Bailey's *Exhibit B* revisits the pathway of European conquest into Africa and then reverses the direction of power. Within post-1994, democratic South Africa, *Exhibit B* resonates as what Jason Kehe calls "a chilling, challenging exercise in seeing and being seen."[41] For Brent Meersman, it "subversively turns exotic spectacle on its head."[42] Kehe notes in his review that while the installation debuted in Europe (in Vienna's Museum of Ethnology in 2010) for predominantly European audiences where "the point was clear: a searing indictment of colonial sins," its transfer to South Africa "muddies that message. Now it's Africa on Africa, implying—possibly—an even darker implication. Who's the spectator, and what's the spectacle?"[43] Bailey adjusted the performance for South Africa; in particular, he removed the installation about Baartman called "Sara." He told me he did this out of respect for her and for the people of the Eastern Cape, not wanting to attempt to imitate or represent her in her motherland, after her remains had been repatriated and buried in Hankey, only 200 kilometers from Grahamstown. He reiterated that the piece was designed for European eyes, where the "Sara" scenario would mean differently in the site of her original display.

Meeting several of the actors after the show in Grahamstown, I listened as they talked candidly about how they draw motivation in their performance from their personal experiences of racism. Bailey has also explained how they developed backstories to each of the scenarios, which helped the actors (all of whom are locals where the installation occurs) focus their performances.[44] The performers in Grahamstown also discussed how different audience members reacted to them. "White people show they are sorry, you see their emotions," company coordinator and performer Luvoyo Yanta told me. "That's not so hard for me," he said. "I can understand that my standing there makes them feel these things." But for him, it was fellow black South Africans who unsettled him. Not carrying the weight of European civilization with them into the performance space, black audiences "judge and stare. And they don't show any emotion," Yanta said. These exchanges mark how the performance functions in two directions: the spectators' experiences of the actors as well as the actors' encounters with their spectators. It also marks the differences and complexities of audiences. We are not a monolith, a generic mass of passive bodies, but rather a collection or assemblage of atomized individual consciousnesses who bring to, and take from, the spectacle our own experiences. For instance, a friend who attended the show with me felt an urgent compulsion to intervene; he said he constantly wanted to unshackle Memani from the bedpost or cut the barbed wire that enclosed Matinyane in her horrible skull-stripping scenario. Sack felt drawn in but also that it was "imperative" that he look away, perhaps to refuse to be complicit in such a gaze. Thus, each audience member experienced the installation autonomously and individualistically. Audience here is anything but passive and unilateral: rather, it is an active exchange, bidirectional, and even reciprocal.[45] In the second half of this essay, I return to audience responses in London and Paris in 2014.

Bailey's call to "have a good look at difference" extends from the nineteenth-century displays and maltreatment of Africans into the present. "A century after the Imperial Age," Bailey writes in the program, "we continue to live in a world fractured by notions of Racial Difference and Otherness."[46] Thus, while the first floor of the Gadra Matric School was focused on nineteenth-century events and evocations, the lower floor brought the stakes of dehumanization of African bodies into much closer, contemporary focus.

As I made my way down the stairs of the Gadra Matric School, I encountered "Found Object #1" (Sbo Ntshebe), a man labeled as "Congolese Immigrant," his vital statistics and refugee status listed on a board next to him. You cannot progress through the exhibit—or through history, Bailey seems to be suggesting—without coming face-to-face, eye-to-eye, with how African immigrants, refugees, and asylum seekers are treated in our contemporary world.[47] Ntshebe and I locked our gazes for a long time; we stood witnessing each other, before I moved down the stairs.

The final tableau, pointedly titled "Survival of the Fittest," consists of a row of airplane seats and a man (Siyabonga Yafele), labeled as Aamir Ageeb from Sudan, duct-taped to the seats, his head, nose, and mouth taped as well, leaving only his eyes staring out at you. This is a horrifying image; a smothered man reduced to nothing but his panicked eyes, pleading with you. The placard gives his birth date and death date and lists the cause of death as "suffocated while resisting deportation by Bundesgrenzschutz officers on Lufthansa Flight LH 588 from Frankfurt am Main to Khartoum. The officers got off with minor charges."[48] Thus, *Exhibit B* connects the history of human zoos, theories of racial hygiene and difference, and gruesome practices against Africans in the past to contemporary European xenophobic practices and immigration anxieties, suggesting that while we might have put the inhumane ways in which Europeans treated and imagined Africans out of our collective minds, there are still lasting impacts—real, material impacts—of that forgotten history. As Sylvie Chalaye[49] suggests, not only is our collective imaginary still framed through phantasmagorical and subconscious colonial images, but such a way of imagining the world has real-life consequences wrought out on the bodies of African refugees like Sudanese Amir Ageeb, Angolan Jimmy Mubenga, Nigerians Joseph Ndukadu Chiakwa and Osamuyi Aikpitanhi, and countless other Africans who have died (usually from asphyxia or cardiac arrest) during forced deportations since 1991.[50] Iizuka reminds us, "In theatre, the dead are always in the room. The dead have a lot to say."[51] And, in the performance installation of *Exhibit B*, it is the live performers who stand in for the dead in Bailey's powerful installation and who speak most persuasively, with their eyes, locking their gaze upon us as their witnesses, without uttering a single word.

The Limits of Racially Charged Artistic Expression

In this second half of the essay, I trace the multiple answers to a question posed by Manick Govinda: "How could a performance *about* racism, performed by black British actors who have maintained a dignified defence of the artwork, be deemed *racist* by predominantly black protesters and anti-racist activists?"[52] The limits of racially charged artistic expression made visible by *Exhibit B* are anchored by three fundamental questions that artistic director of Border Crossings Michael Walling succinctly posed as: Who represents? Who has the right to represent? And who is being addressed in that representation?[53]

Exhibit B tested the stakes and limits of theatre in several ways, including how social media can ignite and proliferate decontextualized misinformation, especially about racially charged issues. In August 2014, Sara Myers, who describes herself as "a Black African mother from Birmingham," started a petition on change.org calling for the Barbican Theatre to stop the "racist Exhibition 'Exhibit B - The Human Zoo'" from performing at their theatre.[54] Calling out the Barbican for "an outrageous act of complicit institutional racism" and branding *Exhibit B* an act of "mental terrorism," Myers threatened to protest outside the theatre if its management allowed the piece to be performed there. In total, 22,973 supporters added their signatures to the petition. The run in London was canceled after Myers and about two hundred protesters got into a shoving match at the Barbican doors. Police in riot gear were called in and the theatre capitulated to the protesters' anger, citing concerns over the safety of both the audience and the actors. A few weeks later, in Paris, a similar protest attempted to shutter the show at the Théâtre Gérard Philipe in Saint-Denis. Despite a judge's ruling in their favor, the performers could complete only two of the eighteen scheduled performances, effectively putting the actors out of work. The protesters never came to see the show, despite Bailey's invitations to them to experience it.

Myers started the petition after reading a preview in the *Guardian* written by John O'Mahony[55] as the play was about to open its run at the Edinburgh Festival a month earlier (where I saw it for the second time). O'Mahony framed the piece as a racially charged power game: he insinuated that Bailey was a dictatorial white director, "spouting the n-word provocatively in his clipped South African intonation" and bullying his black performers—whom O'Mahony describes as "not getting it." He opens the preview with the line: "It's the first Edinburgh rehearsal of *Exhibit B* and there's mutiny in the air." Like a giant game of telephone gone wrong, Myers was (understandably) triggered by O'Mahony's misleading article—Who wouldn't hate this Brett Bailey?—and she and her followers did not see the work, nor did they feel it necessary to do so. Myers said, "You pretty much can go online and see what it looks like. . . . Basically it is black people standing in subservient positions in a subservient way with cages around them and chains around their legs and they're bound and they're gagged. I don't need to really see that."[56]

Operating within this breakdown in communication and understanding and relying solely on images on the internet, the petitioners saw what activist Akala described as "inert black bodies" who were "pornographically disempowered."[57] They read static images as racist without the affective experience of the live tableaux. In *Exhibit A*, we see stylized, simulated degradations of African bodies—as Bailey clarifies a "*staging* [of] a human zoo . . . not a real human zoo"[58]—that ask us to look into the collective colonial past and to see its terrible power and impact. The stylization provides, for some spectators, just enough distance to be able to take in the scene without recoiling in horror or rejecting the performance and leaving. As audience members, we are tasked with translating the silent scenarios of the performers into stories and to transmute what we see into what we think and believe, reflecting on the past and the continuation of mistreatment of Africans in our contemporary world. The experience of spectatorship in Bailey's work demands action on the part of the individual members of the audience. By placing the spectator at the nucleus of the performance, rather than as an inert bystander subordinate to the action of the play onstage, *Exhibit B* shifts the responsibility for the performance—and of the content of the scenarios it depicts—onto us, the audience. We have to find a way to act ethically, to consider carefully the stakes of our gazes, of whether we look and, if so, how we look. And through these acts of looking, we can experience insights about our positions within history and about the power dynamics of the past and the present.

Because the provocative internet images were taken out of context, the protesters read them literally rather than artistically, saw racist surfaces devoid of context, and missed the gaze reversal, which is the central conceit of this work. Bailey said, in response: "I regret that EXHIBIT B[,] a multidimensional performance piece, which has meaning in the intimate dynamic interaction between performers and spectators, has been judged on the basis of 2-dimensional photographs."[59] The piece requires liveness, two live human beings negotiating a gaze; that is *where* the performance happens. Without the experience of that gaze, the still images—which we use as archives of performance or promotional provocations—became a trap. They fixed a scenario in a moment in time and exposed the limits of intelligibility.

"The mob hysteria"[60] that the petition caused is also an example of the limits of clicktivism. Of course, twenty-two thousand people signed a petition that told them a white South African racist was putting black people in cages. Blinkered by assumptions about his whiteness and racism, they judged him without knowing his work or hearing what he had to say. Then, the media frenzy that picked up on the story helped deepen the divide. Journalists, who need to feed the twenty-four-hour news machine, eagerly "cut and paste"[61] this story of yet another act of deplorable white racism, thereby perpetuating the assumptions that O'Mahony started, that Myers was triggered by, and that then twenty-two thousand people were sold. Despite the nuanced and committed way in which Bailey has worked for more than two decades in South Africa to create provocative works of performance art, twenty-two thousand people latched onto familiar narratives of white masters and black slaves, a racist white South African overlord oppressing helpless Africans.

Bailey's forthrightness and willingness to name and discuss the racist legacies into which he was born, and against which he has spent his life fighting, mean that he is often misquoted or misread as being racist, because he talks openly about racism and its power dynamics. Also, his feisty "maverick" personality—part mischievous provocateur, part blunt frankness, and driven by a perfectionist's work ethic—can also feed into misperceptions of him as dictatorial, what Michael Walling calls "the problem of the white director."[62] Walling's question—who has the right to represent?—concerns me here. How can we—can we?—in our contemporary world where whiteness is, justifiably, being called to answer for its sins, remain open to a white artist as he explores racially charged material? Can white artists attempt to interrogate or dismantle racism? Or do we become blinded by what is assumed about white people, especially white South African men?[63]

Walling accepts "that the horrors of colonial history and the neo-colonial present will have a different emotional impact on those people whose ancestors were slaves from those whose ancestors were slave-owners. But that does not mean that only black people can talk about this. Indeed, I would argue that it is essential that everybody talks about it."[64] Ethiopian British poet Lemn Sissay, who supported *Exhibit B*, asks, "Is it really racist to show the shocking facts of the past via theatrical installation?" Citing depictions of the atrocities of the Holocaust as an analog, Sissay asserts, "I am not defined by my scars but by the incredible ability to heal. And part of this healing is to know the story of oppression. These stories must be told by all to all. Like the Jewish community we may not like what we see but we can understand that it must be seen."[65] And Bailey defends his right as a white artist to address race in his work: "Because I am a white South African who spent my first 27 years living under a detestable regime of racism—albeit on the side of privilege—may I not reflect in my work on that system? Should I restrict myself to making anodyne works that don't challenge status quos, that don't confront people with realities that are all too easy to leave festering in the dark?"[66]

Exhibit B also raised questions about definitions of activism. Bailey sees his work as an intervention aimed at dismantling oppressive power structures, a form of performance activism (though he does not use the word "activist" to describe himself; he is an artist). Myers and the other protesters consider themselves activists whose goal it is to call out injustice where they see and experience it. The problem in the racially charged dynamic of these black protesters versus this white artist is that both sides are committed to speaking out about racism, to raising awareness about structures of oppression, and to working toward a more just world. But in this moment in history, whiteness carries too heavy a stigma to be heard and black voices are outraged after centuries of mistreatment by European colonials. So rather than share in antiracist work, which Walling says is everyone's responsibility, the two sides stand on either side of a chasm of mistrust and misunderstanding.

I believe it is incumbent upon white artists to join artists of color in creating work that exposes systems of power, privilege, and white supremacy; in fact, I would argue that it is an imperative that whites address whiteness. *Exhibit B* was aimed at exposing whiteness, but instead, its own whiteness got in the way. Or maybe Bailey's whiteness got in the way? He was written off based on his country of origin: "The fact that he is a white South African seems to be sufficient proof that there is something wrong with the show."[67] And the critique leveled at him was that he used black and brown bodies to teach white audiences about the ills of the racist past. Perhaps this is the tricky stickiness of whiteness in the postcolony: that it can never exist in historical isolation and is always haunted by its own historicity. Can white artists escape the hegemony of whiteness? Or should we, as South African philosopher Samantha Vice[68] suggests, get out of the way?

I return now to the question of "who represents?" In focusing all their attention on Bailey and his whiteness, the petitioners patently ignored the *agency of the performers* involved in the project, all of whom are black and many of whom are African immigrants to Europe. People signed the petition because they assumed Bailey to be a white taskmaster who abused his black actors, playing into an easy and familiar master-slave dialectic that the contemporary public feels righteously indignant about. Petitioners (many people of color included) assumed that the actors were ignorant puppets with no interest in the subject matter and no agency in deciding what they will or will not be involved with. Such assumptions perpetuate the age-old stereotypes held by many Westerners (and propagated though film and other media about the continent) of Africans as ahistorical savages without intellect or agency.

In response to Myers and her followers' claims to speak for them, the Edinburgh and London performers added their own voices to the debate. One of the actors, Avril Nuuyoma, said, "This petition assumes we can't think for ourselves. None of us have been forced to do this, and all of us can leave at any time." In their joint statement, the performers stated explicitly, "We are not objects during the exhibition." They explained:

> In that moment when our eyes meet, we cease to be objectified and become human.
>
> As they move through the exhibit, we watch [people] and witness anger, grief, pity, sadness, compassion. Above all, we witness a dawning of awareness. This is why we keep doing this, and would keep on doing it, if we could.
>
> [Audiences] cry because they didn't know what was done. They cry because they realise how it is still being done. They cry because they realise that the past impacts the present. They cry because they experienced this personally. They cry because they didn't. Reading the pages and pages of comments from the audience left at the end of the exhibit attests to this, but we don't need to read that.
> We see it in their eyes.[69]

Another performer, Priscilla Adade-Helledy, articulated the personal stakes involved for her as a young black female artist. She was deeply disappointed not to be allowed to work at the Barbican, in a role she "felt real investment in...and ownership over." "In all my experiences of racism," she writes, "I've never actually had someone say to me, 'You can't do your art.' We were being totally unvoiced by the people who said they were anti-racists. It was really depressing."[70]

When asked what she thought about Priscilla's claim of being silenced by another, older black woman, Myers dismissed her: "Now she knows how our ancestors felt.... I didn't deny anyone's voice. I didn't shut the show down. The Barbican did that—the Barbican silenced her, not Sara Myers. We just banged drums and protested."[71]

Myers's instinct to question and protest what she perceived as a restaging of a human zoo is based on her lived experience—and frustrations—as a black African in Europe. And the fatigue of forever seeing depictions of abject blackness (such as the framing of Ota Benga as victim, as I discussed in the first half of the essay) also fueled the protests. For T. O. Molefe, "the piece narrows the experience of being black by depicting blackness only as suffering. And it presents this caricature of blackness and the bodies of the performers to white audiences, who can then pick apart the guilt, shame, denial or dissociation they might personally feel from being beneficiaries of and perhaps co-conspirators in racism."[72]

What the protests ask of this piece is: Who is the assumed or ideal spectator? And what happens when the piece triggers deeply felt and suppressed anger about ongoing racism in Europe? While perhaps he intended to activate a different energy around race and racism, Bailey understands *Exhibit B* to be a "lightning rod" that conducted the anger and frustration of Africans, black people, and immigrants in Europe: "This work is...a sharp needle that pricks a skin bloated with fury, frustration and pain. The 'multicultural utopia' of Europe is a myth."[73]

The current refugee crisis in Europe is yet another example of how, when the citizens of empire look to the European metropole for a better life, economic possibility, or to escape troubles at home, they are summarily rejected at the gates. Facing what Ross Douthat calls the "African scramble for Europe," as evidenced in the recent migration influx to the EU from Africa, Europe seems in denial of its inevitable "Eurafrican future."[74] Right-wing parties are on the rise: the nationalist and anti-immigration National Front in France, Freedom Party in Austria, the Golden Dawn in Greece, and Trump's election in 2016 in the United States. Myers and countless other Africans in Europe no doubt face relentless racism on a daily basis. No wonder she defended her decision not to see the show, saying, "As a black woman growing up having experienced racism...there's no need for me to see it because I've *experienced* that"[75] (emphasis mine).

While his lived experience is clearly different, Bailey does understand such frustrations. In a Facebook post from Paris, he reflected on the protesters outside the theater: "[They] are protesting because they are fed up with being second class citizens...with institutionalized racism...with racial profiling and humiliation in the streets and in the media, fed up with lack of access to opportunities…with not having platforms to express themselves…*with being represented as 'other.'*"[76] It is no wonder, then, that two-dimensional images of his show, fueled by the insinuations of O'Mahony's preview article, triggered such an outcry. It is lamentable that the protesters and Bailey's ensemble were not able to join forces in the fight against racism, as was the case in Amsterdam, where activists used *Exhibit B* in allyship with their fight to get rid of the racist blackface character Zwarte Piet.[77]

Exhibit B also tested the limits of freedom of expression. When the Barbican decided to cancel the London run of the show in response to protests, *Exhibit B* became about censorship of artists making racially charged work. Bailey emphatically defends "the right of artists to speak uncomfortable truths, and to challenge status quos. And to disturb. And to offend. I don't want to live in a society in which we silence ourselves in response to every politically correct outcry; in which artists are struck dumb by self-righteous mobs."[78] J. S. Rafaeli, of vice.com, paraphrased Frederick Douglass in stating: "Denying freedom of expression is an act of double violence. You do violence to those who want to speak, but also to those who want to hear. You may have loved to see this piece and decided for yourself whether or not it was worthwhile. But now you can't because some people decided you weren't grown up enough to make up your own mind. And that sucks."[79] Peter Rorvik, of the creative organization Arterial Network, says, "Dissenting voices have a right not to see the work; they do not have the right to force a closure.…The role of artists as agents of change should be celebrated not prosecuted."[80] And for Manick Govinda, "the real problem here is that black people have been censored from the Barbican's decision-making processes in relation to programming and curating."[81] The lightning that *Exhibit B* conducted is thus a more extensive, pervasive, and systemic racism that has saturated Europe to the breaking point; the protesters have had enough and *Exhibit B* became the scapegoat for their frustrations.

To return once again to the question of audience, just as the dynamics of the piece changed when *Exhibit A* transferred from Europe to play in South Africa in 2012, so too did the dynamics shift when people of color were the ones receiving the gaze reversal. *Exhibit B* worked very powerfully for me as a white audience member—a white South African at that—but it is clearly open to many other readings and interpretations. I saw the gaze reversal as a disarming, formidable act of reclamation by the performers to take back and reverse systems of representation; to me, it was all about their agency in the space. In the negotiated gaze space between performer and audience, *Exhibit B*—which is designed for white people, to activate their consciousness and shake Europeans, specifically, out of their complacency and ignorance about the racist practices of the past—worked for me because I was its *ideal* spectator.

But asking people of color to confront the racist history of trauma in the colonial spectatorship relationship—especially as black Africans living in Europe—would reveal very different responses than mine. The scenarios of degradation could be too painful to countenance. And where would a person of color find herself in the work, which is explicitly addressing whiteness? Walling's question "who is being addressed in the representation?" is vital to consider here. A spectator of color might, as T. O. Molefe suggests, have seen "art that turns black bodies into therapeutic objects for white people."[82] Or she may have experienced what Dione Joseph,[83] a woman of color in Edinburgh, did. Joseph was prepared "to witness something startling." But she was unprepared for the emotional collapse she felt upon gazing, in silence, at these scenarios. Her anger was because "it forbids us to speak, to engage, to debate, to have conversation; it is entirely one-dimensional!" Joseph felt trapped and traumatized within a performance that denied her a voice with which to process her experiences. Even though, at the end of each installation, there is a room in which audience members are invited to write their responses to the piece, clearly Joseph needed the communion of other voices, other human beings, with which to process this difficult work that the performance denied her. The Western, logocentric practice of written responses was insufficient for her; she sought out a more African, communal expression and processing and, I would agree, the performance could have benefited from such an audience response redesign. In fact, in the performance I saw in South Africa in 2012, audiences sat around a fire and processed with the performers after the show.

While audiences for *Exhibit B* tended to be populated with white spectators, there have been people of color at every performance of the piece across its five-year run. But in London, protesters made sure many other people never witnessed *Exhibit B*. "This isn't the politics of representation," suggests Rafaeli. "It's the politics of representation of representation."[84] In other words, it became not about who is seen, but who is even allowed to look. Whatever dialogue may have been possible, across the racially charged divide, was effectively silenced and the conversation that the piece was designed to engender never had a chance to occur. And that, to me, is a profound limit. But an even profounder loss is that the larger conversation about institutional racism in Europe seemed never to happen, even after the protests and the Barbican shutdown. As blogger Diasporic Redman from London Town put it, "The challenge has been to the institutional White privilege of the UK arts establishment," but "Bailey, the Barbican, and all the commenters are just further proving how arrogant and out-of-touch they are in being unable to face an authentic discussion of White privilege."[85] Two years after the fact, Barbican Centre director of arts, Louise Jeffreys, admitted that the venue had "failed audiences" by canceling the 2014 performance following protests.[86]

So I return to the title of this essay—until you see the whites of their eyes—as an apt caveat, an expression of the (im)possibility of *Exhibit B* and its consequences. *Exhibit B* illustrates how whiteness haunts our contemporary world, institutions, and mindsets and how it can get caught in the structures of its own creation. The colonial power structures that *Exhibit B* critiques are systems that continue to justify white privilege. The white-sightedness of the Barbican, as stand-in for the larger UK arts establishment, became painfully evident when the institution was willing to censor Bailey's work but not take a good look at its own systems of exclusion and privilege. *Exhibit B* in London attempted to break Steyn's "epistemologies of ignorance" that keep whiteness invisible and unmarked but ended up getting caught in its own white trap. Bailey's display of black and brown bodies was (mis)read as the very practice it aimed to critique, and, simultaneously, he was not prepared for what the fault lines revealed when the assumed ideal audience included Africans who were tired of the very depictions his piece aimed to expose. Bailey's South African whiteness simultaneously positioned him in an impossible identity and, perhaps, taught him about the stakes of representation at the price of his international artistic reputation. There has not been adequate conversation across the divide between white artists (Bailey) and audiences of color (the protesters) about the larger questions and oppressive systems that this piece offers up for consideration. As an exemplar of our contemporary state of global race relations, the *Exhibit B* controversy shows how stalemated in racialized combat mode we still are. Sadly, no one has risked stepping close enough across the divide to see the whites of the other's eyes.

Notes

Epigraph. Brett Baily, World Theatre Day Message, International Theatre Institute ITI (2014), accessed February 20, 2017, https://www.world-theatre-day.org/brett_bailey.html.

1. Melissa Steyn, *Whiteness Just Isn't What It Used To Be: White Identity in a Changing South Africa* (New York: SUNY Press, 2001).
2. Mike Sell, "Activism and/or Ethics? Historicizing the Black Arts Movement," unpublished plenary paper, American Society for Theatre Research annual conference, Portland, Oregon, November 5, 2015.

3. The piece was originally called *Exhibit A* (2010–13) and was focused on German and Belgian colonialism in Africa and later morphed into *Exhibit B* (2012–present) as Bailey added French, British, and other colonial elements to the work to speak to the specific colonial histories of the spaces in which the piece was performed.
4. *Exhibit A*, later *Exhibit B*, performed in 2010 in Vienna (Wiener Festwochen) and Braunschweig (Theaterformen Festival); in 2011 in Helsinki (Kiasma Centre); in 2012 in Brussels (Kunsten Festival des Arts / KVS), Grahamstown, South Africa (National Arts Festival), and Berlin (Berliner Festspiele); in 2013 in Amsterdam (Holland Festival), Ghent (Vooruit Centre), Avignon (Festival d'Avignon), Paris (Le 104), Strasbourg (Le Maillon), and Wroclaw (Dialogue Festival); in 2014 in Edinburgh (International Festival), Moscow (Territoria Festival), Poitiers (TAP), Saint-Denis, Paris (Theatre Gerard Philippe), and Paris (Le 104); and in 2015 in Chile (Santiago a Mil), Galway (Galway International Arts Festival), and Gwangju (Opening Festival of the Asian Culture Complex Arts Theatre). I saw it in Grahamstown (2012) and Edinburgh (2014).
5. When Bailey toured his adaptation of Verdi's *Macbeth* to the Philadelphia Fringe in September 2016, the negative press around *Exhibit B* preceded his arrival. I sat on a panel, hosted by WURD radio host Stephanie Renée, called "Who Gets to Tell the Story?" with local Philly artists of color, all of whom were deeply concerned about Bailey's reputation and the Fringe's decision to bring his work to their city.
6. Bernth Lindfors, *Africans on Stage: Studies in Ethnological Show Business* (Bloomington: Indiana University Press, 2000).
7. A sixteenth-century Arabic word for non-Muslim or infidel, this apartheid-era racial slur is akin to the N-word. Early European cartographers mapped the Southern African coast as the "land of Cafraria."
8. It also frames Benga as a victim, just as much of the discourse around Baartman does. In their 1992 study of Benga's life, for example, Phillips Verner Bradford and Harvey Blume outline "one man's degradation in turn-of-the-century America," chronicling Benga's capture by Verner Bradford's grandfather, his suffering in New York, and his ultimate suicide in 1916. In such narratives, Africans lack any agency and are framed only as helpless victims of colonialism. In her controversial 1996 play about Sara Baartman, *Venus*, Suzan-Lori Parks suggests that Baartman, while victimized, had agency and a modicum of control over her own display.
9. Brett Bailey, Web program, http://thirdworldbunfight.co.za/wp-content/uploads/2015/04/EXHIBIT-B-PROGRAMME-TEXT-FOR-WEBSITE1.pdf
10. Third World Bunfight website, http://thirdworldbunfight.co.za/exhibit-b/.
11. Bailey's oeuvre includes *iMumbo Jumbo* (1997), *Ipi Zombi?* (1998), *The Prophet* (1999), *Big Dada* (2001–2005), *macbEth* (2001), *Safari: C G Jung in Africa* (2003), *medEia* (2003), *Vodou Nation* (2004), *House of the Holy Afro* (2004–2010), *Orfeus* (2007), *Terminal* (2009), *Exhibit A* (2010–2012), *Exhibit B* (2012–present), and *MACBETH* (2014–2016).
12. Brett Bailey, *The Plays of Miracle and Wonder* (Johannesburg and Cape Town: Juta Academic, 2003), 7.
13. Daniel Larlham, "Brett Bailey and Third World Bunfight: Journeys into the South African Psyche," *Theater* 39, no. 1 (2009): 8.
14. Jacques Rancière, "The Emancipated Spectator," *Artforum* (March 2007): 278.

15. The 1820 Settlers, to whom a monument is erected in Grahamstown, were white British colonists brought in to populate the Eastern Cape frontier and defend the Cape Colony from the neighboring Xhosa, whose land the settlers came to occupy. Many of the four thousand settlers were poor and were encouraged to settle in the Cape by the British Crown under a government-sponsored settlement scheme.
16. Brett Bailey, *Terminal* text, unpublished text for waiting room placard. National Arts Festival, Grahamstown, South Africa (2009).
17. Bailey, *Terminal* text (2009).
18. Rancière, "Emancipated Spectator," 277.
19. Daniel Sack, "Regarding the Pain of Others: Brett Bailey's Exhibit B," *Howlround* (October 1, 2013), accessed February 20, 2017, http://www.howlround.com/regarding-the-pain-of-others-part-two-brett-baileys-exhibit-b.
20. Brett Bailey, program for *Exhibit A*, unpublished text for program. National Arts Festival, Grahamstown, South Africa (2012).
21. Audiences were either alone in the room with performers or in contact with other audience members, depending on the nature of each venue site. In Grahamstown, for example, each installation was set up in a different classroom of the Gadra Matric School, which audience members experienced in solitude. In Edinburgh and Avignon, on the other hand, installations were set within the alcoves of the space and audience members encountered other spectators in the open areas of the church or library.
22. In Grahamstown, audiences exited the building to a circle of chairs around a fire, where Bailey (and, later, the actors) met up with us to process the work. (Bailey met audiences after *Terminal* in a similar way.) In Edinburgh, a more formal process was instituted: in a room before the building exit, we were invited to write responses on paper and read the actors' bios and statements under each of their headshots along the wall.
23. Brett Bailey, Berlin installation texts, unpublished text for *Exhibit B* museum placards (2012).
24. Brent Meersman, "'Exhibit B': Look Black in Anger," *This Is Africa* (September 9, 2014), accessed February 20, 2017, https://thisisafrica.me/brett-bailey-exhibit-b-look-black-anger/.
25. Rancière, "Emancipated Spectator," 272.
26. Bailey, installation texts (2012).
27. Sack, *Howlround* (2013).
28. Bailey, installation texts (2012).
29. Laura Mulvey, "Visual Pleasure and Narrative Cinema," *Screen* 16, no. 3 (Autumn 1975): 6–18.
30. Anton Krueger, "Gazing at *Exhibit A*: Interview with Brett Bailey," *Liminalities: A Journal of Performance Studies* 9, no. 1 (February 2013): 3.
31. Sack, *Howlround*, 2013. In my experience of *Exhibit A* in Grahamstown, I rarely encountered other spectators, and, if so, it was a fleeting passing between the rooms. In my experience in Edinburgh, and during Sack's experience in Avignon, we were "always with a collective of other spectators."
32. Sack, *Howlround* (2013).
33. Krueger, "Gazing at *Exhibit A*" (2013): 3.

34. Krueger, "Gazing at *Exhibit A*" (2013): 7–8.
35. Bailey, program for *Exhibit A* (2012).
36. Bailey, installation texts (2012).
37. Bailey, installation texts (2012).
38. Bailey, installation texts (2012).
39. Naomi Iizuka, "What Myths May Come," *American Theatre* 16, no. 7 (1999): 18.
40. Bailey, program for *Exhibit A* (2012).
41. Jason Kehe, "Stare if You Dare," *Cue Online* (June 29, 2012), accessed February 20, 2017, http://cue.ru.ac.za/?p=5983.
42. Brent Meersman, "Resisting the Muse of Imperial 'Science,'" *Mail & Guardian* (June 7, 2010), accessed February 20, 2017, http://mg.co.za/article/2010–06–07-resisting-the-muse-of-imperial-science.
43. Kehe, "Stare if You Dare."
44. See Krueger, "Gazing at *Exhibit A*" (2013).
45. I think it is useful to note the distinction in activity between what Bailey (or Rancière) proposes and Augusto Boal's formulation of an active audience. Unlike Boal's spect-actors, who actively and physically intervene in performance, the locus of activity for Bailey's spectators resides internally, silently in our minds, hearts, and intellects.
46. Bailey, program for *Exhibit A* (2012).
47. In the Vienna performance in 2010, audiences were guided into the space by African refugee children from the city (as children were guides in *Terminal* in 2009). Meersman writes: "I saw how having to take the hand of a black asylum seeker's child had a significant impact on the Viennese patrons" (2014).
48. Bailey, installation texts (2012).
49. Sylvie Chalaye, "Colonial Imaginary: Fantasies and Nostalgia," *Le revue d'Africultures* 43 (2006), accessed February 20, 2017, http://www.africultures.com.
50. The placard by Siyabonga Yafele's tableau lists the names of fourteen people, including those I listed here.
51. Iizuka, "What Myths May Come" (1999): 18.
52. Manick Govinda, "Exhibit B: Artists must Have the Right to Shock," *Free Speech Now!* (September 25, 2014), accessed February 20, 2017, http://www.spiked-online.com/freespeechnow/fsn_article/exhibit-b-we-must-fight-for-the-right-to-be-offensive#.WKsKLRBOE4A.
53. Michael Walling, "Exhibit B: A Response to the Closure," *Border Crossings Blog* (September 25, 2014), accessed February 20, 2017, http://bordercrossingsblog.blogspot.com/2014/09/exhibit-b-response-to-closure.html.
54. Sara Myers, "Withdraw the Racist Exhibition 'Exhibit B - The Human Zoo' from showing at the Barbican from 23rd–27th September," *Change.org petition* (2014), accessed February 20, 2017, http://www.change.org/p/withdraw-the-racist-exhibition-exhibition-b-the-human-zoo.
55. John O'Mahony, "Edinburgh's most Controversial Show: Exhibit B, a Human Zoo," *Guardian* (August 11, 2014), accessed February 20, 2017, http://www.theguardian.com/stage/2014/aug/11/-sp-exhibit-b-human-zoo-edinburgh festivals-most-controversial.
56. Jack Malvern and Gaby Swerling, "Activists Celebrate after Closing Show They Hadn't Seen," *Times* (September 26, 2014), accessed February 20, 2017, http://www.thetimes.co.uk/tto/arts/stage/theatre/article4218426.ece.

57. Akala, "The Human Zoo and the Masturbation of White Guilt," *Huffington Post* (September 15, 2014), accessed February 20, 2017, http://www.huffingtonpost.co.uk/akala/barbican-centre_b_5809508.html.
58. Krueger, "Gazing at *Exhibit A*," 4.
59. Brett Bailey, Facebook (November 30, 2014), accessed February 20, 2017, https://www.facebook.com/photo.php?fbid=10205249573587873&set=a.1640238614827.2087905.1502648785&type=1.
60. Bailey, Facebook (November 30, 2014).
61. Meersman, "Resisting" (2010).
62. Walling, "Exhibit B: A Response to the Closure" (2014).
63. Akala's suggestion that "Mr. Bailey take his foolishness back to where he came from" affirms the commonly assumed implication that South Africa is simply a racist space.
64. Walling, "Exhibit B: A Response to the Closure" (2014).
65. Lemn Sissay, "Brett Bailey's Exhibit B and the Real Human Zoo," Lemnsissay.com (September 26, 2014), accessed May 23, 2017, http://blog.lemnsissay.com/2014/09/26/brett-baileys-exhibit-b-real-human-zoo/.
66. Robyn Sassen, "Brett Bailey's Exhibit B Knots up London Knickers," *Mail & Guardian* (September 5, 2014), accessed February 20, 2017, http://mg.co.za/article/2014–09–04-brett-baileys-exhibit-b-knots-up-london-knickers.
67. Meersman, "Look Black in Anger," (2014).
68. Samantha Vice, "How Do I Live in This Strange Place?" *Journal of Social Philosophy* 41, no. 3 (Fall 2010).
69. "Exhibit B: Is the 'Human Zoo' Racist? The Performers Respond," *Guardian* (September 5, 2014), accessed February 20, 2017, http://www.theguardian.com/culture/2014/sep/05/exhibit-b-is-the-human-zoo-racist-the-performers-respond.
70. J. S. Rafaeli, "Performers in London's 'Racist' Human Zoo Exhibit Are Angry It's Been Shut Down," Vice.com (September 26, 2014), accessed February 20, 2017, http://www.vice.com/en_uk/read/exhibit-b-human-zoo-barbican-178.
71. Rafaeli, "Performers in London's 'Racist' Human Zoo Exhibit Are Angry It's Been Shut Down."
72. T. O. Molefe, "Racism and the Barbican's 'Exhibit B,'" *New York Times* (October 27, 2014), accessed February 20, 2017, https://www.nytimes.com/2014/10/28/opinion/t-o-molefe-racism-and-the-barbicans-exhibit-b.html.
73. Bailey, Facebook (November 30, 2014).
74. Ross Douthat, "Africa's Scramble for Europe," *New York Times* (August 8, 2015), accessed February 20, 2017, https://www.nytimes.com/2015/08/09/opinion/sunday/ross-douthat-africas-scramble-for-europe.html.
75. Malvern & Swerling, "Activists celebrate" (2014).
76. Bailey, Facebook (November 30, 2014).
77. Meersman, "Look Black in Anger," (2014).
78. Bailey, Facebook (November 30, 2014).
79. Rafaeli, "Performers in London's 'Racist' Human Zoo Exhibit Are Angry It's Been Shut Down."
80. Peter Rorvik, "Art's High Price for Freedom of Expression," *Arterial Network* (November 11, 2014), accessed February 20, 2017, http://www.arterialnetwork.org/article/stefMG.
81. Govinda, "Exhibit B: Artists must Have the Right to Shock."

82. Molefe, "Racism and the Barbican's 'Exhibit B,'" (2014).
83. Diane Joseph, "Exhibit B: A Personal Response," The Big Idea (October 11, 2014), accessed February 20, 2017, http://www.thebigidea.co.nz/news/whats-on-show-reviews/2014/oct/148888-exhibit-b-a-personal-response.
84. Rafaeli, "Performers in London's 'Racist' Human Zoo Exhibit Are Angry It's Been Shut Down."
85. Diasporic Redman, "Dismissing the Protest Against 'Exhibit B' as Censorship Is Shutting Down the Very Conversation about Race That Was Intended," *Àse Fountain* (September 30, 2014), accessed February 20, 2017, http://theasefountain.tumblr.com/post/98796884987/dismissing-the-protest-against-exhibit-b-as.
86. Natasha Tripney, "Louise Jeffreys: Barbican 'Failed Audiences' When It Cancelled Exhibit B after Protests," *Stage* (May 13, 2016), accessed February 20, 2017, https://www.thestage.co.uk/news/2016/louise-jeffreys-barbican-failed-audiences-cancelled-exhibit-b-protests/.

Taking the Theatre to the People

Performance Sponsorship and Regulation in Mussolini's Italy

—PATRICIA GABORIK

When Benito Mussolini became prime minister of Italy in October 1922, the men (usually men) of Italian theatre had for some time been wailing its imminent demise. Yet, at the 1934 Volta Convention on the theatre, organized by the Royal Italian Academy (an institution created by the fascist government), experts from around the world—Maurice Maeterlinck, Gerhart Hauptmann, Jacques Copeau, Edward Gordon Craig, Alexander Tairov—came to discuss the state of the art, which had yet to take its last breath. Still ten more years later, in 1944, Silvio D'Amico began to write *The Theatre Must Not Die*, a call for the rebirth of Italian dramatic theatre after a disastrous twenty years (the period known as the *ventennio fascista*), in which the regime's interventions could best be summarized, he wrote, with the Duchess of Chevreau's crack about Richelieu: "The good, he did poorly; the bad, he did well."[1] At every turn throughout his eighty-page essay, D'Amico found reason for complaint, for if he couldn't rightly charge the fascists with doing nothing (at least they, unlike their liberal predecessors, thought the government should support the theatre), he consistently lamented that they should have done more or otherwise. Given his authoritative position—he was a cultured, insightful, and demanding critic and the director of the National Academy of Dramatic Arts, which opened in 1936—*The Theatre Must Not Die*, published in 1945, came to serve as the first major account of theatre history under fascism.

Ever since, that book's characterizations have guided common understanding of dramatic production under Mussolini, which amounts to a series of predictable but not necessarily accurate claims. Underlying it all is the notion that the theatre was losing ground to the fledgling sound cinema, and Il Duce's (the Leader's) preference for the latter only aggravated the situation. All further damage, as typically reported by theatrical and cultural historians, was the result of fascist autarky, paternalism, and cultural vapidity: closed borders and strict censorship killed the creative spirit, the campaign for national unity and against dialect culture marginalized potential audience members and talented artists who could have given rise to the new Italian theatre, explicitly propagandistic performance was a priori devoid of artistic merit (unworthy of further investigation), while state-sponsored shows that were not obvious propaganda do not even fall within a category we might call "fascist theatre." In her recent social history, for example, Patrizia Dogliani recognizes that the theatre received heavy funding but argues that the "principal objective was to ensure that theatrical performances were consonant with the regime's politics and that they were Italian plays, written in Italian."[2]

Such depictions are, however, shaped more by assumptions about what fascism was—and was not—than by the research conducted. They are the result of a generalized view of fascism as a simple *onagrocrazia* ("government by asses"), as Benedetto Croce famously coined it, and of a more complex set of circumstances having to do with the writing of history in a highly charged postwar climate that encouraged the denigration of all things fascist even while several structures and personages of that regime remained standing. In the theatre, there were many of these remaining structures and personnel. And so, the need to criticize and establish distance was felt not only by those who had been ill-disposed to Mussolini's government but also by those who benefited from it regardless of whether they had been particularly sympathetic.[3]

That researchers begin with the premise that an illiberal, violent, and intensely bureaucratic political caste would necessarily manage even its arts in the same illiberal, violent, and blindly bureaucratic fashion is hardly incomprehensible. However, it also means that the area is underresearched, and, at times, studies are poorly framed or inadequately contextualized.[4] This ideological problem is compounded by disciplinary and national-linguistic divides: some solid theatre history pertaining to the period has of course been done, largely by Italian specialists; but their work struggles to find an audience in colleagues who might be interested in the *ventennio* but do not read the language (and thus fall back on the few, very general publications available in English) or among the cultural historians who investigate Mussolini's Italy but are not drawn to what are often rather specialized studies.[5]

An important contribution to the field was made by Günter Berghaus's 1996 collection, *Fascism and Theatre: Comparative Studies on the Aesthetics and Politics of Performance in Europe, 1925–1945*, which set out to conduct a "truly comparative and inter-disciplinary study on the politics and aesthetics of performance in a number of countries governed by fascist or para-fascist régimes," thereby codifying a "generic fascist theatre aesthetics." Despite its many qualities, the volume escapes neither these inadequacies of framing nor occasional tendencies to reassert the commonplaces I refer to. Although it allows for varying perspectives and definitions of fascism itself, a fundamental premise of the book is that the theatre is particularly useful to fascism because of its appeal to an "irrational core that no other form of propaganda can reach," for "mobilising mass audiences and manipulating the emotional impact generated by the event for political purposes seems to be a common trait of fascist theatre." It follows that three of the four essays dedicated specifically to Italy discuss the regime's theatricalization of politics (Emilio Gentile), institutional and regulatory aspects like censorship (Doug Thompson), and the ideologies of propaganda plays (Pietro Cavallo)—as if to suggest though omission that artistry is not at issue. Theatre that was not specifically "fascist" in content remains largely unaddressed; even the paragraph one scholar dedicates to Mussolini's support for Pirandello and Bragaglia liquidates the fact with the negation that their offerings "had anything in common with fascism."[6]

This essay is an initial step in a larger project that therefore seeks to reframe the discussion of theatre under Mussolini's regime. It draws largely on primary and quantitative sources that, while never telling the full story, help to objectify the epoch's disputes and brush away the residue from them that remains on even the most contemporary scholarship.[7] Although partial, it shows that fascist-backed theatre was more varied and vibrant than has ever been acknowledged. This is a truth that must be addressed if we hope to come to a real understanding of what the blackshirts wanted from the theatre and how they tried to get it.

Already back in the 1910s, and thus before fascism's seizure of power, anxiety over the rise of cinema was ubiquitous among thespians (one need only think of the futurist "Variety Theatre" and other manifestoes encouraging a move toward cinematic means and rhythms). The challenges posed by new technologies only increased over time, especially after the first full-length feature with synchronized audio (*The Jazz Singer*) appeared in 1927. Mussolini had also famously declared that the cinema was the state's "strongest weapon" of propaganda, and so it became easy for theatre folk to argue that he watched the stage sputter along while helping the seventh art flourish (even if Mussolini's son Vittorio, the director of an important film journal, attested just the opposite).[8]

The bulk of the data presented in this essay dates to the 1930s, when the institutionalization of performing arts reached its height and is thus most indicative of the government's ambitions; but, as will be shown, actions taken in the 1920s, a period of transformation and exploration, are fundamental for understanding the aesthetic politics of the *ventennio* and the respective places of theatre and film therein. It is true that there was a decisive push to sponsor the film industry beginning in the mid-thirties. However, when a longer and broader view is taken, the theatrical initiatives emerge as more committed and extensive and the theatre more essential to the regime's plans for the unification and would-be fascistization of the Italian masses.

While Mussolini had lauded documentary films as tools of "education and persuasion," for more than a decade, he conceded only half-measures to help the struggling commercial film industry. Until Il Duce's son-in-law Galeazzo Ciano created a Film Department (the DGC, Direzione Generale per la Cinematografia) within the Undersecretariat for Press and Propaganda in 1934, the only substantial move in favor of the industry was the transformation of the Educational Cinema Union in November 1925 into the Istituto LUCE, an entity of the state and its official newsreel and propaganda film producer. In other words, for more than a decade, Mussolini showed interest in the cinema primarily as a vehicle for information.

Even as government involvement in the commercial sector increased in the 1930s, its practices were "schizophrenic," in Vito Zagarrio's words.[9] For instance, laws privileged Italian production in a market dominated by Hollywood, but producers had trouble meeting the demands of these regulations, which therefore created more pressure than relief. Because the regime was only nominally tempted by the possible advantages the industry afforded, it tended to regulate rather than help produce. The DGC appeared, in part, as an antidote to the counterproductive and haphazard regulation that profited neither sector nor government; and after its creation, especially as the 1930s drew to a close, the regime increased support and control in all areas, from production and distribution to censorship and movie hall management. The flourishing of entities like the Experimental Cinema Center (the National Film School) in 1935 and, most famously, Cinecittà (in 1937) is testament to the industry's mounting status; and yet the recurrent time lag between the births of such institutions and their adoption by the state is indicative of Mussolini's reluctance to take responsibility for the field.

The major push to take control of filmic enterprises came along with an unprecedented politicization of cultural production in the late 1930s, a period of continual war, the alliance with Hitler, the racial laws, and fascism's slow decline in popularity.[10] In 1938, the International Exhibition of Cinematic Art and in 1939 Cinecittà fell under regime control, and the well-established (in 1906) CINES film studio became public in 1941. One aspect of this intensification is seen in table 1 and figures 1–4. The first of these divides by producing nation the number of films approved by the censor for projection in Italian cinemas, in 1937 and 1941, respectively.

Nation	Total films projected 1937 / 1941	Approved as is 1937 / 1941	Approved with edits 1937 / 1941	Prohibited 1937 / 1941
Italy	55/78	53 / 77	1 / 1	1 / 0
France	6 / 51	6 / 41	0 / 5	0 / 5
Germany	19 / 88	18 / 82	1 / 4	0 / 2
United States	97 / 46	93 / 37	2 / 1	2 / 8
Other	2 / 27	2 / 24	2 / 0	0 / 3

Table 1. Feature-length films approved and prohibited by the censor: Number of projections by producing nation, 1937 and 1941.

Most striking is the drop in American and increase in German films approved for public showing by 1941, an indication that the alliance with Hitler's Reich was meant to be more than political and military: it was, indeed, economic and cultural as well. Likewise noteworthy, however, is the tighter control of film content, illustrated by the columns showing whether movies required edits before receiving the "visa" that allowed their showing. It is worth repeating, however, that this data speaks to a very particular and extreme handful of years at the close of Mussolini's two-decade reign: the fact that in 1937 American films outnumbered Italian movies 97–55 is a testament to a far "freer" governance in such matters in the first 15 or so years of fascism (it also reflects a rather ambivalent attitude toward American culture).

As figures 1 and 2 show, the dramatic theatre was a stronger vehicle for native production than the cinema (but thespians of all political stripes were keen to defend homegrown voices). All the same, an analogous shift took place, with French plays versus those of the new Reich (see figures 3 and 4).

In both cases, the dominant producers (America in film, France in the theatre) were beaten back. This was in keeping with protectionist policies in the film industry, but in the theatre, the situation was somewhat more complex. Critics and authors had been lamenting the cumbersome presence of French light fare for decades, but its ousting in this period had to do only in part with

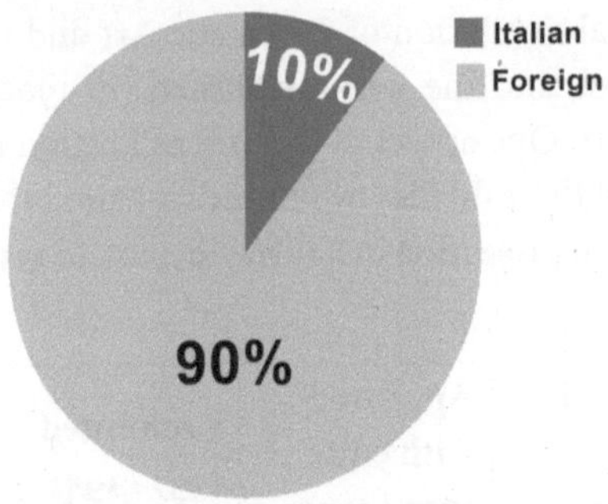

Figure 1. Projected films, Italian vs. foreign, 1937

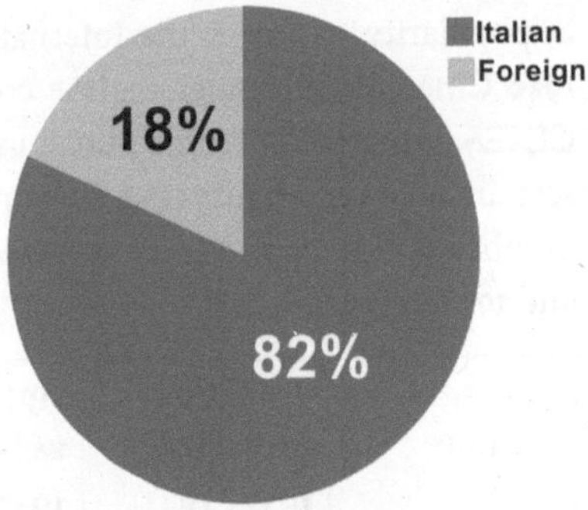

Figure 2. Theatrical productions, Italian vs. foreign, 1937

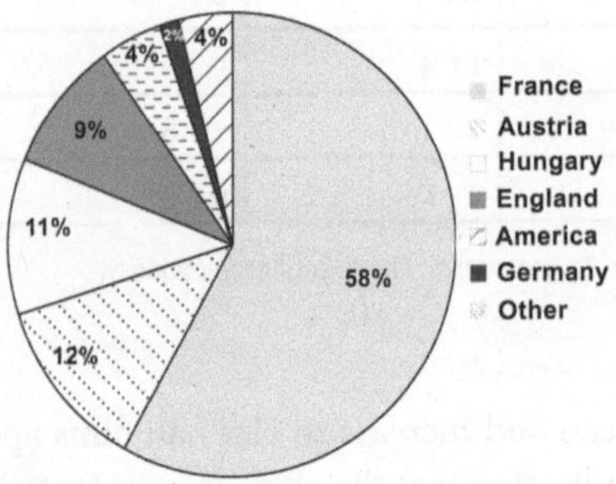

Figure 3. Foreign plays, by author's nationality, 1937

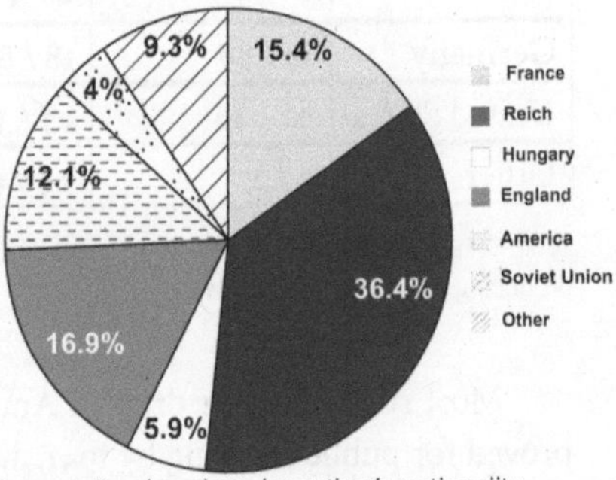

Figure 4. Foreign plays, by author's nationality, 1941

that aversion (which Mussolini shared). Rather, the blackshirts grew increasingly intolerant with France for political reasons, irritated first by its opposition to the 1935 Ethiopian invasion and then responding to its status as official enemy once the Alliance with Nazi Germany was sealed and war broke out. But because the kind of entertainment provided by those French plays was so popular, a replacement was needed, and Hungarian comedies modeled on the French rose in their stead.[11]

Curious—especially in comparison to what happened with cinema—is the upswing of American plays in this later period. Some of it had to do with Anton Giulio Bragaglia's championing of artists like Eugene O'Neill, efforts criticized by some but defended by Mussolini himself (and made under the auspices of the state-sponsored Teatro delle Arti). It may seem strange that US movies were rejected while its plays were increasingly welcomed, and it would be tempting to call forth any number of studies that speak of a pragmatic eclecticism in fascist arts management to once again claim that such apparent inconsistencies were the result of opportunism and ideological emptiness.[12] But here one would have to look closely at repertoire before rushing to such judgement, and, when the American dramatists who made it to the stage were of the type and caliber of O'Neill and Thornton Wilder, also wonder if decisions were not based as much on the kind of product being offered by that market as on provenance alone.

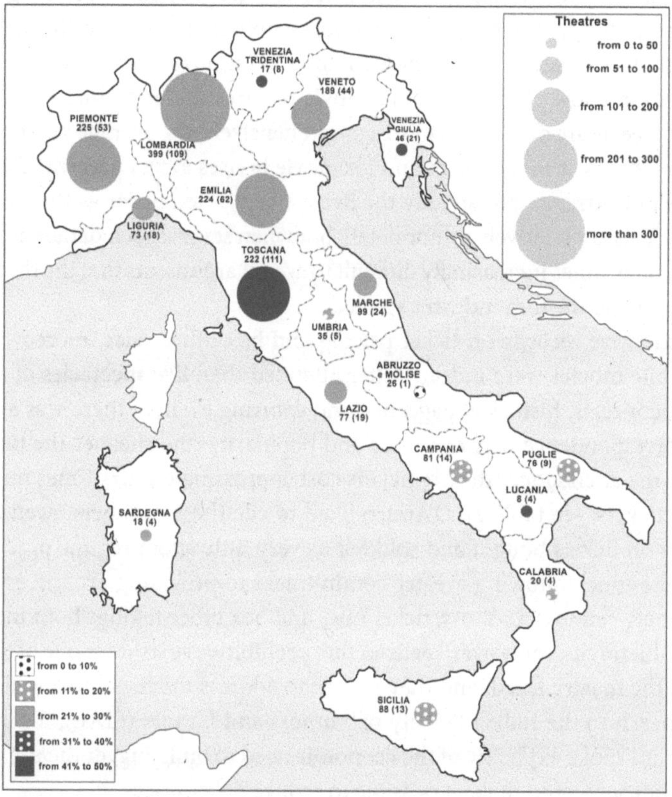

Figure 5. Theatres in Italy, March 1, 1939. There were 1,931 total theatres; numbers in parentheses indicate those run by either the National Fascist Party (PNF) or the National Leisure Organization (OND), which amounted to 525 theatres, or 27.2 percent. In colonial Libya, not pictured, two of every eight theatres (or 25 percent) were run by these government organizations.

Turning back to the divergence between cinema and theatrical support, venue management is a revelatory phenomenon. The government's decision to erect and run theatre and movie houses indicates its eagerness—even in the cinema, where its advances were initially more tentative—to intervene in the public sphere: that is to say, where cultural products came into contact with the public. On the one hand, this could be seen as providing a welcome service, as it ensured access to performance on stage and screen where it had previously been less or unavailable (this was one device for achieving consent among the people). On the other hand, it meant that repertoire could be micro- and locally managed. In any case, in the late thirties, the government ran higher percentages of live theatres than movie houses: only six regions saw fewer than 20 percent of its theatres run by the PNF or OND in 1939 whereas eleven regions saw the same low percentage of its movie theatres under regime management in 1937 (see figure 5). Viewed more comprehensively, the average percentage for theatres looms at 26.2 percent and for movie houses at 22.1 percent. The difference is not extreme, but already the live art begins to appear as the weapon of choice. This is a relatively minor detail, but when several such details are put together, it becomes increasingly difficult to accept arguments that the theatre was neglected and the film industry spoiled.

Extensive records on ticket pricing and box office sales, moreover, show that while movies were indeed better attended than live spectacles of any sort (plays, concerts, historical pageants, and sporting events), there was also a direct correspondence between price and popularity: the cheaper the ticket, the higher the attendance (theatre tickets cost approximately 2.75 times more than movie tickets; see table 2). D'Amico liked to cite these numbers, even if information on tickets bought and sold tell us very little about regime practices. At the same time, following greater commitment to providing art and entertainment, between 1935 and 1937, ticket sales and box office takings both increased. Fascist hierarchs, moreover, realized that prohibitive costs were one of the challenges the theatre faced, and they sought to address the issue. In a well-known 1933 speech to the Italian Society of Authors and Editors (SIAE), for instance, Mussolini spoke explicitly of the economic need to build bigger theatres, whose larger houses would make it possible to reduce ticket prices.[13]

Activity	**Showings**	**Tickets Sold**	**Takings**	**Average Price**
Theatre	73,805	21,426,230	98,001,690.28	4.57
Cinema	543,143	313,974,471	525,117,382.16	1.67
Sport	25,064	8,262,298	30,890,606.08	3.74
Various entertainments	513,407	56,634,076	94,070,430.54	1.66
Totals	1,155,429	400,297,075	748,080,109.06	1.87

Table 2. Comparative entertainment sales and pricing, 1937 (monetary figures in Italian *lire*)

More significant still was the very different evolution of fascist efforts to incorporate the theatre into a cultural scheme. Whereas early in his tenure Mussolini resisted the film industry's advances, he courted theatrical practitioners from day one—and turned to such artists as Eleonora Duse and Luigi Pirandello instead of to the producers of commercial fare. His desire to contribute to the salvation of the form was consistent with his own enthusiasm for theatre and dramatic literature, an interest he shared with many of his "hierarchs."[14] In the very first years after the March on Rome, Il Duce solicited and reviewed numerous proposals for a national theatre and by 1927 had already funded three different art houses, including, most famously, Pirandello's. Later, when the Fascist University Groups (the GUF) formed student theatre companies, their flagship was the Teatro Sperimentale in Florence, where a new generation would write, direct, and produce in hopes of creating the Italian theatre of tomorrow. Mussolini's offices underwrote Bragaglia's avant-garde endeavors for the entire *ventennio*, a fact marked by his 1937 subvention of and visit to the new Teatro delle Arti, which resided within the Fascist Professionals and Artists' Confederation Roman complex and, under Bragaglia's direction, produced Italian classics alongside contemporary foreign work. If funding of the private enterprises among these was never total, it must also be recognized that debates about the advantage of such complete collaboration were as lively among artists as they were among politicians; artists, of course, feared that state funds could never truly come without strings attached. D'Amico's question, "Why is it that fascism, which spent millions on entertainment of dubious quality, never spent a cent on the art theatre?" must therefore, unfortunately, be considered in bad faith.[15] Mussolini and his hierarchs *did* give money to these theatres, pay for renovations on the buildings they used, and, in fully sustaining the GUF experiments and erecting the National Academy, which D'Amico himself directed, look to the future as well as the present moment. Even in the realm of the commercial theatre, directives in the late thirties aimed to make sure that funds went to the companies whose artistic ambitions were the highest. (The boss's soft spot for thespians must have been known, if Theatre Inspector Nicola De Pirro complained that actor-managers would "run directly to Il Duce, as is their custom," in hopes of continued support despite the increasingly selective standards.[16])

Already by the late 1920s, blackshirts turned their attention to open-air spectacles for massive crowds. This was, truth be told, the crux of D'Amico's complaint: he would have preferred that they continued to focus on highbrow endeavors for an elite public even if he would not have used such terms. The government created or helped sustain artistic education and training, single performances and entire festivals, and new (or refurbished ancient) venues to house them.

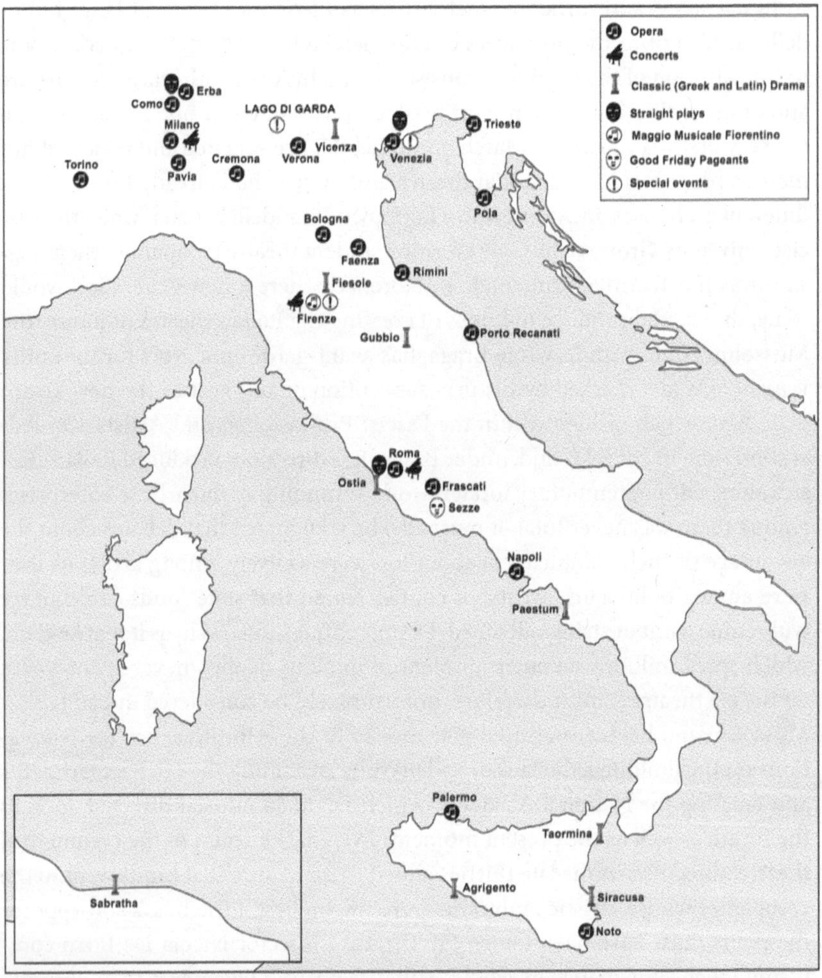

Figure 6. Outdoor theater and music. The types and locations of performances held in outdoor spaces during the spring-summer season, from late April through August, excluding those sponsored by the OND. While most performances indicated here were regular and ongoing, the "special events" were just that, noteworthy both for the regime's support and for the attention they garnered at the time. Florence hosted *18 BL* in 1934, the National Institute for the Representation of Gabriele D'Annunzio's plays opened with *La figlia di Jorio* at the author's Lake Garda villa in 1927, and thanks to an effort spearheaded by Minister of Popular Culture Dino Alfieri, D'Annunzio's *La Nave* set sail on the Venetian Lagoon in September 1938.

As figure 6 shows, there was room for everything, outdoor and in: opera; ancient, classic, and contemporary plays; musical and dance concerts; and religious enactments. First, they founded two national institutes. After seeing impressive productions of *Seven at Thebes* and *Antigone* in the Greek theatre of Syracuse in 1924, Mussolini turned their production company into the INDA, the National Institute of Ancient Drama (on August 7, 1925), charged with producing more such events in ancient theatres and archeological zones all over the country. Then, in late 1926 Il Duce underwrote the new National Institute for the Representation of Gabriele d'Annunzio's plays, an endeavor that can hardly be dismissed as merely propagandistic, despite the poet's heroic nationalist credentials, for he was a remarkable playwright and crucial exponent of late nineteenth- and early twentieth-century European poetry and drama. Both institutes, in fact, trouble the binaries that often accompany characterization of the era's performance: if these plays were performed outdoors for crowds of thousands, they were hardly "popular" in the other sense. D'Annunzio's poetic tragedies found new life in the hands of director Giovacchino Forzano, who knew how to manage both the verse and the onstage crowds that gave them their power (he was an opera librettist and "director," not to mention future collaborator with Mussolini on three historical dramas). For their part, the INDA productions featured new translations of ancient masterpieces; anti-archeological stage designs by Duilio Cambellotti; modern choreography by the students of Hellerau-Laxenburg Eurythmics school, a gymnastic dance style, especially in vogue among female amateurs in the 1930s; and careful attention to direction, a new art in Italy, whose theatre developed differently than that of its neighbors.

Following the advent of these institutes, the regime launched a whole series of programs, festivals, and single shows: year-round, for more than a decade and even into the war years before it became too dangerous to gather massive crowds, it sponsored live performance. These productions showcased existing talents, re-envisioned classic texts, experimented with new aesthetics and technical capabilities, and hosted foreign works and artists. Only a small portion of these were blatantly propagandistic in nature; even the amateur theatrical troupes, who sometimes produced their own original texts and were by far the most prolific writers of "fascist plays," presented a relatively small number of them.[17] And while rather banal entertainment was plentiful in the playhouses, regime-sponsored initiatives were often, simply put, better theatre. An impressive 1933 *Othello* at the Doge's Palace in Venice prompted the Biennale's secretary general to create the Biennale of Theatre. In 1932 at Erba, in the centenary of its author's death, one of Mussolini's favorite plays, *Faust*, had its Italian premiere. One could see Hofmannsthal's *Everyman* with famed Austrian actor

Aleksänder Moisiu and Reinhardt's *Midsummer Night's Dream* or *Merchant of Venice*. Even the play most cited as evidence of Pirandello's supposed anti-fascism, *The Mountain Giants*, debuted under fascist auspices at the Maggio Musicale Fiorentino, a festival that (like the INDA and the Biennale) still exists today. Italy's best actors, from Emma Gramatica to Raffaele Viviani and Annibale Ninchi, and stage designer-architects like Virgilio Marchi (a futurist best known for his work with Pirandello and Bragaglia) brought these projects to life. And of course, the participation of figures like Reinhardt, Copeau, and Gordon Craig in fascist endeavors was important not just for their success but for the contact of both audiences and professionals with foreign developments and perspectives.[18]

Although Mussolini did ask his writers to be "interpreters of our times, which are those of the fascist revolution," as in the aforementioned SIAE speech, he did not ask them to write propaganda. Rather, he declared on this and other occasions that "the state cannot create its own literature. But it can and must support its authors and, above all, honor and encourage talent."[19] This is not to say that the fascist's support for the theatrical arts was devoid of political pragmatism. The contrary was true. However, good theatre was not antithetical to political utility; and political utility was rarely obtained with explicit propaganda.

In her study of the regime's after-work leisure organization, the Opera Nazionale Dopolavoro (OND, referred to as the Dopolavoro), historian Victoria De Grazia in fact made a convincing case for the "deceptively apolitical" nature of the organization's activities, something that is seen time and again in its numerous theatrical exploits and that can be extended beyond that single organization's activities. One example is performance in dialect rather than in the standard Italian that was to be a symbol, and strategy, of national unity from the late nineteenth century and throughout the *ventennio*. As seen in table 3, in 1937, to turn once again to that ideal year (as it represents the apex of fascism's consensus), the OND produced 3.5 percent of all dialect theatre and sold 1.8 percent of tickets to dialect shows. This means that the regime's largest performance sponsor made a miniscule contribution. Given reports on the blackshirt campaign against local vernaculars, this would seem surprising only in that they sponsored any dialect activity at all. And yet, further unexpected details emerge in table 4 and figure 7, regarding the "Theatrical Saturday" program, which made shows in elite bourgeois playhouses (like the Argentina in Rome and La Scala Opera House in Milan) affordable to the working class.[20] That extraordinarily well-attended venture incorporated a substantial number of dialect plays into its repertoire: in 1937, 15 percent of performances were of dialect pieces; over five years, there was an increase (to 19.5 percent in 1938), then

Type of company	Performances	Tickets sold
Primary troupes	1,410	789,911
Regular troupes	5,259	2,111,533
Church troupes	39	7,138
OND troupes	245	54,820
Charity performances	13	6,892
Total	6,966	2,970,294

Table 3. Dialect theater, 1937

Type of show	Performances	Tickets sold
Non-dialect straight plays	186	136,765
Dialect plays	48	46,085
Opera	47	77,206
Operetta	13	11,947
Review	20	18,982
Concert	5	4,108
Total	319	295,093

Table 4. Theatrical Saturdays, 1937

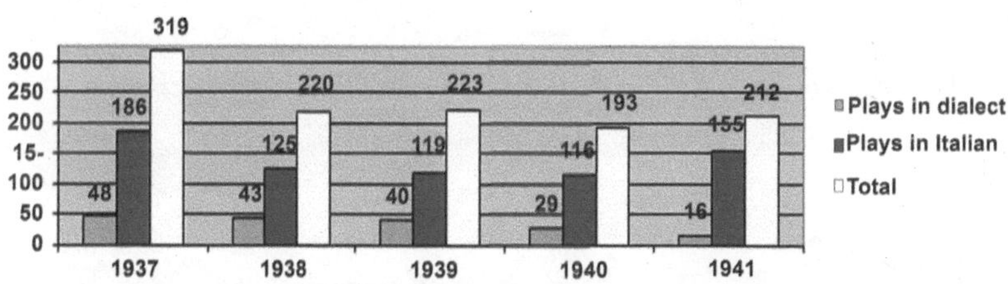

Figure 7. Theatrical Saturdays, dialect shows, 1937–1941

a leveling off (with a range between 15 and 19.5 percent), and finally a drop to 7 percent in 1941.

Numbers for the opera, considered a first-rate expression of Italian genius (but at the time also a "popular" art form), were similar. In this same year, however, the OND hosted 2.4 percent of all dialect theatre, an increase over 1937, which is significant considering that 1941 brought a general decline in dialect performance. In other words, the OND sponsored only a small portion of all available vernacular performances, but, conversely, these comprised a significant part of the OND's production. Statistics for previous years are even more surprising: of a total of 7,511 straight-play performances by the OND's amateur groups in 1932, for instance, 1,566, or 20.85 percent, were in local vernaculars.

These constituted 9.4 percent of all dialect theatre produced, and the total number of dialect performances by all companies increased to 38 percent of all the straight plays performed—a staggering number under a regime known for waging war against local tongues.

A stated goal of offering opportunities to participate in and attend the theatre was the teaching of Italian, but it clearly benefited the fascists to incorporate the popular dialect tradition in their offerings. Nationalization would have to work not around but through local customs and identity—even as Italian was a means of unifying separate communities. The rather significant presence of the

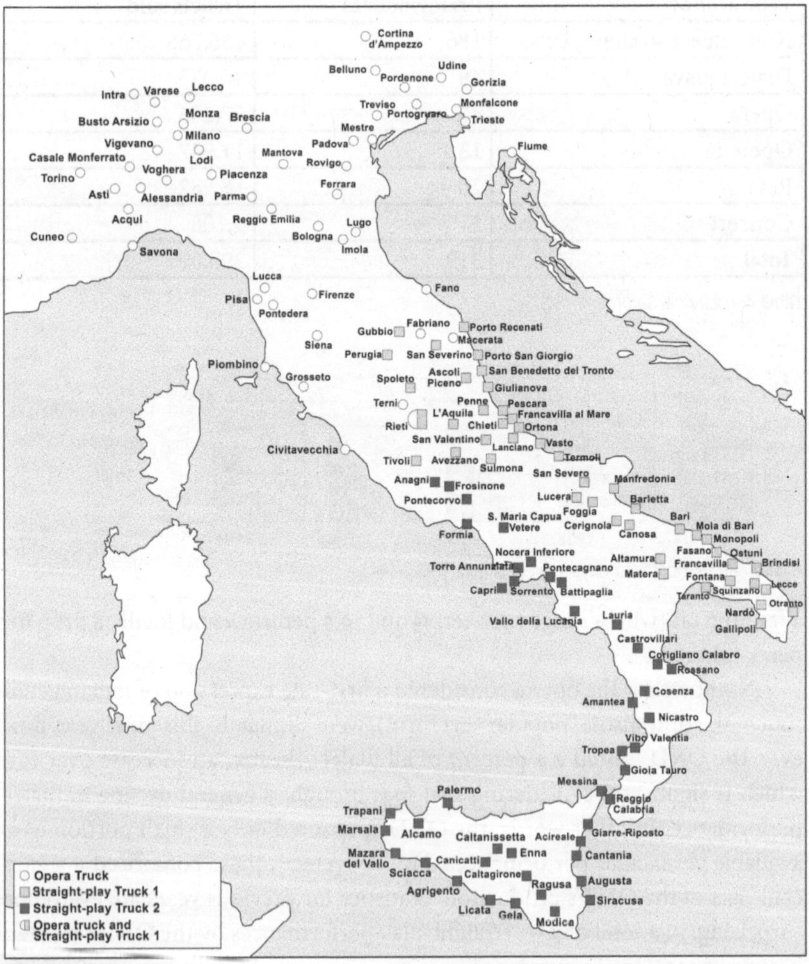

Figure 8. The Thespian Truck tours, 1937.

vernacular in the national repertoire is a cogent example of the pragmatic, "deceptively apolitical" operations De Grazia describes, as well as a particularly interesting piece of support for the notion of the theatre as Mussolini's "most sophisticated weapon": not simple entertainment with pro-fascist story lines, nor a means of disseminating positively inflected news, nor even a vehicle of linguistic imposition, but a chance to build "new Italians" through education, discipline, and a sense of belonging to both a local and a vast national community. This is one area where general historiography on fascist culture would be particularly aided by more attention to the work of theatre scholars, who have addressed the complexities of vernacular performance at the time.[21]

But the party's most innovative and intensive effort to reach the people was the Carri di Tespi (Thespian Trucks) program, which consumed as much as one-fifth of the OND's total budget, more than any other single activity, and reached all but two provinces in the first six years: Zara in the far east and Sondrio in the far north. A traveling theatre program, it literally delivered shows to the urban and provincial masses, whose opportunities to enjoy high quality performance might be rare. Its coverage was vast, as indicated in figure 8. Futurist architect Antonio Valente designed the prototype mobile theatre, a huge stage and house that were transported from town to town by truck brigades and assembled in a few hours' time in the squares, fields, or stadiums that had space for them. The results of the first limited tour in 1929 were so pleasing that the next year one opera and three straight-theatre troupes divided the Italian territory among themselves (in 1936, the number of straight-play trucks was reduced to two).[22]

The variation in frequency and number of performances is notable, as is the breakdown by geographic area: there was special investment in the poorer and generally underserviced south and islands. The director, the aforementioned Forzano, created seasons that were perhaps designed to appeal to local tastes and traditions, producing more straight theatre in the south and islands and larger numbers of operas in the center and the north (nearly 43 percent of straight plays were given in the south yet less than 18 percent of operas). On the whole, however, there were more performances in the south (37.49 percent) than there were either in central Italy (32.96 percent) or the north (29.56 percent). Though the OND is known to have struggled to have an important presence in the south, it expended much energy to take the theatre there.

The propagandistic effect of these occasions—regardless of repertory, which was exclusively Italian and combined rather unsophisticated contemporary plays with classics like Alfieri and Goldoni and authors D'Amico would have preferred, such as d'Annunzio, Pirandello, and the so-called *grotteschi* Pier Maria Rosso di San Secondo and Luigi Chiarelli—was undoubtedly impressive. "The medium

Figure 9. People's Theatre sponsored by the OND. The symbols for the Provincial Thespian Trucks and Mobile Cinema are those from which the trucks began their tours in the first season (1937) and are thus a minimal representation of the phenomenon.

was the true message," Jeffrey Schnapp has claimed, for the Carri's stages, outfitted with the most modern lighting equipment and stage effects, were displays of organization, technical wizardry, and sheer size.[23] Giving an average of 190–200 shows per season to crowds numbering from two to five thousand, the brigades astonished nearly one million spectators. OND director General Corrado Puccetti wrote in 1936 of the assembly that took place before townspeople's eyes: "There they stand before the people, who watch and learn how quickly the regime transforms raw material into style. It's the miracle of transformation, of construction:

the miracle of the corporative age."[24] His words were rhetorical and hyperbolic; but this was nonetheless real progress for the theatrical arts, at least in terms of technical production. Italian scenic practices struggled to keep pace with those in the rest of Europe, but the Carri di Tespi's stages were the best to be had, with revolving stage platforms, Fortuny domes, and complex lighting effects. In short, they had all the spectacular capabilities that make the theatre theatrical (the upgrading that, Bragaglia insisted in a 1929 open letter to Mussolini, would bring about the promised performance revolution).[25]

Given the success of the regular trucks, in 1937 a provincial brigade was set in motion and gave 351 performances for 175,000 spectators. These trucks visited places that were too small to accommodate the larger theatres. Fascist officials proudly claimed, "The people have sensed that the OND—the institution created by Il Duce for their physical, moral, and spiritual well-being—hasn't forgotten anyone."[26] Most surprisingly, not even the Italians in colonial Libya were forgotten. Upon the request of Governor Italo Balbo, a tour with about one hundred shows was organized there by and for the military. As indicated in figure 9, a map of the OND's various initiatives, there was also a traveling cinema program, which supplemented the theatre in larger towns and replaced it in the very smallest ones. According to OND statistics, the weekly projections were propagandistic and educational, and in 1937 alone they were shown in 2,175 rural locations.

The provincial brigades sometimes hosted amateur theatre groups, of which the OND had organized 2,066 by 1936, and thus were tightly tied to another colossal effort to mobilize the masses: the cultural activities competitions, whose numbers and locations are presented in figure 10. These were exhibitions, congresses, and recitals dedicated to music, drama, art, and literature: play- and fiction-writing contests, singers' and musicians' concerts, and photographic (and in a few odd cases, balcony-decorating) displays. These public competitions—picture a 1930s *Italian Idol*—occupied the whole year and every corner of the country; 1937 saw 479 events. Amateur theatrical contests accounted for about 21 percent of these. When one considers all these initiatives alongside the foundation of numerous small playhouses, libraries, and acting schools impossible to discuss in detail here, the centrality of the theatre to the regime's cultural makeup becomes indisputable. Mussolini's government provided, in the words of the OND, "a true gymnasium for training new actors and a launching pad for the theatre."[27] Indeed, all told, the picture starts to look like the nationalization of the thespians.

The frustrations of someone like Silvio D'Amico were, however, completely legitimate. He, along with Pirandello, had been invested in the creation of a

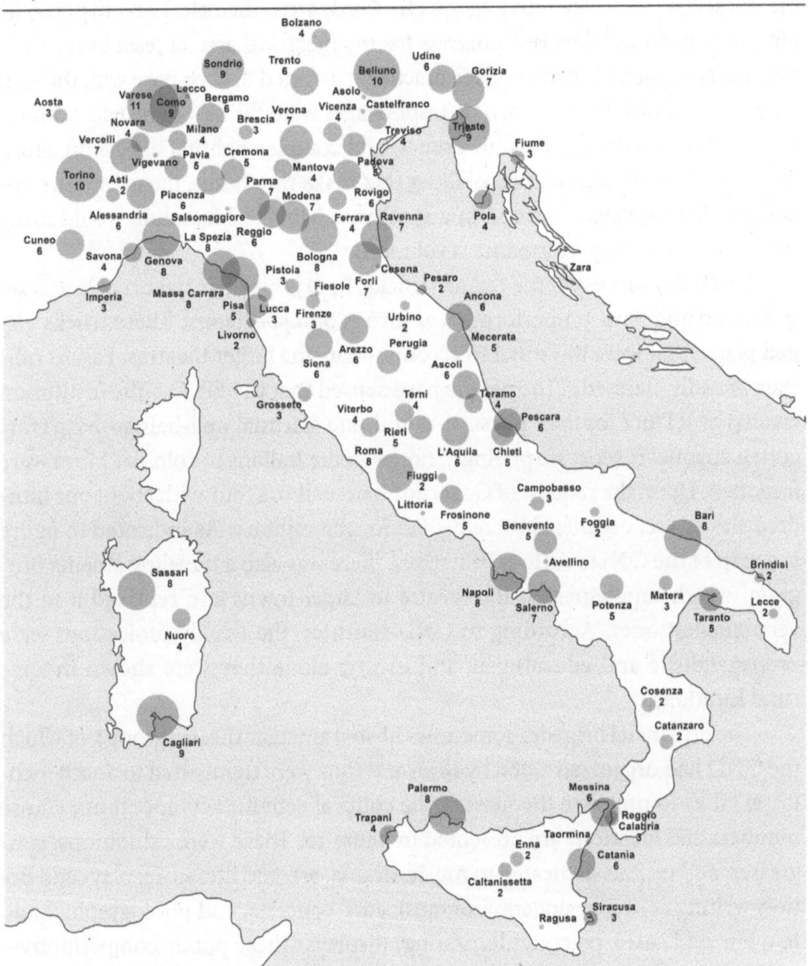

Figure 10. Cultural education activities, Fascist year XV (November 1936 to October 1937); of 479 total events, approximately 21 percent were theatrical competitions.

state-sponsored theatre along the lines of the Comédie-Française, which the regime talked about and planned for but never exactly implemented. Despite the lip service even D'Amico sometimes paid to the *popolo*, he could not have appreciated what appeared to be Mussolini's shift of focus from art houses to open-air shows for crowds of thousands, since the dramatists that fell along the wayside were not Sophocles or Shakespeare or even d'Annunzio, Pirandello, or Eduardo De Filippo, but the lesser-known Italian dramatists who might have been the promise of the current generation. Fascist and commercial initiatives both admitted a variety of authors, as noted, but beyond these bigger names did not center on the most challenging and interesting contemporary dramaturgy. Instead, such authors had to vie for space alongside the classics, more famous colleagues, lighter fare, and some propagandistic drama.[28]

D'Amico thus concluded (in a 1942 article reprinted in *The Theatre Must Not Die*), "By now we've got the horse, the bridle, the harness, the whip, and maybe even the driver: but we don't have the carriage. And so, we continue to go on foot."[29] For D'Amico, that carriage was a fancy theatre in Rome, with perhaps two others in Milan or Turin, with a correspondingly sophisticated repertoire. For the fascist hierarchs, however, the carriage truly was mobile, and multiple. Their National Theatre was not the single impressive edifice in Rome but a vast web of indoor theatres, outdoor theatres, and temporary stages placed in as many gardens, archeological sites, and squares as they could find.[30] (And about repertoire, they agreed only at times.)

Contained within that 1942 venting, however, was an implicit admission that progress had been made. D'Amico's grievances, in some respects, had less to do with the regime's shortcoming than they did with his disappointed expectations and unwillingness to give credit where it was due (at least partly for all the complicated reasons I have outlined). But further, it was about the discomfort of a man born in 1887 and attached to certain cultural and aesthetic traditions that were facing total overhaul in a modernizing society of the masses. The need to respond to a growing public, in the artistic sphere as well as the political one, was hardly a uniquely Italian phenomenon. And from this point of view fascism merely offered a response—totalitarian, as was Mussolini's regime—to a complete metamorphosis of European society (and not just European: consider Roosevelt's America).

D'Amico was right that the 1930s did not produce an important body of Italian dramatic literature; but this was arguably as much the result of a new international tide as it was the fault of fascism or its supposedly draconian censorship practices and collateral self-censorship. This is a complex issue I am unable to treat adequately here, and yet, on this front, too, there are some illuminating statistics. When Mussolini took Italy's helm, preventive censorship already existed; local prefects decided the fate of shows as companies traveled across the peninsula. The centralization of the task under the Ministry of the Interior (in 1931, after nine years in power) often stands as a symbol of the regime's nefarious intentions, even if the principal goal was increased efficiency, requested by the thespians whose humors and budgets were stressed by such uncertainty and inconsistency. Although the changes may well have resulted in greater rigor, it is the means, rather than the meat, that for the most part distinguishes fascist censorship from that which came before and after. A true comprehension of the tangible effects of censorship on performance can only be grasped by a study of reviews and extant scripts. Still, the statistics alone, kept for the duration of censor Leopoldo Zurlo's tenure (1931–43), help contextualize claims about his work that are typically based on what fascist censorship regulations said, rather than what Zurlo actually did.[31]

A first striking piece of information is that approximately 90.6 percent of scripts submitted received the "visa" permitting its performance or radio broadcast. Likewise surprising, especially in light of comedy's undeniably subversive potential and Mussolini's legendary banning of Napoleon in shirtsleeves from the stage, is the information found in figure 11.[32]

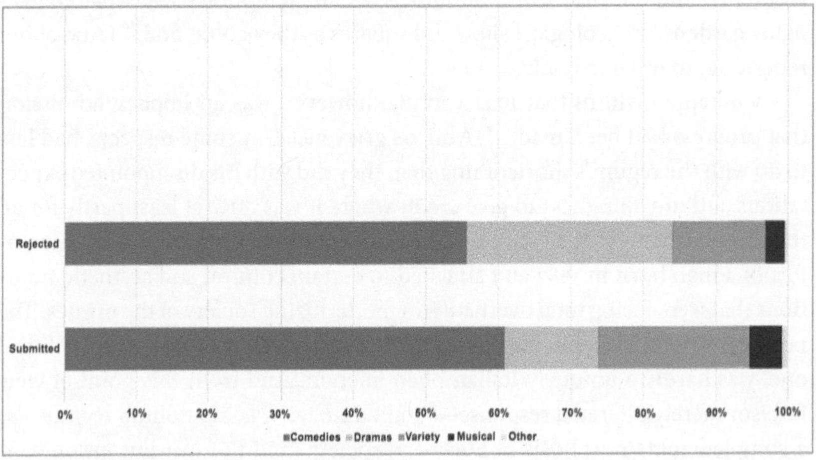

Figure 11. Scripts submitted and rejected by genre

Various types of comic performance (comedies, musical comedies, and variety acts) composed 81.67 percent of submissions received but only 68.52 percent of those rejected, whereas tragedy and drama accounted for 12.94 percent of the total submissions but 28.48 percent—more than double—of those rejected. Scholars typically agree that "moral," rather than "political," concerns girded fascist regulations; and while I would suggest that the two are hardly so separable, these numbers support an argument that strictly political concerns were far from dominant in censorship practices, if only to the extent that the comedy and variety acts, which took more direct satirical aim at the regime, faced fewer restrictions than the dramatic works that represented a whole world view. Moreover, Mussolini and Zurlo, who worked together quite closely in the first few years of centralized censorship, agreed that an outlet was more efficacious than an iron fist.[33]

The numbers are also consistent with a morphing approach over time. When Zurlo's task fell under the umbrella of the Ministry of the Interior (essentially the police force), from 1931 to 1935, it was largely prohibitive; after it moved to what would finally be called the Ministry of Popular Culture, it was increasingly pedagogic. As figure 12 shows, under the Ministry of the Interior, the numbers read as follows: 87.13 percent scripts approved, 8.82 percent rejected, and 4.05 percent suspended; under the Ministry of Popular Culture, instead, 92.12 percent approved, 4.43 percent rejected, and 3.45 percent suspended. The increase in approved texts, and decrease in those rejected, is not a sign of greater openness but a symptom of the new logic, in which the censor himself worked with authors to revise scripts in ways that would make them less offensive to regulations (a labor whose documentation remains in the archives today and that Zurlo recounted in detail in a 1952 memoir).[34]

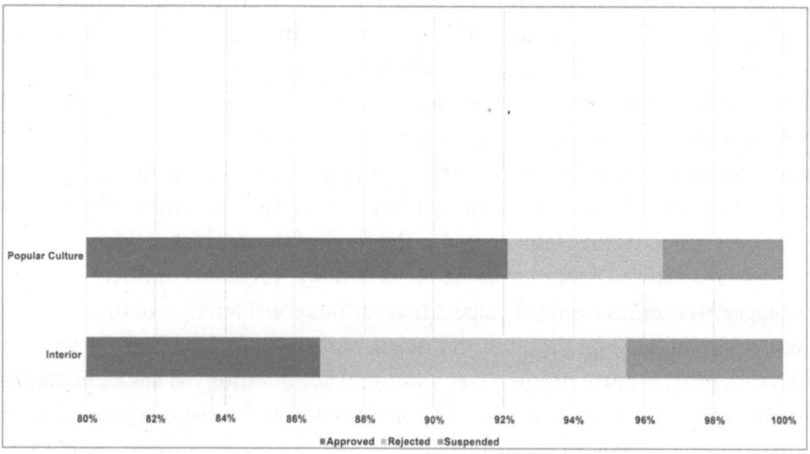

Figure 12. Censorship action

The complexity of the censorship process is underscored by the "suspended" texts, however few they were. These scripts were considered too problematic to be ruled upon; they were archived without decision in the hopes that those who submitted them would not follow through on the request. The reasons for such careful treading varied; one interesting case was when Shaw's *Augustus Does His Bit* was set aside: Shaw was liked by Mussolini and considered a "friend," but tense relations with England at times complicated the approach to his works and, indeed, made decisions on their appropriateness contingent on the most current political situation.[35] Rarely were rulings rubber-stamped: while Zurlo was not loyal to the fascist cause, he was a scrupulous public servant, respectful of the state apparatus, conditioned by the Catholic morality of his day and its sense of prudery, and, most importantly, a cultured individual who was interested in the "elevation" of the entertainment over which he presided. (He had been selected among prefects for the job because he had read "a few more books" than most, he demurred.[36] It is significant, in fact, that one of the few things D'Amico did not find fault with was Zurlo.) Censorship practice offers a prime example of the gray matter to be explored in a picture so often seen in black and white.

Although D'Amico and others, as was common for decades after fascism's fall, have attributed the survival of the theatre to the anti-fascism allowed to flourish in the very entities that produced the next generation of artists, today it seems more fruitful to acknowledge that there was real support on the part of Mussolini and his regime for the theatre, and not little to show for it. At the same time, as noted, statistics and studies of the production apparatus are not enough to tell the whole story of Mussolini and his regime's relationship with the theatrical arts. Political-institutional and aesthetic questions must be explored at one and the same time. That rarely happens, and this is why one specialist who published a thorough study in 1994 could argue that state support required of the performance industry "an almost total submission to the government's will" while conceding that "we still know little about what theatre was performed during fascism."[37] On the level of theatre history, this is unfortunate, as a creative vibrancy in the 1920s and 1930s remains undiscovered. But a bigger loss comes from the impact that serious consideration of theatre of the *ventennio* can have on the study of fascism *tout court*. A close study of this production provides new perspectives on several key questions in fascist historiography: consent, or the dichotomy of collaboration and resistance; fascism's position toward vanguard experimentation (a question where theatre studies lag far behind other disciplines); the regime's apparent aesthetic eclecticism, held to be at odds with ideological consistency and, indeed, totalitarian governance; and especially the Benjaminian paradigm that distills fascism down to the aestheticization of politics, in contrast to the politicization of aesthetics that for the philosopher defined Communist approaches to art.[38] These are questions beyond the scope of this article. But they are pressing. Now more than ever, it behooves us to understand the ways and means of rousing people with theatre—on the left and on the right.

Notes

1. Silvio D'Amico, *Il teatro non deve morire* (Roma: Edizioni dell'Era Nuova, 1945), 61.
2. Patrizia Dogliani, *Il fascismo degli italiani: Una storia sociale* (Torino: UTET, 2008), 237. In general histories, claims range from the necessarily cursory but thus overly simplistic or inaccurate to the purposefully skewed and dismissive. If Dogliani's assessment represents the former, the most egregious example of the latter is probably Denis Mack Smith's best-selling biography *Mussolini* (New York: Vintage, 1982): for an instance of his manipulations of the record, see note 32. Likewise problematic, due both to superficiality of research and to methodological hiccups, is Mabel Berezin, "Organization of Political Ideology: Culture, State, and the Theatre in Fascist Italy," *American Sociological Review* 56, no. 5 (October 1991): 639–51. In a recent publication of stature like Cambridge University Press's *A History of Italian Theatre* (2006), Clive Griffith's "Theatre Under Fascism" seeks to provide a fairly balanced portrait of the epoch but still describes a "drying up of creative talents," going so far as to claim that "even the most politically sympathetic playwrights found it difficult to produce anything of real or lasting value" (346–47), while the author of "The March of the Avant-Garde," Donatella Fischer, writes, "Theatre at this time, apart from the work of Pirandello and Eduardo De Filippo, was very much a vehicle for political propaganda, or a means of mild entertainment" (287).
3. This, for example, was the case with D'Amico: while not a committed fascist, he had direct access to fascist and Vatican officials that certainly aided him in his career both under fascism and after its fall, when the Christian Democrat Party rose to leadership. In saying that Mussolini's regime had done more harm than good, he downplayed the benefits he had received. There were practical reasons for doing so: after the war, anyone who had held a government post under fascism was to be purged, but in practice many bureaucrats continued their careers. Among them was Nicola De Pirro, a good friend to D'Amico and the director general of theatre operations during and after Mussolini's tenure, operations whose basic character saw great continuity from fascist to Christian democrat rule (about which I have written in the *Teatro e Storia* special section "Teatri nel fascismo" cited in note 28). As head of the National Academy of Dramatic Arts, D'Amico was in an analogous situation as a layman: he held great power in an institution created by the regime, but it was not in many people's interest to displace him, an extraordinarily capable and respected thespian, or to dismantle the training center that had served the up-and-coming generation of theatre artists so well.
4. Representative of a persistent refusal to acknowledge the existence of a fascist culture, upon which any productive assessment of the individual arts must be based, is Enrico Ghidetti's preface to *Cultura e fascismo: Letterature, arti, e spettacolo di un Ventennio*, ed. Marino Biondi and Alessandro Borsotti (Firenze: Ponte alle Grazie, 1990). Turning to works specifically interested in the theatre, the difficulty of approaching the period with a different guiding perspective is indicated by the very fact that the only major monographs published in Italy in the last three decades or so, Emanuela Scarpellini's *Organizzazione teatrale e politica del teatro nell'Italia fascista* (Firenze: La Nuova Italia, 1989) and Gianfranco Pedullà's *Il teatro italiano nel tempo del fascismo* (Bologna: Il Mulino, 1994), both look to legislative and organizational issues rather than to aesthetic questions, with

results I note in the conclusion to this essay. Both studies are meticulous but, even when the analysis suggests a more complex picture, generally seek to underscore that the regime, in Scarpellini's words, "aimed at direct and indirect control of all theatrical manifestations," being "interested primarily in [their] economic and strictly political aspects" (xv).

5. In fact, the theatre is hardly a blip on the radar in two of the better and more comprehensive recent analyses of fascist culture: Ruth Ben-Ghiat, *Fascist Modernities: Italy, 1922–1945* (Berkeley: University of California Press, 2001), and Alessandra Tarquini, *Storia della cultura fascista* (Bologna: Il Mulino, 2011).
6. Mario Verdone, "Mussolini's 'Theatre of the Masses,'" in *Fascism and Theatre: Comparative Studies on the Aesthetics and Politics of Performance in Europe, 1925–1945*, ed. Günther Berghaus (Providence, RI: Berghahn, 1996), 134. In the book's eloquent leadoff essay, to give some examples of details, top historian and theorist of fascism Roger Griffin notes that the fascists "were bound to pay closer attention" to cinema than theatre (23), whereas Doug Thompson champions the notion that "rigorous" self-denial "led to a safe but frequently dull repertoire" (103). In his brief introduction, Berghaus addresses some of the volume's shortcomings and gaps and underscores its utility in signaling an area worthy of further research—a call that, as is evident, has yet to be fruitfully answered.
7. This paper has been modified from a much longer version, originally published as "Lo spettacolo del fascismo" in *Atlante della letteratura italiana*, vol. 3, ed. Sergio Luzzatto and Gabriele Pedullà (Torino: Einaudi, 2012), 589–613. Its maps are reproduced here with the kind permission of Casa Editrice Einaudi. The primary statistics sources used for that essay and its graphics are *Annali del fascismo*, [s.n], Roma (1931–1943); Opera Nazionale Dopolavoro, *Annuario dell'Opera Nazionale Dopolavoro* (Novara: Istituto geografico DeAgostini, 1937–1939); Nicola De Pirro, *Il teatro per il popolo* (Roma: Novissima, 1938); Società Italiana degli Editori ed Autori, *Lo Spettacolo in Italia: Annuario statistico* (Roma: SIAE, 1936–1942) and *La vita dello spettacolo in Italia nel decennio 1924–1933* (Roma: SIAE, 1934); ISTAT, *Annuario Statistico Italiano* (Roma: Istituto Poligrafico dello Stato, 1922–1945). In many cases, the final data tabulations are the result of my cross-referencing and calculation. For the same volume, I also completed an analogous study of futurism, "Lo spettacolo del futurismo," 408–22.
8. See D'Amico, *Teatro*, 52, and Vittorio Mussolini, interview with Dario Zanelli, "Mio padre, semmai, amava il teatro," in *Il cinema dei dittatori: Mussolini, Stalin, Hitler*, ed. Renzo Renzi et al., 43 (Bologna: Grafis, 1992).
9. Vito Zagarrio, "Schizofrenie del modello fascista," in *Storia del cinema italiano*, vol. 5 (Venezia: Marsilio, 2006).
10. For a recent and engaging study of the propagandistic "Empire" films produced in this period, see Ruth Ben-Ghiat, *Italian Fascism's Empire Cinema* (Bloomington: Indiana University Press, 2015).
11. See Antonella Ottai, *Eastern: La commedia ungherese sulle scene italiane fra le due guerre* (Roma: Bulzoni, 2010).
12. Marla Stone's *The Patron State: Culture and Politics in Fascist Italy* (Princeton: Princeton University Press, 1998) is representative of this approach.
13. Doug Thompson, for one, acknowledges that the regime "was highly successful in

promoting the idea and the reality of theatre among the working classes, where hitherto it had been the exclusive preserve of the better-off." "The Organisation, Fascistisation, and Management of Theatre in Italy, 1925–43," in *Fascism and Theatre*, 94–112, 107.

14. Mussolini's passion for the theatre is a central concern of my forthcoming monograph, which is the major fruit of the larger project I mention at the start of this essay. The book uses Mussolini as a pivot point, aiming to overcome some of the further divisions that characterize the theatrical (and even literary) studies of the period that too often split their investigations in half, exploring political-institutional questions or aesthetic ones but rarely both at the same time.
15. D'Amico, *Teatro*, 78.
16. Gianfranco Pedullà, *Il teatro italiano*, 145.
17. For a swift overview of the regime's ambivalence toward propaganda, see Pietro Cavallo, "Theatre Politics of the Mussolini Regime and Their Influence on Fascist Drama," in *Fascism and Theatre*, 112–32.
18. International theatrical exchange in Italy prior to and during fascism is the subject of a special dossier, "L'anticipo italiano," *Teatro e Storia* XXII (2008).
19. The SIAE speech is referenced in both Thompson and Cavallo. The original can be found in Benito Mussolini, *Opera Omnia*, vol. 44, ed. Edoardo and Duilio Susmel, 35 vols. (Firenze: La Fenice, 1951–63), 49–50. Some scholars, like Gianfranco Pedullà, argue that this call to represent the times was in itself a call to create propaganda. But such an interpretation is not in line with many other statements and actions; and regime officials' doubts about propaganda, as noted, are well documented. Mussolini himself preferred art that was not explicitly political but in which he found traces of fascist thought (this is why Pirandello appealed to him: as he notoriously had stated it, Pirandello writes fascist plays "without even wanting to").
20. Hailed as a response to Mussolini's call for a theatre of the masses, the program, begun in 1936, boasted 198,970 spectators in the first few months of the 1937 season. The opening performances in Rome, of Aldo De Benedetti's comedy *Two Dozen Red Roses*, accommodated six thousand OND members but reportedly had to send away seventeen thousand other requests, to be fulfilled at future performances.
21. Antonella Ottai's *Come a concerto: Il Teatro Umoristico nelle scene degli anni trenta* (Roma: Bulzoni, 2002), a study of the famed De Filippo siblings' work under fascism, is especially helpful here; also worthwhile are the individual case studies in *Ariel* 2–3 (1993): Sergio Raffaelli, "Mussolini contro il teatro dialettale romangnolo" (139–45), and Mariateresa Zoppello, "Teatro Veneto e censura fascista" (195–206). See also Patricia Gaborik, "Un dialetto nazionale," in *Atlante della letteratura italiana*, vol. 3, ed. Sergio Luzzatto and Gabriele Pedullà, 220–26 (Torino: Einaudi, 2012).
22. For an overview, see Victoria De Grazia, *The Culture of Consent: Mass Organization of Leisure in Fascist Italy* (Cambridge: Cambridge University Press, 1982), chapter 6.
23. Jeffrey T. Schnapp, *Staging Fascism: 18BL and the Theater of Masses for Masses* (Stanford: Stanford University Press, 1996), 21. This monograph is a model study for an approach to fascist theatrical production that works across political-aesthetic boundaries.
24. Paolo Orano, *I Carri di Tespi dell'O.N.D* (Roma: Pinciana, 1937), 19.
25. Anton Giulio Bragaglia, *Il teatro della rivoluzione* (Roma: Edizioni Tiber, 1929), 6–14.

26. Orano, *Carri*, 63.
27. Orano, *Carri*, 63.
28. The pre- and interwar periods also were marked by strong tensions between actors and actor-managers, on the one hand, and playwrights, on the other: the actors who had achieved fame in a star system with a much more histrionic style faced completely unfamiliar challenges in new dramaturgy; and actor-managers and playwrights vied for power in an ever-evolving production system. The relational dynamics, of course, changed a great deal as Mussolini's government increased its control of the sector. Mirella Schino offers an important perspective on such struggles in her preface to the special section of *Teatro e Storia* 38 (2017), "Teatri nel fascismo," eds. Mirella Schino et al.
29. D'Amico, *Teatro*, 177.
30. Patricia Gaborik, "Italy: the Fancy of a National Theatre?" in *National Theatres in a Changing Europe*, ed. S. E. Wilmer (Basingstoke, UK: Palgrave, 2008), 138–150.
31. Particularly problematic in this regard is the Berezin article referred to in note 2.
32. In *Mussolini*, British historian Denis Mack Smith recounted in imprecise (and sometimes downright inaccurate), exaggerated, and condescending tones Mussolini's control of censorship, which, according to Mack Smith, resulted in the immediate banning of "the least hint of satire," and thus plays like Shaw's *Caesar and Cleopatra* because Caesar (like Mussolini) was bald, or plays depicting private moments of great leaders like Napoleon (179). Since then, quality research on censorship has been done, although a tendency to frame the complicated details with caricatured descriptions of the general approach persists—despite rather well-founded arguments by scholars like Antonella Ottai that fascist censorship was less stringent than even Hollywood's Hays Code (*Eastern* 207–10). A good recent study, though the section on the theatre is brief, is Guido Bonsaver, *Censorship and Literature in Fascist Italy* (Toronto: University of Toronto Press, 2007).
33. A wiretapped conversation between Mussolini and censor Leopoldo Zurlo on this very issue is reproduced in Ugo Guspini, *L'Orecchio del regime: Le intercettazioni telefoniche al tempo del fascismo* (Milano: Mursia, 1973), 123.
34. Patrizia Ferrara, *Censura teatrale e fascismo (1931–1944). La storia, l'archivio, l'inventario* (Roma: Ministero per i beni e le attività culturali, 2004), 103. Zurlo self-deprecatingly titled his volume "Useless Memories," in homage to eighteenth-century playwright Carlo Gozzi, who had done the same. *Memorie Inutili. La censura teatrale nel ventennio* (Roma: Edizioni dell'Ateneo, 1952).
35. This is a story yet to be recounted, relying as it does on evidence in the Zurlo archive. It, too, is treated in my forthcoming monograph.
36. Zurlo, *Memorie*, 16.
37. Gianfranco Pedullà, *Teatro*, 38, 42.
38. Regarding vanguardism, and in particular the regime's bolstering of the art of direction, see my article, "*Il Duce*'s Directors: Art Theaters as Instruments of the Fascist Revolution," in *Vanguard Performance Beyond Left and Right*, ed. Kimberly Jannarone, 37–59 (Ann Arbor: University of Michigan, 2015).

To Image and to Imagine

Walid Raad, Rabih Mroué, and the Arab Spring

—ILINCA TODORUȚ AND ANTHONY SORGE

From the "I" to the "We"

In 2010, contemporary arts museum BAK in Utrecht, the Netherlands, curated Rabih Mroué's first solo exhibition, referencing the achievement of a theatre artist breaking into the fine art circuit with the exhibit's playful title wavering between self-celebratory and self-effacing: *I, the Undersigned.* A few months into the exhibit, Mroué crossed out with a bold red line the big lettered title displayed on the pristine white gallery wall and graffitied in cursive Arab lettering underneath: "The People Are Demanding." The slogan had just begun circulating among demonstrating crowds first in Tunisia and then in Algeria, Jordan, Yemen, and Egypt, in a wave of protests that soon came to be named in the media as the Arab Spring. With a single gesture, Mroué drew a line underneath his previous work and hinted at beginning a new chapter. The move from the "I" to the "we" underscored an intent to recalibrate forms and temporalities in a shifted focus from past memories to future aspirations—from an obsession with parsing and (de)ciphering a long history of civil war in Lebanon and marking the present with the signs of trauma to a collective effort to move beyond ghosts and traces to imagine what can happen in an approaching future.

In the same year, Walid Raad, another Lebanese artist who also challenges disciplinary boundaries made similar surveying gestures upon a body of work that seemed to have reached completion. Unlike his *Atlas Group* work, which focused primarily on the Lebanese wars of 1975 to 1991, Raad's current ongoing project, *Scratching on Things I Could Disavow* (which he initiated in 2007) finds Raad shifting his gaze forward, attempting to open "'communication' with the artists of the future" who might emerge out of the "rich yet thorny ground" shaped by conflicts like the Lebanese wars.[1] "Over the past few years, I have been fascinated by the emergence of new art museums, galleries, schools and cultural foundations in cities such as Abu Dhabi, Beirut, Cairo, Doha, Istanbul, Ramallah and Sharjah, among others," writes Raad as an introduction on the project website.[2] For Raad, part of this "communication" with the future involves reopening the lines of transmission between the past and the present, while recognizing that the lines are garbled with the "noise" that accompanies the "telepathic signals" heard across great expanses of time.[3] To this end, in 2010, Raad began *Index XXVI: Artists*, a subset project that collects and catalogs information on past Lebanese artists and invites audiences to correct the mistakes in the information on display, which Raad claims he received "by way of telepathy and/or thought insertion and/or using a future technology."[4] In playful, quasi-mystical language, Raad recounts how renowned dancers and local cooks corrected these mistakes with colorful spray-paint, only to reveal the intention of the future artists to "[distort] the names they communicated to me directly" in order to gain access to the colors of the spray-paint used for the corrections, which were unavailable to them in the future.[5] Like the larger project of which it is a part, *Index XXVI* projects history into a present in development that is moving toward a discernible future, crossing the line from the "I" to the "we" of a collective authorship that includes even the voices of the future.

The wave of popular uprisings in the Arab world that rippled out from Tunisia in 2010 shifted the focus of Mroué's and Raad's art toward a future they attempted to augur through the smoke and rubble of increasingly violent, protracted conflicts. "It was clear that I couldn't continue participating in exhibitions as if nothing was happening, and so the changes became somehow inevitable," Mroué wrote of his initial reaction to the revolutions. "The first thing that struck me was the rallying call from the Arab Spring, 'The People are Demanding.' … It is 'we' who are demanding—as Lebanese, as Arabs, or as unnamed 'people,' if you want."[6] The cry of "We, the People" cannot dissimulate its democratic aspirations as a search for the reestablishment of the agency of common people robbed of their lives, histories, and future over the course of decades of conflicts in regions of North Africa and the Middle East. Democratic—a term that should be deloused of imperialist demagogy—is a useful adjective to describe shifts in subject matter, conceptual frameworks, and points of departure for the two Lebanese artists.

This essay examines how the Lebanese civil war and the Arab Spring inform Raad's and Mroué's continued questioning of visual information, archival remains, and image dissemination as they relate to the project of documenting and producing history. Raad's *Scratching on Things I Could Disavow* and Mroué's performance *The Pixelated Revolution* (2012) find the artists training the lenses they developed during the Lebanese civil war on the fraught revolutions of the Arab Spring and their implications for politics and art in the world at large.

While Raad's and Mroué's bodies of work are substantial, this essay focuses on the following, arranged in chronological order:

Walid Raad
The Atlas Group:
Missing Lebanese Wars (1998)
Hostage: The Bachar Tapes (2001)
I Think It Would Be Better if I Could Weep (2002)
Already Been in a Lake of Fire (2003)
Scratching on Things I Could Disavow: Section 88_Act XXXI: Views from Outer to Inner Compartments (2010)
Index XXVI: Artists (2010)
Preface to the Third Edition (2012–2015)

Rabih Mroué
Come in Sir, We Will Wait for You Outside (1998)
Three Posters (2000)
Secrets in the Open Sea (2004)
I, the Undersigned (2011)
Biokhraphia (2012)
The Pixelated Revolution (2012)

A Shared Project

Walid Raad's and Rabih Mroué's works are rarely discussed in conjunction with each other, even though the generation of Lebanese artists emerging in the 1990s comprises a nexus of friendships, collaborations, and shared artistic interests. Mroué's essay "What Has Slipped Away Is So Far, and What Is Yet to Come So Close," in which Mroué makes a case for the democratic, liberatory power of a theatre that "reconfigures legal paradigms," appears in Eyad Houssami's anthology *Doomed by Hope: Essays on Arab* Theatre (2012).[7] Stephen Barber's *Performance Projections: Film and Body in Action* (2014) places Mroué's *Pixelated Revolution* in the context of other examples of civilian documentation of moments of political upheaval, from Super-8 films of protests in 1960s Tokyo to the frenzied footage of Muammar Gaddafi's assassination.[8] Laura U. Marks's *Hanan Al-Cinema: Affections for the Moving Image* (2015) unfolds the erotics of *The Pixelated Revolution*: the "attitude of vulnerability, of opening oneself to the unknown" that Mroué, like many of the archival artists Marks discusses in the text, models and encourages from his audience.[9] In *Terror and Performance* (2014), Rustom Bharucha inserts Mroué's *Three Posters* into a broader discussion of the performativity of the suicide bomber and Mahatma Gandhi's performance of nonviolence.[10] Walid Raad's name is all but absent from these texts, but Eva Respini's 2015 catalog of Raad's work for the Museum of Modern Art, a thorough and illuminating survey of Raad's *Atlas Group* and *Scratching …* projects, similarly makes no mention of Mroué.

The main reason for this blind spot is that Raad's work is presented and subsequently discussed in gallery contexts by art historians, critics, and curators, while Mroué displays his work primarily on the theatre scene, and therefore he is written about by people active in this field. This compartmentalization discourages the task of analyzing their works as invested in the same issues. The two artists approach the same concerns from different entry points only to arrive at strikingly similar results, not only in subject matter but also in aesthetics and manner of presentation. One obvious similarity is that both have arrived at the presentational model of performance as lecture or artist talk. The two artists have been much more adept at circumambulating boundaries than have institutionally affiliated scholars. Take the example of Raad's most famous project, *The Atlas Group*, which spans a host of subprojects: its material and immaterial products were designed from the start to function in multiple formats, mediums, and venues and existed simultaneously as prints, images, and text blocks to be exhibited in galleries, published on the web, printed in books and journals, and projected and enunciated as performances in theatres, classrooms, and lecture halls. His creation of a foundation named the Atlas Group, a fictitious research organization, fits uneasily between the parameters of conceptual art, performance, historiography, and social practice. "It is difficult enough for me to define the physical limits of some of my works," confesses Raad, "let alone trying to parse the works into their experiential, aesthetic, conceptual, political, critical, personal and historical aspects."[11] The performance part of the project—presenting the images and videos in a lecture setting—has been an important aspect of the work, serving to place and contextualize the visual and material objects in the larger Atlas Group project of reusing and fictionalizing found material or generating and fabricating it to deconstruct and reflect on Lebanese history, trauma, and identity. Through engaging storytelling, the performative lecture suffuses the visual material to be later put on display with a distinct auratic quality. The "fake" archive is given a history, without which it would remain mere snapshot.

Conversely, authentic archival artifacts and visual material are almost invariably integrated in Mroué's performances. *Come in Sir, We Will Wait for You*

Outside, staged in Beirut in 1998, incorporates projected images and sounds (e.g., "pictures of Palestine before the *Nakba*, accompanied by Fayruz's song *O Wooden Bridge*"), video pieces played on TVs onstage (such as "The Lebanese flag flapping in the wind for approximately 3 and a half minutes"), and live feed of performers sitting at desks equipped with lamps.[12] It has been widely noted how the unglamorous setting of desk or table, with the banal chair, sometimes a lamp and a glass of water, are the trademark props in Raad's lectures. Yet here are the same tables, chairs, and lamps appearing as early as 1998 in Tony Chakar and Mroué's piece, which suggest that, like so many other characteristics, the presentational setting is a collective find with diffuse origins linked to the generation of 1990s Lebanese artists.

In *Come in Sir, We Will Wait for You Outside*, a performance that also names itself a presentation, the familiar desk and lamp reveal further connotations intrinsic to the context of Lebanon.[13] When three actors each turn on the lamps, rotate them to shine the bright light in their eyes, and turn on the video cameras to broadcast their faces on the onstage TVs, the tableau sparks with connotations of surveillance and interrogation. The impromptu broadcasting evokes a particular type of TV-messaging in times of war and of propaganda: speeches, abduction tapes, martyr tapes. Both Raad and Mroué regularly hint at this mass-mediatized political use of the image, most directly in works such as the Atlas Group's *Bachar Tapes* and Mroué's *Three Posters*. An obsessive concern with the production and reception of images lodges itself at the very core of both Raad's and Mroué's work, indissociable from the Lebanese context during the years of the civil war, from 1975 to 1991. During this time, a peculiar politics of image in the media aimed to manipulate viewers' perceptions of reality. The particularity of the milieu resulted in the prevalent theme of a reality fabricated though images, of the inextricability of fact from fiction and (mis)representation from reality. *Come in Sir, We Will Wait for You Outside* makes a convincing case for exposing the ontological duplicity of mechanically and digitally recorded images. "Television is too fast. I refuse to understand," runs the line just before images of a man are shown on screens while the actors verbally resist and contradict the signifying power of the image in a manner reminiscent of René Magritte's pipe painting: "This is not a Palestinian," or even "This is not a man."[14] The game has higher stakes than the familiar-sounding aesthetic disputes over representation, intimated when the TV shows images from the Sabra and Shatila massacres of 1982, when upward of 3,500 Palestinians and Lebanese Shiites were killed by an Israeli-backed right-wing militia in and around the Shatila refugee camp in Beirut, from the Armenian holocaust carried out by the Ottoman government from 1915 to 1923, and from Nazi concentration camps.

As Laura U. Marks puts it, archival materials like the images and film clips used in Raad's and Mroué's work are always "discursively framed, sometimes to such a violent degree that they seem to almost erase the past event they record. . . . One has to go digging in the image." Decontextualizing and recontextualizing these images reminds the viewer of this discursive framing and what it leaves out while drawing attention to the plentiful "perceptibles" waiting to be found within an image by the eye that is encouraged to "look askance."[15] Political contexts, along with the politics of representation, inform Raad's and Mroué's aesthetic manipulations of images, even if the Lebanese landscapes, situations, and events merely provide the silent backdrop to apparently innocuous images, such as setting suns filmed over Beirut's seaside promenade in Atlas Group's *I Think It Would Be Better if I Could Weep*.[16] Both Raad and the anonymous Lebanese army intelligence officer who provided the film used in this piece model this method of "looking askance," along with its potentially subversive political dimensions. "From 1997 on," Raad explains, "the officer decided to videotape the sunset instead of his assigned target. This videotape recounts the operator's story and concentrates on the footage he was permitted to keep after his dismissal."[17] While the thought of a soldier choosing to focus on natural beauty rather than the horrors of war might evoke some platitudes about the triumph of the human spirit in the face of atrocity, Raad resists such impulses, insisting on the significance of the act of *choosing* images, rather than the images themselves. "I just woke up and the weather in the mountains is beautiful," Raad wrote to a friend during Israel's attack on Lebanon in 2006. "The weather again: the best way to naturalize a disaster, to think of something else to write, to think, and to feel."[18]

A similar scene in Mroué's *Come in Sir*, a comparably straightforward and simple critique of image manipulation, gives the public a lesson in "the way to shoot a dramatic scene," by manipulating found visual material, decontextualizing it, and setting it in a different, fabricated context.[19] In this performance, lively traditional music plays over a black-and-white montage of scenes from Palestine before the Israeli occupation, before the TV monitors begin to convulse in seizures of flickering, distorted images culled from footage shot during the occupation. Shots of a grandmother figure wiping sweat from her brow at a family dinner are cut from the reel, magnified, put in slow motion, and emotionalized with a music score. The result renders the old woman as if she's crying: a posterized image of the iconic innocent victim. However, "a picture prevents you from seeing," wryly warns the performance. While this contextualization of the footage of this woman almost demands a specific emotional and political response from the viewer, the chorus of actors addressing the audience from the TV monitors following this footage suggests otherwise. "This is not our contribution in liberating Palestine," one actor informs the audience. "You are not watching us. We are watching ourselves," the next explains. Just as the anonymous intelligence officer models an alternate way of seeing his reality, of digging in an image, of peeking beyond its frame, of attempting to perceive that from which one's eyes have been averted—choosing to look at a sunset rather than his "target"—these three pairs of eyes watch themselves, or representations of themselves in the form of the Palestinian men and women in the footage, to encourage the same kind of critical, intentional viewing from the audience. "Stay where you are. Palestine will not be liberated," the third televised head explains, as much a warning as an instruction: "Liberation," Mroué suggests, requires a change of one's position, one's orientation, a "looking askance" at what is in front of you to "liberate" that which is held captive, though never fully invisible, within the repressive confines of the discursive framing.[20]

Three Posters by Mroué and Elias Khoury, devised and performed in 2000 in Beirut, focuses on a particularly astounding practice of image broadcasting during the civil war period, namely the martyr tapes aired on Tele-Liban, the public television channel. The performance was conceptualized after discovering the unedited recordings of resistance fighter and Communist party member Jamal Sati, who in 1985 carried out a suicide mission against the occupying Israeli Army. The recording shows Jamal Sati trying out different versions of his speech and negotiating his performance, revealing the moments of uncertainty and hesitation that were edited out of the broadcast message. Mroué exposes the fabrication by first performing himself three versions of a martyr speech visible onstage through a live feed on a TV while he is hidden from view. At first, the visual document seems authentic, filmed as a "period piece," in combat costume and against the background of posters and images from the 1980s. But when the door of the filming booth opens, and the audience glimpses the inside of the recognizable setting, the fabrication is exposed. "Fiction intermingled with reality; from this moment on, the audience was led to question everything that followed," writes Mroué in the introduction to the published piece.[21] The audience, now trained by that revelation to be critical in their reception, is subsequently shown the three versions of Jamal Sati's authentic martyr speech. After the lesson in discernment, spectators are more capable of capturing the subtle mechanisms that draw attention to the manipulations of reality made visible in the video document. The authority of the image, of so-called unquestionable evidence, served to the populace on the eight o'clock news (when the martyr tapes were aired on Tele-Liban) falls to pieces. "The video demanded that we consider the limits of truth and its representations" by destabilizing the authority of the image. "This threw radically into question the status of the video as a record, a representation," leading to the realization that image and representation carried more weight and political power than the real, which faded behind the screen of images. In the case of Jamal Sati, "the video was more important than his actual mission," and the record of his death more valuable than his actual death.[22]

The question posed by Mroué about "how an artwork can be critical of the notion of 'truth,' while claiming to convey 'truth,' but at the same time 'being a fabrication of truth'" is taken on by Raad in the same context of broadcast messages one year later, in 2001, in *Hostage: The Bachar Tapes*.[23] The sixteen-minute testimonial video of Souheil Bachar recounts experiences from being the sole Arab protagonist in "The Western Hostage Crisis," held in captivity "for 3 months in 1985 in the same cell as five American men: Terry Anderson, Thomas Sutherland, Benjamin Weir, Martin Jenco, and David Jacobsen," as stated in the descriptive blurb of the project.[24] While the much-mediatized hostage crisis is an event that some of us might remember, and the names of the imprisoned combatants are real ones (even the short-termed presence of an Arab among them seems to be a historical fact), "Souheil Bachar" is a character played by an actor, and the testimonial tape is an Atlas Group fictional document. But in the context in which the video weighs more heavily than the referenced event, as the main agent impacting reality, the fictionalized real Jamal Sati and the realized fiction Souheil Bachar objectively reach a dangerously equal ontological plane of realness. In fact, Bachar, even as a work of fiction, imparts to the viewer more authentic knowledge on the recounted event than the edited, manipulated, and performed recoding of Jamal Sati that played on Tele-Liban.

A frustratingly theatricalized reality—one in which everything from state-sanctioned news media to suicide bombers' carefully rehearsed video testimonials offers a performance of ostensible truth-telling—leads Lina Saleh playing the "Artist" in Mroué's *Biokhraphia* (2002) to unequivocally declare, "I reject theatre and all things related to theatre."[25] Another exploration of the real persona behind layers and screens of representation (literally materialized onstage through transparent screens serving as projection surfaces, which will evocatively be filled with a milky liquid to render images blurry), *Biokhraphia* makes the Lebanese subject lament the manipulation through image happening on TV: "I believed in it. A lot of my friends were martyred."[26] The anti-theatrical sentiment wails against the cheap, but simultaneously painfully real, melodrama of the civil war. "If I had brought a cameraman, and we had actually shot what happened, it would have been a great performance," the Artist tells an interviewer (also played by Saleh) as she recounts a confrontation with the militia.[27] In an antimelodramatic move, the Artist aspires to the leveling of theatrical action, wherein every minute and quotidian action, event, and artifact turn into carriers of meaning: "It's enough that someone does something … anything. For example, someone passing by … crossing the street and another person is watching… . This act, in itself, is enough to be theatre."[28] Just as *Biokhraphia* mocks and destabilizes the familiar formats of the documentary and the artist interview, calling attention to their theatrical nature as their subject rails against the theatre, Raad's Atlas Group lectures, with their familiar academic trappings undermined by pre-planned technical difficulties, scripted questions from the audience, and Raad's ever-thickening Lebanese accent, function on the premise that the images presented are inherently theatrical, showing traces of a lived reality that has become complexly theatricalized.

Despite his efforts to highlight the theatrical, performative, and, indeed, fictive elements of his *Atlas Group* work, the visual allure of the documents in these pieces, coupled with Raad's convincing performance of scholarly authority figure, invariably leads some segments of his audience to believe in the authenticity of the facts, histories, and documents presented. As Eva Respini puts it, the success of the *Atlas Group* project "hinges on our need to believe in official narratives."[29] These seemingly "official" narratives, no matter how blatantly theatricalized or fabricated, offer to quench the audience's thirst for truth, especially for those in the audience who might not have experienced the realities of the Lebanese civil war, shattered in contending sides (Raad refers to the period only in plural, as "Lebanese civil wars").[30] However, in the civil war context, the archive stands not as a record of historical truth but as the institutionalization of lies; those who try to drink from that fountain will find themselves only further dehydrated.

A crucial dimension of Lebanese daily life in the 1990s was the loss of a noncentralized, private archive recording life before the civil war. In a 2002 article titled *Le Feu! Histoires de Beyrouth* published in Canadian art magazine *Parachute*, Mroué evokes the incineration of Lebanese memory and identity contained in privately held books, letters, postcards, magazines, journals, and photographs—all burned to ashes as a preventive and protective measure in the face of the Israeli occupation. The portrait resembles the old war tactics of invaded people, who react to the threat of a much bigger invading force by setting fire to their crops and lands before retreating in impoverishment, relegating themselves to inheriting their own self-imposed amnesia:

> Tout fut rassemblé, jeté, et brulé. Tout le monde brulait ses documents: sur les toits, les balcons, dans les rues… . Des mots qui brulaient, illuminant les nuits de Beyrouth plongées alors dans l'obscurité à cause de la guerre. Beyrouth essayait de cacher son histoire politique, en effaçant toute trace, tout document qui pourrait être d'une utilité quelconque au Mossad israélien. Mais ainsi, elle effaçait aussi

> une partie essentielle de son histoire … ainsi que les détails de sa vie quotidienne, privée et individuelle.
>
> Everything was collected, thrown out, and burned. Everybody burned their documents: on rooftops, in their balconies, on the streets. . . . Words on fire illuminated the nights of Beirut, a city thrown into obscurity because of the war. Beirut tried to hide its political history by erasing all trace, all documentations that could have been useful in any way to the Israeli Mossad. Only this way, the city also erased an essential part of its history … as well as the details of its private and individual daily life.[31]

In the hollowed-out history, the contending factions during the civil wars filled the vacuum with a programmatic policy of image making, archive production, and reality manufacture. The broadcast martyr testimonies previously discussed constitute one exemplary practice. "Videotaping resistance fighters testifying before executing their suicide missions was a common event of the time," wrote Mroué in the prefatory note to *Three Posters* about this almost surreal use of the public image.[32] A politics of image production and dissemination becomes an integral part of war reality: "When the resistance films its operations, it's to prove their existence. Because, in their opinion, one can't be real unless one's captured on film."[33] Carrying out a military operation means to "conquer, raise the flag, film the event, withdraw."[34] In other words, producing the image of victory and power equates to having power, irrespective of the events, deaths, and victims themselves. Reality, the operation's actual impact, gets lost behind its representation.

A fabricated war archive contaminates the public sphere and disseminates through the physical city and the media: "One day, suddenly, we would see the poster of a friend hung on the walls of Beirut, or a photograph or video on the TV announcing his or her death."[35] Raad explains that *Secrets in the Open Sea* was inspired by the oddity of "the appearance in early 1990s Lebanese newspapers of scores of tiny black-and-white group portrait photographs," while *Already Been in a Lake of Fire* "developed in response to the coverage by Lebanese newspapers, which typically dispatched photographers to record the location where each bomb's explosion had propelled the destroyed car's engine to land."[36] These incidents betray the relentless efforts of government officials to control reality through documentations.

Another front in the process of the fictionalization of reality is the coverage of the war in international media. Jayce Salloum's 1994 documentary *This Is Not Beirut* edits short clips from the many sensational news reporting on

Lebanon, collects the many names Beirut has been called through history and in the media, and presents the numerous conflicting views on the political situation. As Sarah Rogers points out, "throughout the 1970s and 1980s, the media declared Beirut a breeding ground for snipers, kidnappings, suicide bombers."[37] The film's *via negativa*, deconstructing to reject the plethora of plastered images and narratives on top of the city, cannot find what *is* Beirut. The viewer watches people in the video repeatedly attempting and failing to schematize a coherent picture of the civil war—who's fighting who, what are the factions, the allegiances, the political and religious sectarians—or an explanation of what being Lebanese means.

The multiple and layered manipulations in the hands of the many factions, secular political groups, and religious sectarians lead to a history of post–World War II Lebanon that seems impossible to parse through the thicket of representations. In Lebanese textbooks, history stops in 1946, "after a committee of historians repeatedly failed to produce a narrative of the war satisfactory to the country's sectarian factions."[38] The difficulties in parsing real from fabrication leads Raad to say in a *BOMB* interview that "the Lebanese civil war refers to an abstraction."[39] After decades of civil war, and layered heaps of misrepresentations, in ruins is not only the physical landscape but also the psychic buildup of its residents.

The poignant sense of mourning that the image Mroué painted of a Beirut illuminated by the fire of its own burning memory exudes can partly explain Raad's project of (re)creating and fabricating the types of documents that have been lost in the war. Facing the paucity of genuine documents, and the inadequacies of those extant, a sensible reaction to the lack of unadulterated documents is to invent them. Conjuring the existence of private and collective memories recorded in photographs, newspaper cutouts, diaries, and marginal notes is an effort to salvage Lebanese history and identity from the fire of passing time.

The imagined history surrounding many Atlas Group "found" documents evokes a sense of miraculous rescue and fortuitous occurrences: the Fakhouri files that extraordinarily survived the war and were donated to the Atlas Group, microscopic images unearthed from the rubble of Beirut (*Secrets in the Open Sea*), or an exceptional surveillance cameraman who for a few minutes a day disobeyed orders and produced a personal document (*I Think It Would Be Better if I Could Weep*). The desire to rescue memories, identities, and histories through salvaging images, documents, and archives is shared among artists in the region. These efforts aim toward the building of a counter-archive to the official discourses. Collectively founded in 1996, the Arab Image Foundation came into being as a reaction to the lack of authentic visual documents that can function as an archive for the history of the region. I say "authentic," because images themselves are not lacking.

But how are we to represent histories where there is no evidence remaining, no thread of continuity, but rather a fracture, a vacuum of erasure and amnesia? In 1991, the Lebanese government granted a much-debated general amnesty for war crimes, a gesture that betrays not only government corruption but also an effort to forget a traumatic past. How can unearthing or conjuring archival evidence of violence and trauma contest imposed amnesia, and how can it heal a present scarred by the past? Perhaps, Raad and Mroué seem to suggest, the act of constructing a past by assembling and creating images to fill the blanks, bullet holes, and craters in an official archive can prefigure the collective creation of the future.

Raad has referred to the images produced and exhibited in the Atlas Group archive as "hysterical documents," because they are imaginary documents standing as "fantasies erected from the material of collective memories."[40] Raad's projection of mental states onto documentary objects allows us to observe the connections between image, history, and trauma. Alan Gilbert construes even the manner of presentation as traumatic, since, he tells Raad, "the objects, individuals and histories represented in your work always elude direct representation, however obsessively you represent, follow or record them … the way trauma can rarely speak directly."[41] Achim Borchardt-Hume notices how Raad's work invokes post-traumatic amnesia "by way of its elusiveness, its circling around the event, by way of its dissociative and distant relation to a violent past, evoked but not foregrounded."[42] Sarah Rogers suggests that the use of performance comes out of a need for narration in the talking cure, tying the projects of the Atlas Group with the psychoanalytic treatment of traumatic memory and Freud's theoretical writings on hysterical symptoms.

Yet to some extent, all considerations of history are traumatic. While trauma might figure in the inquiry, the projects run much deeper, into questioning the possibility of ever being able to know and record history. As a landmine of contending and contradicting representations, history loses its solidity as fact, and what become foregrounded are the efforts and mechanisms themselves of recording and preserving history. These efforts are always, in all times and places, at least tinged with error, due to the very nature of archival acts. But civil war Lebanon is a time and place that makes the difficulties evident. Reality and its representations, historical events and their documentation, fact and fiction are not clear-cut binaries but undiscernibly comingled. Raad insists that "the Atlas Group produces and collects objects and stories that should not be examined through the conventional and reductive binary of fiction and nonfiction. . . . This distinction is a false one."[43] Mroué also suggests that his work is not primarily about unearthing or exposing a traumatic past or attempting a programmatic setting straight of history, since, as he writes: "I do not think my work is about a requirement to 'understand' things in the conventional meaning of the word."[44]

The uncertainty principle of historiography is nowhere more evocatively manifested than in the Atlas Group's *Missing Lebanese Wars*. The narrative behind the project's collection of images depicting racehorses close to the finishing line imagines a clique of historians gathering every Sunday at the races. The historians play the game of fortune among themselves, placing their bets not in the customary manner on horses but on marginal errors: who can get the closest millisecond approximation to correct the photographic document's error in portraying the winning moment, that is, the exact time when the horse touches the finish line. The image never shows a horse's snout *just* touching the finishing line; it shows it just before or right after the winning moment. Under each image, the historians' bets in milliseconds are arranged in order of accuracy. As André Lepecki observes, the newspaper cutouts of horses just before or just after crossing the finish line, with marginal notes recording the historiographical game of taking a chance with error, show how we "will always fail to document the passing of the instant that marks the event. . . . History seems never to be exactly where it is supposedly taking place."[45] In Raad's words, this "inability to be present at the passing of the present" is the main obstacle in writing and recording history.[46] The newspaper cutouts of horses just before or just after crossing the finishing line, a collection of "blurred, never-on-time, always-to-the-side images" represent unmanipulated and raw archival documents that do not hide their imperfections in recording the present.[47] The imperfections expose the seed of absurdity in the historical task of recording reality and the impossibility of completely catching the ever shifting and immaterial historical present in the fixed form of the document. The historical uncertainty principle is a product of the spatial and temporal limitations of the document, of the forever faulty recording mechanisms, and finally of the inherent biases of whomever does the recording. One description scribbled by Dr. Fakhouri about the winning historian reads: "Well, he was an evil man. Epochal and irrelevant at the same time." His version of history is doomed to be just as irrelevant, and maybe even "evil." As many winners, as many histories, suggests Raad.

Given the inherent error of documentation and embracing archival impossibilities, Raad's and Mroué's projects turn to examining "how history gets imaged and written."[48] By bypassing easy dichotomies of fact and fiction, their interest lies not in "images of war but in what war does to images."[49] Raad and

Mroué have nothing to say, only to show, in the belief that images do and undo reality. Their practice takes a critical stance toward the image, especially images officially produced through media channels, unsettling the ontological realness of the document as an unquestionable reproduction of reality.

If much of Mroué and Raad's work made in response to the Lebanese civil war challenges the official narratives of the past—theatricalized, reductive historical narratives sanctioned or created by the state, the academy, or other rigid institutions and passed off as "true"—their more recent work shows their response to a troubling provocation of the Arab Spring: What happens when the official narratives of the present and the future are disrupted? What new narratives can emerge in the fissures created by crumbling autocratic regimes, and in whose voices will they be told?

The Recorded Revolution, the Pixelated Future

The shift from the "I" to the "we," from critical examinations of a problematic past to a hopeful look into the future, involves an overcoming of the trauma paradigm. Mroué's *The Pixelated Revolution* evidences this shift, being a work that is so clearly indented in the overarching project of assessing the production of history through imagery and yet takes a clear turn toward a positive reassessment of the possibilities of a democratic and more truthful production of images and documents.

The lecture performance revolves around anonymous Syrian citizens who disseminate via social media (YouTube, Facebook, etc.) videos and images they shot with handheld devices (such as phone cameras) of the immediate, unadulterated situations of their violent reality. Tanks, bombings, and the people behind the guns doing the fatal kind of shooting appear recorded in fugitive clips. Mroué assumes that people are indiscriminately filming what they are seeing on the streets, without edits, producing a spool of images that does not lie: "The filming eye does not want the murderer to be granted amnesty in the future."[50] With such a democratized archive and direct evidence of aggressors, general amnesties and glazings over of oppression cannot be as easily achieved in the future. *The Pixelated Revolution*, in which the image becomes a weapon on the side of the aggressed, not an instrument of top-down reality manipulation, is not concerned with deciphering, writing, or rewriting history to reflect on the present but moves beyond historical trauma to talk in an unprecedentedly direct manner about the instantly recorded now.

In a fortuitous turn of events corroborated by ease of access to recording devices and means of disseminating information through the web, the 2012 performance represented the actualization and the incarnation of image producers that Raad and Mroué previously had only imagined. The democratization and decentralization of the production and dissemination of information facilitated by the "tools of today ... , new technologies, from digital cameras and mobile phones to the internet, wireless connection, and other devices," provide the material support in the writing of an "alternative history" or, in other words, a counter-archive.[51] A fiction come true, so to speak, *The Pixelated Revolution* stars actualized versions of the previously only imagined historians and the nonexistent documents that only years before Raad had to conjure in the *Atlas Group* project. The people on the streets of Beirut with cameras on their cell phones are all Dr. Fakhouris: "Between 1976–78, Dr. Fakhouri was in the habit of carrying a photographic camera wherever he went." The people in the streets documenting the present instinctually and without hidden motivations—besides the desire to show the world what they are seeing, recording so close to the instant that they document the unmistakable presence of shooting bullets—are all recording the historical moment as close to the horse's finishing line as possible.

Like the archival traces of more authentic documentation previously unearthed by Raad and Mroué, those "blurred, never-on-time, always-to-the-side images," the photos and videos produced by Syrian civilians resisting and documenting their own oppression are technically of low quality, are "pixelated," and betray the emotional state of the holder of handheld devices in shaky recordings.[52] Through their lack of official standards of archival quality, the images testify to their authenticity as counter-archive to the media-generated nicely shot images from tripods by professional image manipulators. "The importance of digital images and of their pixelated and low resolution resides in the fact that they originate outside of regulated systems and official institutions," says Mroué during the lecture, as contrasted to "those unshakable pictures ... highly suspicious and most probably untruthful and fabricated."[53] The nonprofessional methods of image production stand as testimony to the people's taking over of the archive. The people are armed with the weapons of affordable recording devices to create their own history.

As everyday users become distributors of archival content across an unregulated field of image sharing, the divides between amateurs and professionals, between passive masses and active citizens, crumble. Gaining control of the image can be a first step to accessing political agency. If a nation's level of democracy can be measured by its access to the archive, then the recent shaping of a movement of counter-archiving by recording what usually remains silenced and buried stands as a powerful act of resisting suppression. The counter-archive opens possibilities, because it arms people with the power to image and imagine, to resist and to at least shoot the criminal shooting.

On the other hand, crimes aren't stopped when "the Syrian protesters are [merely] recording their own deaths."[54] To imagine the act of image making as a weapon, and shooting a video as having the power to incapacitate the enemy, can be an artist-as-archivist utopia. The utopian dimension becomes problematic if "one is shooting with a camera and the other is shooting with a rifle"; there is, after all, still only one victim.[55] Mroué is aware of these limitations and chooses instead to focus on the practical teaching of "guerilla filmmaking," sharing a manifesto describing counter-archival methods of production and reception of documentary materials. With clarity and discernment, a precautionary note veers away from the utopian. "Wars and revolution happen by way of the image," says Mroué during the lecture, but "images alone are not enough to achieve victory."[56]

As in his *Come in Sir* performance, wherein an actor instructs and challenges the audience, "Stay where you are. Palestine will not be liberated," Mroué's comment about the limits of "images alone" underscores his insistence that his audience engage with the issues he presents in his art. "Showing a diagram that aligns the sniper, the recordist, and the viewer, [Mroué] argued that we who view the videos can prove that the recordists are not dead," Marks explains, recounting Mroué's *Pixelated Revolution* performance in Vancouver, British Columbia, in 2012. This "deeply ethical work of magical thinking … requires that those who view also act to prevent the killing and, even more, to bring the dead back to life."[57] Mroué makes this point even more emphatically in video loops in which the recordists collapse to the ground only to rise again as the film is reversed; even more explicitly, a series of flip-books allowed audience members to literally hold these recordists' lives in their hands, as they flipped back and forth to create animations of the videographers' deaths and resurrections while listening to their lo-fi recordings of gunfire and cellphones clattering to the ground. It is clear that for Mroué, "victory" in the context of a conflict like the Syrian civil war does not simply mean the replacement of one political system with another: it is also the victory of memory over erasure, of life over death, of possibility over circumscription, of the "we" over the "I." In other words, it is a victory for pixelization.

Pixelization, often the effect of enlarging or zooming in on a low-resolution image, results in the grainy blurriness that characterizes the videos and stills in Mroué's lecture-performance. Pixelization is often the result of amplification and scrutiny, whereby that which appears to be solid, flat, and monochrome reveals itself to comprise countless individual units of color. Understood this way, pixelization does not simply allude to the increasingly accessible digital technology that allows everyday citizens to document the history unfolding before them; rather, it refers to the very democratic aspirations at the heart of the Arab Spring revolutions and of Mroué's work. Resisting the "simplification of thorny issues into easy binaries," Mroué calls for a theatre—and a society—that "emphasizes differences, not consensus … a place of uncertainty, of conflicting ideas."[58]

In a sense, then, while Raad's post-2010 work does not bear the digitized mark of the cheap, damaged cellphones that produced the images in Mroué's piece, his conception of "revolution" is no less "pixelated." *Scratching on Things I Could Disavow* appears to find Raad picking up where his *Atlas Group* work left off: digging through the archives that have played a role in shaping the reality of the Arab world and presenting his "findings" with a mix of mischievousness and earnestness. This time, Raad's focus is the history of Arab art, from the canonical to the contemporary. However, another distinction separates *Scratching* from the *Atlas Group* work: a preoccupation with a future Raad invites his viewers and audiences to cocreate along with institutional and "immaterial" forces already at work in shaping the future as they have the past and the present. Indeed, *Scratching* seems as concerned with the effect of the institutional and the "immaterial" on the past, present, and future as Mroué's work is concerned with the political and the military. Raad's 2013 contribution to his *Preface to the Third Edition* series, comprising a portfolio of canonical Islamic art (assembled, according to Raad, by a female artist in 2026) and an accompanying text explaining the proposed transport of these art pieces from France to the Louvre's new museum in Abu Dhabi sometime between 2016 and 2046, predicts that exactly twenty-eight of these art pieces will undergo a variety of material and aesthetic changes in this process. Raad predicts that the historians, curators, and conservators who initiated this journey will attribute these changes to the weather, "asserting that the 'corrosion' began soon after the exquisitely crafted, climate-controlled crates were opened in the Arabian desert. But a rare few will correctly surmise that the objects opted to dissimulate: they traded skins, limbs, faces, and organs with each other."[59] Raad goes so far as to speculate that some of these changes will be the result of "the dreams and disorders of the non-Emirati workers constructing such temples of culture."[60] By prophesying how these iconic works of art, selected by the types of "experts" Raad frequently parodies in his lecture-performances, will morph and mutate as they make their way to Abu Dhabi, Raad envisions a dynamic future in which a construction worker's dreams can play as great a role as nature itself, and the fixed, static ambassadors of an officially sanctioned "past" wriggle free from their discursive constraints to present themselves anew.

Like *Index XXVI*, with its invitation to the public to help correct the mistakes of the past and in so doing enter into communication with the future, *Preface to the Third Edition* offers a hopeful vision of a future in which art, artists, and art viewers free themselves from a variety of rigid constraints, discursive or otherwise: even "colors, lines, shapes, and forms" themselves might feel safe enough to come out from their hiding places in "fonts, covers, titles, and indices" and return to the artworks from which they retreated after the Lebanese wars.[61] However, Raad is careful to temper his optimism about the democratic, liberatory potential of the future, especially in light of the trajectory of many of the Arab Spring uprisings. In a text accompanying 2010's *Section 88_ Act XXXI: Views from Outer to Inner Compartments*, Raad describes a scene that will take place between 2014 and 2024, when a "proud local resident" attempts to enter "a new museum of modern and/or contemporary art in an Arab city" only to be barred by an invisible wall he senses blocking the entrance. As he warns the other museumgoers not to enter, "he is removed from the site, severely beaten, and sent to a psychiatric facility," where, according to the newspaper documenting the event, he "Claims World Is Flat."[62] However, as haunting as this prognostication may be, it is only one of many within the works that comprise *Scratching* and, as such, constitutes just one pixel within a massive image, the whole of which we are unable to see.

The Pixelated Revolution and *Scratching on Things I Could Disavow* continue to teach us how to read traces of the real into an image, how not to be fooled by manipulated images, and also how to add in shyly hopeful, democratic training manuals for shooting unadulterated documents, how to destabilize even the most fixed of images, and how to augur perceptible futures in archival materials seemingly frozen in time. Raad and Mroué's projects of performative historiography are still heavily invested in interrogating archival documents and destabilizing easily accepted representations, but at the same time they are invested in searching for unedited, less manipulated, alternative image sources and modes of production. As liberal commentators in the United States bemoan the advent of the "post-truth era" ushered in with the election of President Donald Trump, Raad and Mroué remind their audiences of the ways that the true, the "post-true," the fictive, and the yet-to-be-true can stand next to each other in a constantly shifting, pixelated image of reality that we can help create, if only we know where, and how, to look.

Notes

1. In Eva Respini, *Walid Raad* (New York: Museum of Modern Art, 2015), 110.
2. Accessed May 8, 2013, www.scratchingonthings.com.
3. In Respini, *Walid Raad*, 134.
4. Accessed August 21, 2017, http://www.sfeir-semler.com/hamburg/exhibitions-hamburg/2010/2010-01-16-walid-raad.html.
5. In Respini, *Walid Raad*, 134–35.
6. In Maria Hlavajova and Jill Winder, eds. *Rabih Mroué: A BAK Critical Reader in Artists' Practice* (Utrecht: BAK, 2012), 20.
7. Eyad Houssami, ed. *Doomed by Hope: Essays on Arab Theatre* (London: Pluto Press, 2012).
8. Stephen Barber, *Performance Projections: Film and the Body in Action* (London: Reaktion, 2014).
9. Laura U. Marks, *Hanan Al-Cinema: Affections for the Moving Image* (Cambridge: MIT Press, 2015), 209.
10. Rustom Bharucha, *Terror and Performance* (London: Routledge, 2014).
11. Walid Raad, *Miraculous Beginnings*, ed. Achim Borchardt-Hume (London: Whitechapel Gallery, 2010), 15.
12. Rabih Mroué and Tony Chakar, "Come in Sir, We Will Wait for You Outside," *Discourse* 24, no. 1: 100–101.
13. "The idea of this presentation is very simple: Stay where you are and we will bring you Palestine." Mroué, "Come in Sir, We Will Wait for You Outside," 100.
14. Mroué, "Come in Sir, We Will Wait for You Outside," 102.
15. Laura U. Marks, *Hanan Al-Cinema: Affections for the Moving Image* (Cambridge: MIT Press, 2015), 202.
16. Accessed May 8, 2013, www.mediacultuur.net/bronnen/i-think-it-would-be-better-if-i-could-weep.
17. In Respini, *Walid Raad*, 94.
18. Ibid., 37.
19. Mroué, "Come in Sir, We Will Wait for You Outside," 106.
20. Accessed August 21, 2017, https://www.youtube.com/watch?v=5zC6QxpLTdU&t=50s.
21. Rabih Mroué and Elias Khoury, "Three Posters," introduction by Rabih Mroué, *TDR: The Drama Review* 50, no. 3 (T191): 184.
22. Mroué, "Three Posters," 183.
23. Ibid., 184.
24. Accessed May 8, 2013, www.ubu.com/film/raad_bachar.html.
25. Rabih Mroué and Lina Saneh, "Biokhraphia," *TDR: The Drama Review* 52, no. 1 (T197): 172.
26. Mroué, "Biokhraphia," 169.
27. Ibid., 170.
28. Ibid., 173.
29. Respini, *Walid Raad*, 29.
30. The 1990s generation of Lebanese artists, Raad and Mroué being no exceptions, emerged from a shared reality of war sourcing their art: "You're all the war generation. You lived

the civil war. You were affected by it. It's imprinted on you," runs a line in *Biokhraphia*. Mroué, "Biokhraphia," 171.

31. Rabih Mroué, "Le Feu! Histoires de Beyrouth," *Parachute* 108: 54. Author's translation.
32. Mroué, "Three Posters," 183.
33. Mroué, "Biokhraphia," 173.
34. Ibid., 173.
35. Mroué, "Three Posters," 184.
36. In Janet A. Kaplan, "Flirtations with Evidence," *Art in America* 92, no. 9: 137, 169.
37. Sarah Rogers, "Out of History: Postwar Art in Beirut." *Art Journal* 66, no. 2: 9.
38. Rogers, "Out of History," 9.
39. Walid Raad and Alan Gilbert, "Walid Raad," *BOMB* 81: 40.
40. *BOMB*, "Walid Raad," 40.
41. Ibid., 40.
42. Raad, *Miraculous Beginnings*.
43. *BOMB*, "Walid Raad."
44. Interview in Hlavajova, *Rabih Mroué*.
45. Mroué, "Three Posters," 92.
46. *BOMB*, "Walid Raad," 42.
47. André Lepecki, "After All, This Terror Was Not Without Reason: Unfiled Notes on the Atlas Group Archive," *TDR: The Drama Review* 50, no. 3 (T191): 42.
48. *BOMB*, "Walid Raad," 39.
49. Mroué in Hlavajova, *bih Mroué*.
50. Rabih Mroué, "The Pixelated Revolution," trans. Ziad Newfal, introduction by Carol Martin, *TDR: The Drama Review* 56, no. 3 (T215): 30.
51. Mroué, "The Pixelated Revolution," 32.
52. Lepecki, "After All, This Terror Was Not Without Reason," 42.
53. Mroué, "The Pixelated Revolution," 32.
54. Ibid., 25.
55. Ibid., 29.
56. Ibid.,35.
57. Marks, *Hanan Al-Cinema*, 207.
58. In Eyad Houssami, ed., *Doomed by Hope: Essays on Arab Theatre* (London: Pluto Press, 2012), 119.
59. In Respini, *Walid Raad*, 148.
60. Ibid., 164.
61. Ibid., 141.
62. Ibid., 125.

Where Has the Political Theatre in Israel Gone?

Rethinking the Concept of Political Theatre Today

—SHULAMITH LEV-ALADGEM

Since the 1990s, Israeli scholars and practitioners have contended that the public theatre—once critical, politically combative, and a theatre of values—has become a theatre of high production values—more populist, escapist, devoted to the box office than before, and thus bad theatre.[1] Against a vast supply of such nonpolitical performances on the central stage, intellectuals draw attention to those few performances in the fringe theatre that still dare to challenge, resist, or subvert the sociopolitical status quo in Israel.[2]

Since for many years my concern as a theatre scholar and practitioner has not been the central stage but noninstitutional community-based theatre, I agreed with this contention, in that it reinforced my argument that community-based theatre in Israel should be regarded as a distinct and singular form of political theatre.[3] The ideological roots of both assertions, that of the public theatre as nonpolitical and that of community-based theatre as political, are embedded in the so-called critical discourse that has been growing in Western culture in recent decades and that denounces the political potential of contemporary dominant cultural practices ruled by the market in favor of a political art of the oppressed that might be found far from the center, in geographic, cultural, economic, ethnic, and national peripheries.[4]

Recently, however, following a perplexing experience of a number of community-based performances, I realized that it has become difficult to perceive "politicalness" not only in the public theatre but also in the community-based theatre, which I had previously advocated as a clear case of political theatre. Rather than denouncing the entire theatre field as nonpolitical, however, perhaps it is time to reconsider the acknowledged concepts and assumptions with which we, theatre intellectuals in Israel and elsewhere, are used to experiencing and giving meaning to theatre and performance articulations in the established theatre venues as well as in nontraditional contexts. There may indeed be a need to look for new sources of inspiration that will stir us into thinking beyond the already acknowledged insights of what political theatre is. Thus, the intention here is to present Jacques Rancière's radical concept of the political as such a revisonary source and to demonstrate this through a discussion of several case studies taken from the Israeli theatre.

The Failure of the Tripartite Interpretative Key

One afternoon in 2012 I attended a theatre project held at the Center for the Blind in Tel Aviv. It was initiated by Peter Harris, a veteran and leading facilitator and director of community-based theatre in Israel. The idea was to provide a dramatic encounter between students from the Department of Theatre Arts at Tel Aviv University and blind and partially sighted members of the Centre for the Blind, with the intention of challenging social stereotypes of the blind. The encounter was founded on the appropriation of theatrical and performative devices to create an original script, based on the self-texts of the participants, that would then be devised into a public performance. During a nine-month period, the collaborative participants met on a weekly basis and explored together through playing and improvisations what seeing and/or non-seeing mean from the point of view of people in both groups.

The final performance, *The 6:6 Inn*, was a colorful collage of skits, dramatic scenes, monologues, songs, and dance routines in which it was difficult to distinguish the sighted from the blind performers. It was a high-spirited theatrical event, celebrating mostly the joy of mutual creativity and togetherness while also delivering from time to time satirical comments on the discriminatory nature of society.

As is my practice, I immediately tried to read the performance through the tripartite interpretative key, which I introduced in 2010, in my book *Standing Front Stage: Resistance, Celebration and Subversion in Community-Based Theatre*.[5] This model is based on three modes of political theatre by which to explore community-based theatre projects: resistance, co-optation (celebration of the status-quo), and subversion. In my model, I argue that the height of radical community-based theatre in Israel occurred during the 1970s, when it both emerged from and fueled the social agitation of the radical Black Panthers (Hapnterim Hashchorim) movement, which led a strong social protest among young Mizrahi residents of underprivileged urban neighborhoods. This type of community-based theatre produced, for about a decade, radical, original performances that resisted the domination and discrimination of the Mizrahi Jews (originating from Muslim countries) by the Ashkenazi Jews (originating from Europe and America). In 1977, following the right-wing Likud Party's rise to power, through the massive support received from the Mizrahi Jews, and the promise of the newly elected government to improve the social conditions of the Mizrahim, community-based theatre generally lost its political drive. Within the appeased social atmosphere of the 1980s, community-based theatre became more celebratory and consensual, a co-opted legitimized tool of the institutional welfare programs. In the 1990s, against the background of the disappointment of the Mizrahim with the national welfare projects, on the one hand, and the opening of Israeli culture to new voices from below, on the other, community-based theatre strove to regain some of its politicalness by adopting tactics of subversion and negotiation.[6] This was reflected mainly in the women-based community theatre that emerged in Israel at the time, which became the almost exclusive space for feminist theatre. The greater number of younger Mizrahi women than Mizrahi men in the local ensembles generated a feminist, resistant theatre by means of which these women conducted a subversive and complex negotiation of gender-based issues with both their communities and the Israeli hegemonic culture at large.[7]

Seeking to analyze *The 6:6 Inn* by means of this tripartite model hindered my enthusiastic spontaneous response to the performance. I could not interpret it as radical since, unlike the Israeli radical community-based theatre of the 1970s, it did not deliver a direct and sharp protest against a specific oppression, nor did it strive to encourage the audience to move out from the auditorium and become activists in real life. Nor could I interpret it as subversive, since unlike the Israeli subversive community-based theatre in the 1990s, *The 6:6 Inn* did not articulate radical messages in a subtle and less abrupt manner in order to be accepted. However, to interpret it as a co-opted performance that celebrates the status quo also seemed inappropriate and totally in contrast to my emotional experience that something different and important was indeed happening on the stage. The consequence of this disturbing feeling, which I had also recently experienced as a spectator on a few other occasions, reinforced my impression that there is a need to refresh the acknowledged perceptions of what political theatre is.

Jacques Rancière's Alternative Idea of Equality

Jacques Rancière provides an original and radical concept of the political to confront traditional left-wing politics in general and the "critical discourse" of post-structuralism in particular. Intervening by linking politics with aesthetics, Rancière attempts to interrogate forms of description and interpretation that have become too self-evident.

My presentation of Rancière's singular concept of the political does not mean that I recommend Rancière as a new guru of political activism and/or political theatre. I'm also well aware that from our point of view as theatre intellectuals, Rancière's attitude to theatre is somewhat perplexing. He displays little direct interest in theatre and clearly prefers to wander among other art fields, such as poetry, literature, cinema, and installation art. This becomes even more perplexing in his well-known text on theatre "The Emancipated Spectator," in which he explicitly negates both Brecht's and Artaud's theatrical innovations regarding the role of the audience and theatre for political ends.[8] Nevertheless, I wish to discuss here his original concept about the political as a useful stimulus from which to think anew political theatre.

To grasp Rancière's novel and bold proposition, it is necessary to review the current, central approaches of what is the political, as discussed in a special issue published in 2009 of *Theory and Criticism*, a leading Israeli academic journal in the social sciences. There are basically two main answers today to the question of what is the political: The first answer, hailing from the school of "political liberalism," which is mostly influenced by Carl Schmitt, indicates that politics and the political are parallel. The control of the law, on which the liberal state is based, is unable to identify or seriously deal with those of its enemies that utilize the law against the state. Thus, the specific political distinction to which political actions and motives can be reduced is that between friend and enemy, and, accordingly, the political exists in the binary poles of the sovereign and the partisan or terrorist.[9] The second answer is that of the critical school based on Foucault, who extended the political beyond the restricted context of the state only to include the exception of any formal or informal system. Accordingly, it is not that everything is political but rather that nothing is political until it is politicized and thus becomes political. The political may emerge in unusual and amazing forms, and thus what is important is not the ontological meaning of the political but how we can identify it. As Foucault argues, the political is identified as the exceptional that operates exceptionally against any governmental or cultural authority. The political exposes and undermines the authoritative system by, first, defining it as violent and, second, demanding that the authoritative system identify itself as such.[10] The perception that the political is a rare, exceptional, and temporal surprise can, on the one hand, be directly connected to Rancière, who was influenced by Foucault. On the other hand, Rancière takes his concept of the political to a much more revolutionary configuration of exceptionalism. His radicalism and originality stem first and foremost from his deliberate rejection of the prevalent leftist political and cultural discourses to which most of us as theatre scholars and practitioners still belong. For him, the prevalence of such discourses have turned into a dangerous consensus of restoring and recycling stereotypical criticism as if it were still defiant and critical, while in fact it leads the political as well as political art into obsolescence.[11]

Rancière is not the only individual on the left who sought an alternative to Marxism after the events of 1968, but he is definitely original in his reimagining of equality, the core component of his political thought, in a way that interrogates not only the traditional concepts of the left but also the entire discourse of equality that we have inherited throughout history. The main point is that we have become accustomed to think of equality as a future goal for which democratic societies must fight. Equality for Rancière, in contrast, is not a duty or responsibility of governments. It is not to be given by the powerful to the powerless but rather to be taken and to be enacted by the nonprivileged, who do not count within a society: "not an equality decreed by law or force, not a passively received equality, but an equality in act, verified."[12] Most of all, such equality is "not an end to attain, but a point of departure, a *presupposing* to maintain in every circumstance."[13] It is equality as a premise that engenders political change, and the fight for it has to be not in the social reality, the realm of the economic conditions of production, but in that of aesthetics. Such a radical perception of equality as an axiomatic, a priori point of departure, which constitutes the pivot of Rancière's singular idea of what the political should be, challenges the politicalness of activist performances that are perceived almost automatically as the epitome of political theatre.

One clear example of this is *Legislative Theatre at Holot*, a performance I attended in 2015 at Tmuna, the leading fringe theatre in Tel Aviv.[14] The performance was originally created and performed at Holot, the detention camp for African asylum seekers, in the far desert of southern Israel, and since June 2016, the performance has been playing throughout the country. It is a joint project by the theatre activist Chen Alon, who facilitated and directed the performance, and the filmmaker Avi Mograbi, who produced a documentary film, based on the performance *Between Fences*, which was invited to participate in the latest Berlin film festival—the sixty-sixth Berlinale. The ensemble comprises a mixed group of asylum seekers and Israelis who have come together to represent the asylum seekers, who are not represented in the Israeli parliament and suffer from a violation of basic human rights. The political intention of the performance is to persuade the government to implement the 1951 Refugee Convention and international law. The group explored various techniques, exercises, and improvisations, inspired by Augusto Boal's *Theatre of the Oppressed* and *Legislative Theatre*. The performance is based on personal testimonies of the asylum seekers and acted out on a bare stage, through short scenes. For example, in one scene an asylum seeker asks his boss to let him be present at his child's birth. The boss aggressively rejects his request while approving the same request by another, Israeli, worker. In another scene, repeated three times, a doctor enters the camp and orders the sick asylum seeker not to approach him but to keep his distance. Without any examination, the doctor abruptly recommends each time Acamol (paracetamol), the most common nonprescription medication. In the second part of the performance, Alon conducted a discussion with the audience while inviting us to come onstage and become *spectactors* who reenact a given scene to suggest possible solutions.

This form of theatre, which is acknowledged today all over the world as a political-activist theatre, gives a chance to those who suffer from inequality to use the theatre as a committed tool for fighting for equality. I value and identify with such a form of political theatre; however, precisely because of this, I saw it as challenging to determine how Rancière's unusual idea counter-acts the politicalness of *Legislative Theatre at Holot*, in which the stage represented a fictionalized inequality that would perhaps change only in the real future. The inspiring question that arises from this is what Rancière's idea might mean for us, theatre scholars and practitioners, to posit equality at the outset of any political project rather than at its end? How might we articulate "equality in act," verified through theatre? I certainly did not experience such an approach or form of equality in *Legislative Theatre at Holot*. Is that what I experienced in *The 6:6 Inn*? "The equality of anyone and everyone," no matter who can see and who are blind and thus can not, acted out and verified from the beginning of the performance to its end?[15] The answer requires here further elaboration upon Rancière's alternative thinking of the political and its application in political theatre.

The New Interpretative Key of Jacques Rancière

While the perception of reality as socially constructed through the partition of power (or power relations) has become a matter of commonsense for most of us, by also applying it to the interpretation of the theatre field, Rancière offers a new key, an aesthetic key, which he calls the partition of the sensible (*le partage du sensible*), referring to an a priori meta-sensory system that organizes both the life world and the art world, and thus defines politics or the political very differently from its long-standing accepted meaning.

The historical moment that inspired Rancière to formulate this interpretative key occurred in the mid-nineteenth century, after the outbreak of the French and the American Revolutions that generated a third revolution—that of aesthetics. What interests Rancière, and might be stimulating for us too, is not the political revolutions themselves but how the special atmosphere generated a new way of "thinking democracy" and, thus, of "thinking aesthetics." Reading Friedrich Schiller's *Letters on Aesthetic Education* (1795), Rancière emphasizes the experiential turn that Schiller brought about: how for the first time aesthetics was thought not simply in relation to beauty or works of art but as an autonomous sphere of a new status of experiencing full freedom. The free aesthetic experience that "*grants[s] freedom by means of freedom*" is redefined by Rancière as also a political experience of full emancipation, democracy, and equality.[16] Inspired by another philosopher of the mid-nineteenth century, Joseph Jacotot,[17] Rancière proposes his radical idea that equality should be articulated as an axiomatic, a priori point of departure, as already mentioned. Moreover, Rancière extends the experiential perception of aesthetics into an alternative interpretative key of the partition of the sensible, which means the distribution of the perceptible that allots to each his/her proper role and function and thus determines what can be said, thought, and felt. It is the way in which abstract and arbitrary forms of symbolization of hierarchy are embodied by the evidence of a perceptible universe—a material and symbolic reconfiguration of the given state of things. Such a system not only determines the ways of being of both the life world and the art world in a given place and time but also keeps these two spheres in a constant simultaneous condition of connection and disconnection.[18]

To formulate the conditions that bring into being the political moment—an aesthetic expression and experience of equality, democracy, and emancipation—Rancière presents first *the police order*: the socio-aesthetic fabrication that usually manages to prevent it. A given society or community, according to Rancière, is a sensory fabric constructed not through the hierarchical division of power but upon a specific, a priori, hierarchical division of the sensuous, which determines the boundaries and borders of human experience. In other words, each polity performs a certain system of allocation, shaping its community by means of the sensuous experience that is shared—unequally—among the people of the community and thus giving rise to differences and inequalities while also bringing the people together around that which they can share.

Although any police order (social order) generates inequality, it advocates itself as the best and correct system for the entire community, fostering a consensus that negates any form of dispute and keeping everyone "in their place, in their class, taken up with the duty allocated to them, and equipped with the sensory and intellectual equipment appropriated to that place and duty."[19]

For Rancière, what is at stake is not whether a police order "is sweet and kind"[20] or the opposite, a "cold monster imposing its rigid order on the life of society."[21] He insists, no matter how strange and irritating it may sound, that since every social system is based on inequality, there is never one correct and ultimate police order to imagine for all times to come.

An Israeli performance group that seems to follow this approach is Public Movement, which since 2006 has been creating critical public events in-between art and reality, across Israel, Europe, and the United States. The international appeal of their performative actions lies in their "sense of 'glocality' ...—a territorial overlap between sovereign local space and action space, which also has characteristics of a non-local artistic 'Every nation.'"[22] Thus, the group offers "radical configuration[s] of social and ritualistic patterns embedded in power structures, such as national and military ceremonies, as well as in civic behaviour,"[23] which are not specific to the current sociopolitical order in Israel but challenge in general "social structures and counter-structures, which include hierarchical relations."[24] Using Rancière's vocabulary, the intention of these performative interventions is to generate dispute by impelling the participant out of his "proper" place, class, duty, and "the sensory and intellectual equipment appropriated to that place and duty."[25] In Public Movement's *Positions*, for example, "two performers stand on either side of a public space, while other group members mark out the performance space with red-white caution tape. The two announce: 'You are asked to choose a side, to take a stand!' and audience members are required to choose and position themselves on one side as two diametrically opposed stances are proclaimed—i.e., men/women, smokers/non-smokers, capitalism/socialism.... For every proclamation, the action space is divided into two, but for a while an intermediate zone is left between the caution tapes, briefly trapping those who waver between the two poles."[26] *Positions* evokes the issue of how much choice is indeed allocated for each of us by the police order, and it does so in line with Rancière, without advocating it as a "'rehearsal' of specific activism."[27] However, like the other interventions of Public Movement, it is still only a partial expression of Rancière's genuine concept of the political moment. It should be clearly noted that Rancière has no interest in providing a compelling recipe or practical goal-oriented guideline with his theories. Although his concept invites a kind of doing that anyone, at any moment, can take up, it is nevertheless not a progressive doing with an assured climax and a successful end that fixes the police order.

The Political Moment: The Aesthetic Counteraction of the Police

Rancière's formulation of politics or the political has nothing to do with the prevalent, accepted view of politics, which can be at best associated with his concept of the police order. The political for Rancière is an alternative, new aesthetics that shatters the police order's consensual fabric of collectivity through unauthorized disagreement, declassification, dispute, deregulation, and disorder, generating a new "redistribution of space and time, place and identity, speech and noise, the visible and the invisible."[28] Thus the political, as Rancière redefines it, is an ongoing potentiality, occasionally appearing as a brief aesthetic event that provides a new opportunity of experience, which liberates new sensory data and stimuli, opening up options for establishing new relations between things and their meanings. This means that, unlike our prevalent thinking, strikes, demonstrations, elections, and even revolutions are not political in themselves but are all part and parcel of the police order. They might, however, become political in that extraordinary moment in which the places of their occurrence, the involved subjects, the texts that are being said, and the symbolic actions that are being carried out all depart from their ordinary, legitimate social status and functions. Accordingly, any activist theatre is also not political in itself. Rancière purports that the police order also influences the artistic order—that partition of the sensible that organizes, regulates, and determines the art world in a specific historical and cultural moment. Art, accordingly, has never existed in general but, rather, as various orders or regimes of identification, which have been historically and politically constructed, each indicating a particular way by which art is identified as art and perceived as art at a specific time and place.[29] Thus, as much as artists may hate to admit it, the art world, similarly to the life world, is also restricted and policed, directing artists to follow artistic regulations, such as that of political theatre in our case, that have been defined and accepted a priori.

The political moment for Rancière is the culmination of freedom, emancipation, democracy, and equality in its fullest appearance and sense (experience and meaning) only if the political subject, as already indicated, practices and verifies equality from the outset through creative and poetic expressions and proposes a new form of collectivity that is still not possible in the given police order.[30]

Furthermore, the political subject, who may belong to a given oppressed, marginal, or excluded group, does not appear in the political moment in his formal, allocated identity but as an equal member of his community. The political subject is thus an emerging, new subject who, despite not being officially accounted equal, imagines and invents himself as a new equal subject born out of his alien, dissenting, aesthetic activity in the political moment. This new meaning that Rancière assigns to *the oppressed, the people, the demos, the proletariat, the artisan*, and so on seeks to reject the Aristotelian division between the privileged men of logos, who have the capacity to reason and thus to make claims about justice and injustice through speech, and the unprivileged men of *pathos*, who have only the capacity to express pain or pleasure. This approach, as Rancière indicates, has come down to us through history in various variations until it reappeared as the leftist accepted stand that the workers cannot rebel by themselves but need the intellectuals to educate them to revolution.

Rancière's political pedagogy negates any intellectual partition between activity and passivity, thinking and feeling, and thereby between the worker and the thinker, the student and the schoolmaster, the artist and the audience, and so on.[31] Such an approach might seem problematic since it calls into question the basic tenet regarding political/activist theatre that a given audience/group needs consciousness-raising through theatre to reach sociopolitical consciousness. However, reading Piscator's manifesto of 1920 on the workers' theatre in light of Rancière's presupposition of universal equality of intelligence reveals the singularity of Piscator in envisioning (if not fully practicing) the workers themselves as capable of standing front stage and of acting out their own texts, in their own artistic style, without the tutelage of the elite experts.[32] It was Brecht who, impressed by the unique acting ability of the workers, wrote in his *Two Essays on Unprofessional Acting* that there is a special "simplicity to be found in their acting, a kind that does not result from a lack of origins but from a specific outlook and a specific concern."[33] They "often shed a surprising light on the complex and baffling relationships between the people of our time."[34]

The relevance of Rancière's concept of the political to theatre artists and scholars further extends to the artificial, creative, playful, and theatrical qualities that Rancière assigns to the political event. I find it informative that the Rancière who, as already said, has no particular concern with theatre as an art form is that same Rancière who proposes the political not only as an aesthetic and a poetic event but, more concretely, as a theatrical event. Rancière assigns to theatre in general a special politicalness as a gathering place for heterogeneous audiences, which are displaced from the places, times, and functions allotted to them by the police through the power of mimicry.[35] His indication that theatre is "effective in organizing a sensory space where plebeians happen to speak *like* patricians" is highly evocative if we ask ourselves how we might realize this maxim in practice, assigning new possibilities of politicalness for theatre, both mainstream and fringe.[36]

More concretely, I argue that since Rancière conceptualizes the political as a constant potentiality that can never be fully materialized but only appears in the eruption of a sudden, moment, he appropriates theatre in two ways: First, he utilizes theatrical components to express the political as theatrical. For example, "Politics is primarily a conflict over the existence of a common stage and over the existence and status of those present on it … a litigious play that sets up the political stage."[37] Politics is "performing or playing in the theatrical sense of the word, … which means first setting it up as theatre."[38] "It introduces new objects and subjects onto the common stage."[39] "Politics sets up scenes of dissensus."[40] "This scene-mise-en-scene exercises democracy."[41] "Democracy as a mode of being … a more playful notion of democracy."[42]

Second, what is embedded in Rancière's description is that the political moment comes into being through and as a unique theatrical event. The political subject that, as noted before, is a new, artificial, not-yet existing equal subject, who must express a new, not-yet formed type of communality and who acquires first and foremost the theatrical will and ability to act as if, like an actor, as if he were someone else, to become that someone, even if for a brief moment, as if he is already an equal participant in the political process, but in fact he is not. Accordingly, the theatrical modes of action appropriated by the political subject are: acting, performing, playing, and improvising, turning any space—found, created, or site-specific—into a specific aesthetic space for playing new fictional parts, playing new modes of living together, and facilitating an experience of equality and pure freedom. Here, again, it should be stressed, even though it may be difficult to accept, that Rancière's notion of pure freedom and equality are not associated with any form of revolutionary movement. The political-ness of the political event lies in the in-between theatrical space of experience that expresses poetically a sense of hope that things could be and can be otherwise and bears the promise of "a new topography of the possible."[43]

Looking at the Israeli public theatre, it seems to me that such politicalness can be traced in *Sea Breeze*, an adaptation by Ofira Henig and Khalifa Natour of the book *My Secret Relations with Carla Bruni* by the Palestinian author Ala

Chalichal, directed by Ofira Henig in the Haifa Municipal Theatre in 2011. In a recent interview with Ofira Henig, an internationally acclaimed Israeli director, who has lately worked as an independent artist, she stated that her work has become more personal and thus more political, "not in the sense of actuality, but in the philosophical sense."[44] When I asked her what she meant by that, she replied that she "has no interest in the prevalent perception of political theatre in Israel, which usually refers directly to local political issues. I rather strive to create a more poetic political theatre that would provide the spectator with a new perspective on his life."[45] She added that "in the rehearsal room, all of us, Jewish, Arabic, and German artists, despite our high political consciousness, we don't talk about any of it. We create together, maintaining the atmosphere of full equality as a utopian alternative to the inequality of reality outside the room."[46] A similar space of equality can be traced in *Sea Breeze*, which depicts the everyday life of both Israeli Palestinians and Israeli Jews, living in Akko and Haifa, two mixed cities in northern Israel, in time of war in both Lebanon and Gaza. The Palestinians are not represented as oppressed or marginalized; and the Jews are not represented as the powerful and the rulers. All the characters onstage appear and act as equal human beings, striving, each in his own way, to get through their day within the complicated situation.

Two poetical moments are embedded in the show that demonstrate the mode of Rancière's politicalness. The first focuses on a Palestinian mother arriving with her daughter at the beach. On the stage, there is a fence of green shrubbery that hides the sea from the sight of the audience. The daughter tries to persuade the hesitating mother to enter the water. After a pause, the mother takes of her shoes, climbs up the fence, with her back to the audience, releases a cry of liberty, and jumps into the water with her clothes on. The daughter, following her mother, takes off her shoes, releases the same cry, and lands in the water, too, with all her clothes on. The audience hears the joyful voices of the two playing women, the sweet, familiar sound of the water, and sees the spray of water drops. This poetic expression of a moment of utter freedom and a microcosm of emancipation captured the audience, which responded with sporadic soft clapping and smiling at each other. This was a momentary experience of hope encompassing both the stage and the auditorium, signaling that things could be and can be otherwise.

The second moment happens at the end of the performance. Two of the Palestinian characters decide to celebrate the Jewish carnivalesque holiday of Purim, which commemorates the saving of the Jewish people in ancient Persia and in which the tradition is to wear masks and costumes. One of the characters is dressed as a stereotypical cowboy and the other as a stereotypical Sheikh (an

Arab tribal leader), each sitting on top of a ladder, as if these were the saddles of two horses, riding into the sunset, while the stage lights fade out. This dialectical image expresses, on the one hand, an option of a new form of community that although not yet possible in the given Israeli police order nevertheless signifies that things might be otherwise. Such a play of disguise and masquerade is nonetheless a subversive poetic device by means of which the subjects onstage manage to foil and disrupt the police order, for while a cowboy is a popular costume among young Jewish children, that of a Sheikh is usually not. Thus, this playful moment of multilayered playing offers a new option, which "consists in setting out the encounter and possibly the clash of heterogeneous elements."[47] Political art for Rancière is exactly such an expression of negotiation and relation between opposites, creating a mixture "to provoke a break in our perception, to disclose some secret connection of things hidden behind the everyday reality."[48] The cheerful response of the audience to this absurdist and humorous Arab Purim reveals that the spectators, like the actors, had experienced a moment of comfort and a glimpse of the hope that all people in Israel need so much today.

Conclusion

There is much more that can be discussed regarding Rancière's political concept, and no less so regarding his idea of political art, but I must leave that for another opportunity. My intention here has been to argue that there is a need today to embark on an intellectual journey to reconfigure the accepted concepts of political theatre, which has become less distinct and thus more problematic to identify.[49] As Ken Nielsen and Lisbet Jørgensen write, "although all theatre can be said to have political content in some form, theatre has no inherent capacity for being politically radical or influencing political change."[50] Different forms of aesthetic production can now be understood as political (or a-political) depending on the time, place, and context of the event, and as the result of negotiation between a certain way of doing and a certain way of seeing. The judgment is often based on a preconception of what political performance should be or do or what forms of political performance are no longer effective or relevant in today's world. While there is still "a political modality that shapes our experiences . . . , it morphs and changes day by day."[51] Janelle Reinelt's conclusion is that political theatre today is enormously varied and takes place in various settings, such as national as well as fringe theatres, galleries, installations, and site-specific venues. "Some of it is devised; some of it emphasizes the physical, some of it engages spectators directly. . . . Some of it is discursive, some of it is poetic, some of it is musical, and some of it is incoherent."[52] Indeed, looking at the Israeli scene, mainly at the fringe, there are still occasionally traditional, issue-based performances that focus on urgent sociopolitical local problems, as in interventional community-based theatres, queer theatre, disability theatre, women-based performances, site-specific performances, and forms of Boalist activist projects. Generally, however, as already noted, theatre is mostly assessed as escapist and nonpolitical.

This article does not advocate giving up or negating the current accepted concepts of political theatre but refreshing, extending, and renewing them. I chose Rancière as one possible guide for such a journey, since he strives to provide a new way of thinking the political. The critical alternative key that Rancière offers lies in the principle of a counter-partition of the sensible that generates the political moment, a moment that can change something of our world by providing an exceptional experience that transforms our regular and habitual relations between words, things, and their meaning. Since it is aesthetic strangeness that can not be colonized by the police order, the political efficacy is thus an aesthetic efficacy of dissensus, of thwarting the standard by inventing new combinations. Accordingly, the political in both the life world and the art world constitutes those rare theatrical events that can change the cartography of the perceptible.

It is precisely Rancière's original move of shifting theatre from the realm of art into the realm of politics, and his unique way of seeing politics as a theatrical event, that reveals the political power of theatre from a new perspective. In staging the political as theatrical, Rancière implies that theatre contains the appropriate means and faculties by which to produce political moments. He provides us with directional and dramaturgical guidelines not only for how to imagine new modes of political events but also for how to re-search contemporary performances that would otherwise be considered nonpolitical.

Having reached the end of this article, it is time to go back and re-search the politicalness of *The 6:6 Inn*, the community-based performance that I originally had felt constrained to consider as nonpolitical despite the special, invigorating experience that I had undergone. The leading questions of this re-search, following Rancière's key, should thus be: Did it create an exceptional experience? In what ways? Did the performers present themselves as new equals, as not yet accounted for subjects? Did they offer a new form of living together? And did they manage to change the usual way we experience and give meaning to blindness? The answers are already encapsulated in the title of the performance, which indicated not only the Inn as the central artistic stage-image but also its invented, political singularity as an a priori starting point of absolute equality and not as a future goal to be accomplished at the end of the performance. The literal and metaphorical equality of the sign 6:6 (20:20 vision) was manifested in the leading, reprised song onstage: "Welcome all to the 6:6 inn/ a place of fun and joy/ everybody is invited/ here we are always open/ here everyone fits in/ everybody is in the circle, connected, never alone." Thus, the performance managed to create the overall effect of an inability to distinguish the sighted from the blind performers, as already noted. However, the form of communality suggested on the stage was not a uniform and unified ideal collectiveness but, rather, one that contributed a mode of living together-and-apart. This was expressed through the fragmented, collage structure of the skits, dramatic scenes, monologues, songs, and dance routines and through the content of this mixture, which delivered heterogeneous voices, feelings, and thoughts. Above all, the 6:6 form of community epitomized the politico-aesthetic potential of the theatrical space to bring people together and celebrate human joy, creativity, expressivity, and, more than anything, a sense of hope—a promise that things could be and can be otherwise!

Acknowledgments

This article is based on a keynote speech presented at the *International Research Workshop of The Israel Science Foundation: Rethinking Political Theatre in Western Culture*, at the Theatre Arts Department, Tel Aviv University, Israel, March 2–4, 2015.

This research was supported by the Israel Science Foundation (grant no. 435/10).

Notes

1. Shoshana Weitz, "From Combative to Bourgeois Theatre: Public Theatre in Israel in 1990," in *Theatre in Israel*, ed. Linda Ben Zvi (Ann Arbor: University of Michigan Press, 1996), 101–16; Avraham Oz, *The Political Theatre* (Tel Aviv: Zmora Bitan and Haifa University Press, 1999) (Hebrew); Sosh Avigal, "Repertoires 2001–2002: The Scale of Risks," *Teatron* 6 (2001): 60–66 (Hebrew); Shimon Levi, "A Drop of Cold Water on a Hot Stone," *Teatron* 9 (2002): 4–6 (Hebrew); Yuval Meskin and Haim Nagid (2003), "People of Currency, People of Silence- Following a Colloquium at Tzavta," *Teatron* 10 (2003): 12–15 (Hebrew).
2. Shimon Levi, "'Have I Slept when the Others Suffered?' On Theatre and Reality Here, Now," *Teatron* 8 (2002): 70–71.
3. Shulamith Lev-Aladgem, "Ethnicity, Class and Gender in the Israeli Community Theatre,"

Theatre Research International 28, no. 2 (2003): 181–92; Shulamith Lev-Aladgem, "Whose Play Is It?: The Issue of Authorship/Ownership in Israeli Community-Based Theatre," *The Drama Review* 48, no. 3 (2004): 117–34.

4. Baz Kershaw, *The Radical in Performance: Between Brecht and Baudrillard* (New York: Routledge, 1999), 5, 16.
5. This book was the first academic comprehensive study on community-based theatre in Israel.
6. In English, see, for example, Shulamith Lev-Aladgem, "Ethnicity, Class and Gender in the Israeli Community Theatre," *Theatre Research International* 28, no. 2 (2003): 181–92; Shulamith Lev-Aladgem, "Whose Play Is It?: The Issue of Authorship/Ownership in Israeli Community-Based Theatre," *Drama Review* 48, no. 3 (2004): 117–34; Shulamith Lev-Aladgem, *Theatre in Co-Communities: Articulating Power* (London and New York: Palgrave Macmillan, 2010), 77–99.
7. Shulamith Lev-Aladgem and Anat. First, "Community Theatre as a Site for Performing Gender and Identity," *Feminist Media Studies* 4, no. 1 (2004): 37–50.
8. Jacques Rancière, "The Emancipated Spectator," in *The Emancipated Spectator*, by Jacques Rancière, trans. G. Elliott (London: Verso, 2009), 1–25.
9. Carl Schmitt, *The Concept of the Political*, trans. Leo Strauss (Chicago: Chicago University Press, 1996 [1925]); Carl Schmitt, *The Theory of the Partisan: A Commentary/Remark on the Concept of the Political*, trans. Clint, A. Goodson (East Lansing: Michigan State University Press, 2004 [1963]).
10. Michel Foucault, *Security, Territory and Population*, trans. Graham Burchell (New York: Picador, 2003).
11. Jacques Rancière, *Disagreement: Politics and Philosophy*, trans. J. Rose (Minneapolis: University of Minnesota Press, 1999).
12. Jacques Rancière, *The Ignorant Schoolmaster: Five Lessons in Intellectual Emancipation*, trans. with an introduction by Kristin Ross (Stanford, CA: Stanford University Press, 1991 [1987]), 72.
13. Ibid., 138.
14. On this performance, see, for example, http://www.haaretz.com/news/israel/.premium-1.660913.
15. Jacques Rancière, *Disagreement*, 17.
16. Jacques Rancière, "Our Police Order—What can be Said, See, and Done. Interview with Jacques Rancière," *Palinurus: Engaging Political Philosophy* (electronic Journal, 2007), 1–5, quote, 3. Also published in *Le Monde Diplomatique* (Oslo), November 8, 2006.
17. Jacques Rancière, *The Ignorant Schoolmaster*.
18. Jacques Rancière, "Contemporary Art and Politics of Aesthetics," in *Community of Senses: Rethinking Aesthetics and Politics*, ed. Beth Hinderliter, Vered Maimon, Jaleh Mansoor, and Seth McCormick (Durham, NC: Duke University Press, 2009), 31–50; Jacques Rancière, "The Politics of Literature," in Jacques Rancière, *The Politics of Literature*, trans. Julie Rose (Malden, MA: Polity, 2011), 3–30; Jacques Rancière, *Mute Speech: Literature, Critical Art, and Politics*, trans. James Swenson, with an introduction by Gabriel Rockhill (New York: Columbia University Press, 2011).
19. Jacques Rancière, "The Misadventures of Critical Thought," in *The Emancipated Spectator*, Jacques Rancière, trans. Gregory Elliott (London: Verso, 2009), 35–49, quote, 42.
20. Jacques Rancière, *Disagreement: Politics and Philosophy*, 30.

21. Ibid., 29.
22. Daphna Ben-Shaul, "Critically Civic: *Public Movement*'s Performative Activism," in *Performance Studies in Motion: International Perspectives and Practices in the Twenty-First Century*, ed. Atay Citron, Sharon Aronson-Lehavi, and David Zerbib (London: Bloomsbury, 2014), 118–30, quote, 123.
23. Ibid., 118.
24. Ibid., 119.
25. Rancière, "The Misadventures of Critical Thought," 42.
26. Daphna Ben-Shaul, "Critically Civic: *Public Movement*'s Performative Activism," 129.
27. Ibid., 130.
28. Jacques Rancière, "The Politics of Literature," in *The Politics of Literature*, by Jacques Rancière, trans. Julie Rose (Malden, MA: Polity, 2011), 3–30, quote, 4.
29. Jacques Rancière, *The Politics of Aesthetics: The Distribution of the Sensible*, trans. and introduction by Gabriel Rockhill (London: Continuum, 2004).
30. Jacques Rancière, *Dissensus: On Politics and Aesthetics*, ed. and trans. Steven Corcoran (London: Continuum, 2010).
31. Jacques Rancière, *The Philosopher and His Poor*, ed. and introduction Andrew Parker, trans. John Drury, Corinne Oster, and Andrew Parker (Durham, NC: Duke University Press, 2004 [1983]); Jacques Rancière, *The Ignorant Schoolmaster*.
32. Erwin Piscator, "The Program of the Proletarian Theatre," in *Modern Theories of Drama*, ed. George W. Brandt (Oxford: Clarendon, 1998 [1920]), 220–23.
33. Bertolt Brecht, "Two Essays in Unprofessional Acting," in *Brecht on Theatre*, by Bertolt Brecht, ed. and trans. John Willett (London: Methuen, 1964), 148–53, quote, 148.
34. Ibid., 149.
35. Jacques Rancière, *Names of History: On Poetics of Knowledge*, trans. Hasan Melehy and forward by Hayden White (Princeton: Princeton University Press, 1994).
36. Rancière, *Disagreement*, 25.
37. Ibid., 26.
38. Ibid., 88.
39. Rancière, "The Politics of Literature," 4.
40. Jacques Rancière, "The Politics of Aesthetics," *Beaver Group ARTicles* 16 (2006): 1–8, quote, 2.
41. Davide Panagia, "Dissenting Words: A Conversation with Jacques Rancière," *Diacritics* 30, no. 2 (2000): 113–26, quote, 125.
42. Ibid., 118.
43. Rancière, "The Misadventures of Critical Thought," 49.
44. Gad Kaynar (Kissinger), "An Interview with playwright and director Ofira Henig: 'I have nothing to do here, and it's sad.'" *Teatron* 40 (2015): 30–37, quote, 37 (Hebrew, translation is mine).
45. Shulamith Lev-Aladgem, "Mail Correspondence with Ofira Henig," February 14, 2016.
46. Ibid.
47. Rancière, "Contemporary Art and Politics of Aesthetics," 41.
48. Ibid.
49. Rikard Loman, "The Politics of Indifference," *Nordic Theatre Studies* 16 (2004): 107–21.
50. Ken Nielsen and Lisbet Jørgensen, "Introduction: Political Theatre Revised and Redefined," *Nordic Theatre Studies* 16 (2004): 5–11, quote, 8.

51. Janelle Reinelt, "What Is Political Theatre Today?" A Lecture Presented in Wickham Theatre, Department of Drama, Bristol University, May 6, 2008, accessed May 16, 2016, http://www.str.org.uk/events/lectures/archive/lecture0805w.shtml.
52. Ibid.

"Equal Rights by All Means!"

Beatrice Forbes-Robertson's 1910 Suffrage Matinee and the Onstage Junction of the US and UK Franchise Movements

—CHRISTINE WOODWORTH

On the afternoon of March 31, 1910, hundreds of people filled the Maxine Elliott Theatre in New York City for an afternoon of suffrage drama and variety entertainment. The event was organized by British actress Beatrice Forbes-Robertson to benefit the Equality League of Self-Supporting Women, created by Harriot Stanton Blatch, daughter of Elizabeth Cady Stanton. The suffrage matinee serves as a fulcrum in the genealogy of the US suffrage campaign, reaching back to the first convention in Seneca Falls, New York, in 1848, drawing together the suffrage activities of Seneca Falls and nearby Geneva, New York, at the turn of the century, and looking ahead to dozens of US performances of British pro-suffrage propaganda plays as well as other performative protest methods inspired by the iconic suffragettes across the Atlantic. By the early twentieth century, many of the protest strategies of American and British suffrage proponents differed widely. An examination of the eclectic series of performances at the 1910 suffrage matinee reveals how the movements became intertwined onstage, laying the foundation for future transatlantic transfers of activists, artists, texts, and tactics while illustrating the various journalistic attempts at dismissing such activism.[1] When the curtain rose on this performance in 1910, a new era commenced, marking a turning point in the US suffrage campaign.

In the early twentieth century, most high-profile US suffrage performances, parades, pageants, and protests were staged in large metropolitan areas. The

1910 suffrage matinee in New York City was no different. Yet the genesis of the US suffrage movement was located in the much smaller upstate New York community of Seneca Falls, host to the first Women's Rights Convention in 1848. While the early beginnings of the US suffrage movement are firmly rooted in Seneca Falls in the mid-nineteenth century, its neighboring community of Geneva housed an organization that was instrumental in the transformation of the theory and tactics of the US suffrage campaign at the turn of the century. The political activism in Geneva, although several hundred miles away from New York City, may have laid some of the groundwork for the pivotal performance at the Maxine Elliott Theatre. Much of the archival evidence of the 1910 suffrage matinee (as well as countless other events in the US suffrage campaign at this pivotal time) survives in scrapbooks compiled by Elizabeth Smith Miller and her daughter, Anne Fitzhugh Miller. As the cousin of Elizabeth Cady Stanton, it is hardly surprising that Elizabeth Smith Miller found her way to the suffrage cause. Residing a few miles away from Seneca Falls, Elizabeth and Anne created the Geneva Political Equality Club in 1897, which served as a hub for transatlantic exchange between US and UK suffrage proponents. The Geneva Political Equality Club hosted meetings, speakers, performances, and study clubs. They also often sent delegations to Albany and New York City as part of legislative action or to participate in protest or advocacy events. Through it all, Elizabeth Smith Miller and Anne Fitzhugh Miller painstakingly saved newspaper clippings, photographs, circulars, letters, programs, and other ephemera, creating an invaluable archive of turn-of-the-century US suffrage documents. The result is seven scrapbooks housed at the Library of Congress as part of the Miller National American Woman Suffrage Association (NAWSA) Suffrage Scrapbooks, 1897–1911 collection.[2] Were it not for this collection, the 1910 suffrage matinee would be known only through anecdotal accounts in memoirs and sardonic reviews in anti-suffrage newspapers, such as the *New York Times*. The geographic, familial, and political connections between Seneca Falls, Geneva, and New York City are exemplified through the suffrage matinee. Examining the matinee's possible inception reveals the vital role Geneva played in the US suffrage campaign in the early years of the twentieth century.

The 1910 matinee was part of a sea change in the early twentieth-century US suffrage movement. The iconic foremothers of suffrage—including Elizabeth Cady Stanton, Susan B. Anthony, and Lucy Stone—were gone and with them the tactics of nineteenth-century protest and legislative reform.[3] Early suffragists attempted to work within the system to shift laws, initially on a state and eventually on a federal level. This technique of legislative reform had yielded little progress by the turn of the century. Elizabeth Cady Stanton's daughter Harriot Stanton

Blatch recounted in her memoir *Challenging Years*, "The suffrage movement was completely in a rut in New York State at the opening of the twentieth century. It bored its adherents and repelled its opponents."[4] Given this, it is hardly surprising that the twentieth century brought a new generation of suffrage leaders into positions of influence. Emblematic of the bold New Woman, suffragists and suffragettes employed a variety of approaches in the United States, beginning to borrow heavily from the methods of the scandalous Women's Social and Political Union (WSPU) in the United Kingdom. Frances Diodato Bzowski, in an article addressing the shifting tactics of the US suffrage campaign, noted that Blatch and Alice Paul, having both lived in England and worked as part of the British suffrage campaign, were new "generals" who would "lead the newly intensified movement."[5] Largely due to the influence of the British suffrage campaign, a variety of new US suffrage organizations were founded in the early years of the twentieth century. Among them was the Equality League of Self-Supporting Women, created in New York City in 1907 by Harriot Stanton Blatch.

Blatch grew up in the nexus of the women's rights movement in the United States, helping to host house guests like Sojourner Truth, traveling with her mother for public speaking engagements all over the country, and, following college at Vassar, helping her mother and Susan B. Anthony edit a volume of *History of Woman Suffrage*.[6] On one of her many transatlantic crossings, Harriot Stanton met the man who would soon become her husband, William Henry Blatch. Together they spent twenty years living in England, where Harriot became involved in a variety of suffrage circles, including a short-lived suffrage committee, which brought her together with Emmeline Pankhurst when they were both young mothers. Pankhurst would go on to found the WSPU in 1903, the most high-profile suffrage organization in the United Kingdom, known for their motto "Deeds Not Words" as well as their at times violent protest strategies. Blatch's engagement in political circles in England increased, and she eventually took on leadership roles in several suffrage organizations, which led her to become a member of the Fabian Society.[7] Her affiliations with the Fabians led to several meetings with George Bernard Shaw, including one at her home in Basingstoke, where he read from *Candida*. Politics and theatre were thus woven together for Blatch throughout her engagement with activism.

Upon their return to the United States to live in 1902, Blatch recollected, "I was eager to help win the vote for women, eager to finish the work my mother had begun."[8] Blatch regularly traveled to Geneva, New York, to participate in events hosted by the Geneva Political Equality Club. She also joined the Women's Trade Union League in 1905, igniting her desire to create a suffrage organization that was predominantly targeted at working women.[9] Perhaps in anticipation of later performative protest tactics, Blatch recalled of the early meetings, "We all believed that suffrage propaganda must be made dramatic, that suffrage workers must be politically minded. We saw the need of drawing industrial women into the suffrage campaign and recognized that these women needed to be brought in contact, not with women of leisure, but with business and professional women who were also out in the world earning their living."[10] The Equality League of Self-Supporting Women (which would later be renamed the Women's Political Union) began with a meeting of about two hundred. Within a year and a half, however, the organization boasted more than twenty thousand members. The membership of the Equality League included women from a variety of professions, including "doctors, lawyers, milliners and shirtmakers."[11] Eventually the Equality League was affiliated with a wide array of trade unions (including those of garment workers, typographers, and bookbinders) as well as intellectuals and social reformers.[12]

Not surprisingly, the inception of the Equality League was met with scorn and infantilization. On January 3, 1907, the *Brooklyn Daily Eagle* noted, "The Equality League of Self Supporting Women springs from its bassinet, helmets its youthful self in gory-hued aigrettes, and challenges all comers." The writer's condescension for the Equality League members leaps off the page. The deployment of language that invokes signs of bourgeois femininity (namely bassinets and aigrettes) was common among journalists looking to undermine or dismiss the political work of suffrage activists, and many high-profile suffrage meetings, protests, and performances were reduced to descriptions of women's apparel. The writer goes on to claim, "It follows that when the Equality League (etc.) has whipped all jousters to a finish … public offices will no longer be manned with clerks and bookkeepers, doortenders, messengers, and stenographers. Instead they will be womanned with telephone girls, and housemaids, bad cooks, seamstresses, and school teachers, broken down by overwork." The writer concludes by reassuring readers, "Fortunately, for the world's peace of mind, most reforms are slow, very slow of consummation."[13] Unfortunately for the writer, merely ten years after the formation of the Equality League, New York State legalized suffrage for women.[14]

The Equality League of Self-Supporting Women was initially localized in its advocacy, organizing delegations to the New York State legislature to testify about bleak working conditions. Soon the Equality League expanded its focus through an event that initiated the transatlantic transfer of suffrage protest tactics. In December 1907 WSPU member and former political prisoner Anne Cobden-Sanderson delivered a speech in New York City. Defying a ban on her entrance to the United States, Cobden-Sanderson snuck over the border from

Canada, giving talks in Philadelphia and Chicago before addressing the overflow crowd at Cooper Union, described by some as "Manhattan's labor temple." She discussed the labor activist roots of the WSPU, protest strategies, and her experience in prison. According to suffrage historian Ellen DuBois, "Cobden-Sanderson's visit to New York catalyzed a great outburst of suffrage energy; in its wake, Blatch and a handful of other new leaders introduced the WSPU tactics into the American movement, and the word 'suffragette' became as common in New York as in London."[15]

Almost two years later, Blatch was instrumental in organizing the speaking tour of another notorious British suffragette: none other than Emmeline Pankhurst herself, leader of the WSPU. Many of the clippings related to this tour were preserved in the Miller scrapbooks that were created in Geneva, New York. Additionally, Blatch recounted her memories of the tour in her memoir. Pankhurst wrote to her friend Blatch, asking for advice and guidance on a US speaking tour. Having invested a great deal of her own money into the suffrage cause, Pankhurst was in need of income to help with medical costs for her son.[16] Pankhurst addressed an overflowing crowd in Carnegie Hall on October 25, 1909. As the *New York Times* noted the next day, although the theatre held more than three thousand people, "more than 300 were sent away, and there was still a line of persistent ones extending up the street and around the corner" for more than two blocks.[17] Hundreds of people sat on the platform. There were representatives from a number of suffrage and trade organizations (e.g., Blatch's Geneva cousin Anne Fitzhugh Miller, which may partly explain why news clippings were so carefully preserved in the Miller scrapbooks) and from a wide array of professions, including teachers, doctors, dentists, actresses, journalists, bookbinders, cigar makers, hat trimmers, textile workers, and many more. Additionally, as the *Times* noted, "Three Maori women from the Hippodrome, with tattooed faces, were there, invited as peers. In their own country, New Zealand, they have voted." Following introductory remarks by Blatch and a performance of a suffrage song, Pankhurst spoke about the history of the suffrage movement in England, the arrests of protesters, and the horrors of force-feeding. In lieu of detailing the grim content of her speech, the *New York Times* devoted an entire paragraph to describing the dress that Pankhurst wore, noting its connection to the cause: "She was attractively gowned in a mauve Empire frock of velvet. The lining of the large, loose sleeves was of a dull shade of green, little green danglers hanging from them, green embroidery on the front, with a hint of a green skirt, of the same shade beneath and with the white of the close-fitting undersleeves and the neck making the three colors of the English suffragette, purple, white, and green."[18] It seems that even the most iconic and influential suffragette of the twentieth century would be reduced to the exterior trappings of her femininity through descriptions of her attire.

Emmeline Pankhurst's North American tour took her to many large cities. It also brought her to the small city of Geneva, where the Geneva Political Equality Club hosted her lecture at the Smith Opera House on November 22, 1909.[19] Anne Fitzhugh Miller once again took the stage with Pankhurst, this time to introduce her on behalf of the Political Equality Club. In a newspaper article printed the next day, the writer described how the Smith Opera House was decorated to represent the history of the US suffrage movement, including Political Equality Club banners, yellow chrysanthemums, and a large portrait of Susan B. Anthony. The colors of the UK suffrage campaign were depicted on the program from the event.[20]

In addition to hosting high-profile suffrage figures such as Emmeline Pankhurst (and, later in 1911, her daughter Sylvia[21]), the Geneva Political Equality Club sponsored theatre-related events. At a meeting of the Elizabeth Smith Miller Study Club (an offshoot of the Geneva Political Equality Club) on January 3, 1910, it was decided that the organization would present a production of *How the Vote Was Won* by Christopher St. John and Cicely Hamilton in April 1910. Harriot Stanton Blatch was responsible for this suggestion, as several newspaper clippings recounting the meeting indicated. Noting the comic tone of the play, one article assured readers, "The three meetings preceding this occasion will lead up to the subject of 'Votes for Women' but in a more serious vein than is revealed in the play."[22] The Geneva production of *How the Vote Was Won* was ultimately staged on May 18, 1910, just under two months after the suffrage matinee was held at the Maxine Elliott Theatre in New York City, where Hamilton and St. John's play was also featured. The Geneva production was presented in the St. Francis DeSales Hall and was directed by and starred a local high school teacher. The production was a benefit for the local public library.[23] It is unclear at what point plans were made for the New York City production, principally organized by Beatrice Forbes-Robertson. The meeting of the Study Club, at which Blatch, visiting from out of town, was a special guest, was a full two months prior to the suffrage matinee in New York City. Regardless of which production was in the planning stages first, Blatch was the common denominator between them, advocating for the use of British suffrage drama to advance the cause in the United States.

Ultimately, it was actress Beatrice Forbes-Robertson, who, in conjunction with Blatch, organized the suffrage matinee as a benefit for the Equality League in March 1910 in New York City. Several months later, in November 1910, Forbes-Robertson was brought to Geneva by the Geneva Political Equality Club to offer a recitation and speak in favor of suffrage. In the article announcing her engagement in Geneva, the author references both the New York City and Geneva productions of the Hamilton and St. John play, thereby linking them together again through their commonalities. The article reads, "Last spring Miss Forbes-Robertson organized and carried to a successful finish a suffrage matinee presenting three suffrage plays to a large audience at Maxine Elliott's theater in New York City, netting $1,000 profit for the Equality League of Self-supporting women. One of the plays, 'How the Vote Was Won,' was presented in this city last spring under the auspices of the Elizabeth Smith Miller Club."[24]

The Miller family and the Geneva Political Equality Club were responsible for much of the surviving documentation (scant as it may be) of the suffrage matinee in New York City. The timing of the New York and Geneva events and the involvement of Harriot Stanton Blatch in the administration of both could suggest that Blatch and the Geneva Political Equality Club may have had a role in the genesis of the fund-raiser at the Maxine Elliott Theatre. Forbes-Robertson's visit to Geneva was part of a larger speaking tour to several upstate New York communities. However, her prior relationship with Blatch as well as Blatch's familial and political relationship with the Smith Miller family uniquely situate the Forbes-Robertson visit to Geneva within a larger matrix of the twentieth-century suffrage campaign and the transatlantic transfer of activists, propaganda techniques, and new performance traditions that employed theatre as a tool for change.

Before the twentieth century, theatre was no stranger to the suffrage cause. Bettina Friedl's anthology *On to Victory: Propaganda Plays of the Woman Suffrage Movement*, illustrates how both pro- and anti-suffrage plays were read or staged in homes as early as the 1850s, largely as entertainment. Parlor theatricals were popular throughout the nineteenth century in the United Kingdom and the United States. Indeed, in her memoir, Blatch opens with an explanation of how even her mother, Elizabeth Cady Stanton, and cousin Elizabeth Smith Miller were known in the family for their parlor minstrel performances. Blatch recounts how notice of her birth was sent via a letter in 1856 from her mother to her mother's cousin Elizabeth Smith Miller. Rather than addressing her cousin by name, Stanton hailed her as "Julius" and referred to herself as "Massar Johnson" because, as Blatch clarifies in a footnote, "Elizabeth Smith Miller and my mother were often called Julius and Johnson after two comedians in the Christy minstrels whom they imitated much to the amusement of their families."[25] Friedl explains how suffrage propaganda plays fit within parlor performance traditions: "The earliest plays, written immediately before and after the Civil War, were true parlor farces written for those bourgeois audiences who had already heard of the Woman Question and were in turn troubled, amused, or perhaps genuinely interested by its implications."[26] It was not until the early twentieth century that suffrage drama for propaganda purposes abandoned the parlor and took center stage.

Approximately one year before the 1910 suffrage matinee at the Maxine Elliott Theatre, a production of Elizabeth Robins's *Votes for Women* was staged at Wallack's Theatre in New York by the Actors' Society. Unlike the three short propaganda plays presented as part of the suffrage matinee, *Votes for Women* is a slightly melodramatic three-act text. The *New York Times* reviewer did not find it to be an especially well-written drama or a convincing piece of propaganda but did rave about the performances, especially that of Mary Shaw in one of the principal roles. The reviewer opened by asserting: "It is a little difficult to know just what to say about Miss Elizabeth Robins's 'Votes for Women,' which was acted for the first time in this country at Wallack's Theatre last night. A play, in the sense of a work of rational movement and well-balanced part, it certainly is not; and as an argument to carry conviction to any one who stands in opposition to the cause which Miss Robins and her fellow-suffragettes are supporting, it is undoubtedly weakened by the case described."[27] The author of "The Lounger" column in *Putnam's Magazine*, however, noted, "It was a great night for woman suffrage—and for Socialism."[28] While Robins's play is set in London and had its premiere in London at the Court Theatre in 1907, Robins was an American actress and writer. Her citizenship prevents *Votes for Women* from being designated as a British drama. However, its setting, characters, production history, and Robins's own engagement with both the British Theatre and British suffrage organizations meant that the 1909 New York production was cloaked in a sense of British-ness. This production may have also helped lay the groundwork for the 1910 suffrage matinee. Present in the audience for *Votes for Woman* was Mrs. Clarence Mackay (Katherine Duer Mackay), who purchased a box and would go on to become one of the patronesses of the suffrage matinee one year later. Representatives from the Equality League took up the circle of the first balcony, according to a cutting in the Miller scrapbook.[29]

The 1910 suffrage matinee at the Maxine Elliott Theatre was a fund-raiser, generating more than $1000 in donations to the Equality League of Self-Supporting Women. It also served as a moment when the UK and US suffrage movements converged onstage as British and American actresses performed three short suffrage plays originally produced by the well-known Actresses' Franchise League (AFL) in London. Actresses in the British theatre were themselves self-supporting women, earning a living or scraping by in a field dominated by male managers, agents, producers, directors, and playwrights. Women in the theatre, particularly noncelebrity women who appeared in choruses, had minor parts, or were perennial understudies for more famous performers, were in especially vulnerable positions. Noncelebrity performers were contingent labor, working contract to contract, facing constant threats of sexual harassment and exploitation, and responsible for paying for their own costumes as well as their travel and lodgings when appearing on provincial stages.

While some actresses were engaged in the more militant tactics of the WSPU, most avoided such engagement, because a night (or several nights) in prison could effectively end a career. The AFL was founded as an alternative. Dale Spender, in the introduction to the first published collection of British suffrage plays noted that the first meeting of the AFL in December 1908 at the Criterion Restaurant "was a glittering affair with four hundred actresses present."[30] While officially the organization was not affiliated with either the WSPU or the more conservative National Union of Women's Suffrage Societies, the majority of the membership found themselves sympathetic to, or members of, the WSPU. The AFL provided invaluable creative support to the suffrage cause. In her foundational study of activist actresses, *Innocent Flowers: Women in the Edwardian Theatre*, Julie Holledge asserts that entertainment had long been woven into political meetings through music or recitation. The AFL soon offered a new form of political entertainment through the creation of a play department run by Inez Bensusan.[31] Bensusan recruited writers to create short plays and monologues for the AFL repertory and organized the performances of a wide array of texts at political meetings throughout England.

One of the most popular pieces to emerge from the AFL was *How the Vote Was Won*, by Cicely Hamilton and Christopher St. John (formerly Christabel Marshall). The original production of *How the Vote Was Won* was directed by Edy Craig, who was St. John's partner, daughter of the iconic actress Ellen Terry and, later, founder of the Pioneer Players. The play premiered in 1909 as part of a larger WSPU exhibition. Beatrice Forbes-Robertson originated the role of Winifred.[32] As with many of the suffrage plays that were restaged in a variety of locations and contexts, with each subsequent staging of *How the Vote Was Won*, new casts had to be assembled and rehearsed as previous performers were booked into other roles in the British (or American) theatre and unable to perform.[33] Set within an imaginary general strike by women, all female relations of suffrage foe Horace Cole arrive at his house to be taken care of as his female servants depart for their own families. The frenzy of their arrival as well as the economic toll of their new dependence on him causes Horace to emphatically convert to the suffrage cause. The short farce quickly became a crowd favorite throughout England. It is hardly surprising, then, that it would soon become "a runaway hit on both sides of the Atlantic."[34]

Beatrice Forbes-Robertson, who was an active member of the Actresses' Franchise League (and would eventually become one of the vice presidents), was the principal organizer of the 1910 suffrage matinee in New York. As the reviewer for the *New York Times* claimed, "Miss Beatrice Forbes-Robertson certainly, if not positively militant, has courage of the suffragist convictions, for she arranged the matinee, came in strong in the honors that were awarded in Mrs. Blatch's speech, and acted in two of the plays herself, each time being a definite symbol in the cast of WHAT WOMEN DO WANT."[35] *How the Vote Was Won* was the final play on the bill for the matinee. Two more somber pieces, *Before the Dawn*, by Bessie Hatton, and *A Woman's Influence*, by Gertrude Jennings, preceded the popular comedy.

The circular advertising the New York City Suffrage Matinee confirms the fund-raising success of the event, describing it as "a triple bill ... consisting of three new and successful Suffrage Plays." A handwritten note on the circular reads, "This is the performance referred to in Miss Robertson's letter. $1000 profit for" and a line is drawn to "Equality League of Self-Supporting Women." The circular lists some of the actors and actresses that were to appear, a mix of American and British performers. Additionally, the lengthy list of "patronesses" was included at the bottom of the page.[36] These included noted suffragists as well as theatre celebrities including Ethel Barrymore, who Blatch claims in her memoir also performed.[37] In addition to Barrymore, the performers and patrons for the event included familiar theatrical names such as Ruth Holt Boucicault (wife of Dion Boucicault's son Aubrey) and Johnston Forbes-Robertson, as well as iconic figures from the suffrage movement, such as Mrs. John E. Milholland (mother of Inez Milholland), Katherine Duer Mackay (socialite suffragist and founder and president of the Equal Franchise Society), and Harriot Stanton Blatch.[38]

Although the advertisement for the suffrage matinee does not include mention of the other elements of the performance, the *New York Times* reviewer noted, "In the intervals between the plays addresses were made by Johnston Forbes-Robertson and Mrs. Harriot Stanton Blatch. During the former's address one voice was raised louder than the speaker but whether in protest to the sentiment of the occasion could not be determined. It was the voice of an infant hidden somewhere in the balcony." The reviewer also indicated that other prominent attendees were situated in reserved boxes and that suffrage banners adorned the interior of the theatre. Most of the review is dedicated to summarizing the plots of the three plays.[39]

In addition to the rousing speeches, satirical poems were delivered by celebrity figures. Charlotte Perkins Gilman's poem "Women Do Not Want It" (published in 1893) was one of the pieces performed. Maxine Elliott had donated the use of the theatre, and she herself performed Gilman's poem.[40] In the poem, Gilman responds to the anti-suffragist claim that had gained traction at the end of the nineteenth century that women do not actually want the vote.[41] The concerns she raises reflect the multifaceted concerns of the suffrage movement that persisted well into the twentieth century. The poem opens:

> When the woman suffrage argument first stood upon its legs,
> They answered it with cabbages, they answered it with eggs,
> They answered it with ridicule, they answered it with scorn,
> They thought it a monstrosity that should not have been born.[42]

Gilman proceeds to ask, "Have we women always wanted what you gave to us before?" and then answers her own questions with examples of domestic violence, control over attire, and exclusion from governance and facets of religion. She then writes,

> Did we ask to be forbidden from all the trades that pay?
> Did we claim the lower wages for a man's full work today?
> Have we petitioned for the laws wherein our shame is shown:
> That not a woman's child–nor her own body–is her own?[43]

Although the Equality League of Self-Supporting Women initially approached suffrage from the perspective of labor activism, Gilman's poem illustrates the breadth of the women's rights movement in the early twentieth century, extending beyond concerns of work and the vote.

The review of the matinee published the next day in the *New York Times* did not delve into the content of the poem to address the women's call for equal pay for equal work, custody rights, or bodily autonomy. Instead, the unnamed reviewer once again focused on the clothing of the performer, noting, "The poem was very agreeably recited by Miss Maxine Elliott, quite becomingly feminine and charming in a very smart gown of cream broadcloth, with white furs, and a big, smashing black tulle hat, which, however, made ingress and egress through the narrow first entrance somewhat difficult." The girth of Elliot's apparel notwithstanding, following the conclusion of the event the reviewer proclaimed, "If

Equal Rights will result in many more entertainments as pleasant as the one arranged in aid of the Equality League of Self-Supporting Women at the Maxine Elliott Theatre yesterday, then Equal Rights by all means!"[44]

The suffrage matinee on March 31, 1910, ignited a series of other performances and creative spectacle events in support of women's suffrage in the United States. Beatrice Forbes-Robertson staged subsequent performances of *Before the Dawn*, *A Woman's Influence*, and *How the Vote Was Won* in Washington, DC, Chicago, and Philadelphia.[45] Approximately one month after the initial New York City suffrage matinee, Beatrice married Swinburne Hale, who became smitten with her after witnessing her deliver a speech at a suffrage rally.[46] She returned to the New York stage in 1911 with three different plays (including one by Charlotte Perkins Gilman) and a Pageant of Protest, all staged as a fund-raiser for the Woman Suffrage Party.[47] Forbes-Robertson-Hale would eventually give up theatre but maintained her active involvement in suffrage campaigns, speaking and writing about the cause. Fola La Follete, who had appeared as Ethel Cole in *How the Vote Was Won* for the 1910 suffrage matinee, created a one-woman version of the play, in which she performed all the characters. She toured this production to great acclaim throughout the United States.[48]

The Equality League for Self-Supporting Women (now the Women's Political Union) also continued to produce theatricals as fund-raisers for their cause including tableaux and a benefit matinee of *Lysistrata*, both at the Maxine Elliott Theatre.[49] The organization even created pro-suffrage silent films. On May 21, 1910, the Equality League sponsored a parade that brought together hundreds of suffrage activists from an array of organizations. They marched down Fifth Avenue to Union Square, accompanied by an army of mounted police. Once in Union Square, an audience of more than ten thousand people listened to the rallying speeches, according to a *New York Times* article published the next day. The *Times* deemed it "the biggest suffrage demonstration ever in the United States."[50] The demonstration possessed theatrical flair as representatives from the Collegiate Equal Suffrage League marched in caps and gowns as well as sashes of purple, green, and cream, and the more than ninety automobiles involved in the procession were draped in yellow sashes and ornamented with yellow flowers. The parade also featured a baby carriage that carried lemonade and sandwiches for the participants, thus subverting the anti-suffrage image of the empty baby carriage, which they feared would be the result of women's enfranchisement. This parade ignited a tradition of elaborate suffrage processions in New York City. In the next seven years, six more parades would march down Fifth Avenue, with one in 1915 boasting as many as fifty thousand participants.[51]

The Maxine Elliott Theatre was a site of convergence in 1910. The rich histories of British and American suffrage campaigns were interwoven as artists and activists from both nations inhabited roles together onstage. The suffrage matinee was also a pivotal moment in the genealogy of US suffrage history, weaving together the significant New York State activist hubs of Seneca Falls, Geneva, and New York City. The performance of the suffrage propaganda plays, recitation of poetry, and delivery of stirring speeches ignited a new mode of performative protest strategies, marking a unique chapter in the history of the US suffrage campaign. The Equality League of Self-Supporting Women brought together working women from an array of socioeconomic and educational backgrounds and lines of work. Once the organization adopted some of the spectacular measures and texts of the British suffrage campaign, they were catapulted into the spotlight. Had the writer for the *Brooklyn Daily Eagle*, writing shortly after their first meeting, had any inkling of the grandiose nature of the Equality League's performative protests and the ways in which their work would go on to shape suffrage protests throughout the United States, he may not have been so quick to conclude his article with the following statement: "Mere man, lower-case man, looks on with more amusement than agitation."[52] Women got the last laugh, however, first in 1917 when New York State enfranchised women and again in 1920 when the Nineteenth Amendment was passed.

Notes

1. Frances Diodato Bzowski, "Spectacular Suffrage; Or, How Women Came Out of the Home and into the Streets and Theaters of New York City to Win the Vote," *New York History* 76, no. 1 (January 1995): 56–94. In her article, Bzowaski offers several examples of performative protest that predate the 1910 suffrage matinee. While many groups were employing the tactics of the British suffrage campaign, the numbers engaged in these endeavors were much smaller than what would emerge with the matinee and the other large-scale pageants, parades, and performances it inspired. This matinee was also unique in that it offered a direct lineage to the origins of the US suffrage campaign in Seneca Falls, New York, in the nineteenth century.
2. Miller NAWSA Suffrage Scrapbooks, 1897–1911, Rare Book and Special Collection Division, Library of Congress. These scrapbooks have been digitized and can be accessed through the Library of Congress website: http://memory.loc.gov/ammem/collections/suffrage/millerscrapbooks/index.html.
3. Lucy Stone died in 1893, Elizabeth Cady in 1902, and Susan B. Anthony in 1906.
4. Harriot Stanton Blatch, *Challenging Years: The Memoirs of Harriot Stanton Blatch* (New York: G. P. Putnam's Sons, 1940), 92.

5. Bzowski, "Spectacular Suffrage," 66.
6. Blatch, *Challenging Years*, 17, 61.
7. Ibid., 77.
8. Ibid., 92.
9. Nancy F. Cott, *The Grounding of Modern Feminism* (New Haven: Yale University Press, 1989), 24–25.
10. Blatch, *Challenging Years*, 93–94.
11. Ellen Carol DuBois, *Woman Suffrage and Women's Rights* (New York: NYU Press, 1998), 191; "Self-Supporting Women Organize to Get Office and Other Things," *New York Times*, January 3, 1907, 6.
12. Cott, *The Grounding of Modern Feminism*, 24–25.
13. "A New Giantess," *Brooklyn Daily Eagle*, January 3, 1907, 4.
14. Much like the subsequent Nineteenth Amendment to the US Constitution, this was not evenly applied to all women. Voting rights remained stripped from indigenous men and women and many Asian immigrants and restricted for African American women through exclusive, racist legislation. Louise Michele Newman's book, *White Women's Rights: The Racial Origins of Feminism in the United States* (Oxford: Oxford University Press, 1999), offers a fuller analysis of this exclusion.
15. DuBois, *Woman Suffrage*, 196.
16. Blatch, *Challenging Years*, 113.
17. "Great Throng Hears Mrs. Pankhurst," *New York Times*, October 26, 1909.
18. Ibid.
19. The Smith Opera House opened in 1894, funded by William Smith, who also created the women's college in his name that still exists today, affiliated with Hobart College for men.
20. "Mrs. Pankhurst a Good Entertainer," November 22, 1909, Scrapbook 8, pp. 21–22, Miller NAWSA Suffrage Scrapbooks, 1897–1911, Rare Book and Special Collection Division, Library of Congress.
21. "Miss Pankhurst Drew Big Crowd," February 14, 1911, Scrapbook 9, p. 38, Miller NAWSA Suffrage Scrapbooks, 1897–1911, Rare Book and Special Collection Division, Library of Congress.
22. "First Meeting of the Season," January 3, 1910, Scrapbook 8, p. 9, Miller NAWSA Suffrage Scrapbooks, 1897–1911, Rare Book and Special Collection Division, Library of Congress. Of the two articles on this page of the scrapbook that recount Blatch's recommendation of the comedy, one refers to the title as "How They Won the Vote" while the other dubs it "How the Ballot Was Won."
23. "For Benefit of the Free Library: 'How the Vote Was Won' To Be Presented by Junior Suffrage Club," May 18, 1910, Scrapbook 8, p.13, Miller NAWSA Suffrage Scrapbooks, 1897–1911, Rare Book and Special Collection Division, Library of Congress. Humorously, a smaller notice of the production on the same page of the scrapbook misattributed the title as "How the Boat Was Won."
24. "Beatrice Forbes-Robertson, English actress, speaks at Geneva Political Equality Club meeting," November 10, 1910, Scrapbook 9, p. 23, Miller NAWSA Suffrage Scrapbooks, 1897–1911, Rare Book and Special Collection Division, Library of Congress.
25. Blatch, *Challenging Years*, 3. From its inception, the US suffrage campaign rightly faced criticism for its exclusion of women of color. It is important to note how the practice of blackface minstrelsy was a reflection of structural racism, woven so deeply into the

culture that even one of the most iconic social justice activists of the nineteenth century was complicit in its perpetuation. While Blatch relates the memory of Sojourner Truth's visit to their home as part of a suffrage speaking tour, engagements such as this do not negate the fraught race relations among early suffragists.

26. Bettina Friedl, "General Introduction," *On to Victory: Propaganda Plays of the Woman Suffrage Movement* (Boston: Northeastern University Press, 1987), 5.
27. "MARY SHAW SUPERB IN 'VOTES FOR WOMEN': Elizabeth Robbyn's [*sic*] Suffragette Play Produced by Actors' Society. A TRAFALGAR SQUARE SCENE Interesting Study of a Crowd, but Play Unconvincing as Drama or Argument." *New York Times*, March 16, 1909, 9.
28. Excerpts from "The Lounger," *Putnam's Magazine: An Illustrated Monthly of Literature, Art and Life* 6: 255.
29. "Votes for Women," Scrapbook 7, p. 112. Miller NAWSA Suffrage Scrapbooks, 1897–1911, Rare Book and Special Collection Division, Library of Congress.
30. Dale Spender, "Introduction," *How the Vote Was Won and Other Suffragette Plays* (London: Methuen Theatrefile, 1985), 7–13.
31. Julie Holledge, *Innocent Flowers: Women in the Edwardian Theatre* (London: Virago, 1981), 62–63. The AFL contributed to the suffrage campaign in vivid ways including costuming and performing in pageants and processions and providing disguises for suffragettes temporarily released from prison due to hunger strikes and the "Cat and Mouse Act." The most iconic and enduring contributions to the cause, however, came in the form of suffrage drama.
32. Christopher St. John and Cicely Hamilton, *How the Vote Was Won* (Chicago: Dramatic Publishing Company, 1910), 3.
33. Holledge, *Innocent Flowers*, 66–67.
34. Ellen Ecker Dolgin, *Shaw and the Actresses Franchise League: Staging Equality* (Jefferson, NC: McFarland, 2015), 138.
35. "Suffragist Plays at Benefit Matinee," *New York Times*, April 1, 1910, 11.
36. "Suffrage Matinee organized by Beatrice Forbes-Robertson for benefit of Equality League of Self-Supporting Women at Maxine Elliott's Theatre," March 31, 1910, Scrapbook 9, p. 24, Miller NAWSA Suffrage Scrapbooks, 1897–1911, Rare Book and Special Collection Division, Library of Congress. The letter referenced in the note does not appear to have been preserved in the scrapbook.
37. Blatch, *Challenging Years*, 138.
38. Milholland advocated for the participation of African American women in the suffrage movement. W. E. B. Du Bois published a short editorial by Milholland in *Crisis* in December 1910. Mrs. John E. Milholland, "Talks About Women," *Crisis*, December 1910, 28.
39. "Suffragist Plays at Benefit Matinee," *New York Times*, April 1, 1910, 11.
40. Elliott's sister Gertrude was married to Beatrice Forbes-Robertson's famous uncle, English actor and theatre manager Johnston Forbes-Robertson, which may have been useful in securing the venue. Lee Shubert sanctioned the free use of the theatre. In a thank you letter to Shubert a few weeks after the matinee, the then acting president of the Equality League wrote, "We wished to express to you our sincerest thanks for your kindness in joining with Miss Elliot in lending us the theatre for our Benefit Matinee. We feel that having the use of such a beautiful theatre added very much to the attractiveness of the entertainment." Elizabeth Ellsworth Cook to Lee Shubert, April 20, 1910, New York

City, General Correspondence 1909–1910 EN-ER, Box 28, Shubert Archive, New York City. The author would like to thank the staff of the Shubert Archive for their assistance in locating this letter.

41. Judith A. Allen, *The Feminism of Charlotte Perkins Gilman: Sexualities, Histories, Progressivism* (Chicago: University of Chicago Press, 2009), 139.
42. Charlotte Perkins Gilman, *Charlotte Perkins Gilman's* In This Our World *and Uncollected Poems*, ed. Gary Scharnhorst and Denise D. Knight (Syracuse, NY: Syracuse University Press, 2012), 91.
43. Ibid., 91.
44. "Suffragist Plays at Benefit Matinee," *New York Times*, April 1, 1910, 11.
45. Barbara Cohen-Stratyner, "How the Vote Was Won, and Exported," *New York Public Library*, February 20, 2015, https://www.nypl.org/blog/2015/02/20/how-vote-was-won?utm_source=feedburner&utm_medium=feed&utm_campaign=Feed%3A+NYPLAllBlogs+%28NYPL+Blogs%29. "Smart Set Folk Hard Pressed by the Social Whirl," *Philadelphia Inquirer*, January 29, 1911, 20.
46. "Actress Suffragist to Marry Lawyer," *New York Times*, April 29, 1910, 9.
47. "Benefit for Woman Suffrage: Three One-Act Plays and a Pageant to be Presented Today," *New York Times*, March 21, 1911, 11.
48. Margaret Mary Finnegan, *Selling Suffrage: Consumer Culture & Votes for Women* (New York: Columbia University Press, 1999), 88.
49. Blatch, *Challenging Years*, 138.
50. "SUFFRAGE PARADE HAS POLICE GUARD," *New York Times*, May 22, 1910, 11.
51. Linda J. Lumsden, *Rampant Women: Suffragists and the Right of Assembly* (Knoxville: University of Tennessee Press, 1997), 75.
52. "A New Giantess," *Brooklyn Daily Eagle*, January 3, 1907, 4.

"Why I Wrote the Phyllis Wheatley Pageant-Play"

Mary Church Terrell's Bicentennial Activism

—LURANA DONNELS O'MALLEY

Sometimes I joke in rehearsal, "If this was truly a period piece, I'd be in chains somewhere."
—OKIERIETE ONAODOWAN

Hamilton: An American Musical, the groundbreaking creation of Lin-Manuel Miranda, broke that ground in part by casting actors of color as key historical figures of the American Revolution and its aftermath. On Broadway, African American actors played three US presidents: Okieriete Onaodowan (James Madison), Daveed Diggs (Thomas Jefferson), and Christopher Jackson (George Washington).[1] Jackson, however, was not the first man of African descent to portray George Washington on the American stage. More than eighty years earlier, in 1932, a black man played the role in a production that explored the relation between America's founding fathers and the people they enslaved: Mary Church Terrell's *Historical Pageant-Play Based on the Life of Phyllis Wheatley*.[2] As critic Lyra D. Monteiro notes about *Hamilton*, there is "a truly damning omission in [*Hamilton*]: despite the proliferation of black and brown bodies onstage, not a single enslaved or free person of color exists as a character in this play."[3] In contrast, the 1932 production of Terrell's script placed the eighteenth-century poet Phillis Wheatley front and center as an enslaved African American character with agency and impact.

Mary Church Terrell (1863–1954) was an African American educator, writer,

Figure 1. Portrait of Mary Church Terrell, courtesy of the Moorland-Spingarn Research Center, Howard University Archives, Howard University, Washington, DC.

suffragist, and civil rights activist. Terrell (figure 1) was a founding member of the National Association for the Advancement of Colored People (NAACP), the first president of the National Association of Colored Women, and the first black woman in the United States appointed as a member of a board of education, in Washington, DC. Although Terrell was a prolific writer (the author of numerous essays and articles in addition to her autobiography), to my knowledge she wrote only two scripts, both intended as contributions to the 1932 bicentennial celebration of George Washington's birthday: a pageant about the African American soldiers who fought in the Revolutionary War and a biographical pageant-play on Phillis Wheatley. The former was never staged; the latter was performed as part of the official Washington, DC, festivities for Washington's bicentennial.

Terrell's stated goal for both historical pageants was to combat the negative and demeaning images of African Americans she had encountered in other plays and pageants planned for the Washington bicentennial. In *Phyllis Wheatley*, Terrell exposes the injustice of authentication rituals, as Wheatley is again

Figure 2. Engraving of Phillis Wheatley, 1773, attributed to Scipio Moorhead. Library of Congress Rare Book and Special Collections Division, Washington, DC.

and again asked to prove the validity of her talent as a writer. Ironically, Terrell herself faced such judgment from two sides: from black critics opposed to the Washington bicentennial's representations of African Americans and from production staff and supporters who questioned the historical authenticity of her pageant-play. Although the production faced numerous obstacles and was considerably downsized from the original plans, the performance, created by a dozen artists and staff members, featured a cast of more than two hundred African Americans, most of them public school youths performing for their own community. *Phyllis Wheatley* was ultimately the only staged birthday bicentennial event to place African American history at center stage and in a positive light.

As Terrell knew, the historical Wheatley (figure 2) was not only contemporaneous with Washington but also had an unusual connection to him. In October 1775, Wheatley composed a poem in honor of General Washington and sent it to him at his headquarters in Cambridge along with a brief note; in February 1776, Washington wrote a reply to thank her for it.[4] Wheatley's poem first appeared in print in the *Virginia Gazette* in March 1776; titled "To his Excellency

George Washington," the panegyric praises Washington but also requests that he be guided by the goddess Columbia.[5] This documented interaction between Wheatley and Washington inspired Terrell to dramatize the major events of Wheatley's life, from her capture in Africa to her wedding, featuring the Washington poem as the centerpiece. Terrell addresses several of her goals for the script in her short essay "Why I Wrote the Phyllis Wheatley Pageant-Play," including her intention "to increase the colored youth's respect for his African ancestors by showing the native ability and the brilliant literary success of an African girl stolen from her native land and sold as a slave in this country, when she was but a small child."[6] As Terrell includes a similar passage in her autobiography, *A Colored Woman in a White World* (1940), she evidently saw her involvement with the Washington bicentennial as a significant example of her own negotiation within a white world.[7]

Bicentennial Inclusion

The United States Congress established the federal George Washington Bicentennial Commission in 1924 via a joint resolution, signed by Calvin Coolidge. The bicentennial celebration (officially held between February 2 and November 24, 1932) was a federally sponsored initiative to commemorate the first president's date of birth through publications, educational outreach, and public events.[8] The commission's associate director and driving force was New York congressional representative Sol Bloom (figure 3). Bloom was no doubt appointed in part because of his prior association with the entertainment industry; most notably, he coordinated the Midway Plaisance entertainments for the Chicago World's Fair in 1893. Bloom and the federal commission encouraged schools, clubs, and civic organizations to create a variety of public programs such as observances, speeches, ceremonies, plays, and pageants, many of which were overseen by local commissions. Bloom estimated that "an average of some sixteen thousand individual programs—by churches, schools, civic bodies, patriotic societies, and fraternal orders—were held in all parts of the United States each day of the nine months' Celebration," totaling a staggering 4,760,345 "separate and distinct" programs honoring Washington nationwide.[9] The commission printed extensive educational resources related to the history of Washington and his era, and it specifically encouraged theatrical representations through two pamphlets. One gave advice for would-be producers and the other listed dozens of scripts and pageants related to Washington, many of which were written under the commission's auspices.[10] A final statement by the federal Play and Pageant Division stated, "The reports to the Commission indicate that several hundred thousand persons, principally children, took part in these plays and pageants."[11]

Figure 3. Costumed children with Sol Bloom. Library of Congress Prints and Photographs Division, Harris & Ewing Collection.

Terrell was spurred to write her pageant-plays when she realized that plans for the birthday bicentennial celebration were excluding African American heritage and history, echoing their exclusion from similar US occasions in the past. The 1893 World's Columbian Exhibition (popularly known as the Chicago World's Fair) is a prominent example of how the contributions of African Americans to their country were overlooked by the organizers of national celebrations and exhibitions. African American activist Ida B. Wells created a pamphlet protesting the insufficient coverage of African American achievement at the exhibition: "The exhibit of the progress made by a race in 25 years of freedom as against 250 years of slavery, would have been the greatest tribute to the greatness and progressiveness of American institutions. We can only hope that ...

in another great National endeavor the Colored American shall not plead for a place in vain."[12] When exhibition planners created a single "Negro Day" (August 25) to placate critical African Americans, Frederick Douglass attended the event and gave a keynote address, but Wells refused to participate.[13]

Over two decades later, in 1921, James Weldon Johnson and W. E. B. Du Bois succeeded in their quest for inclusion in the America's Making Exhibition, a celebration of the diverse immigrant cultures of the United States. The exhibition, which emphasized assimilation and "a single loyalty" to America, was held at Seventy-first Regiment Armory in New York from October 29 to November 12.[14] Johnson and Du Bois created the "Americans of Negro Lineage" pavilion, also known as the "Negro pavilion." Its main exhibition booth was designed as an Egyptian temple, with Meta Fuller's sculpture "Ethiopia Awakening" as its focal point. Du Bois contributed a pageant, *The Seven Gifts of Ethiopia to America*, performed on November 11; he firmly believed in the power of pageantry as "a means of uplift and education."[15]

In the 1930s Terrell and other African American activists continued to make their pleas for inclusion. While the Great Migration was bringing millions of black Americans into previously white-dominated urban centers, African Americans continued to face substantial social obstacles and injustices throughout the country, such as voting disenfranchisement, lynching, and segregation. Since the New Negro Renaissance of the 1920s had brought African American artistic styles and themes into the larger American cultural sphere, the planned bicentenary events of 1932—from parades to ceremonies and pageants—offered a new and significant opportunity to include the African American story within a national commemoration.

Because the principal aim of the bicentennial celebration was to celebrate Washington's achievements—as a general, as a founding father, and as the nation's first leader—the year's activities nationwide were predominantly adulatory in tone. Many African American historians and intellectuals, familiar with Washington's status as a slaveholder and his opposition to the recruitment of black soldiers for the revolutionary army, had a different perspective. One such voice, that of the eminent black historian Carter G. Woodson, spoke out in terms reminiscent of Wells and her opposition to the Chicago World's Fair. Woodson's critique was indirectly aimed at Terrell, in relation to her membership on a bicentennial subcommittee with a very long name: the Committee on Coordinating Activities among Colored People for the George Washington Bicentennial Celebration in the District of Columbia (hereafter referred to as CCAACP). The CCAACP was a subcommittee of the District of Columbia Commission for the George Washington Bicentennial, headed by Cloyd H. Marvin (president of George Washington University). The DC commission oversaw events in the nation's capital and was therefore in charge of some of the most prominent events of the bicentenary. In August 1931, Marvin appointed Terrell to serve on the CCAACP.[16] In addition to Terrell, some of the most prominent African American citizens in the DC community served on the committee, including its chair, Garnet Wilkinson, who served from 1924 until 1951 as first assistant superintendent of Public Schools of the District of Columbia, in charge of DC's African American schools (Division 10–13).

On December 12, 1931, Woodson published a critique of the bicentennial preparations in the *Afro-American* (a Baltimore-based newspaper with a wide Atlantic-coast circulation). In the essay, titled "George Washington Bi-Centennial Commission Has Colored Sideshow," Woodson explains that his office at the Association for the Study of Negro Life and History (ASNLH) has received "numerous inquiries as to what we are going to do about the George Washington Bicentennial celebration."[17] Woodson states that it is a mistake to assume that he and the ASNLH have "charge of the affair, or that, if we have not, somebody more liberal-minded than the Herbert Hoover–Sol Bloom commission now directing it should have the work in hand." The article's "sideshow" is a not-so-veiled reference to Sol Bloom's past life as an entertainment entrepreneur for the Chicago World's Fair Midway Plaisance, where he popularized the "hoochie-coochie dance" as part of his Algerian village exhibit. Woodson evidently associated Bloom with the erasure of black presence within a large celebratory context.

After commenting on the segregated approach to the bicentennial events, Woodson then writes, with bitter understatement, "Right here in Washington we have been asked to register our names as willing to play the part of slaves in the celebration which will be staged in the capital of the nation, and it is highly probable that most of us who will be selected by the management handling these various celebrations will be better qualified to serve as slaves than as anything else. Unfortunately many of us have never been willing to play any other part."[18] On one level, Woodson calls attention to the irony of being asked to willingly volunteer to perform as enslaved people as part of a tribute to the country's slaveholding first president. He also accuses the bicentennial's African American collaborators (likely the CCAACP, to which Terrell belonged)[19] of playing the part of slaves in their cooperation with bicentenary plans. Further, Woodson argues that a focus on enslavement does not express the full force of African American experience and achievement in the United States; he follows by noting the contributions of Crispus Attucks and Benjamin Banneker as well as Wheatley. It is possible that the article was the germ of Terrell's idea for her Wheatley pageant-play.

A few weeks after his first essay, Woodson continued to criticize the CCAACP. In an article titled "Eliminating the Negro from the George Washington Bicentennial," he again sarcastically criticizes the CCAACP members as "compromising mediators" who "bartered away the claims of the Negro in return for such cheap recognition as service upon a committee to provide for a jim-crow celebration." "It was an easy matter to eliminate the Negro from the preparation for the George Washington Bicentennial.... These genuflecting Negroes were told that the colored people who would doubtless expect to take a part in the celebration should make some preparation among themselves and have their own demonstration."[20] Woodson concludes by asking his readers to completely reject participation in the bicentennial celebration: "There cannot be any honor in the segregating recognition which has been provided for here in the District of Columbia. To acquiesce in any such arrangement is tantamount to accepting a jim-crow section in a theatre or a jim-crow car."[21]

In a later article (January 2, 1932), Woodson chastises the organizers for neglecting to acknowledge the contributions of Crispus Attucks: "The Negroes of this country therefore should resist any effort of the George Washington Bicentennial or that of the genuflecting Negroes who are cooperating with them to eliminate these significant facts by a biased dramatization of American history."[22] Almost forty years after the Chicago World's Fair, yet another occasion was on the way to becoming a lost opportunity.

Terrell: "Yes I Can"

By mid-January 1932, not long after Woodson's critiques appeared, Terrell was put in charge of a new aspect of the CCAACP, perhaps created in direct response to Woodson: the pageantry committee.[23] Later that month, the *Afro-American* published a straightforward article with the attention-getting headline "Group Plans to Ban Jim Crow Celebration." The article, which reports on the January 29 meeting of the CCAACP, lacks the condemnation of Woodson's pieces on the topic. The anonymous article mentions Terrell as pageantry chair and may have been written by one of the committee members in response to Woodson's earlier criticisms: "Every precaution will be taken to see that colored people do not participate in any feature of the program where their self-respect is likely to suffer."[24]

In fact, Terrell had concerns that reflected Woodson's, as seen in her essay on the origin of her pageant-play about Wheatley: "I read many pageants written especially for the George Washington Bicentennial Commission. Without exception, the colored people mentioned in them were objects of ridicule. They were all slaves, of course, and their imperfect English with their mirth-provoking antics was used to make the audience laugh."[25] Like Woodson, Terrell recognized the communicative power of visual representations of black Americans clad as slaves, whether portrayed as happy or abject. Many of the numerous works listed in *Pageants and Plays Depicting the Life of George Washington and His Time* featured demeaning scenes of happy enslaved characters in Washington's service.[26] Terrell saw that a counter-narrative was needed, a "pageant about a creditable representative of our group who lived in George Washington's time of whose career our young people would have reason to be proud," and she pressed for it with the CCAACP: "At the next meeting I said again it would be a pity and a sad reflection upon us if we should let the bicentennial celebration year pass without producing a pageant depicting the achievement of somebody with African blood in his veins. Again my friend challenged me by saying 'Why don't you write one yourself? I believe you can do it.' In a sort of a dare-devil spirit I replied, 'Yes I can and I will.' As soon as I got home I started to write the pageant."[27] That inspiration seems to have led her to write two scripts, each treating subject matter referred to by Woodson. According to an article about the March 4 meeting of the CCAACP,[28] Marie Moore Forrest, head of pageantry for the DC bicentennial, had approved two pageants by Terrell: one about Phillis Wheatley and another titled *Depicting the Bravery of Colored Soldiers During the Revolutionary War*.[29] Although Wilkinson instructed the schools of Division 10–13 to cooperate with Terrell and her pageantry committee to produce both pageants,[30] there is no evidence that this second script was ever staged. Plans for *Phyllis Wheatley*, however, were well underway by March 1932.[31]

In brief, the plot of Terrell's *Phyllis Wheatley* moves from an initial scene of Wheatley's capture in Africa, to a scene depicting her purchase by the Wheatley family, and then to several scenes showing her acquisition of literacy in the Wheatley household. Her writing talent is revealed gradually, first to her owners and then more publicly in several authentication scenes featuring various guests to the household. The reading of Wheatley's correspondence with George Washington and her visit to his camp fall roughly at the center of the pageant-play. Wheatley then briefly visits England before returning to help her ailing mistress. The pageant-play ends on an uplifting note with Wheatley's wedding to John Peters; it does not depict her difficult marriage to him, nor her death in poverty. In general, Terrell highlights the positive aspects of Wheatley's story, emphasizing her bond with the Wheatleys over her enslavement by them; such choices are unsurprising, given both Terrell's target audience of African American youth and the overall celebratory nature of the bicentennial year. Yet Terrell also takes care to display a vibrant African homeland, and in later drafts, Wheatley expresses longing for the mother she was torn away from.[32]

Envisioning a production, Terrell saw the genre of pageantry—with its combination of history, spectacle, and ceremony—as the most appropriate format for a bicentenary event. By 1932, African American men and women had written and produced pageants in communities and schools for decades; Du Bois's *The People of Peoples and Their Gifts to Men* (1913), later revised and staged as *The Star of Ethiopia*, was the genre's most famous example.[33] Terrell's script, which she terms a "pageant-play," combines dialogue with spectacle (historical costuming, detailed exterior locations such as the African village or the slave market, and entertainments such as music at the garden party and songs at the wedding). Interlude dances serve as transitions between acts. Director Marguerite Williams, who was the first African American to receive a doctorate in geology in the United States and served as chair of the division of geology at Miner Teachers College, was involved with the production from its onset. Together, she and Terrell planned the involvement of numerous school and community groups, each forming the cast of a section of *Phyllis Wheatley*.

There were, however, many surprises in store for Terrell over the next few months. Like most African Americans at the time, Terrell was a loyal supporter of the Republican Party (the "party of Lincoln"), despite today's perspective that Herbert Hoover's presidency was detrimental to black interests. For the 1932 election, Terrell was appointed by the Republican Campaign Committee as "director of work among the colored women of the East."[34] In the fall of 1932, Terrell was forced to prioritize her commitment to Hoover over her involvement with the production of *Phyllis Wheatley*; she moved to New York for much of the autumn to work for Hoover's campaign. Although she recalls in her memoir that her office was "in the beautiful Waldorf Astoria Hotel," her correspondence also shows how much she wished she were in DC to consult on the production.[35]

A Change of Venue

As the performance drew nearer, a change to the production venue undermined Terrell's original ambitious vision. Just as Terrell changed location, so did the *Phyllis Wheatley* production; this move served to decrease its status as a bicentenary event. The *Afro-American* reported in March 1932 that Terrell had chosen a site for both of her planned pageants: "These plays are expected to be presented in the Sylvan Theatre, at the base of the Washington Monument."[36] The Sylvan Theatre would have been quite a spectacular location for the production. First used in 1917, it is an outdoor stage located to the southeast of the Washington Monument (figure 4). The Sylvan was the brainchild of theatre artist Alice Pike Barney, who initially staged classical plays there as well as her own writings.[37] It was designed for eight thousand spectators but could hold many more between

Figure 4. Flag Day exercises at Sylvan Theatre, 1919. Library of Congress Prints and Photographs Division, Harris & Ewing Collection.

the stage and the foot of the monument. Certainly, the Sylvan had the potential to host a glorious public event in honor of George Washington and was in fact used for at least two other bicentennial performances in 1932.[38]

But the venue for *Phyllis Wheatley* changed from the Sylvan Theatre to the Washington Auditorium and then to the auditorium of Armstrong Technical High School sometime between the newspaper account in March 1932 and an October letter received by Terrell. The letter, written by the production's costumer Carrie Watson (of the Department of Household Arts for the DC Public Schools), broke the news of a second site change: "The Pageant has been changed from the [Washington] Auditorium to Armstrong High School. This was done by the Co-ordinating Committee, after Mr. Wilkinson had thought it best to change in the face of 'depression.'"[39] Washington Auditorium, built in 1924, was an indoor auditorium holding more than five thousand spectators; it was located at the corner of Nineteenth and E Streets NW (just two blocks west of the White House) (figure 5). Although by 1932 it was struggling to make ends

Figure 5. Washington Auditorium interior. Library of Congress Prints and Photographs Division, National Photo Company Collection.

meet (its last major event, Franklin D. Roosevelt's 1933 Inaugural Ball, was held only two months after the Wheatley pageant-play), the Washington Auditorium was still a prestigious venue located in the heart of DC.[40]

Armstrong Technical High School, located in northeast DC, was a vocationally oriented school for African Americans (figure 6), a rival to the more academic Dunbar High. Primarily a technical school, Armstrong was also known for its applied curriculum arts (painting, music, and design), and its 1,100-seat auditorium regularly served as a site for black theatrical performances. The 1915 "Community Center Use of Buildings" act allowed for "the supplementary use of public school buildings for educational purposes—civic meetings, social centers, and centers of recreation."[41] In the move from the Washington Auditorium to the high school, both the visibility and the status of the *Phyllis Wheatley* pageant-play dramatically decreased. Nine days after Watson's letter, Wilkinson himself wrote to Terrell to explain the change: "The Committee, after careful consideration of all the difficulties attendant upon securing a full house for the

Figure 6. Armstrong High School exterior, photograph by Marjory Collins, 1942. Library of Congress Prints and Photographs Division, Office of War Information Collection.

Washington auditorium, decided to transfer the pageant-play from the Washington Auditorium to the Armstrong High School Auditorium."[42]

In all likelihood, the CCAACP moved the pageant-play indoors to the Armstrong auditorium because they saw the initial outdoor setting, at the foot of the grand Washington monument, as too public a site for a pageant performed by and about African Americans. Moving the pageant-play to Armstrong Technical High School's smaller auditorium circumscribed the event as an experience meant primarily for African American audiences. An undated letter from Marguerite Williams alludes to this thinking: "The nature of the play has caused us to change the place from the Auditorium to the Armstrong High."[43] The cast itself may have been the most significant concern. Given that African American schools and community groups had a long-standing practice of cross-racial casting in pageantry, there were probably no white actors involved in the *Phyllis Wheatley* production. A notice, perhaps written by Williams, asked teachers and other coordinators to "note which of your characters are supposed to represent our people and which are to represent the other race."[44] Williams commented to Terrell, "I have selected one of my own boys for General Washington"; the Armstrong program credits Robert Harlan in the role of Washington. Harlan was a 1930 graduate of Cardozo High School (a black public high school in DC) who then attended Miner Teachers College; he would have been twenty-one years old when he performed as Washington.[45] Perhaps Wilkinson and other planners did not feel that white audiences in DC were ready to see a young black man play George Washington.[46] The shift to the less prominent auditorium of an African American high school would have ensured a mostly segregated audience, undermining the black community's desire for inclusivity and representation of the African American experience within the bicentennial celebrations. The Armstrong auditorium, however, was an ideal location for reaching the audience Terrell sought to educate and inspire: African American youth.

Authentication Rituals

Changes to the site may have been disappointing, but Terrell must have been far more troubled by questions raised about her script's accuracy. In the pageant-play, several groups of eminent white authorities call upon Phyllis Wheatley to demonstrate her knowledge and skills. These authorities range from friends of Wheatley's owners, John and Susanna Wheatley, and the eighteen Boston men who sign a declaration of Wheatley's competence to the assembled guests of the Countess of Huntingdon in England. Terrell, like Wheatley, was forced to authenticate her knowledge when several of her collaborators, both black and white, called her competence into question.

Writers of historical drama must find a balance between historical accuracy and aesthetic purpose. Terrell did her research diligently, closely basing the pageant-play on several available biographical accounts of Wheatley's life. Early Wheatley biographers, however, introduced various factual mistakes that were replicated in many later sources, including in Terrell's script.[47] One early biographer, Henri Grégoire (1808, translated into English by Warden in 1810), established the basic story of her life, partly based on a letter from a French consul in Boston, who claimed to know Wheatley's husband, John Peters.[48] The next account, by Margaretta Matilda Odell, appears in the 1834 edition *Memoir and Poems of Phillis Wheatley*. Odell, a descendant of Susanna Wheatley, gives many details that Terrell made use of, such as Phillis Wheatley at the slave market being covered only with a carpet.[49] Most nineteenth-century accounts repeat versions of the Grégoire and Odell narratives. A 1916 account by DC lawyer G. Herbert Renfro, partly based on Odell, relays events in a lively prose style that might have caught the playwright's eye.[50] The African American literary historian Benjamin Brawley included a biographical statement, along with a serious assessment of Wheatley's poetry, in his 1918 survey *The Negro in Literature and Art in the United States*; James Weldon Johnson also cataloged her significance in his *Book of American Negro Poetry* (1922).[51] According to later biographers such as William Robinson and Vincent Carretta, all of these accounts contain numerous factual errors, some of which became references or scenes in Terrell's pageant-play.[52] For instance, accounts of Wheatley's life typically assert that she personally met with luminaries such as George Washington and the Countess

Figure 7. Marie Moore Forrest, courtesy of National Woman's Party Collection at the Belmont-Paul Women's Equality National Monument, Washington, DC.

of Huntingdon.[53] Although these meetings never actually took place, they became dramatically significant scenes in Terrell's pageant-play.

Late into the rehearsal process for *Phyllis Wheatley*, a white woman, Marie Moore Forrest, raised questions about the authenticity of the pageant-play's chronology. Wilkinson informed Terrell in a letter in late October that he had appointed Forrest as general advisory director for the production.[54] Forrest, the head of Pageantry and the Drama in the Community Center Department of the DC Public Schools, was an active member of the National Woman's Party, as well as a celebrated writer and director of large pageants on topics related to patriotism and suffrage (figure 7).[55] In 1932, she served as head of pageantry for the DC Bicentennial Commission, and it was she who had originally given approval to Terrell's two proposed plays in March 1932. Although her late involvement with *Phyllis Wheatley* may seem surprising, Forrest had a long-standing working relationship with the African American theatre community in DC. After coaching acting for many years for the Howard University Dramatic Club under Ernest Just, she then worked with Montgomery Gregory and the acclaimed Howard Players beginning in 1919.[56]

By the time she joined the *Phyllis Wheatley* production team, Forrest had already directed three major pageants for the birthday bicentennial. In February, she codirected Percy Mackaye's "folk-masque" *Wakefield* in Constitution Hall; in June, she directed a large-scale pageant titled *The Great American* (a standard biographical chronology of events in Washington's life) in the Sylvan Theatre, where it played to a total of twenty thousand spectators.[57] Forrest then wrote and directed a more symbolic pageant titled *The Vision of George Washington: A Pageant of the American Harvest*, performed in mid-October 1932, also in the Sylvan Theatre. Forrest staged all these pageants, which required minimal involvement by black performers, in highly public spaces.[58]

Wilkinson probably deemed it necessary to bring Forrest on board because of Terrell's absence and Marguerite Williams's lack of experience. At the earliest, Terrell returned home to DC only a week before the pageant-play's premiere on November 19 and so had little to do with its rehearsal process.[59] Williams collaborated with Terrell from the beginning as the coordinator of the various schools' participation and seems to have worked tirelessly for the success of the project (she is listed as general director in the program). Forrest, however, was a famous and experienced theatrical practitioner. Likely it eased many minds to have her onboard once Terrell left for New York.

Wilkinson, writing in his capacity as chairman of the CCAACP, informed Terrell of Forrest's initial objection to the pageant-play's chronology in his letter dated October 27 (only weeks away from the November 19 performance): "It has been called to Mrs. Forrest's attention that, according to James Weldon Johnson in his book on American Negro Poetry and Brawley's Negro in Literature and Art, Mrs. Wheatley died in 1774 and Mr. Wheatley in 1778. The significant thing in this connection is that you picture Mrs. Wheatley as present in such events as the George Washington incident and both Mr. and Mrs. Wheatley present at the wedding ceremony, the first of which occurred after the death of Mrs. Wheatley and the second of which occurred after the death of Mr. Wheatley. In other words, the pageant calls for the presence of Mr. and Mrs. Wheatley in incidents that really occur after their deaths, according to the foregoing authorities."[60] Wilkinson's observations concerning dates, based on the authority of two African American authors, are both correct. Even if Wheatley had visited George Washington's camp in 1776, which in all likelihood she did not, Susanna Wheatley could not have been present at it (as in Terrell's original version of act 5), since she died in 1774.[61] Nor could she and John Wheatley have been present at Phillis Wheatley's wedding in 1778, as John died several months before the wedding.[62] Wilkinson goes on to ask Terrell to either refute the errors or to make a change in the script: "We should greatly appreciate a statement from you as to your authority for connecting Mr. and Mrs. Wheatley with events coming after 1774 and 1778, respectively." Wilkinson closes by urging that Terrell consider the matter immediately: "This office is anxious that there should be no valid ground for criticism of the historical accuracy of the incidents in the Phyllis Wheatley Pageant. Accordingly, it is respectfully requested that you advise me in writing at once what you think we should do under the circumstances." Wilkinson's anxiety that "there should be no valid ground for criticism" may have been due to the public nature of the planned theatrical endeavor and to the fact that, as the black head of a black committee writing to a black writer with a criticism initiated by a white director, he himself felt authentication pressures.

Terrell's responses hint strongly that she was displeased by the questions. She responded immediately via almost identical letters to Wilkinson, Forrest, and Williams, each dated November 2. She wrote to Forrest: "I hear that there is some criticism of the pageant play because the events do not follow in chronological order. Everything which I have written is historically correct, but I have transposed certain events so that they would produce the best dramatic effect. I have a perfect right to do that, as I understand it. . . . If I have not the right to present the events in the chronological order which will produce the best effect on the audience, please tell me so. If I have sinned against the canons of dramatic art, I am perfectly willing to change the order of the acts, so that they will conform to the dates. Incidentally I don't think the dates in which the events occurred amounts to a row of pins, as compared with the dramatic effect which will be greatly improved by transposing them."[63] Her reference to religious transgression, of sinning "against the canons of dramatic art," reveals her strong feeling, as does her use of the phrase "a row of pins," which indicates at least a modicum of scorn for the questioning of her artistic integrity. Terrell's letter to Williams contains similar first passages but a different conclusion: "Of course if some sticklers insist on having a play arranged in chronological order, I can do it, although I do not want to do it. It will not be nearly so interesting to the audience, as the way in which it is arranged at present."[64] In communicating to her African American collaborator, she is much more direct in her rejection of the changes proposed by the white authority. Terrell's replies, however, did not end the matter.

Forrest, who as the instigator of the questions on chronology must have been one of the main "sticklers," wrote to Terrell again immediately with yet another criticism of the play's order. Forrest first placates with this assurance: "I received your letter this morning and think perhaps you did not understand the changes which were necessary in the Pageant. We have not changed your order at all. You have a perfect right for dramatic effect to change the chronological order of events." Forrest then explains that she has uncovered what she calls another "mistake"—that Susanna Wheatley had died by the time Phillis Wheatley traveled to England, so Susanna could not have accompanied her there. Forrest states that she has fixed the problem by changing a character name: "So as it was a very minor thing, Phyllis being the principal character, I had another name substituted for Mrs. Wheatley. I believe you will like it perfectly well and if not it will be very easy to change this little minor thing after you get home after election."[65] But now it is Forrest who is incorrect about the chronology. Although the historical Susanna Wheatley did not go on this voyage to England in 1773 (her son Nathaniel Wheatley made the trip), she had not yet died when Wheatley set sail.

Terrell wrote a second letter to Forrest to insist that she never intended for Susanna to go to England as Forrest implies. (In the various undated versions of Terrell's manuscripts, however, sometimes it is Susanna Wheatley who offers to accompany Phyllis; sometimes it is John or Nathaniel). Whether Terrell was innocent of the specific charges put by Forrest, she was "guilty" of other historical inaccuracies in the service of artistic impression. In raising these questions, Forrest uncovered Terrell's deliberate structural alterations to the chronology of Wheatley's life. Terrell admits as much: "Everything is historically correct, except as I have already stated, I have not followed the chronological order of the events depicted."[66]

Terrell protests Forrest's changes: "If other parts of the play have been as incorrectly quoted and presented as this, I do not know what has happened with my little dramatic effect."[67] It is complex, however, to sort out Terrell's original choices of chronology for the dramatization versus the changes made by Forrest in the interest of precision. Ironically, Forrest's changes created their own inaccuracies. In summary, in Terrell's manuscripts the reading of the George Washington poem (read aloud by Phyllis Wheatley in act 4 at a sewing bee) and the meeting at Washington's camp (act 5) occur before Wheatley's meeting with the governor and the other Bostonian gentlemen (act 6), which precedes Wheatley's trip to England in act 7. In reality, however, the Boston meeting of authenticators took place in 1772 (with Susanna Wheatley present), three years before Wheatley wrote the George Washington poem, in 1775. And while Terrell is defensive about the question of Susanna Wheatley and England, in most drafts of the pageant-play she erroneously makes Susanna Wheatley the instigator of the reading of the George Washington poem.[68] Since Susanna Wheatley had died in 1774, she never read the Washington ode, written by Wheatley in 1775; neither could she have visited Washington's camp in 1776, as indicated in most drafts, even if such a visit had happened.

For the production, Forrest and Williams seem to have solved this problem (that Susanna Wheatley died before the writing of the Washington poem) by changing act 4's sewing bee to take place at the home of Mrs. Lathrop (the married name of the Wheatleys' daughter, Mary), with a notation in the program that the scene is "Two Years After the Death of Mrs. Wheatley." Forrest did not want Susanna Wheatley present in the Cambridge camp scene if it was not historically accurate and so "killed her off" at this point in the production. In all likelihood, since it would have been difficult to change the scene order at the late date when all of this came to a head, Forrest substituted Mary Lathrop for Susanna Wheatley for the rest of the pageant-play, starting with act 4.

Terrell never explicitly presents her exact objections to the changes to her "little dramatic effect," but in my opinion Terrell altered the historical chronology of events in Wheatley's life in order to strengthen the bond between Phyllis Wheatley and Susanna Wheatley.[69] This relationship was central to Terrell's creation of her drama in its earlier drafts; John Wheatley is a shadow figure, scarcely present in any scene in the manuscript. Terrell's earlier drafts feature Susanna Wheatley in most pivotal moments. In the Moorland 1 typescript, written before the change of Susanna Wheatley to Mrs. Lathrop, the act 4 sewing bee scene shows Susanna Wheatley bursting with pride at Wheatley's writing and using the George Washington poem as an example for her friends. In act 4, scene 2, when Mary charges in with the letter from General Washington, Mr. Wheatley suggests that the three women (Susanna, Mary, and Phyllis) should visit the camp together. In act 5, the only act in which George Washington appears, the manuscript highlights his courteous interaction with these three women. Dramatically speaking, this scene of bonding helps to justify the later scene in which Wheatley leaves England to return to her ailing mistress (even though in reality Wheatley wrote the Washington poem years after the trip). The George Washington poem was Terrell's inspiration for creating the pageant-play as part of the bicentennial celebration. Although Terrell's letters do not explain her placement of the two Washington-related scenes (the reading of the poem and the camp scene), perhaps she envisioned these scenes as demonstrating the strong connection not between Wheatley and Washington but between Phyllis and Susanna Wheatley.

When Forrest changed Susanna Wheatley into her daughter Mary Lathrop for all scenes following act 4, the impact on Terrell's vision was enormous. What Forrest saw as a "minor thing"—"I had another name substituted for Mrs. Wheatley"—led to a major change. The substitution of Mrs. Lathrop does not accord with the centrality of Susanna Wheatley in the earlier manuscripts. Furthermore, Forrest's changes created more errors in later scenes. By changing act 6 to take place in Mary Lathrop's garden rather than in the home of Susanna Wheatley, Forrest removed Susanna Wheatley from the scene of authentication by the Bostonian dignitaries, despite the historical fact that she was there and was in fact its instigator. Thus, Terrell's vision—the bond between a mistress and an enslaved person—was largely lost. Terrell, returning from New York, was too late to save it. The wording of her letters indicates that this second-guessing of her artistic choices frustrated Terrell. She must have felt keenly the parallel to the pageant-play's scenes of authentication.

A Performance at Armstrong

Despite the tribulations leading up to it, a single performance (titled on the program *Phillis Wheatley: A Bicentennial Pageant*) did take place at Armstrong High School on November 19, 1932. I have been unable to unearth any photograph of the event, but Terrell's archives at Howard University and at the Library of Congress each contain extensive documentation. The Armstrong program indicates the contributions of twenty-four staff members. Students from Division 10–13 played supporting roles, the ROTC of Howard University performed the military camp scene, Miner Teachers College students acted in the scene set in England, and unspecified "civic and church groups" performed the wedding scene. Actors playing major roles such as Susanna Wheatley or Mary Lathrop

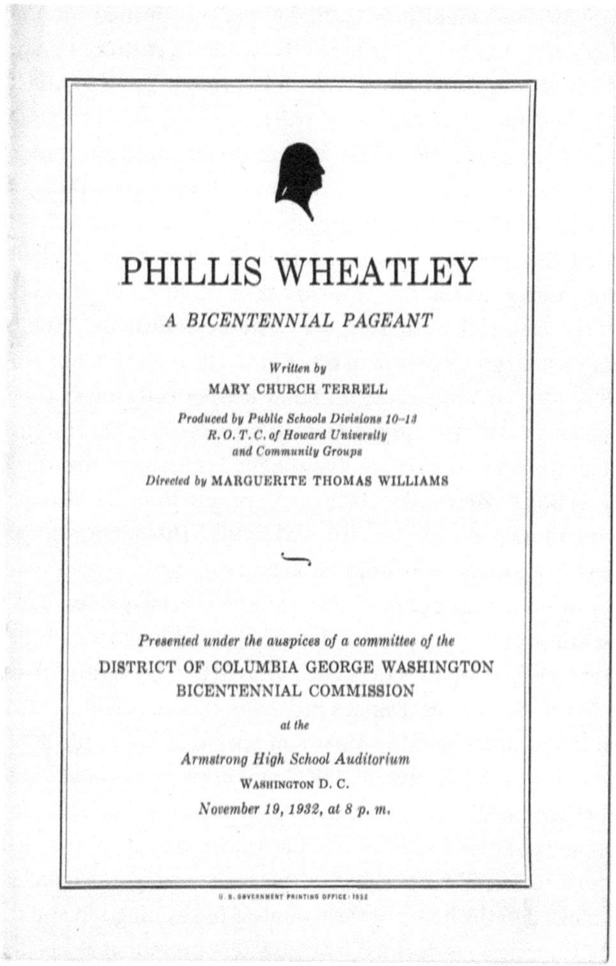

PHILLIS WHEATLEY

A BICENTENNIAL PAGEANT

Written by
MARY CHURCH TERRELL

Produced by Public Schools Divisions 10–13
R. O. T. C. of Howard University
and Community Groups

Directed by MARGUERITE THOMAS WILLIAMS

Presented under the auspices of a committee of the
DISTRICT OF COLUMBIA GEORGE WASHINGTON
BICENTENNIAL COMMISSION

at the

Armstrong High School Auditorium
WASHINGTON D. C.
November 19, 1932, at 8 p. m.

U. S. GOVERNMENT PRINTING OFFICE: 1932

Figure 8. Cover of program, *Phillis Wheatley: A Bicentennial Pageant* (November 19, 1932), Mary Church Terrell Papers 102, Box 6, Folder 163, courtesy of the Moorland-Spingarn Research Center, Manuscript Division, Howard University, Washington, DC.

persist from scene to scene. Three different actors played Phyllis Wheatley at various ages. In addition to several glee clubs and choruses who sang, a total of 235 African American performers of all ages had roles in the story.

While African Americans were the primary creators of the production, Carrie Watson's acquisition of the production's costumes is a story of interracial cooperation. A costume list itemizes 162 costumes needed for the pageant-play, including suits for twenty-four military privates, twenty-five "ladies' dresses for a colonial wedding," and thirty Louis XV period court costumes (perhaps for the garden party in act 7).[70] The list of these period costumes demonstrates the production's scale and ambition. Watson informed Terrell in mid-October that George C. Havenner, executive vice chairman of the DC commission, was very supportive of the production. "Mr. Wilkinson arranged a meeting for me with Dr. Havenner concerning 'my' costumes… . A very splendid conference with him yesterday resulted in my selection of what ever I needed in the 'costume room' at the Bicentennial Headquarters, and the making up of what I did not find to suit. Can you beat it?"[71] Watson goes on to note with enthusiasm that other whites were also bolstering her costume endeavors. "The bride's outfit, Dr. Peters' outfit, and a number of other are to be made for 'our children' by the white help in the costume room and they are perfectly lovely to me. Mrs. Forrest has taken a most un-tiring interest in my work and Dr. Havenner has given me a 'make-up' man."[72] In her autobiography, Terrell notes that the DC commission gave $1,000 to defray the costs of the production; she also quotes in full a post-production letter of thanks from Marvin.[73] This support for the CCAACP from the DC Bicentennial Commission and the "white help" demonstrate how the preparations for the performance bridged a racial divide.

Both music and dance provided entertaining yet historically based complements to the pageant-play's action; each infused the story with African American culture to varying degrees. Dances in *Phyllis Wheatley* fell into two categories: social dances included within scenes and symbolic "interlude dances" between scenes. The 1916 pageantry handbook *Community Drama and Pageantry* distinguishes between ordinary illustrative dances (giving the example of a minuet at a colonial wedding) and symbolic illustrative dances, also called interpretative dances.[74] In Terrell's pageant-play, the former category includes the "Verona Minuet" danced in the home of the Countess of Huntingdon and the folk dance "Roger de Coverley" performed by characters present at Wheatley's wedding. The interlude dances, most of which were arranged and directed by Adrienne Marshall, an African American teacher of dance in DC, provided more opportunity for creativity and symbolism. Although nothing is known of their choreography, the interlude dances seem to have been abstract reflections on the content of the upcoming scene; as *Community Drama and Pageantry* states, the interpretive dance aims to "bring out the poetic meaning of a scene."[75] The program from the Armstrong production identifies eight interlude dances, one before each of the pageant-play's eight acts.[76] The dances varied in number of performers and probably in style. Thirteen women danced "Candle Light Dance," performed before the first scene in the Wheatley household; thirteen male high school cadets performed in "Dance of the Soldiers," which preceded the scene at Washington's camp. Two women performed the final prewedding interlude "Dance of Love." Perhaps these two dancers are the ones described in the costume list as "Greek women, material white with gold and silver trimming."[77] Such faux-Hellenic attire, typical of pageant conventions, would have further emphasized the allegorical function of their dance. If "Dance of Love" is any indication, the interlude dances were not particularly expressive of African American culture, with one exception. The inclusion of an interlude dance called "Cotton Needs Pickin'" was probably inspired by a 1928 book of the same name by Charles H. Williams, who taught physical education at Hampton Institute (an African American secondary school in Virginia) and later founded the Hampton Institute Creative Dance Group.[78] Williams's book provides sheet music, movement notes, and photographs that document the re-creation of eight dances drawn from African American folk traditions. For "Cotton Needs Pickin'," the photographs show four male and four female dancers; these numbers align with the cast list in the Armstrong program, suggesting the possibility that the *Phyllis Wheatley* production used Williams's instructions for male/female couple movements. The evidence indicates that the pageant-play's varied dances, whether historical or abstract or a combination of both, must have provided the production with entertaining spectacle as well as moments for reflective contemplation.

The production's music conjoined its subject's two worlds: the world of George Washington and the world of the enslaved African people who surrounded him. Although archival documents list the titles of numerous musical selections, the typed words scarcely convey the impact of choral voices and instrumental music in performance.[79] The program credits "orchestral accompaniment for the scenes and interlude dances" to the Washington Civic Orchestra; the pageant-play's concertmaster Louia Vaughn Jones was professor and head of the music department at Howard. Music director Alfred H. Johnson, head of music for the public schools' Divisions 10-13, led choral classes and glee clubs in various songs. Numerous songs and orchestral pieces evoked the Revolutionary era; sheet music for two of these pieces was included in *Music from the Days of George Washington*, a 1931 collection gathered by two experts from the Music Division of the Library of Congress and issued by the Bicentennial Commission.[80] The instrumental "Mrs. Washington's Minuet" that accompanied the "Candle Light Dance" was probably the piece "Minuet Danced before Mrs. Washington" included in the collection, one of two 1792 minuets by Pierre Landrin Duport. For "Dance of the Soldiers," the orchestra played "President's March" (circa 1790) by Philip Phile, included in another book issued for the bicentennial.[81] Resources published by the Bicentennial Commission clearly enhanced the production. In addition to this march and minuet, the pageant-play included other common songs published in numerous popular music collections, such as "Yankee Doodle," "Rule Britannia," and "Drink to Me Only with Thine Eyes."

Fittingly for an event that sought to integrate African American experience into the Revolutionary-era story, African American folk music also pervaded the production. The *Phyllis Wheatley* pageant-play organizers drew on the work of R. Nathaniel Dett, a music teacher at Hampton Institute. Carter Woodson later advocated for the study of African American music in his 1933 book *The Mis-Education of the Negro*, as part of his overall vision for reforms in African American education. Woodson noted that most African American colleges "do not even direct special attention to Negro music in which the Negro has made his outstanding contribution in America."[82] Hampton Institute was an exception. Dett first published an edition of "cabin and plantation songs as sung by the Hampton students" in 1874; by the 1927 edition, the compilation consisted of more than one hundred and fifty songs.[83] The recurring theme in the Armstrong production of *Phyllis Wheatley* was "L'Envoi," described in Dett's book as an "old Negro melody transcribed from the singing of Dr. Robert Russa Moton, Principal, Tuskegee Institute."[84] In Dett's arrangement into chorale form, "L'Envoi" recurred numerous times in the production. The song's words introduce into Phyllis's story a note of melancholy: "I'm a going to travel/I'm ready to fly; Come quickly to bear me/To God in the sky."[85] The script, which ends with Wheatley's wedding celebration and never hints at the difficulties to come, does not portray her death; "L'Envoi," however, hints at the transitory nature of Wheatley's life and at the obstacles she faced. Plantation songs in the production, such as "Go Down Moses," "We are Climbing Jacob's Ladder," and "I'm So Glad Trouble Don't Last Always" (also in arrangements by Dett), express a religiously derived belief in a glorious afterlife in contrast to present toils.

The production also included at least two musical selections with strong ties to African and African American dance traditions: for act 1 (Africa), the orchestra played a "war dance" interlude based on a selection from Henry Krehbiel's 1914 resource *Afro-American Folksongs*.[86] Spectators also heard "Bamboula (African Dance)," from Samuel Coleridge-Taylor's *Twenty-Four Negro Melodies* (1905).[87] The bamboula instrument and its associated dance, which had origins in Africa and later manifestations in the West Indies and in Congo Square of New Orleans, symbolized the continuity of African heritage in the diaspora.[88] Clearly, the pageant-play's creative team enlisted a multitude of available resources in their quest to provide historically, culturally, and symbolically appropriate music and dances. As Woodson desired, music became a means for African Americans to learn both history and culture; the music of *Phyllis Wheatley* evoked Wheatley's African past as well as her African American adaptation.

I have not been able to locate any firsthand responses from black spectators beyond a review published in the African American publication the *Washington Tribune*. The review, while remaining mostly objectively descriptive, does opine that "the acting was very good. Some of the dancing was rather poor."[89] The official 1933 report by the DC Commission considered the production a success: "The auditorium was packed for the occasion and the pageant ... was admirably presented."[90] Months after the production, in April 1933, Forrest wrote a gushing letter to Terrell: "The story of this wonderful negro girl should be known to every colored child as an incentive to the child to perfect its own life.... We are thankful that she brings to her race the message which is so instructive and inspirational. We hope that many cities will produce this beautiful pageant."[91] Despite her praise, Forrest undermines Wheatley's talent by questioning its source: "To those of us who have delved more or less deeply into the psychology of life the question of the prodigy arises to confront us, which can of course be answered only by the theory of reincarnation, but no matter how or from when she comes, we are thankful that she brings to her race the message which is so instructive and inspirational."[92] The idea that Wheatley may be the reincarnation of another talent recalls the many pressures of authentication both depicted and experienced by Terrell.

Another letter of congratulation came from C. K. Berryman, political cartoonist for the *Washington Star* and Pulitzer Prize winner: "I went to Armstrong NOT EXPECTING MUCH, but I take pleasure in telling you how very agreeably I was surprised and I wish to congratulate you upon your splendid work and the excellent manner in which it was presented."[93] Despite the patronizing attitude toward African American community performance likely at the source of Berryman's low expectations, Terrell seems to have highly valued this letter; her archives contain numerous copies, and she offered it as publicity material for a May 1933 production of the pageant-play in Baltimore.[94] After all of her struggles to work within the white power structures of the bicentennial celebration, she must have appreciated this objective perspective from a prominent white artist.

Mary Church Terrell never stopped fighting for the rights of African Americans and remained a sought-after speaker late in life. She famously continued her activism into her late eighties, with a successful fight to integrate DC restaurants, a process begun in 1950 and decided by a Supreme Court ruling in 1953.[95] She died in 1954, at the age of ninety. Terrell's *Phyllis Wheatley* was a revolutionary pageant-play about the Revolutionary era. While today black actors do indeed play George Washington in *Hamilton* on Broadway and on tour around the United States and the United Kingdom, creator Lin-Manuel Miranda does not bring African American characters to the forefront of his Revolutionary story. Terrell's pageant-play portrayed the enslaved Phillis Wheatley as the heroine of a compelling success story, and the production at the Armstrong auditorium was a complex cultural spectacle featuring hundreds of African American performers from numerous schools and civic groups. Despite the impediments Terrell faced—Woodson's attacks on the CCAACP, the restriction of the production to an African American venue, and the calls to authenticate the accuracy of her script—she met her goal: "We must teach our children that we are citizens of this country and as such, whenever the opportunity is afforded, we must take part in every national movement in which other groups join."[96] The 1932 production of *Historical Pageant-Play Based on the Life of Phyllis Wheatley* is a testimony to Terrell's dogged efforts to include African American representation within a national celebration.

Notes

1. Epigraph is Onaodowan quoted in Mark Kennedy, "3 Presidents in 'Hamilton' Put 'Blood into the Statues,'" *Salon.com*, July 15, 2015.
2. Since Terrell uses the spelling "Phyllis" in her play's title and all manuscripts rather than the more typical "Phillis," I will use the former spelling whenever I refer to this character and the latter when referring to the historical Wheatley. Phillis was evidently named for the slave ship that brought her across the Atlantic. Terrell named her own elder daughter Phyllis in 1898.
3. Lyra D. Monteiro, "Review Essay: Race-Conscious Casting and the Erasure of the Black Past in Lin-Manuel Miranda's *Hamilton*," *Public Historian* 38, no. 1 (2016): 93.
4. George Washington, "From George Washington to Phillis Wheatley, 28 February 1776," *The Papers of George Washington*, Revolutionary War Series, vol. 3, January 1, 1776–March 31, 1776, ed. Philander D. Chase (Charlottesville: University Press of Virginia, 1988), 387.
5. Phillis Wheatley, "His Excellency General Washington," *Virginia Gazette* (Dixon and Hunter edition), March 30, 1776, no. 1286, p. 1. URL: http://research.history.org/DigitalLibrary/va-gazettes/VGSinglePage.cfm?IssueIDNo=76.DH.14.
6. Mary Church Terrell, typescript, "Why I Wrote the Phyllis Wheatley Pageant-Play," Mary Church Terrell Papers 102, Box 6, Folder 156, Manuscript Division, Moorland-Spingarn Research Center, Howard University (hereafter cited as MCT Moorland-Spingarn). This document is undated, but it was written sometime before November 1933.
7. Mary Church Terrell, *A Colored Woman in a White World* (Washington, DC: Ransdell, 1940), 456.
8. United States George Washington Bicentennial Commission, *Activities of the Commission*

and Complete-Final Report of the United States George Washington Bicentennial Commission, volume 5 of *Report of the United States George Washington Bicentennial Commission* (Washington, DC: United States George Washington Bicentennial Commission, 1932).

9. Sol Bloom, preface, United States George Washington Bicentennial Commission, *Activities of the Commission and Complete-Final Report*, xii.
10. Esther Willard Bates, *How to Produce a Pageant in Honor of George Washington* (Washington, DC: United States George Washington Bicentennial Commission 1931); United States George Washington Bicentennial Commission, *Pageants and Plays Depicting the Life of George Washington and His Time* (Washington, DC: US Government Printing Office, 1931).
11. United States George Washington Bicentennial Commission, *Activities of the Commission and Complete-Final Report*, 563.
12. Ida B. Wells-Barnett, *The Reason Why the Colored American Is Not in the World's Columbian Exposition: The Afro-American's Contribution to Columbian Literature*, ed. Robert W. Rydell, reprint of the 1893 edition (Urbana: University of Illinois Press, 1999). http://digital.library.upenn.edu/women/wells/exposition/exposition.html.
13. Alessandra Lorini, *Rituals of Race: American Public Culture and the Search for Racial Democracy*, Carter G. Woodson Institute Series in Black Studies (Charlottesville: University Press of Virginia, 1999), 49; Barbara J. Ballard, "African-American Protest and the Role of the Haitian Pavilion at the 1893 Chicago World's Fair," in *Multiculturalism: Roots and Realities*, ed. C. James Trotman (Bloomington: Indiana University Press, 2002), 119.
14. John H. Finley, "Foreword," *The Book of America's Making Exposition* (New York: City and State Departments of Education, 1921).
15. W. E. B. Du Bois, *The Seven Gifts of Ethiopia to America*, *The Papers of W.E.B. Du Bois* (Sanford, NC: Microfilming Corporation of America, 1980), Microfilm Reel 87: Essays, Forewords, and Student Papers; Novels, Pageants, and Plays, frames 1459–1464; W. E. B. Du Bois, "The Drama among Black Folk," *Crisis* 12, no. 4 (1916): 173.
16. Cloyd H. Marvin to Mary Church Terrell, August 10, 1931. MCT Moorland-Spingarn, Box 2, Folder 32.
17. C. G. Woodson, "George Washington Bi-Centennial Commission Has Colored Sideshow," *Afro-American* (December 12, 1931): 19. See also C. G. Woodson, "The Side-Show of the George Washington Bicentennial," *New York Age* (December 12, 1931): 9, and C. G. Woodson, "Communications," *Journal of Negro History* 17, no. 1 (1932): 103–6.
18. Woodson, "George Washington Bi-Centennial Commission Has Colored Sideshow," 19.
19. In this and later essays, it is not always clear whether Woodson is writing about Bloom's federal commission, the DC Bicentennial Commission, or the CCAACP.
20. C. G. Woodson, "Eliminating the Negro from the George Washington Bicentennial," *New York Age*, December 26, 1931.
21. Ibid., 9.
22. C. G. Woodson, "The George Washington Bicentennial Eliminates March 5th, Crispus Attucks Day," *New York Age*, January 2, 1932.
23. Wilkinson asked Terrell to chair this committee in this letter: Garnet C. Wilkinson to Mary Church Terrell, January 18, 1932. Mary Church Terrell Papers, Library of Congress (hereafter cited as MCT LOC), Microfilm Box 9, Reel 7, "Correspondence."
24. "Group Plans to Ban Jim Crow Celebration," *Afro-American*, January 30, 1932.
25. Terrell, "Why I Wrote."

26. United States George Washington Bicentennial Commission, *Pageants and Plays.*
27. Terrell, "Why I Wrote."
28. "Group Plans to Observe Attucks Day," *Afro-American*, March 5, 1932.
29. Mary Church Terrell, "Pageant-Play Depicting Heroism of Colored Soldiers in Revolutionary War." Undated typescript in MCT Moorland-Spingarn, Box 2, Folder 26. Terrell may have written this play as a direct response to Woodson's call for an acknowledgment of Attucks and other black soldiers, as the existing manuscript does exactly that. There are numerous drafts of *Phyllis Wheatley* in MCT Moorland-Spingarn, Box 6, Folders 158–161. An eight-page script on legal-size paper seems most complete and may have served as the working script for the initial production planning (Folder 159). Several of the scripts in the Terrell papers at the Library of Congress are longer and more fleshed-out, so they are likely from a period much closer to the production (MCT LOC Microfilm Box 25, Reel 18. Subject File: "Phyllis Wheatley Pageant, 1932–33.") In this essay, "LOC 1," "LOC 2," and so on are my own designations for scripts in the order as they appear in the microfilm.
30. Garnet C. Wilkinson to Mary Church Terrell, March 8, 1932. MCT LOC Microfilm Box 9, Reel 7, "Correspondence."
31. Garnet C. Wilkinson to Mary Church Terrell, March 8, 1932. MCT LOC Microfilm Box 9, Reel 7, "Correspondence." In addition to Terrell, two other significant activists wrote bicentennial plays focused on African American characters. Mary White Ovington, a white woman who was one of the founding members of the NAACP, published *Phillis Wheatley: A Play*, and W. E. B. Du Bois published *George Washington and Black Folk: A Pageant for the Bicentenary, 1732–1932* in his *Crisis* magazine. Neither play seems to have been produced. Mary White Ovington, *Phillis Wheatley* (New York: Schulte Press, 1932); W. E. B. Du Bois, *George Washington and Black Folk, Crisis* 41, no. 4 (April 1932): 121–24. For analysis of the latter, see Lurana Donnels O'Malley, "The Witch of Endor Slept Here: W. E. B. Du Bois and the Crisis of the George Washington Bicentenary," *MELUS: Multi-Ethnic Literature of the United States* 41, no. 4 (Winter 2016): 32–54.
32. LOC 1, MCT LOC Microfilm Box 25, Reel 18. Subject File: "Phyllis Wheatley Pageant, 1932–33," 14–15.
33. Errol Hill and James Vernon Hatch, *A History of African American Theatre*, Cambridge Studies in American Theatre and Drama (Cambridge: Cambridge University Press, 2003), 199–202.
34. Terrell, *Colored Woman in a White World*, 457.
35. Ibid., 457.
36. "Group Plans to Observe," 7.
37. Robert Benedetto, Jane Donovan, and Kathleen Du Vall, *Historical Dictionary of Washington, D.C.*, Historical Dictionaries of Cities of the World (Lanham, MD: Scarecrow Press, 2003), 211.
38. District of Columbia, *Report of the District of Columbia Commission, George Washington Bicentennial* (Washington, DC: US Government Printing Office, 1933), 17.
39. Carrie Watson to Mary Church Terrell, October 18, 1932. MCT Moorland-Spingarn, Box 2, Folder 40.
40. The auditorium was demolished in the 1960s.
41. Allan Keiler, *Marian Anderson: A Singer's Journey* (New York: Scribner, 2000), 198. Keiler documents Marian Anderson's performances at Armstrong in 1936 and 1937 and analyzes

in-depth the controversy of her bid to play in the auditorium at the all-white Central High School in 1939, following the DAR's refusal to have her play in Constitution Hall. Armstrong was deemed too small to house her concert.

42. Garnet C. Wilkinson to Mary Church Terrell, October 27, 1932. MCT Moorland-Spingarn, Box 2, Folder 40.
43. Marguerite Williams to Mary Church Terrell, undated, MCT Moorland-Spingarn, Box 2, Folder 40. Likely date is between October 11 and 18, 1932.
44. Typescript, "Notice. To be sent to teachers in charge," MCT Moorland-Spingarn, Box 2, Folder 158. The document is undated but was written sometime before May 24, 1932.
45. Marguerite Williams to Mary Church Terrell, October 27, 1932. MCT Moorland-Spingarn, Box 2, Folder 40; *Phillis Wheatley: A Bicentennial Pageant* (program) MCT Moorland-Spingarn Box 6, Folder 163; Harlan went on become a government attorney and a civil rights program officer; "Robert J. Harlan," Obituary, *Washington Post* (December 24, 1989).
46. In summer 2018 a person of color did play Washington in DC, when the Haitian American actor Carvens Lissaint portrayed him in *Hamilton* at the Kennedy Center.
47. William Henry Robinson, *Phillis Wheatley: A Bio-Bibliography*. A Reference Publication in Afro-American Studies (Boston: G.K. Hall, 1981), xii–xiv.
48. Henri Grégoire, *An Enquiry concerning the Intellectual and Moral Faculties, and Literature of Negroes*, trans. D. B. Warden. Reprint of 1810 edition (College Park, MD: McGrath, 1967). French original: Henri Grégoire, *De la littérature des Nègres, ou, Recherches sur leurs facultés intellectuelles, leurs qualités morales et leur literature* (Paris: Chez Maradan, 1808).
49. Margaretta Matilda Odell, "Memoir," in *Memoir and Poems of Phillis Wheatley, a Native African and a Slave* (Boston: Geo. W. Light, 1834), 9. See Vincent Carretta, *Phillis Wheatley: Biography of a Genius in Bondage* (Athens: University of Georgia Press, 2011), 175–76, on why Odell's account should be viewed with skepticism.
50. Phillis Wheatley, *Life and Works of Phillis Wheatley*, ed. Herbert G. Renfro. Reprint of 1916 edition (Freeport, NY: Books for Libraries Press, 1970).
51. Benjamin Griffith Brawley, *The Negro in Literature and Art in the United States* (New York: Duffield, 1918); James Weldon Johnson, *The Book of American Negro Poetry* (New York: Harcourt, Brace, 1922).
52. Robinson, *Phillis Wheatley*; Carretta, *Phillis Wheatley*.
53. For example, see Johnson, *Book of American Negro Poetry*, xxviii.
54. Garnet C. Wilkinson to Mary Church Terrell, October 27, 1932.
55. Betty Miles, "Mrs. Marie Forrest, Prominent Pageanteer Here," *Evening Star* (Washington, DC), December 4, 1956.
56. Bernard L. Peterson, *The African American Theatre Directory, 1816–1960: A Comprehensive Guide to Early Black Theatre Organizations, Companies, Theatres, and Performing Groups* (Westport, CT: Greenwood, 1997), 98; Cedric J. Robinson, *Forgeries of Memory and Meaning: Blacks and the Regimes of Race in American Theater and Film before World War II* (Chapel Hill: University of North Carolina Press, 2007), 177.
57. District of Columbia, *Report of the District of Columbia*, 10.
58. For *The Great American*, however, correspondence between Forrest and Terrell shows that Forrest and her personnel coordinator, Maud Howell Smith, made an effort to include African American characters and performers by consulting with Terrell and the

CCAACP (MCT Moorland-Spingarn, Box 2, Folder 26). I have not yet been able to determine the degree to which this effort came to fruition in the production.

59. A letter from Williams indicates that Terrell was back in DC by at least Monday, November 14. Marguerite Williams to Mary Church Terrell, November 14, 1932. MCT Moorland-Spingarn, Box 2, Folder 40.
60. Garnet C. Wilkinson to Mary Church Terrell, October 27, 1932.
61. Carretta, *Phillis Wheatley*, 157.
62. Despite Forrest's concern, none of the existing manuscript drafts specify that Susanna Wheatley is present at the wedding.
63. Mary Church Terrell to Marie Moore Forrest, November 2, 1932, MCT LOC, Microfilm Box 9, Reel 7.
64. Mary Church Terrell to Marguerite Williams, November 2, 1932, MCT LOC, Microfilm Box 9, Reel 7.
65. Marie Moore Forrest to Mary Church Terrell, November 3, 1932, MCT Moorland-Spingarn, Box 2, Folder 26.
66. Mary Church Terrell to Marie Moore Forrest, November 4, 1932, MCT LOC, Microfilm Box 9, Reel 7.
67. Ibid.
68. Of all the drafts, only LOC 1 and LOC 2 put the reading of the poem at Mary Lathrop's house.
69. Such an interpretation is present in many accounts of Wheatley's life. See, for example, Brawley, who refers to Susanna Wheatley as Phillis Wheatley's "best friend" (21).
70. Typescript, "List of Costumes Required," MCT LOC, Microfilm Box 25, Reel 18.
71. Carrie Watson to Mary Church Terrell, October 18, 1932.
72. Ibid.
73. Terrell, *Colored Woman*, 457.
74. Mary Porter Beegle and Jack Randall Crawford, *Community Drama and Pageantry* (New Haven: Yale University Press, 1916), 199–200.
75. Beegle and Crawford, *Community Drama and Pageantry*, 200.
76. The interlude dances are present in the manuscripts from the earliest drafts, but their exact names vary from draft to draft.
77. Typescript, "List of Costumes Required," MCT LOC, Microfilm Box 25, Reel 18.
78. Charles H. Williams, *"Cotton Needs Pickin'": Characteristic Negro Folk Dances* (Norfolk, VA: Guide, 1928).
79. Typescript, "Incidental Music for the Phyllis Wheatley Pageant," MCT LOC, Microfilm Box 25, Reel 18.
80. Carl Engel and W. Oliver Strunk. Reprint of 1931 edition. *Music from the Days of George Washington: A Collection of Patriotic and Military Tunes, Piano and Dance Music Songs and Operatic Airs* (New York: AMS, 1970).
81. John Tasker Howard, who also composed the music for Mackaye's *Wakefield*, edited a volume that gave a historical overview as well as suggestions of where to find published music for use in bicentenary events. John Tasker Howard, *The Music of George Washington's Time*. Reprint of 1931 edition (New York: AMS, 1976), 21–22.
82. Carter Godwin Woodson, *The Mis-Education of the Negro*. 1933 (Nashville, TN: Winston-Derek, 1990), 90.
83. The pageant also used Dett's "Prelude (Night)" from his "In the Bottoms" suite as the

accompaniment for the interlude dance between act 1 (Africa) and act 2 (slave market scene). R. Nathaniel Dett, *In the Bottoms: Characteristic Suite for the Piano* (Chicago: Clayton F. Summy, 1913).

84. R. Nathaniel Dett, *Religious Folk-Songs of the Negro*. Reprint of 1927 edition. (New York: AMS, 1972), xiii.
85. Ibid., xiii.
86. Reference to musicologist Henry Krehbiel occurs in "Incidental Music for the Phyllis Wheatley Pageant" (MCT LOC Microfilm Box 25, Reel 18). Possibly the choice was selection 6 in Henry Edward Krehbiel, *Afro-American Folksongs: A Study in Racial and National Music* (New York: G. Schirmer, 1914), 61.
87. Samuel Coleridge-Taylor, *Twenty-four Negro Melodies*: Op. 59 (Boston: O. Ditson Co., 1905). Coleridge-Taylor's publication popularized the Bamboula melody, which he based on writings by Krehbiel. Source: Jeffrey P. Green, *Samuel Coleridge-Taylor, a Musical Life* (London: Pickering & Chatto, 2011), 182.
88. Du Bois also specified "Bamboula" to accompany his African scene in his unproduced script *George Washington and Black Folk*.
89. "Phyllis Wheatley Pageant Given Saturday Night," *Washington Tribune* (November 25, 1932), 15.
90. District of Columbia, *Report of the District of Columbia Commission*, 20.
91. Marie Moore Forrest to Mary Church Terrell, April 30, 1933. MCT Moorland-Spingarn, Box 6, Folder 156.
92. Ibid.
93. C. K. Berryman to Mary Church Terrell, November 26, 1932. MCT LOC, Microfilm Box 9, Reel 7, "Correspondence."
94. Harry J. Hunt to Mary Church Terrell, March 17, 1933. MCT LOC, Microfilm Box 9, Reel 7, "Correspondence." There were at least two other post-bicentennial performances of the play: May 26 and 27, 1933, at the Booker T. Washington Junior High School in Baltimore, under the direction of Harry J. Hunt, and March 28, 1941, by the Dunbar Community Center of DC. The 1933 program lists two notes in parentheses about episode 7 (in England): "(Chronology here has been sacrificed for dramatic climax)" and "(Fall of curtain denotes the passage of time)." Program, MCT LOC, Microfilm Box 25, Reel 18.
95. Dennis B. Fradin and Judith Bloom Fradin, *Fight On!: Mary Church Terrell's Battle for Integration* (New York: Clarion, 2003).
96. Terrell, "Why I Wrote."

The Lasting Theatre of Dario Fo and Franca Rame

—JULIET GUZZETTA

Once a year I teach an intermediate Italian language course at my large state university in the Midwest.[1] I follow a textbook that is organized around cultural themes, and through these, the authors introduce new vocabulary and grammar. When I was editing my syllabus for the fall of 2016, I had not noticed that the beginning of the fourth chapter, the one on politics (with the sophisticated title *Il valore delle idee* [*The Value of Ideas*]), would coincide with the most contentious presidential election of my lifetime. On Monday, November 7, 2016, after working our way through a few introductory ideas, I invited the students to converse in small groups using a conversation section in the textbook that I often turn to for how it incorporates new vocabulary. The atmosphere in the room suddenly grew tense as the questions invited my students to ponder, "Is there a political party to which you feel close? Did you vote in the last election? Is there a politician in particular that you admire?"[2] As I walked around the room to different groups, I noticed that many students were awkwardly avoiding responding. Finally, the students began to speak up—to me, in English. "These are awfully personal." Another student: "This isn't a political science class."

At that point, I guided the conversation to come together as a whole class and I briefly defended these questions as a cultural example of the fundamental importance of civic engagement. "In Italy," I told them, "politics is for everyone, not just students of political science," ending with my joke, "so when you're in Italy and go to *il bar* to have your morning *cappuccino*, be prepared to talk about two topics: politics and soccer." That day, my students helped me realize that there was something far more valuable to the conversation questions than practicing spoken Italian with new vocabulary. Those questions speak to a fundamental Italian principle: no matter the political affiliation, everyone has the potential, the right, and even the responsibility to engage in political discourse, even if they are not politicians. One hears the echoes of Antonio Gramsci's magnanimous declaration that everyone is an intellectual, even if not by profession.

It was this idea, among others, that Dario Fo (1926–2016), the 1997 Nobel laureate for literature, and Franca Rame (1929–2013), also a writer, actor, producer, and politician but most known as Fo's partner in life and art, internalized and embraced as a guide for their theatrical practice. Fo, who both the public and even critics often solely credit for the work that he and Rame created collaboratively, for decades held the distinction of having been the most performed living playwright in the world from the early 1960s until his death in 2016.[3] Literary scholar Joseph Farrell points out, however, that in fact it is the works that are jointly signed with Fo and Rame as coauthors that are most frequently staged.[4] From Chile to Romania, South Africa to China, Fo's admirers have hailed him as a champion for the people who, in a revised Brechtian mode, aims to educate as much as entertain. Fo and Rame's poetics, both in their solo shows and with larger casts, is fundamentally dialectical as it melds the tradition of the medieval *giullare*, a figure that combines clowning and wisdom like the English court jester, with a Gramscian orator who contemplates current events from the perspective of a revised Marxist philosophy. Most of their theatre, including the well-traveled plays such as *Mistero buffo* (*Comic Mystery*, 1969), *The Accidental Death of an Anarchist* (1970), and *Can't Pay, Won't Pay* (1974), directly aims not only at questioning the conditions of the working class and challenging then-current political matters but also at inspiring their audiences to question and actively challenge the authority in their lives. Their plays attempt to demonstrate how ordinary people have been persecuted by those in power for centuries, and, even more importantly, they aim to rectify this mistreatment by providing a space wherein their audiences can voice opinions and engage in debate.

In part to pay homage to the late Fo and Rame, with a focus on Rame as a gesture that aims to correct her frequently subordinated status, this essay explores some of the ways in which they created a unique theatrical poetics by and for the working class with the clear intention of provoking their audiences into an active commitment to civic responsibilities. It then shifts to focus on a more recent theatrical form known as the Theatre of Narration, arguing that this genre developed Fo and Rame's political engagement for a new time. In conversation with the Theatre of Narration, the longevity and creativity of Fo and Rame's work can be understood broadly. It is both a potent source of political theatre in the long 1970s and a legacy that was reborn via an entirely new theatrical genre that became widely popular in Italy in the mid-1990s. The lingering effects of their work, then, is twofold: Fo and Rame first emboldened audiences worldwide, and especially in Italy, over decades, but most effectively from the mid-1960s to the early 1980s. Secondarily, they extended their reach, albeit unintentionally, through the development of the still rising phenomenon called the Theatre of Narration. Together, Fo and Rame, and the Theatre of Narration demonstrate not only how different tactics are necessary in different times and contexts but also that continuous reinvention is essential for political dialogue to remain an unthreatening and vital part of civic duty, whether on a stage or in an Italian language classroom.

The Theatre of Narration

Teatro di narrazione is a theatrical style consisting of solo artists who both write and perform their shows, much in the spirit of Fo and Rame. Scholars typically divide narrators (so-named to distinguish from actors) into two generations of artists: those born in the 1950s (Marco Baliani, Laura Curino, Lella Costa, and Marco Paolini are among the most celebrated) and those born in the 1970s (Ascanio Celestini, Davide Enia, and Giuliana Musso), and they largely credit Fo as the genre's "grandfather."[5] On the one hand, his and Rame's influence in terms of political impact has been underestimated or applied with broad strokes, which this essay counters by exploring some of their more subtle influences, namely, with respect to audience relationship. On the other hand, Fo's impact in terms of poetics has been largely overestimated insofar as his performance aesthetic is very different than even the most animated narrators. The physicality of the narrator varies considerably from that of Fo, who is known for the plasticity of his face, his large gestures, and his physical comedy. Narrators, by contrast, often stand at a podium or simply downstage center, or sometimes sit in a chair or on a bench, and do not engage in the level of physical acting that made Fo a celebrated clown.

The Theatre of Narration also draws on influences from other important twentieth-century figures such as Jerzy Grotowski, with his invention of a Poor Theatre, and Judith Malina, whose work in Italy with the Living Theatre was particularly important for the feminist movement. It is also part of a direct lineage of solo actor-authored theatre practices in Italy, with Fo and Rame as its closest relatives.[6] Similar to Fo and Rame's monologue performances is the minimalist aesthetic that also characterizes the Theatre of Narration and allows it to travel cheaply and easily, since there is almost never backdrop scenery and rarely properties or elaborate costumes, save a chair or a scarf or coat, which the actor might manipulate to suggest different characters. While the first generation of narrators was active in the theatre, specifically in community performances and children's theatre, as early as 1974, when some of them were still in high school, the genre began to gain momentum only in 1987, when Laura Curino first performed her *Passione*, followed by Marco Baliani's *Kohlhaas* (performed in repertory since 1990). Marco Paolini's *The Story of Vajont* (debut 1993) catapulted the genre onto the national scene when a 1997 performance was televised live and uninterrupted on Rai 2, a state-run network. It is still common in the late 2010s for national networks to televise several performances of Narrative Theatre every year.

While the poetics of each narrator is their own, with their unique deliveries and concerns, the main aspect that links them, in addition to the formal choices of performing solo with a minimalist aesthetic, is how they revisit historical events of national importance from local perspectives. Through an overarching story that is neither autobiographical (though often involves autobiographical sequences) nor episodic, narrators demonstrate how ordinary people have major influences on the legacies of the past. In *Vajont*, for example, Paolini revisits the 1963 tragedy in northeastern Italy when a landslide caused by the construction of what was then Europe's largest dam (and a source of pride for postwar Italian industry and science) resulted in a massive flood that decimated seven towns and killed approximately two thousand people in just over four minutes. He distances the story from the maudlin reportage that focused on the disaster, concentrating instead on how and why it happened and recounting overlooked records of protest by local villagers, politicians who visited the site, and geologists' warnings that construction of the dam was happening too quickly to assure the stability of the mountains that supported it. As with Paolini's production, part of the potency of the Theatre of Narration lies not only in its ability to render the great and tragic histories and historical figures of Italy meaningful on an intimate scale but also in how it demonstrates that anyone can influence the public past by incorporating their connections into the narrative. The Theatre of Narration continues into the 2010s with those first- and second-generation artists, in addition to new groups of practitioners that might come to be known as the third generation as they sustain their contributions and explore new modes of expression within the genre that might, for example, involve the digital scape.[7]

There are also notable similarities between the Theatre of Narration and other contemporary theatrical practices, and though an in-depth comparison would constitute a different essay, a brisk overview will help to situate this practice among its interlocutors. In particular, the Theatre of Narration will call to mind different monologuist and/or research-based traditions from a wide range of countries and times. Theatres that "claim a relationship to reality," as Carol Martin describes the "Theatre of the Real," share research methods and in some cases a similar historical perspective to that of the Theatre of Narration.[8] Documentary Theatre especially, with its echoes of New Deal Era initiatives such as Living Newspaper productions, is a closely related cousin. Perhaps the most important difference, however, is the fluidity of the "documentary" status in the Theatre of Narration. Even while productions are heavily researched and employ documentary techniques such as oral accounts of an event or archival evidence, they are used to create a single Aristotelian structure that narrators embellish with elements of autobiography, or simply their imagination, which is also important in the theatre of Fo and Rame.

Though scholars have written extensively about Fo as a revolutionary, even militant, playwright and performer, focusing on both his complex relationship to politics and his versatile poetics to explain and explore his dedication to the working classes, few have examined how his and Rame's work has a life independent of them. While the Theatre of Narration espouses a complicated practice tied to several theatrical traditions and sociopolitical moments, understanding Fo and Rame's goals of audience engagement emphasizes both the longevity and reach of their ideas and sheds light on the intimate rapport between narrators and their audiences. To understand the nuances of how the Theatre of Narration is a potent, but also sometimes compromised, form of political theatre, one must first grasp the strategies of Fo and Rame in their own times. In considering how the narrators adapt Fo and Rame's political objectives, one can observe, first, that the Theatre of Narration renegotiates the need to attract primarily working-class audiences and instead aims to create conversation across class lines. Second, related to both the different audience composition and the different zeitgeist of the decades in which they work, narrators have developed a much more nuanced nonpartisan political agenda. The major difference is that as Fo and Rame performed in the 1970s, they invoked current events largely to strengthen an argument about contemporary politics, whereas the narrators contemplate the historicity of a particular event to understand the present more dynamically.

The Urgency of Fo and Rame

Fo and Rame's oeuvre represents a long artistic evolution that traverses several media, from television and radio to writing, drawing, and performing onstage, and includes the creation, dissemination, and re-creation of several theatre companies, with performances ranging from satire and political commentary to serious dramatic topics. Their reputation as revolutionary refers to their far-left ideas, famously left of the Italian Communist Party (PCI) itself, adhering to the belief that "a better society will be created out of mass struggle and not by laws coming out of parliamentary chambers" even if advanced by PCI politicians.[9] Historicization is important here. Fo and Rame created some of their most renowned plays in the late 1960s and early 1970s, a time when there were many tensions intra-party, not just inter-party. For example, on the heels of the "Hot Autumn" of 1969, which saw continuous revolts in factories for better pay and conditions, tensions between union leadership and workers began to rise, paving way for the concept of the "conservative" union leader who developed deeper loyalties to the company than to the employees whose work he oversaw.[10] Differing ideals across the left challenged a unifying vision, and Fo and Rame were caught in the middle.

One might say that they were lucky to be in the "right moment at the right time," since the popular European uprisings of 1968 and 1969 that continued in Italy through 1980 were hugely influential on their own intellectual formation and served as a launching ground for them to connect with new audiences. Unlike France, for example, Italy saw sustained activism from the people throughout the 1970s, as well as both far-right and left terrorist activities, in which extra-parliamentary organizations bombed public places such as banks and train stations. While most of these gruesome attacks targeted ordinary people, one of the most glaring acts of violence was the kidnapping of former prime minister Aldo Moro. The kidnapping involved murdering five of his body guards, holding him hostage in a "people's prison" for fifty-four days, and his eventual assassination by the leftist group the Brigate rosse in 1978.[11] The tragedy is widely considered to mark the point of no return for the PCI. As Antonio Negri describes the situation in a reflection written almost twenty years later, the PCI suffered considerably after the kidnapping and assassination because its leadership felt they had to fracture ties with social movements so as not to appear sympathetic to the Brigate rosse. Quickly the party became politically marginalized and morphed into the bureaucratic power-hungry organization that it never intended to be.[12] In many ways, it was this new identity of the party that was already on the rise but sealed with the Moro tragedy, against which Fo and Rame reacted.

In terms of their artistic and intellectual response to Moro, Fo and Rame were hardly alone. It is testament to the complexity of the 1970s and the psychic trauma of the violence against Moro that innumerable books, television programs, feature films, and plays have attempted to comprehend those years and specifically that event.[13] Narrators have also explored this moment, as in Marco Baliani's *Corpo di stato* (*Body of State*, performed in repertory since 1998), which takes a highly personal viewpoint questioning the role of violence in the social movements of the 1970s and also commemorating the young anti-Mafia activist Giuseppe "Peppino" Impastato who was killed by the Mafia on the same day as Moro. Part of what is successful about Baliani's production, which he wrote and performs solo as is typical in the Theatre of Narration, is his intimate rapport with the audience, which is made possible by his confessional, even diaristic, recollections of being a student in Rome in the mid-1970s and how conflicted he felt while negotiating the pressures that surrounded different approaches of activism.

Dario Fo, by contrast, had a much more difficult time creating a show that could digest the Moro incident and, more broadly, the seemingly incessant acts of terrorism in Italy, while in the midst of such emotionally wrought chaos. Fo based his play, which he called simply *La tragedia di Aldo Moro* (*The Tragedy of Aldo Moro*, 1979), on Moro's letters while he was kidnapped, in which he pleaded with the government to negotiate for his life. It was a very different play than is typical of Fo's repertoire, bereft of comedy and satire and rather something akin to a Greek tragedy. In fact, it was loosely structured after the story of Sophocles's *Philoctetes*, the title character abandoned by his countrymen when he was wounded. When asked in an interview years later if there was ever a subject Fo felt he was unable to render fit for the stage, his response was the Moro kidnapping, despite how necessary he believed it was for people to discuss. His play, he remarked, proved to be a cultural exercise rather than a piece of theatre. The continuous flow of new information regarding the kidnappers, along with the continued terrorism in Italy, rendered it impossible.[14] In 1981, however, he produced one of his more successful plays *Clacson, trombette e pernacchi* (*Trumpets and Raspberries*), which took up the theme of terrorism again, borrowing a small amount from Moro's letters but inventing an entirely different narrative surrounding the wealthy Agnelli family (of FIAT cars), all in Fo's trademark satire.

Even this brief overview of how Baliani and Fo handled the topics of terrorism and the Moro murder point to an important difference between the two styles of theatre. Fo is at his best when he is a clown, while the Theatre of Narration relies on the intimacy of a conversation. Baliani's introspective style works to encourage audience members to similarly ask themselves how this national tragedy affected them personally and how their subjective viewpoints come together to shape the national narrative of the tragedy. The element of grotesque, however, in Fo and Rame's theatre often worked to incur live (and not necessarily reflective, but rather spontaneous) reactions, which they aimed to foster into conversation. In fact, after many of their shows, they and accompanying cast members stayed onstage to have discussions with their audiences about what they just saw. This became so frequent that it was known as "the third act" of their productions, and the level of emotion in these direct engagements with the audience could often rival any stage drama.

To an extent, the idea of the third act was also a product—a welcome one—of the tensions of the 1970s. Accompanying the social movements, the atmosphere was suffused in an energy that encouraged dialogue and exchange among ordinary citizens, artists, and intellectuals. Seizing on the interest and efforts of the working class in particular, Fo and Rame used the theatre to continue the conversations that were to a large extent already taking place. What was unique about their effort was that it meant creating a new audience for theatre. Their theatre was to be a theatre for the people: the factory workers, students, those fighting for women's rights, essentially the populations engaged in political activity, who were not the typical theatre audience of, for example, Ionesco.[15] Fo and Rame took concrete steps specifically to nurture a majority working-class audience, not one that was necessarily heterogeneous, which is more important in the Theatre of Narration. Indeed, as the theatre scholar Paolo Puppa notes, one can examine Fo's (and Rame's) career as an ongoing invention of new tools for engaging the working class.[16] They articulated this priority gradually and only once they had achieved considerable success among the middle and upper classes, after performing regularly in large theatres and by 1962 even having their own television show. When their television program *Canzonissima*, a sketch-based variety act, so quickly led to national controversy in an era during which censorship was common practice in Italy, they began to believe that their popularity and success had backfired on them.[17] It made them reflect upon one of the simplest yet most meaningful professional questions: for whom was their work?

Almost existentially, their widespread popularity, which had led authorities to attempt to censor their writing, caused an ideological clash: a Gramscian battle of the popular against official culture. Fo and Rame's work was becoming victim to a textbook example of cultural hegemony in which the dominant capitalist class reinforces the system by coercing the underclasses to accept ruling-class values. As Marx and Engels famously wrote, "The ideas of the ruling class are in every epoch the ruling ideas."[18] Those with capital power are those with the intellectual power to control the culture industry, and by reinforcing their own beliefs, they write both history and ideological values that cohere with their own sense of purpose. When the state-run network insisted on censoring Fo and Rame's program, the gesture blatantly exemplified the very heart of this idea and incited a problem for the two artists. If Fo and Rame were emerging as democratic voices of the left, how could they allow the state to heavily redact their skits and alter their ideas, presenting an ideology to the public that was entirely different from their own?

By 1963 they had left *Canzonissima*, and they were barred from Italian television for the next fourteen years. Pouring their energy into theatrical production, they began to reflect on the relationship of their practice with its publics. While political, their theatre was above all entertaining. The bourgeoisie made fun of itself by permitting Fo and Rame's mockery, which significantly lessened the political punch in their work. Having aimed to create a didactic and subversive form of theatre by using comedy to engage with the working class, they were displeased with what they had in fact come to symbolize.[19] Rame herself notes that by the end of the 1968 season it dawned on them that without meaning to, they had become the "jesters at the court of the fat and intelligent bourgeois."[20] Rather than changing the political status quo by holding up a mirror to the bourgeoisie, they were its clowns: talented performers, irreverently poking fun at the ruling classes who laughed obligingly but, ultimately, dismissively. They experienced for themselves the "safety valve" that Bakhtin articulates as the raison d'etre for the continued existence of carnival and other illusory performance apparatuses under dominant hegemonic regimes. Their success with these audiences not only risked their ability to reach the working class but also undermined the actual principles on which they built their work.

As a result, they created a new theatre company, the Associazione Nuova Scena, and wrote a didactic text just before the first productions of *Mistero buffo*, which in some ways would be the creative counterpoint to the goals they articulated in the manual (figure 1). Fo explains that a couple years later, in 1970, they were looking for "a new public, the workers, the proletariat, in order to demonstrate an exercise in the corruption of the 'system' with the obvious intention to solicit change."[21] Back in 1960 Rame had actually joined the PCI, and though Fo never did, they both depended upon their relationship to the party to help guarantee the audiences with whom they wanted to dialogue. One of the ways in which they took advantage of their close rapport with the PCI was by performing in many of the cultural centers across Italy run by the party's cultural and creative branch known as Associazione Ricreativa e Culturale Italiana (ARCI) to build an audience of workers. Quickly, Nuova Scena became dependent upon ARCI for both their venues and their audiences, but the PCI leadership was largely in control of ARCI, and Fo and Rame found them too entrenched in bureaucracy to advance the changes that they advocated. Thus, during the 1970s, they experienced firsthand so much of what the left was experiencing: namely, the splintering of relationships that had been based on unifying ideals that now were fraying in different directions. They had to reassess, yet again, how they could create a theatre practice that gave voice to the people offstage as much as those on the stage.

Figure 1. Dario Fo in a nationally televised production of *Mistero buffo*, 1977. He invites the audience to sit with him and converses with them throughout the show.

In August 1968, Fo and Rame and other company members first began to articulate the goals of Nuova Scena by collaboratively reflecting upon Marx, Gramsci, and Lenin with a focus on ideas of how the bourgeoisie manages culture. Fo and Rame underline that in their work they aim to create not just artistic entertainment for the working classes but a type of Gramscian cultural activity.[22] This notion of activity is particularly salient in its suggestion of energetic possibilities and calls to mind Gramsci's musings on the distinction between a "war of maneuver" and a "war of position." As Gramsci explains in his *Prison Notebooks* (8), unlike the war of maneuver, which requires a blunt assault against the state, the war of position will be much more complex and difficult, requiring exceptional qualities of patience and inventiveness.[23] Regarding the war of position, as literary scholar Joseph Francese has argued, Gramsci had shifted his thinking from a short-term effort to one with long-lasting potential that extends in perpetuity.[24] In his notebooks, Gramsci underlines that the military metaphor can be only indirectly linked to political science and the social theory that he espouses, but given the atmosphere in Italy from late 1968 to 1980, it holds newfound relevance in conversation with the revolutionary energies in the air.

Fo and Rame's desire to interact with working-class audiences and dialogue with them demonstrates a dialectical interaction with Gramsci's war metaphors. As sociologist Daniel Egan summarizes, "For Gramsci, the classical model of revolution through military insurrection (war of maneuver) has been supplanted within advanced capitalism by a cultural struggle of much longer duration and complexity (war of position)."[25] The play *Morte accidentale di un anarchico (Accidental Death of an Anarchist*, 1970) and the pre-show lecture from Fo, for example, demonstrate the desire both to spark a revolutionary flame in the audience as though it were a war of maneuver and also to stimulate a more methodical, calculated, and long-term resistance, as in his formulation of the war of position. The play frankly addresses a controversy unfolding almost in real time when the show first opened. Based on the probable defenestration of Giuseppe Pinelli when he was in police custody under interrogation as a suspect in the December 1969 Piazza Fontana bombing, Fo uses humor to underline the outrageous absurdity of the Milanese police, who claimed that the death of Pinelli, an anarchist, was a mysterious accident.

Fo plays a mentally unstable con artist with the character name "the Maniac" in police custody who outsmarts the officers by impersonating various people including another officer and especially the judge in the Pinelli case, who has come to investigate the "accident." It is not a narrative play in which the plot develops the action or character, but it progresses through the momentum of a series of accumulating farcical scenes, in which the Maniac, and eventually a journalist, originally played by Rame, challenges the police's story and, with that, their authority. After some tongue-and-cheek dialogue, the journalist gets to the serious questions. "On the subject of the window, the abandoned inquiry failed to include the report on the trajectory taken by the body of the presumed suicide. . . . It would establish whether, when he emerged from the window, the anarchist was still alive . . . or less than alive."[26] This level of specificity highlighting the lack of detail, and indeed seriousness, in the police investigation after the death of Pinelli is meant to slowly ignite outrage. The journalist builds her case: "Also missing from the evidence in that inquiry, and this is even more alarming, is a tape that recorded the exact time at which an ambulance was called. . . . The ambulance was called five minutes before the anarchist took off out of the window. Can any of you explain this curious talent for anticipation?"[27] As her interrogation increases in intensity, with the help of the Maniac in the room, the many unanswered questions and the implication that the police are hiding information become increasingly clear. Given the proximity to the actual events when this play first premiered, the potential for audience members to protest was real.

While Fo and Rame were developing strategies that work both in and across multiple historical and situational contexts, their efforts were fully focused in the Gramscian realm of maneuver, where critical issues, such as the death of someone in police custody, would eventually become less important with time. According to Gramsci, what is needed to result in long-lasting change is a situation in which decisive positions are at stake.[28] Echoing Gramsci's strategy, Fo and Rame demonstrate, more than this case of the anarchist, the long-term need for both journalists and ordinary people like those in the audience to question the police and hold them accountable. Their performance is not just one of character. They are performing the gestures that the audience can take up: directly and politely questioning authority. Relatedly, the very presence of the Maniac represents the insanity of the situation, paralleling their world at the time, but the journalist, and the audience who is meant to identify with her, hold the potential to correct that insanity by insisting that those in power assume responsibility when they are responsible. In the words of the literary critic Mario Mignone, they are attempting to address political corruption in a "veiled attack against the antidemocratic and repressive nature of Italy's ruling institutions in general, and exhibit a genuine concern for the conditions of the common people who are the victims of economic and social injustices."[29] They do so not just through the content of their plays but also in their dedication to creating and empowering new audiences of traditionally disenfranchised peoples.

The extent to which Fo and Rame were harassed by police and far-right groups as a result of their success in attracting new audiences to discuss leftist ideology cannot be overstated and points both to their achievement at rousing audiences and to the state's deep fear of such potential. One could measure their success at dialoguing with new publics by the degree to which they roused a state-initiated campaign that sought to silence them through cruel and belligerent tactics of fear and intimidation. At times, this directness on the part of Fo and Rame had dire consequences, but they courageously embraced even those tactics that were meant to silence and suppress them and shared them with their audiences. I am thinking here of the monologue *Lo stupro* (*The Rape*, 1983), written and performed by Rame in which she draws on her traumatic personal experiences after she was kidnapped, tortured, and gang raped in 1973 by a neofascist group that was discovered to have been commissioned by several high-ranking Milanese police officials. This horrific crime speaks to the long 1970s in Italy as much as it does to the agitation that Fo and Rame's theatre created. Their work attempted to shine a light on much of the chaos and state-sanctioned violence and inspire their audiences to think through the intellectual positions of the lower and middle classes in order to then join in their struggles.

The Fo and Rame Legacy in the Theatre of Narration

Just as the political turmoil of the 1970s is a vivid background in much of Fo and Rame's work from that period, it is likewise influential for the Theatre of Narration, since some of the most celebrated narrators came of age during the decade. Fo and Rame, however, engage with political upheaval differently than the narrators. The main contrast is the directness with which Fo and Rame approached current events through the lens of their overt political ideologies; this directness compares to a much more nuanced presentation from narrators, who cast a much wider net for the make-up of their audience and are, after all, reflecting retrospectively, not in present time. While the narrators may or may not share Fo and Rame's political opinions, they certainly share the aim of creating a space for conversation. But unlike Fo and Rame, their aim does not skew toward the revolutionary with performances that could incite protest or another form of action. It is worth recalling that when Fo and Rame were performing in the 1970s, they were already widely known, and the period itself was rife with social protests on the streets and in organizations, whether for workers' rights or women's rights. The Theatre of Narration, by contrast, did not have a large following until Paolini's *Vajont* was aired on national television in 1997 to much acclaim. By then, like the Clinton era of the 1990s in the United States, the culture of protest from the 1970s in Italy had been dimmed by, among other reasons, the Trump-esque leadership of the wealthy media tycoon Silvio Berlusconi, who was on and off prime minister from 1994 to 2011.[30]

One of the key developments in the work of Fo and Rame effected by the narrators is how they engage with political messages. As discussed, Fo and Rame worked closely with the Italian Communist Party. They performed in the party's spaces. They propagated many of the party's beliefs regarding the worker and class in particular. The politics of the Theatre of Narration is much more complex and subtle, to the point where it risks going undetected. In *Corpo di stato*, for example, as Baliani reflects on the death of Moro, he is more interested in bringing the audience to question what it means to be a part of a political moment, as he was when he was a university student in the 1970s, rather than persuading them to a particular set of party beliefs. Curino's *Olivetti* plays (performed in repertory since 1996), for which she is perhaps most known, on a superficial level seem to celebrate the Olivetti family, famous for their typewriters, design, and their magnanimous company policies for factory workers, which has a left-leaning sentiment, but she stops short of an argumentative position. Rather, even more subtly, by portraying the matriarchs of the Olivetti family, she presents the possibility that much of what is celebrated about the Olivettis is thanks to the women in the family.[31] This suggestion, however, is delicate and nuanced, as the play is largely about the Olivetti men, even if it is told through the voices of the women, giving them the rare opportunity to narrate history.

The theatre of Fo and Rame and the Theatre of Narration present political intention along a range, from the subtle to the overt. This range highlights the epic range of the Brechtian spectrum of *verfremdungseffekt*, or estrangement effect, that is inherent in both. Frederic Jameson argues that it is important to understand Brecht's theories in the context of a debate concerned with literary form, rather than in the context of modernism's challenge of realism. Brecht's ideas were part of a debate in which mass culture superseded literature in general.[32] The binaries of entertainment versus education, and distancing oneself from the art to partake in both, assume a political relevance when contemplated in the realm of the masses and the popular. Stylistically, and substantively, the narrators operate in an understated mode compared to Fo and Rame, whose approach to both entertainment and education are big and bold, with raucous comedy, satire, and pronounced political positions. Fo was an exceptionally gifted comical actor, and his physical theatre played well to popular audiences. It was, after all, designed specifically to reverberate with them. He and Rame also controlled the physical space by arranging how the audience was seated (often on the floor around the actors rather than far off, as in hierarchical bourgeois theatres with the actors on raked stages) and creating a debate-like environment by speaking candidly out of character before their plays, in addition to during the third act afterward.

By contrast, the poetics of the Theatre of Narration strikes a far more intellectual tone that is already distant from the entertaining moments that comedy or dramatic portrayals may provide, even if the energy in the performance space is intimate and contained. Compared to the way that Fo and Rame attempted to incite their audiences to partake in many of the strikes and protests around them and unite to bring about a longer-term change, these choices might appear to make the Theatre of Narration less intentionally political, and to an extent it is. In different ways, however, narrators are making strong political choices on a formal scale. By adhering to a more intellectual even didactic representation of theatre, rather than playing for laughs, they play instead to the intellectual in everyone, as Gramsci stated. Their theatre is as much for the working class as it is for immigrants or for aristocrats, and by alternating their venues, broadcasting the occasional performance, traveling all over Italy from small hill towns to major cities, and performing for free as part of summer festivals (paid by local municipalities), the message is that everyone has an equal voice. Fo and Rame wanted to privilege the voice of the working class to compensate for centuries of being silenced, and this effort is not lost in the Theatre of Narration, even if it aims to be more inclusive.

There might be no greater tribute to Dario Fo and Franca Rame than when Laura Curino, who often incorporates a feminist approach, discusses the couple at the end of her play *Passione* and then quotes one of Rame's scenes from *Mistero buffo* by performing a large portion of it. In many respects, Curino's homage to Rame is a far more direct reference to the powerful influences of the couple's theatre than any implicit echoes of Fo that scholars emphasize. I suspect that this lack of acknowledgement of Rame in much of the criticism is due to Fo's principal authorship, especially of the early plays, even though Rame wrote or coauthored many of her monologues with Fo and exerted an acute editorial acumen over Fo's scripts. She also assumed the role of artistic director in their companies, which was a hugely intensive time commitment and necessary to their continuing livelihood, yet largely thankless in terms of artistic value. The issue of Rame receiving fair credit is complicated by the unique partnership of an artistic couple in which continual conversation about work was a part of their lives in the theater as much as it was at home. At times Rame fully credited Fo with authorship, while at other times she attempted to assert her role in the creation of their plays.[33] Her mixed feelings likely relate to the status of women in the second half of the twentieth century, and yet Fo continues to be more celebrated even in the late 2010s. While Curino nods to both Fo and Rame, it is refreshing that she highlights Rame's influence and also draws attention to the extent to which Rame is often marginalized in favor of Fo.

With *Mistero buffo* in particular, Fo and Rame repopularized monologuist traditions. The production consists of twelve mini *canovacci*, or scenarios, divided into two sections of commentary and then biblical accounts of the Passion (figure 2). As with the Theatre of Narration, there is barely a set or elaborate costumes. Fo employs political satire and involves the audience through eye contact and direct address, which integrates them into the performance itself, making the event an opportunity for dialogue, debate, and even confrontation.[34] Improvisation is another strategy that both Fo and the narrators use to bring audience members closer to the material as well as the performance itself. This episodic organization presents monologues linked by didactic interpretations that create a continuous dialectical exchange between the past and the present, history and the current moment, culture and politics. Theatre scholar Simone Soriani points out that the way the metanarrative is interrupted by smaller moments allows Fo to connect medieval fiction and contemporary realism. Many narrators also invoke this formal technique of macro-to-micro accounts as a tool to connect the past and the present.[35] Unlike *Mistero buffo*, however, Narrative Theatre productions do not contain a series of freestanding sections. Narrators recount stories, and whether they veer toward realism or *affabulazione*, they still have a beginning, a middle, and an end.

Highly autobiographical, in *Passione*, Curino shares her memories of moving from Turin as a young child to a suburb of the city called Settimo Torinese, because it was seven (*sette*) kilometers north of the city border. The name is relevant, as she describes a place that was built by industry for the families of its workers, so business could flourish. In her account, it was entirely soulless and lacked even its own name, having instead a name that described it in relation to a real city. In a bildungsroman of sorts, she poignantly describes, often with humor, coming of age in a place where developers cared more about their commodities than the well-being of those who made them. She recalls how on one rare occasion a theatre troupe came to town and notes the huge impression it made on her, inspiring her to become a writer and actor. Although she does not mention the couple by name, Curino recalls the moment when the two actors came to Settimo to perform *Mistero buffo*. That they were performing in Settimo, where so many workers lived, and not in the big city of Turin is another key point in Curino's *Passione*, and a choice that the narrators copy in their own performance tours when they visit working-class towns. With that detail, Curino underlines the cultural importance of Rame and Fo's theatre in working-class towns like Settimo. The room where they performed the piece was, in Curino's words, "full of communists, priests who had misinterpreted the title and came to hear about the historic compromise [between the Christian

Figure 2. Franca Rame in the nationally televised production of *Mistero buffo*, 1977, performing Maria.

Figure 3. Laura Curino performs Rame's Maria in *Passione* circa 1995 at an outdoor production in Dro (Trentino-Alto Adige). Photographer: Paolo Rapalino

Democrats and Communist political parties], and even two bishops who came to excommunicate the priests for coming … and the two performers from Milan; the man with the teeth that stick out, who always makes you laugh even when there's not much to laugh about, and his wife, the brunette (who I know is now blond, but I think she tints her hair) who played the Madonna reciting in an antique dialect."[36] Gently poking fun at the actor with the big teeth and his wife who now dyes her hair, and also noting that the church found many of their works scandalous, Curino mentions them as a way to honor the influence that they had over her and the Theatre of Narration's creative development.

Shortly after this, Curino performs Rame's Madonna monologue in a strange and serious pause in her melancholy comedy (figure 3).[37] Hauntingly, she conjures Rame and the hazy pathos of the past by maintaining the barely decipherable archaic dialect of Fo and Rame's original script of Mary under the cross of her dying son. Her homage points to the continuing, multilayered, and reconfigured influence of Fo and Rame not just on the narrators but also on Curino's audience members. In quoting one of the most wrenching monologues in their entire repertoire, and one that Rame, not Fo, uttered, Curino summons the seriousness of their plays and of their message at a time when the famous couple worked diligently to inspire their audiences to participate in the political movements all around them, when there was energy and support for social justice causes. Curino's performance, intertwined with a commentary on and indeed a criticism of the heartlessness of industry, draws a strong parallel to audiences in the late 1980s through the 2010s, as she continues to perform *Passione* as part of her repertoire. Without being as overt as Fo and Rame, in invoking them, she nonetheless signals their commitment to rouse their audiences, and, even more importantly, she carries that work to a new audience, in a different time, and with her own emphasis and interpretation.

On Wednesday morning, November 9, 2016, when my Italian class next met, it felt like a new world. Many of us had not gotten much sleep and several students were not present. I regretted not having encouraged them to engage more with the political questions that we had encountered at our last meeting. I had not wanted to take advantage of my position as their professor, but even in classes other than political science, such as theatre classes, literature classes, and language classes, should we not connect our work with students to ideas of civic duty that we can discuss together? The artists who I study would certainly ask, "If not in humanities classes in university, *where* can we have these conversations?" Having learned from them, I would answer, "In the theatre. And also in class."

Notes

1. The author wishes to thank Zarena Aslami, Nancy Marino, and Patrick O'Donnell; the editors of this issue, Brian E. G. Cook and Sara Freeman; and the two anonymous reviewers for their helpful criticism and conversation.
2. Anne Cummings, Chiara Frenquellucci, and Gloria Pastorino, eds., *Immagina: L'italiano senza confini* (Boston: Vista Higher Learning, 2016), 119. All translations are my own unless otherwise noted.
3. Christopher Cairns, "Italy," in *European Theatre 1960–1990: Cross-Cultural Perspectives*, ed. Ralph Yarrow (London: Routledge, 2014), 130. See also the extensive record of international performances maintained in the online archive of Dario Fo and Franca Rame, accessed January 29, 2017, http://www.archivio.francarame.it/Estero.aspx.
4. Joseph Farrell, *Dario Fo and Franca Rame: Harlequins of the Revolution* (London: Methuen, 2001), 200.
5. For two of the most seminal book-length investigations on the practice (both in Italian), see: Gerardo Guccini, *La bottega dei narratori: Storie, laboratori e metodi* (Rome: D. Audino, 2005); and Simone Soriani, *Sulla scena del racconto* (Arezzo: Zona, 2009).
6. For a helpful investigation of many actors who are also authors in Italian theatre history, see Donatella Fischer, ed., *The Tradition of the Actor-Author in Italian Theatre* (London: Legenda, 2013).
7. I am thinking here of Daniele Timpano, who performed his award-winning *Aldo morto—tragedia* in 2012, followed by a project in collaboration with the Teatro Orologio in Rome called *Aldo morto 54* in which Timpano live-streamed 24/7 an experimental performance art project in which he lived in a 3x1 meter room for fifty-four days, the length of time the former prime minister of Italy, Aldo Moro, was held hostage after he was kidnapped by the Brigate rosse, a leftist extremist group, before they assassinated him in 1978. The play on words in the title adds a "t" to Moro's actual name to make the word *morto*, which means "dead."
8. Carol Martin, *Theatre of the Real* (London: Palgrave Macmillan, 2013), 5.
9. Tom Behan, *Dario Fo: Revolutionary Theatre* (London: Pluto, 2000), 3.
10. Ibid., 31.
11. At the time of his kidnapping, Moro was heavily involved in talks known as the "historic compromise," in which the major parties, the Christian Democrats and the Communists, were attempting to create an alliance, but when Moro was kidnapped the talks eventually crumbled. For a thorough analysis of the economic and legal complexities that surround this incident, see Richard Drake, *The Aldo Moro Murder Case* (Cambridge, MA: Harvard University Press, 1995).
12. Antonio Negri, "Reviewing the Experience of Italy in the 1970s," *Le Monde Diplomatique*, n.d., http://mondediplo.com/1998/09/11negri.
13. Some of these artistic renderings begin shortly thereafter, as in the left-leaning writer and politician Leonardo Sciascia's *L'affaire Moro* (1978), published the very year of Moro's murder and based on his prison letters, which takes to task the leadership for not doing enough to save him. Among the more critically acclaimed films is Marco Bellocchio's *Buongiorno, notte* (*Goodmorning, Night*, 2003), loosely based on the autobiography of one

of the kidnappers, Anna Laura Braghetti, which interjects a provocative gendered slant on the attack.

14. Chiara Valentini, *La storia di Dario Fo* (Feltrinelli Editore, 1997), 186.
15. I allude here to Fo's given reason for breaking up the successful company that he, Franco Parenti, and Giustino Durano began in 1953 that staged the publicly and critically acclaimed *Il ditto nell'occhio* (*A Finger in the Eye*). In the midst of their success, Pareti wanted to follow with an Ionesco production, an idea Fo not only disagreed with but also opposed so vehemently that he decided that they could no longer work together. This speaks to how Fo saw the leftist avant-garde as elitist, a point on which he would never compromise. See Joseph Farrell and Antonio Scuderi, eds., *Dario Fo: Stage, Text, and Tradition*, (Carbondale: Southern Illinois University Press, 2000), 7–8.
16. Paolo Puppa, *Parola di scena: Teatro italiano tra '800 e '900* (Rome: Bulzoni, 1999), 296.
17. The second state television channel, RAI 2, was generally more lenient than the first, particularly in the early 1960s, when the Socialist Party had joined a coalition with the dominant centrist party, the Christian Democrats, which was the majority party in postwar Italy until it dissolved under corruption scandals in 1994. While it was the state that imposed censors on *Canzonissima*, given that it aired on a state-run national channel, one must also acknowledge the power that the Roman Catholic Church wielded within the party. The censorship of Fo and Rame can be understood as a precursor to the tumultuous relationship they would always have with the Roman Catholic Church, particularly during *Mistero buffo* productions, which followed them to Catholic communities outside of Italy as well and created near-constant protest. For the most part, the criticism did not appear to deter Fo and Rame, given the extent to which they continued to satirize the corruption of the Roman Catholic Church in many of their plays, often in a grotesque and bawdy style.
18. Karl Marx and Frederick Engels, *Collected Works: Volume 5, 1845–47* (New York: International Publishers, 1975), 59.
19. Antonio Scuderi, "Dario Fo and Performance Theory," *Italian Culture* 12 (1994): 244.
20. Dario Fo, *Le commedie di Dario Fo* (Torino: Einaudi, 1975), vii.
21. G. Br., "Nel «Mistero» di Dario Fo sete di giustizia sociale: La forza rivoluzionaria di un Vangelo interpretato dagli umili," *Gazzetta del Popolo*, January 14, 1970, 6.
22. Dario Fo and Vittorio Franceschi, *Compagni senza censura* (Milan: Mazzotta, 1970), 7.
23. Antonio Gramsci, *Passato e presente: Le Idee 57, Quaderni del carcere* (Rome: Editori Riuniti, 1971), 103. From notebook 8.
24. Joseph Francese, "Thoughts on Gramsci's Need 'To Do Something Für Ewig,'" *Rethinking Marxism* 21, no. 1 (January 2009): 54–66.
25. Daniel Egan, "Rethinking War of Maneuver/War of Position: Gramsci and the Military Metaphor," *Critical Sociology* 40, no. 4 (March 20, 2013): 521–22.
26. Dario Fo, *Accidental Death of an Anarchist* (London: Methuen Drama, 2009), 58.
27. Ibid., 59.
28. Gramsci, *Passato e presente*, 103–4.
29. Mario B. Mignone, "Dario Fo, Jester of the Italian Stage," *Italian Quarterly* 85 (Summer 1981): 49–50.
30. Berlusconi was the prime minister in Italy from May 10, 1994, to January 17, 1995; from June 11, 2001, to May 17, 2006; and from May 8, 2008, to November 16, 2011, for a combined total of approximately nine years.

31. Juliet Guzzetta, "At Work, at Home: Women, Labor, and Laura Curino's Olivetti Plays," *Annali d'Italianistica* 32 (2014): 291–306.
32. Fredric Jameson, *Brecht and Method* (London: Verso, 2000), 38.
33. Farrell, *Dario Fo and Franca Rame*, 194–201.
34. Mignone, "Dario Fo, Jester of the Italian Stage," 47.
35. Simone Soriani, "*Mistero buffo*, dal varietà al teatro di narrazione," in *Coppia d'arte: Dario Fo e Franca Rame con dipinti, testimonianze e dichiarazioni inedite*, ed. Concetta d'Angeli and Simone Soriani (Pisa: University of Pisa Press, 2006), 104.
36. Laura Curino, Roberto Tarasco, and Gabriele Vacis, *Passione* (Novara: Interlinea, 1998), 59.
37. Paolo Puppa has briefly compared other interpretations of Rame's monologue from *Mistero buffo*, noting that of Curino and focusing especially on the work of actress Lucia Vasini when she and Paolo Rossi performed *Mistero buffo* in 2013–14. Paolo Puppa, "La scrittura femminile di Franca: la paura del tragico," *Cuadernos de Filología Italiana* 21 (2014): 295–305, 300.

Chavez Ravine

Culture Clash and the Political Project of Rewriting History

—ASHLEY E. LUCAS

On a piece of once-sacred land, where hundreds raised their children and buried their dead, a young Mexican baseball player named Fernando Valenzuela took the mound to pitch for the Los Angeles Dodgers in the 1981 opening day game at Dodger Stadium. Born in poverty, Valenzuela would become, soon after this game, a baseball legend, symbolizing the immigrant success story in the United States. The stories that preceded and enabled Valenzuela's taking this mound, however—the stories of the more than eighteen hundred Mexican American families who were forced out of their homes for the construction of Dodger Stadium—have not fared as well as his. On May 17, 2003, a Latino theatre group premiered a play that told the stories of those former residents and asked LA audiences to reconsider the history of their city, its government, and its people. In doing so, they embodied and promoted an alternate version of the past, foregrounding the actions and concerns of Latina/os and working-class people.[1]

With a cast of characters ranging from Abbott and Costello to J. Edgar Hoover, the Latino performance trio Culture Clash bridges the gap between history and performance in *Chavez Ravine*, a play about land, community, and power in the heart of Los Angeles.[2] The extensive archival research and interviews conducted by the playwright/performers laid the foundation for a script that is based in historical fact as much as it is constructed as a dramatic fiction. Theatre historian Freddie Rokem describes the way performances about the past link an awareness of the "failures of history" with "the efforts to create a meaningful work of art."[3] In *Chavez Ravine*, the failures of history signify the oppression and marginalization of a Mexican American community and the absence of that community from traditional histories. Richard Montoya, Ric Salinas, and Herbert Sigüenza, the three members of Culture Clash, create a complex and multivocal version of the past in which the displaced people speak louder than the city leaders. In doing so, these playwright/performers make visible what Latina/o theatre scholar Jon Rossini describes as "the need to imagine an alternative that transforms not only the self but also the very structures of representation."[4] *Chavez Ravine* offers an experiential and performative version of Los Angeles history, challenging both who has the right to define the past and how the experiences of our ancestors are transmitted to a new generation.

Chavez Ravine clearly establishes an alternative version of the history of Dodger Stadium and at the same time asserts the right of the contemporary Latina/o community in LA to make and tell their own histories. It insists that the residents of the neighborhood be as much a part of the story line of US history as the hard-won success of Fernando Valenzuela. This play uses elements of fiction and theatricality to point toward larger truths and to reassert the agency of people who were robbed of their land and the opportunity to tell their own stories. *Chavez Ravine* uses the live, racialized bodies of its actors (and some creative staging) to reinscribe meaning on the past and to offer Latina/os in Los Angeles a measure of space, authority, and visibility in the present.

The History of a Place and a Play

The neighborhood of Chavez Ravine was home to more than eighteen hundred families before Dodger Stadium opened for business in 1962.[5] The land was originally settled by the Tongva people, who occupied the entire Los Angeles basin region before the Spanish arrived to explore and later colonize the area in 1542.[6] The land eventually became part of Mexico, and in the 1840s city councilman Julian Chavez acquired the land (then appraised at $800.00), which at that time was near the center of the Pueblo of Los Angeles.[7] On February 2, 1848, the signing of the treaty of Guadalupe Hidalgo redrew the borderline between Mexico and the United States, and a huge portion of Northern Mexico, including much of what we now know as the states of Arizona, California, New Mexico, Colorado, Utah, and Nevada, suddenly became part of the United States. The residents of this new US territory had the choice to stay and become US citizens or migrate south of the new border.[8] Migration in and out of the ravine continued for the next one hundred years. In 1910 and 1911, social unrest caused by the Mexican Revolution prompted a number of refugees from the war to settle in Chavez Ravine.[9] The neighborhood appears to have been inhabited by settlers of various origins at least since the land's occupation by the Tongvas until the evacuation of the last of the ravine residents enabled the construction of Dodger Stadium in 1959.

In the 1940s and 1950s, a group of the mostly Mexican American residents of Chavez Ravine resisted the city's plans to build a housing project on the land where their families had lived for generations.[10] The city used the law of eminent domain to force families to sell their homes to the government, with promises that affordable community housing projects would be built on the land where their private homes now stood.[11] City officials had so much trouble severing the community's ties to the land that local sheriffs physically removed the last of the homeowners (the Aréchiga family) from their home in 1959. The Ravine families and their supporters protested to the City Council about the removal, but their efforts could not defeat those of the city's leadership, notably City Councilwoman Rosalind Wyman and Mayor Norris Poulson, who staunchly defended the urban renewal of Chavez Ravine. Mayor Poulson's political support came from the Chandler family, owners of the *Los Angeles Times*, who had financial and business interests in the property. The promised housing project never materialized. Eventually the city subsidized Dodgers owner Walter O'Malley's bid for the more than three hundred acres of Chavez Ravine.[12] O'Malley then oversaw the construction of Dodger Stadium on this site just north of what had become downtown LA.

To tell their version of the story of this neighborhood, Culture Clash premiered *Chavez Ravine*, their first history-based play, at the famous Mark Taper Forum in Los Angeles on May 17, 2003.[13] This production was the fifth highest grossing production in what was then the Taper's thirty-five-year history.[14] The play was revived and sold out most of its performances at the smaller Kirk Douglas Theatre in Culver City in 2015 with a few notable changes in the script.[15]

Chavez Ravine differs structurally from the plays in the group's earlier *Culture Clash in AmeriCCa* series, on which they began work in 1994.[16] Their previous site-specific work was set in the present time and was episodic and often monologic, without a clear plotline or recurring characters.[17] These plays do not follow the story of an event and do not present any kind of cohesive journey for the characters.[18] *Culture Clash in AmeriCCa* broadly describes the intersections of various ethnic groups in specific US cities in a time frame loosely defined as the present.[19] *Chavez Ravine*, on the other hand, develops a historical narrative that jumps back and forth through time. It also maintains a clear story line and brings certain characters back to the stage multiple times to ground the audience in their narratives as the history of the neighborhood unfolds. In a research and writing process that took two years to complete, Montoya, Salinas, and Sigüenza conducted interviews, did archival research, and worked with dramaturg John Glore as they reconstructed the history of Chavez Ravine.[20]

Bringing all this research to the stage, Culture Clash revives the struggle over land rights, socioeconomic privilege, and ethnicity by performing *Chavez Ravine*.[21] They act out their version of history and challenge widely accepted constructions of the past, such as those seen in government documents, newspaper articles, and mainstream history texts. These representations of history construct Chavez Ravine as a neighborhood unworthy of being saved. The play functions as a combination of ethnography, history, fiction, and art, leaving audiences to wonder how much of this representation of culture, time, and place has been invented or shaped by the writers' dramatic interpretation. *Chavez Ravine* not only provides an alternative version of history but demands that its audiences reconsider the nature and function of history in general as it relates to notions of politics, social stratification, and ethnicity. The members of Culture Clash not only tell a version of history that their spectators might not have heard before but also expose how and why other narratives about this community's past have deliberately obscured the agency of Mexican Americans in Los Angeles, destroying what Tara J. Yosso and David G. García refer to as "the cultural wealth present in these communities."[22]

The First Scene of *Chavez Ravine*: Setting the Stage for a New Look at the Past

In this play, Culture Clash stages a comparative history, drawing multiple parallels between time periods, dominant and marginalized cultures, and the shifting landscape of Los Angeles. The group opens their two-act play with characters based on familiar public personas. Montoya plays the legendary Dodger announcer Vin Scully broadcasting the start of the 1981 opening day baseball game, while Sigüenza takes the mound as Dodger pitcher Fernando Valenzuela: "Today will be quite a test for young Valenzuela. Imagine folks, here's a young kid, speaks no English, and a little more than a year ago was playing far away, in the childhood sandlots of a sleepy Mexican village, in a place called Etchohauaquila, Sonora. This screw-balling south paw is the youngest player since Catfish Hunter to start an opening day game. And after a quick scratch of the crotch, here we go."[23] This narrative about Valenzuela identifies him as an immigrant success story. He came to the United States from what the character of Scully implies was a backward and impoverished Mexico and then became a legendary ballplayer. This depiction of the theatrical character of Valenzuela reinforces the popular perception of the historical figure of Valenzuela and makes the character both familiar and believable. Wearing a bad toupee and anglicizing the pronunciation of the name of Valenzuela's home town, Montoya plays up the contrast between Valenzuela, the racialized immigrant, and Scully, the symbol of the white, mainstream media. This contrast continues to function in a multiplicity of ways throughout the text as the corporate presence of Dodger Stadium overtakes the Mexican American community of Chavez Ravine.

Since the play begins in Dodger Stadium, the audience gains a sense of the current geography of the Ravine before the layers of the past are revealed in the course of the production. The staging works to make the audience members feel as though they were seated in Dodger Stadium. Valenzuela and later a stagehand dressed as team manager Tommy Lasorda both make entrances through the audience, and at one point the actors ask the audience to stand and sing "Take Me Out to the Ball Game" while ushers dressed as concession sellers wander through the aisles tossing bags of popcorn into the audience.

The audience takes in this heightened yet recognizable version of characteristically American baseball history, and immediately after situating themselves comfortably in the ballgame, a piece of history that generally goes unrecognized drops into the scene, literally: "*Small houses gently fall from above onto the outfield. Like ghosts from another era, two Chavez Ravine residents enter... They look toward Fernando.*"[24] In the staging of the play at the Taper, homes the size of dolls' houses lower from the fly space above the stage and hover in the air above the actors' heads. They do not distract from the action of the play but remain there as a visual contrast to the action in Dodger Stadium. Closer to the audience's and Valenzuela's fields of vision, a house about the size of a microwave sits down stage left, as though it were on the baseball field.

With the emergence of the houses in the outfield of Dodger Stadium, time collapses through a conflation of historical moments in the same space. Siblings Henry and Maria Salgado Ruiz, 1940s residents of the Ravine, visit Valenzuela in 1981 and teach him about the piece of land where he will make history as a great baseball player.[25] Henry says he "was born behind second base," mapping out the past on the landscape of the present and staking his claim to a space now seen as a piece of corporate and commercialized property.[26] The theatrical scene captures the space in two different modes, each dearly loved by loyal communities. Maria describes the Ravine as sanctified ancestral space: "These are sacred lands you're pitching on Fernando. Long ago burial grounds for the Tongva, Chinese, and Jewish gente."[27] When Maria inserts a Spanish word as she lists the "Jewish gente," she evokes the Mexican and Mexican American ancestors who are not explicitly included in her list. This passage also contextualizes Maria and her family/community as a bilingual group honoring many different former inhabitants of this land. As she says this, the audience sees Henry and Maria in 1940s period dress standing in the middle of a physical representation of Dodger Stadium, visually marking the sharp contrast between their claim to this land and the Dodgers' investment in it.

The 2015 revival production preceded this opening scene in the stadium with film footage from 1959 of the actual evictions of the Ravine's last residents, including scenes of bulldozers demolishing houses and of police carrying an elderly woman out of her home.[28] This more violent beginning to the play seems apt in light of the heightened awareness of police brutality against people of color in the wake of the deaths of Tamir Rice, Michael Brown, and Eric Garner in 2014.[29] The projections of Don Normark's photos of Chavez Ravine in the 1940s, which were interspersed throughout the revival production, further contribute to the palpable sense of loss experienced by the displaced residents of the neighborhood as well as the grief and strife of the political moment in which the audience lives in 2015.[30]

These additional juxtapositions of historical imagery with live performance further bridge the gaps between what Diana Taylor calls the archive (unchanging records) and the repertoire or "embodied memory… all those acts usually thought of as ephemeral, nonreproducable knowledge." The repertoire, she argues, lends performers and audiences alike a measure of agency in the making of meaning in the present moment.[31] By foregrounding historical images in the midst of a performance, *Chavez Ravine* demands that the archive be reevaluated in the shared context of each live performance of the play. Culture Clash works hard to keep their audiences on their toes as they move through broad landscapes of space and meaning in this play.

Changing Notions of Space in a Shifting Landscape

Chavez Ravine, like most Culture Clash plays, makes huge leaps in time and in the changing landscape of a place. Both the Mark Taper Forum theatre and Chavez Ravine itself are the stationary sites for the play, but over the course of the play and the many decades of the Ravine's gradual conversion from a residential neighborhood to Dodger Stadium, the space changes dramatically. The play has suggestive, minor set changes, but no major walls or backdrops move on or offstage during the show. The light-colored wooden floor of the Taper stage had one panel in it that could be flipped over to reveal a solid green rectangle to suggest the grassy field in Dodger Stadium. A table and chairs were sometimes onstage to create either a family home in the 1940s neighborhood or the office of Los Angeles mayor Poulson. At one point three actors sitting in a group of chairs huddled close to one another create a helicopter flying above the city, with actor Herbert Sigüenza standing on another chair behind them swinging a rotating apparatus in the air above his head to serve as the helicopter's propeller (see figure 1). Creative but not literalized staging allows the actors to move through a long series of fragments of settings and recognizable characters from Los Angeles, showing the audience that the writer/performers have specific knowledge of the city. The performers become living embodiments of the people of LA as they act out the struggles of the characters that are drawn from the community.

Figure 1. Production photo from *Chavez Ravine* at the Mark Taper Forum in 2003. Back row: Herbert Sigüenza. Front row, from left to right: Ric Salinas, Richard Montoya, Eileen Galindo. Photograph by Craig Schwartz. Courtesy of the Mark Taper Forum.

The shift from community to corporate space in *Chavez Ravine* encompasses not just land but ideologies and life practices. Chavez Ravine changed from a place in which people could live and raise children to a place where people paid money to witness a performance of commercialized, masculine, competitive culture in the United States. As the play so tellingly reveals, money did serve as the driving force behind the transformation of Chavez Ravine. In supplanting the communities that lived and died in the Ravine, Dodger Stadium monumentalized the power of US capitalism, Walter O'Malley (owner of the Dodgers), the Chandler press, and commercialized US culture, as embodied by the national pastime of baseball. Historian Cecilia O'Leary notes that the events and icons that publicly identify a culture serve to build a sense of nationalism and "unite disparate communities" under a symbol of the nation.[32] Dodger Stadium serves that function both in the play and in the actual community of Los Angeles.

Chavez Ravine recognizes the power of the stadium as an icon, but it also recognizes the people whose way of life is being destroyed by it. The stadium is a place that welcomes all the residents of LA, and it invites them to shed their differences and participate in an "All-American" sporting event. The former residents of the ravine are able to return to the land as Dodgers fans. However, in the stadium, the families who lived on this land cannot bury the umbilical cords of their children under the homes of their ancestors or participate in any of the other cultural practices that were once among the defining characteristics of the neighborhood. If they return to the land, they have to do it on the Dodgers' terms.

A group of unnamed minor characters in the play are being displaced from their land but do not seem to mind much, because, as one of them puts it, "Fight or no fight, we all love baseball."[33] This sense of inclusion in the love of baseball and the stadium itself as a symbol of US nationalism encourages this subset of sport-loving characters to shift their loyalties from the neighborhood community to a US national pastime. They maintain a different claim to the land and take pride in the fact that this monument to sport culture will be constructed upon their ancestral homes. O'Leary comments on the implications of buying into the symbols of nationalism: "Never neutral, nationalism always creates, reflects, and reproduces structures of cultural power."[34] The admiration and sense of inclusion that Dodger Stadium evokes from these men make them easy to manipulate in this situation. They do not fight the city because they have bought into the power structures represented by the stadium.

Other characters in the play do not shift their loyalties. The women of the Ruiz family reject Dodger Stadium and the nationalist sentiment attached to it.

Maria Ruiz puts her faith in her rights to protest this injustice and to vote on measures that might allow the residents of the Ravine to keep their property. Her political efforts to claim the land ultimately fail, but she uses these experiences to align herself with a different sense of inclusion in the nation: "It's true we lost, but what's important is that we helped create a culture of resistance. The struggle for Chavez Ravine prepared me for civil rights, the Farm Workers Union, my labor work with Bert Corona and the Chicana Movement. Chavez Ravine was huge for me. It made me the person I am today."[35] Though Maria was not a real person who Culture Clash interviewed, she was based on a combination of activists, including Judith Baca (former director of the Citywide Mural Project in LA), Dolores Huerta (cofounder of the United Farm Workers), and Alice McGrath (activist for the Sleepy Lagoon Defense Committee).[36] She represents the activist ideologies that Culture Clash and their collaborators embody in all their performances. When Maria looks at Chavez Ravine, she sees the struggle instead of the stadium, and that is her national symbol.

The Politics of Performance and the Performance of Politics

As David Román notes, "Culture Clash . . . bears the influence of early Chicano theatre and the belief that performance should remain oppositional to the exploitative practices of the dominant Anglo culture."[37] Early Chicano theatre was born out of the Chicano Movement and its politics of resistance. From the short *actos* first performed by El Teatro Campesino on the backs of flatbed trucks in the 1960s to the present, Chicana/o theatre has consistently challenged structural racism and asserted the agency of displaced and downtrodden people.

Luis Valdez, the founder of Teatro Campesino, argues that the practice of foregrounding oppressed peoples—Chicana/o or otherwise—enables artists to reconstitute ideas of national belonging: "It's incumbent on all writers and people who tell stories of America to reexamine the idea of America. And if you're talking about the basic issue of human rights, then the idea of America begins to shine."[38] Valdez did precisely this in 1978 when his landmark play *Zoot Suit* became the first Chicana/o play to receive a professional production at a major theatre. Setting a precedent for later works by Latina/o playwrights, *Zoot Suit* premiered at the Mark Taper Forum, where *Chavez Ravine* was produced in 2003. As the premier venue for professional theatre in Los Angeles, the Taper has a vested interest in producing plays about its legendary hometown. In the decades after the original production of *Zoot Suit*, the Taper launched many significant productions about LA by writers of color, including Anna Deavere Smith and Luis Alfaro. From 1995 to 2005, the Taper was the home to the Latino Theatre Initiative, developing and producing new works by Latina/o playwrights.[39] *Zoot Suit*'s extended run in 1978 and its subsequent production on Broadway opened the doors for men and women of color and Latina/os in particular to gain access to professional theatre spaces in Los Angeles and beyond.

As *Zoot Suit* delved into the wrongful conviction and eventual exoneration of a group of Mexican American youths in the 1940s, it also revived the culture of the *pachuca/os*, making them salient symbols of political resistance in the 1970s and beyond.[40] *Chavez Ravine* draws on many of the same types of research materials as *Zoot Suit* (interviews, newspaper archives) and also meaningfully grapples with LA history in the 1940s. *Chavez Ravine* challenges the public, as *Zoot Suit* did, to understand citizenship, community, and national identity differently because of the lives and actions of the Mexican Americans who helped to make Los Angeles what it is today.

Culture Clash draws on the political legacies of earlier Chicana/o theatre in deliberately exposing how the white men who ran the LA city government and press in the 1940s and 1950s forced a long-standing Mexican American community off their land. The playwrights make no attempt whatsoever to give equal weight to the vast range of characters in their plays, because they are strategically bringing previously silenced voices to the forefront of their work. Joining these voices in a single performance creates a larger historical and artistic picture, not just of the past but of class and racial conflict in Los Angeles. This version of history has a deliberate bias, but even the privileged viewpoints in this play offer a variety of perspectives on this community.

The four actors in the play portray fifty-one characters who offer up a complex dialogue about the negotiation of space, time, and power.[41] Each voice in this play has a different claim to the history and the land, and those claims often compete with one another. The text of *Chavez Ravine* brings together the languages of different time periods, social classes, ethnicities, and political perspectives. Culture Clash makes a multifaceted critique of the displacement of the families from Chavez Ravine by using their words, voices, and bodies to perform, rather than merely describe, the struggles surrounding this piece of land. Culture Clash implicates the press, McCarthyist sentiment, and the Los Angeles city government in the series of events that forced the Ravine families off their land.

Theatre scholar Antonia Nakano Glenn calls *Chavez Ravine* "an act of reclamation."[42] The members of Culture Clash look for the unsung voices of Chavez

Ravine's history in a way that resembles what Anna Deavere Smith identifies in her own work as the search "to find America in its language."[43] Smith uses the words of her interviewees to capture meaning and perspective in connection to the situations of social conflict that her plays describe. In this way, she uses reported speech to seek out a sense of what it means to be living in the United States in a given moment, and in her landmark play, *Twilight: Los Angeles, 1992*, she took to the same stage at the Taper to represent this city's history through the eyes of some of its disenfranchised people.[44] Culture Clash takes on a similar project in chronicling the history of this piece of land and the people tied to it.

However, the plays of Culture Clash and Smith differ in the weight given to the various voices in the performance. In an *L.A. Times* review of Culture Clash's play *Bordertown* (which is part of the *Culture Clash in AmeriCCa* series), theatre critic Laurie Winer criticized Culture Clash for privileging some voices over others. She praised Smith in contrast to Culture Clash, saying that the Latino trio "does not possess [Smith's] gift for giving equivalent moral weight and serious consideration to each of her subjects."[45] Winer identified a key distinction in the ways that Culture Clash and Smith construct their plays, but her critique of Culture Clash outright rejects the politics of representation being deployed by Culture Clash in their plays. *Chavez Ravine* has no interest in being objective. It offers a multi-perspectival take on history yet also deliberately unravels the narrative threads of injustice that have so thoroughly concealed the shady business dealings behind the stadium and the agency and desires of the displaced residents.

Unlike Anna Deavere Smith, whose strict use of verbatim interview texts creates a sense of legitimacy for all her ethnographic plays, Culture Clash makes deliberate use of fiction for the sake of humor, theatricality, and continuity. Audiences overhear private conversations, listen to musical numbers about flushing toilets, and hear commentary from a dead poet. When a ghost speaks, we know that Culture Clash did not uncover the words of an otherworldly spirit through empirical research, yet the fictive event provides insight into cultural practices, modes of speech and behavior, and, at times, vital information.

Staging Unseen Histories: Using Fiction to Suggest the Facts

Much of the difficulty in staging the struggles of the Ravine's residents derives from a need to represent masked forces of domination. Norman Chandler, the publisher of the *L.A. Times* from 1940 to 1960, had the ability to shape public discourse on a large scale, and Culture Clash takes on the Chandler press in film noir–style scenes where three actors in trench coats and fedoras make underhanded deals to further their financial investments in the Ravine.[46] Montoya and Salinas play characters named Mover and Shaker, while Sigüenza embodies a mysterious mastermind character known as the Watchman. These characters, who serve as allegories for the press and certain government agencies, conspire to halt the City Housing Authority's plans for public housing in the Ravine so that they can make a larger profit by selling their land holdings to the investors in Dodger Stadium:

WATCHMAN: ... You wanna stop the Housing Authority?
SHAKER: Sure we do, plenty awful.
WATCHMAN: We need to kill this public housing project by calling it socialistic see? We need to convince everyone that the top brass at the City Housing Authority are communist infiltrators, see?
MOVER & SHAKER: We see.
WATCHMAN: Maybe we'll get Joe McCarthy to make a house call.[47]

The invocation of McCarthyism links the events of Chavez Ravine to similar manipulations of power by the House Un-American Activities Committee at that time. Mover, Shaker, and the Watchman all have hidden identities. They serve as allegorical figures, like those in medieval morality plays or the *actos* of early Chicana/o theatre, and in doing so, they give physical form to the hidden political forces behind the actions of members of the press and government officials.[48]

The joy of watching Culture Clash lies in their ability to transform again and again, imitating humankind in a vast array of characters. The remarkable talent of the interviewer/writer/performers to transmute themselves into so many different, culturally distinct people has attracted diverse audiences in theatres around the country.[49] Culture Clash plays with the fine lines between cultural truths and stereotypes in the communities they portray. They use stereotypes to make the characters recognizable and then add nuances that make the characters more complex, to the point of eventually questioning the basis of such performative types. Because of the intricacy of their performances, and because their minimal stage directions fail to indicate many important parts of the relevant physical action, their plays lose a great deal when read on paper. The performance itself also makes the lines between fact and fiction more difficult to track, because an audience member must take in the information at the speed of the actors' delivery.

The Indecipherable Melding of Fact and Fiction in Culture Clash's Characters

Though they do not have academic training in ethnography or history, the members of Culture Clash used many of the same research techniques as academics use as they prepared the script of *Chavez Ravine*. They conducted interviews with city councilwoman Rosalind Wyman and other political figures from the time, as well as with several people who lived in the Ravine during the land struggle.[50] They did archival research, and a time line of the significant events appeared in the program to the premiere production of the play. Historian Eric Avila states: "The people whose stories are shown by Culture Clash are those who leave very little traces of their history in letters, reports, books, or papers, the kinds of documents traditionally valued by historians. . . . As Culture Clash shows through their research—which is exactly how an academic historian does research—there are multiple realities which all need to be told and made accessible to everyone."[51] The genius of Culture Clash lies in their ability to use humor and physicality in performance to draw the audience into history from their perspective. The performance exhibits historical accuracy in terms of many of the facts it shares with the audience, but the actors also capture an intuitive and experiential sense of the historical events to which the audience can relate.

Culture Clash takes creative license in the presentation of history to challenge previous versions of the same events and to make people care about what happened. Activist and writer Lucy Lippard describes the vital contributions that artists of color make in the writing of alternative histories: "Drawn to the illusory warmth of the melting pot, and then rejected from it, [artists of color] have frequently developed or offered sanctuary to ideas, images, and values that otherwise would have been swept away in the mainstream."[52] In the program to the play, above the list of characters, the playwrights assert: "Some characters depicted in *Chavez Ravine* are based on real people, some are composites of several people, others are fictional. We are grateful to all." The playwrights announce their presence as researchers, editors, comedians, and artists engaged in the process of both creating and re-creating history. In doing so, they humanize not only themselves but the actual people whom the play describes, inviting the audience to connect the facts presented about various injustices with the people onstage and in the communities outside the theatre.

To emphasize the interrelation of history and art, Culture Clash based the narrator of the play on a poet from the Ravine named Manazar, whose poems they discovered while conducting research for the show.[53] The character of

Manazar operates in ways that the real poet could not have done: "Quivole, my name is Manazar, I am a poet who grew up aqui in La Bishop. When I died, not too long ago, they spread my ashes all through these hills. Now, before we proceed with the play, I have to take you back to the beginning, the genesis of this place. Hey, it's my job as your dead poet/slash/ghost presence/slash/narrator device que la chingada ... any similarity between me and the Stage Manager in *Our Town* is purely coincidental."[54] Based on the play alone, the audience member who had never heard of the real Manazar would have no way of knowing whether he really existed. Indeed, Manazar's humor, ghostliness, and omniscience about the world of the play would probably lead most audience members to believe that he is an entirely fictional character.

Manazar's presence in the play would defy the traditional logic of a historian, but in performance an audience suspends disbelief to allow the dead to speak. Freddie Rokem asserts that all historical figures represented onstage have a "ghostly" dimension to them because they embody the past.[55] In that sense many, if not all, of the characters in *Chavez Ravine* are spirits, but Manazar appears to be ghostlier than the rest because he is both dead and metatheatrical. He travels beyond the grave and through time and all the while realizes that he is part of a play as a "narrator device que la chingada."[56] By describing himself in these terms, Manazar appeals to both a traditionally white subscriber audience and a Latina/o audience. He succinctly describes his function in the play while code-switching between English and Spanish to show his ability to navigate both cultures and have a sense of humor at the same time. He also can see and speak directly to the audience members, and he makes an intertextual reference to *Our Town*, a work with which the actual Manazar may or may not have had any familiarity. Whereas these aspects of a historical figure in an academic text would be immediately contested, in performance the character's flexibility and obvious fictions add humor and a degree of continuity to the play.

Manazar also makes political commentaries as he narrates the play: "Things might have been slow in the Ravine, but the mayor's office was about to get as busy as a triple baptism at San Conrado church on a Sunday afternoon. Now watch me make myself invisible. (*Spins and picks up a broom*) Orale."[57] This passage introduces the next scene in the mayor's office and allows Manazar to overhear the conversation that takes place, but more than that, Manazar critiques the dominant culture's tendency to ignore the working class. He becomes invisible when he embodies the role of a custodian. Even though he remains in the mayor's office throughout the scene, the other characters proceed as if he did not exist. The audience gets the mayor's perspective on the struggle over the Ravine, but the presence of Manazar contextualizes the mayor's voice and prevents him from dominating the process of history-making, as politicians are wont to do.

A good number of the characters in *Chavez Ravine* appear only briefly, as snapshots of different opinions or viewpoints on the situation. They make up the landscape of the neighborhood and influence how other voices are received. The play contains many characters with various types of public and official authority: Vin Scully, Walter O'Malley, Frank Wilkinson (site manager of the City Housing Authority), Richard Neutra (architect), Pete Seeger (folksinger), Mayor Norris Poulson, and J. Edgar Hoover, to name just a few. The audience listens to and perhaps even sympathizes with some of these characters, notably Wilkinson, but these official voices speak in the context of the unofficial ones that also populate the play, including Henry and Maria Ruiz, Señora Ruiz (their mother), Manazar, Uri (the sheepherder), Lencho (the resident drunk), and the Dodger Dog Girl.[58] These unofficial voices often have more potent and memorable things to say than their more authoritative counterparts.

Embodying the Past: The Power of the Live Body in Performance

The audience understands the history of the Ravine as experienced by all the characters, but the manner in which the characters speak and the kinds of stories they tell greatly influence the audience's sympathies. In the most powerful scene of the play, Señora Ruiz takes up her shotgun and defends her home when the sheriffs come to forcibly remove her:

> MOTHER: We are not the Mullhollands.
> (*We hear the pump action of a shotgun*)
> We are not the Lankershims or the Van Nuys,
> (*We hear the pump action of a shotgun*)
> but you'll remember this name, Arechiga
> (*The pump action of a shotgun*)
> Cabral, Casos y Lopez . . .
> (*Shotgun*)
> Perez
> (*Shotgun*)
> Ramirez
> (*Shotgun*)
> You took our sons to fight your war,
> And now you take our homes.

> (*Shotgun*)
> Our land ... Mi casa no es tu casa. ¿Sabes que? Why don't you tell the pinche sheriff to build a stadium in his own goddamn backyard.[59]

Richard Montoya plays the character of the mother, and though several of the earlier scenes with this character are funny, this depiction of Señora Ruiz is not an attempt to achieve humor through the use of drag. Rather, the cross-gender performances in the play only add to the sense that the four actors onstage symbolically mediate a diverse and multifaceted community.[60]

The most powerful moments of transformation occur when the actors become characters who are developed as people rather than presented as staged cartoons, such as the town drunks, the helicopter pilot, Vin Scully, and others. Señora Ruiz, among others, has the presence of a full person, even though the audience never loses sight of the fact that she is being played by a man. In the staging of this scene in the 2003 production, Montoya wore a housedress and apron over the pants and shirt that serve as his basic costume for the show.[61] He wore a wig with one long braid hanging down his back and defiantly pumped his shotgun throughout the speech. The other actors and musicians onstage held up huge photographs of the real families of the Ravine being carried out of their homes by law enforcement agents while members of the press crowded around to record the event.

This scene establishes the community of people displaced from *Chavez Ravine* as living beings who take physical shape on the stage of the Taper. Drawing on a Brechtian notion of actors as demonstrators, Rokem states: "The notion of performing history emphasizes the fact that the actor performing a historical figure on the stage in a sense also becomes a witness of the historical event."[62] In this regard, when he portrays Señora Ruiz, Montoya becomes a witness of the families resisting the forced evacuation of their homes, as do the other actors onstage. The audience, of course, witnesses this reincarnation of the past as well, and they are implicated in and participating in a community with a shared history as they watch the play. Culture Clash more directly involved the audience by making jokes about Gordon Davidson (then artistic director of the Taper), the Taper subscribers, and even ad libs about people present in the audience at a particular performance.[63] With these techniques, Culture Clash reinvents their audience as a community united with the actors onstage, and in doing so they displace hegemonic concepts of who has access to the creation of public discourse and the telling of history.

Creating an Alternative Discourse: Significance Beyond the World of the Play

Is Señora Ruiz's version of history less than truthful or accurate because she is a composite of several real people? Audience members may not be able to distinguish the many factual parts of this character's background or pinpoint their origins in the primary source material from Culture Clash's research. Even as I researched the play and the history of the Ravine, I waded through many uncertainties that I have only begun to sort out with much help from the playwrights. *Chavez Ravine* does not aim to get across precise and traceable information. The vivid language and memorable staging that convey this character's struggle point to a visceral and emotional sense of the real lives of the families displaced from the Ravine, and this may motivate some audience members to connect these struggles to their own lives or those of communities suffering in the present. The sort of historical information conveyed by the character of Señora Ruiz might not be particularly useful to an academician or government official who needs to be able to document her findings. General audiences, people with emotional or familial ties to Chavez Ravine, and even cultural historians might glean more from Señora Ruiz's life onstage than they would from reading/hearing all the research Culture Clash needed to do to construct her. More than facts, Culture Clash asserts that the histories of the people Señora Ruiz represents need to be told.

The version of history presented in *Chavez Ravine* has the potential to resonate in impoverished communities, particularly those that are also communities of color, across the United States. Beyond that, it raises awareness of the politics of gentrification in audiences who might not otherwise see the effects of urban development on the communities that are displaced by such practices. When Congress passed the Federal Housing Act in 1949, it also set aside $10 billion for cities that would demolish and rebuild their poorest neighborhoods. Wealthy investors capitalized on the opportunity to build more expensive properties in the locations where low-income housing once stood. Fifteen years after the passage of the Federal Housing Act, more than 609,000 poor people, two-thirds of them people of color, had been displaced from their homes in these neighborhoods nationwide.[64]

With or without federal incentives, developers and government officials continue this cycle to this day, displacing low-income communities in many major US cities. *Chavez Ravine* certainly addresses the Los Angeles community, but it also has something to say to other groups of Latina/os being displaced in more recent times: Puerto Ricans in New York City were forced out of their homes to enable the construction of Lincoln Center, and many other communities face similar circumstances in the face of major commercial or government development. Urban renewal disproportionately affects people of color and reinforces structures that maintain white hegemony.[65]

Chavez Ravine clearly aligns itself with the displaced rather than with those who invoke the power of eminent domain. Culture Clash, in a manner similar to that of many contemporary social scientists, identifies their own biases and reveals them to the audience rather than attempting to mask their version of history with the pretense of objectivity. *Chavez Ravine* offers us a different way to learn about culture and history and challenges often unquestioned ideas about dominant power structures and the structures of "knowledge" that support them. *Chavez Ravine* acknowledges and portrays the losses of sacred land, a way of life, and an array of opportunities.

Questions remain as to whether this piece of theatre has had or can have a direct and/or lasting effect in people's lives. Did viewing *Chavez Ravine* change anyone's mind about the practices of urban renewal and gentrification? Did anyone with the power to alter such a situation behave differently after seeing this play? We might also ask whether *Chavez Ravine* changed people's notions of Latina/o identity or affected their sense of cultural heritage.

These questions prove difficult to answer, but the extraordinary popularity of the play suggests that such ideological transformations might be possible for audience members. Something in the performance drew audiences night after night, in two separate productions and years, to return to the theatre to contemplate how a group of poor and largely forgotten Mexican American families lost their homes and neighborhood. If empathy for those families (or even the desire to see Latina/os onstage) can motivate ticket sales across time, then it is possible that *Chavez Ravine* could also have had a larger impact on individuals' actions or behavior regarding their neighbors in the city. Culture Clash's ability to consistently book their plays in mainstream, predominantly white, regional theatres makes them an exceptional group, unrivaled by any other Latina/o performance collective in their level of popularity and visibility in US regional theatres. Culture Clash took advantage of the commercial power of their name when they chose to stage an alternative version of the history of Chavez Ravine. Artistically and stylistically, this play stands as the culmination of their work up to the play's premiere, in 2003. Several years later, in 2010, Richard Montoya and Herbert Sigüenza teamed up with a larger cast to stage a Culture Clash production of a similar play titled *American Nightmare: The Ballad of Juan José* at the Oregon Shakespeare Festival.[66] Where *Chavez Ravine* tells a local story,

American Nightmare offers a national portrait of racism and immigration in much the same narrative style as its LA-focused predecessor. The later play riffs on the style of the earlier one and suggests that the same sorts of institutionalized racism and exclusion that forced the residents of the Ravine off their land have functioned to enshrine inequality throughout the United States.

Herbert Sigüenza sums up the political function of *Chavez Ravine* this way: "America is full of cultural amnesia. History gives a sense of place and cultural pride. Ultimately with this play, we want people to realize that together we are making history and that we built this city together."[67] Sigüenza suggests that both the community of Los Angeles and its history continue to be built and rebuilt by all Angelenos, past and present. Lin-Manuel Miranda's casting of actors of color in all the roles in *Hamilton* asserts something similar about US history by bringing the voices of the marginalized to the forefront of a conversation about national identity.[68] *Chavez Ravine* gives voice to a necessary version of history, one that asserts the presence of Latina/os in LA today as much as it records their past. If Culture Clash can make audience members care about the people removed from the Ravine, then hopefully they can change not only that audience's relationship to the past but also influence their perception of the present and the future.

This desire to overcome American cultural amnesia is at the root of all of Culture Clash's ethnographic plays. Culture Clash identifies the historical power structures that have prevented people of color in the United States from having equal access to land, education, government, the press, and the process of history-making. In doing this, Montoya, Salinas, and Sigüenza are reinscribing the narrative of American cultural citizenship and exposing the flaws, prejudices, and limitations inherent in the ways in which mainstream concepts of American identity have been constructed against oppressed and minoritized groups within the nation. By demanding that audiences notice the ways gentrification rewrites US history, Culture Clash gestures toward a more complexly imagined picture of the United States, one that is fuller and truer because it includes those unimagined Angelenos whose bodies are buried under the Dodger Stadium pitcher's mound.

Notes

1. Throughout this article, I use the terms Latina, Latino, and Latina/o to describe people of Latin American descent in the United States. These terms were popularly used by scholars and members of Culture Clash during both major productions of *Chavez Ravine*, in

2003 and 2015. For this reason, I continue to use this language rather than shifting, as many contemporary academics and activists have at present, to the term Latinx.

2. The group we now know as Culture Clash originally formed under the name Comedy Fiesta. On Cinco de Mayo 1984, visual artist Rene Yañez brought together six actors, comedians, and poets for their first performance together as a performing troupe. When Marga Gómez and Mónica Palacios split off from Comedy Fiesta to pursue their careers in solo performance, Richard Montoya, Ric Salinas, Herbert Sigüenza, and José Antonio Burciaga formed Culture Clash. The four performed monologues and sketch comedy together until Burciaga left the group to spend more time with his family. The remaining three members began writing full-length plays. The early Culture Clash plays—*The Mission* (1988), *A Bowl of Beings* (1991), *S.O.S.—Comedy for These Urgent Times* (1992), and *Carpa Clash* (1993)—reflect the performers' backgrounds in stand-up comedy, with their reliance on monologues and sketch comedy. These early plays focus on the experiences of Latinos in the United States and often refer directly to the lives of the writer/performers.
3. Freddie Rokem, *Performing History: Theatrical Representations of the Past in Contemporary Theatre* (Iowa City: University of Iowa Press, 2000), 3.
4. Jon D. Rossini, *Contemporary Latina/o Theatre: Wrighting Ethnicity* (Carbondale: Southern Illinois University Press, 2008), 7.
5. Eric Avila, *Popular Culture in the Age of White Flight: Fear and Fantasy in Suburban Los Angeles* (Berkeley: University of California Press, 2004), 164; Negotiations for the land began in 1957, but the stadium was not fully constructed and open to the public until 1962. Los Angeles Dodgers Website, accessed March 20, 2005http://losangeles.dodgers.mlb.com/NASApp/mlb/la/ballpark/index.jsp.
6. See the Gabrieleno/Tongva website, accessed March 9, 2005, http://www.tongva.com.
7. Culture Clash, *Chavez Ravine*, *American Theatre* 20, no. 9 (November 2003): 39.
8. Rodolfo Acuña, *Occupied America: A History of Chicanos* (New York: Harper and Row, 1988), 19.
9. Ibid.
10. Ibid., 296.
11. Eric Avila, "Revisiting the Chavez Ravine: Baseball, Urban Renewal, and the Gendered Civic Culture of Postwar Los Angeles," in *Velvet Barrios: Popular Culture and Chicana/o Sexualities*, ed. Alicia Gaspar de Alba (New York: Palgrave Macmillan, 2003), 125.
12. Avila, *Popular Culture in the Age of White Flight*, 163.
13. Unless otherwise noted, all descriptions of the staging and performance and quotes from the script of *Chavez Ravine* refer to the premiere production in 2003. I saw three performances of that run of the play as well as an early private reading of the script for the production team and lawyers for the Dodgers and former LA city councilwoman Rosalind Wyman. I did not see the 2015 revival but have read the revised script used for this production.
14. Ric Salinas, e-mail to author, March 10, 2005.
15. Most the changes to the script used for the 2015 revival lie in the reordering of scenes. The most significant textual addition occurs in the final monologue given by Maria Ruiz, which has added language about more recent political struggles related to policing, immigration, and prisons: Culture Clash, *Chavez Ravine: An L.A. Revival*, unpublished manuscript, 2014, 106. The information about the sold-out performances of the 2015 revival comes from Ric Salinas, e-mail to author, May 16, 2017.

16. After Culture Clash's early success with a series of often autobiographical comedies, which ended with the production of *Carpa Clash* in 1993, the Miami Light Project commissioned Culture Clash's first site-specific, ethnographic play, *Radio Mambo: Culture Clash Invades Miami*, which premiered in 1994. Since then, Culture Clash has written and performed four other full-length plays in this style: *Bordertown*, about San Diego and Tijuana, *Nuyorican Stories*, about New York City, *Mission Magic Mystery Tour*, about San Francisco, and *Anthems: Culture Clash in the District*, about Washington, DC. Montoya, Salinas, and Sigüenza go into a major city for a few months, research the city's history and its current events, interview people from a variety of ethnic communities, and write and perform a play that offers a view of the city from a multiplicity of perspectives, often privileging the voices of racialized and minoritized groups. They have performed these site-specific plays individually and as a compilation show called *Culture Clash in AmeriCCa*, which juxtaposes vignettes about different sites to create a sense of the diversity of identities and cultures in the United States.
17. The only recurring characters in the earlier site-specific plays are the characters of Montoya, Salinas, and Sigüenza as themselves or "the interviewers." Their earlier plays, site-specific or not, are full of self-referential humor, but *Chavez Ravine* does not reference the playwrights or their public personas explicitly.
18. The possible exception to this would be *Anthems*, which deals somewhat peripherally with the tragedies of 9/11 and follows Montoya as "The Writer" in a very fragmented journey through the play.
19. The notion of all events in *Culture Clash in AmeriCCa* happening in the present is somewhat complex. *Anthems*, their play about Washington, DC, takes place in a specifically post-9/11 context, but the other plays in the series were all written before 9/11. When the plays are edited together and staged as *Culture Clash in AmeriCCa*, all events seem to take place in a generalized present moment that does not set vignettes from *Anthems* apart as temporally distinct from, or even more specific than, the scenes from other plays.
20. Herbert Sigüenza, interview by author (Los Angeles), June 5, 2003.
21. *Chavez Ravine*, dir. by Lisa Peterson, set by Rachel Hauck, costumes by Christopher Acebo, lighting by Anne Militello, sound by Dan Moses Schreier, Mark Taper Forum (Los Angeles: Mark Taper Forum's New Work Festival), May 17, 2003.
22. Tara J. Yosso and David G. García, "'This Is No Slum!': A Critical Race Theory Analysis of Community Cultural Wealth in Culture Clash's *Chavez Ravine*," in *Aztlán: A Journal of Chicano Studies* 32, no. 1 (Spring 2007): 147.
23. Culture Clash, *Chavez Ravine*, 40.
24. Ibid.
25. No accents were used in the characters' names, either in the printed programs for *Chavez Ravine* or in the published version of the script.
26. Culture Clash, *Chavez Ravine*, 40.
27. Ibid.
28. Deborah Vankin, "Trio's Bite Back: Culture Clash Feels a Timely Pull to Update Its Play 'Chavez Ravine' Amid Gentrification Trends," in *Los Angeles Times* (January 29, 2015), E1.
29. Rich Juzwiak and Aleksander Chan, "Unarmed People of Color Killed by Police, 1999–2014," http://gawker.com/unarmed-people-of-color-killed-by-police-1999-2014-1666672349, May 17, 2017.

30. Salinas, e-mail to author, May 16, 2017.
31. Diana Taylor, *The Archive and the Repertoire: Performing Cultural Memory in the Americas* (Durham: Duke University Press, 2003), 19–20.
32. Cecilia Elizabeth O'Leary, *To Die For: The Paradox of American Patriotism* (Princeton: Princeton University Press, 1999), 4.
33. Culture Clash, *Chavez Ravine*, 57.
34. O'Leary, *To Die For*, 4.
35. Culture Clash, *Chavez Ravine*, 61.
36. Richard Montoya, e-mail to author, April 30, 2005.
37. David Román, "Latino Performance and Identity" in *Aztlán* 22, no. 2 (Fall 1997): 157–58.
38. Luis Valdez quoted in Jorge A. Huerta, "El Teatro's Living Legacy," in *American Theatre* 33, no. 10 (December 2016): 30.
39. Diane Rodriguez website, www.diane-rodriguez.com, July 29, 2017.
40. I have argued this more fully in another article: Ashley E. Lucas, "Reinventing the *Pachuco*: The Radical Transformation from the Criminalized to the Heroic in Luis Valdez's Play *Zoot Suit*," *Journal for the Study of Radicalism* 3, no. 1 (Spring 2009): 61–88.
41. The 2003 production of the play featured the three members of Culture Clash and actress Eileen Galindo, and the 2015 revival cast Sabina Zuniga Varela alongside Montoya, Salinas, and Sigüenza.
42. Antonia Nakano Glenn, "Breaking Ground: Culture Clash Unearth Stories Long Buried in Chavez Ravine" in *L.A. Alternative Press* 2, no. 3 (May 14–27, 2003): 20.
43. Anna Deavere Smith, *Talk to Me: Listening Between the Lines* (New York: Random House, 2000), 12.
44. Anna Deavere Smith, *Twilight: Los Angeles, 1992* (New York: Anchor, 1994).
45. Laurie Winer, "*Bordertown* Hits Barriers," in *Los Angeles Times* (June 2, 1998), F1, F8.
46. Los Angeles Times Media Center Website, http://www.latimes.com/services/newspaper/mediacenter/la-mediacenter-milestones,0,117814.story?coll=la-mediacenter-footer, March 9, 2005.
47. Culture Clash, *Chavez Ravine*, 47.
48. *Actos* are short, political sketches that can be performed in any location. This form of theatre has been a vital component throughout Chicana/o theatre history and is certainly a type of theatre with which the members of Culture Clash are very familiar. The best known *actos* were scripted by El Teatro Campesino: Luis Valdez, *Early Works: Actos, Bernabé, and Pensamiento Serpentino* (Houston: Arte Público, 1994), 11–134.
49. Ethnographic theatre has provided an entrée into the regional theatres not just for Culture Clash but also for Anna Deavere Smith and other less well-known performers, such as Heather Raffo and Michael Keck.
50. Ric Salinas describes their interviews with Ravine residents: "We got to interview about six to eight residents from the Ravine, ranging in age from sixty to ninety years of age. The sixty-year-olds were most helpful. They were second generation and remember their last days as children in those three neighborhoods. We spoke to some of the eighty to ninety-year-olds. Many were young adults that moved there when their parents migrated, mostly from Mexico." E-mail to author, March 10, 2005.
51. Tiffany Ana Lopez, "*Chavez Ravine* by Culture Clash: A Discovery Journal," in *Innovative Theatre and Creative Education for Young People: Performing for L.A. Youth* (Mark Taper Forum Theatre Education Program, 2003), 8.

52. Lucy Lippard, *Mixed Blessings: New Art in a Multicultural America* (New York: Pantheon, 1990), 5.
53. Sigüenza, interview by author.
54. Culture Clash, *Chavez Ravine*, 44.
55. Rokem, *Performing History*, 6.
56. The phrase *que la chingada* is difficult to translate. It suggests that Manazar is calling himself a "badass." When asked about how to translate *que la chingada* in this context, Ric Salinas notes that this phrase was written as a tribute to Luis Valdez's character El Pachuco from *Zoot Suit* and points out that the real Manazar was a *pinto* (prisoner) at one point and that he would likely have spoken in "the vernacular of badass pachucos." Salinas, e-mail to author, March 10, 2005.
57. Culture Clash, *Chavez Ravine*, 53.
58. The young women who sold hotdogs at Dodger Stadium were called Dodger Dog Girls. The character in the play was not based on a specific person but rather on an idea of what a Dodger Dog Girl might have been like. This character loves Fernando Valenzuela so much that she literally levitates with joy at seeing him play.
59. Culture Clash, *Chavez Ravine*, 60.
60. Ibid., 83.
61. In the 2015 production, Sabina Zuniga Varela, the lone actress in the show, played this role rather than Montoya.
62. Rokem, *Performing History*, 9.
63. On one of the three occasions when I saw the play performed in 2003, Richard Montoya as Vin Scully ad-libbed a joke about several elderly women in the front row of the theatre who were crunching loudly on the popcorn that the ushers had passed out during the song "Take Me Out to the Ballgame."
64. Acuña, *Occupied America*, 295.
65. George Lipsitz, *The Possessive Investment in Whiteness: How White People Profit from Identity Politics* (Philadelphia: Temple University Press, 1998), 6–7.
66. Richard J. Montoya, *American Night: The Ballad of Juan José* (New York: Samuel French, 2015).
67. Lopez, Chavez Ravine *by Culture Clash*, 4.
68. Lin-Manuel Miranda and Jeremy McCarter, *Hamilton: The Revolution: Being the Complete Libretto of the Broadway Musical, with a True Account of Its Creation, and Concise Remarks on Hip-Hop, the Power of Stories, and the New America* (New York: Grand Central, 2016).

Part III

ESSAY FROM THE CONFERENCE

The Robert A. Schanke Award-Winning Essay

The Heavy Lifting

Resisting the Obama Presidency's Neoliberalist Conceptions of the American Dream in Kristoffer Diaz's *The Elaborate Entrance of Chad Deity*

—NOE MONTEZ

Macedonio (Mace) Guerra walks into a wrestling arena moments before making his debut as a ringside manger. The grappler is positioned for the first time in his career as not just an invisible journeyman but as a character recognized by the sport's audience. Guerra has assumed the alias Che Chavez Castro, a caricature of the United States' most insidious imaginings of Mexican identity. He is paired with his protégé—an Indian American immigrant portraying a Pakistani villain known as The Fundamentalist. Whereas global wrestling monopoly THE Wrestling and its all-powerful CEO Everett K. Olson once rendered Macedonio a bit player, in this moment, surrounded by a mise-en-scène that fuses communist symbolism, Islamic iconography, and Latin American stereotypes, Mace has become an integral component of THE Wrestling's story line. His character has been written into a plot that will lead The Fundamentalist to battle and defeat world champion and American hero Chad Deity. In playwright Kristoffer Diaz's Pulitzer Prize–nominated script *The Elaborate Entrance of Chad Deity*,

Guerra's transformation is powerfully depicted, detailing Mace's rise from boyhood aspirations of becoming a professional wrestler to becoming rapidly subsumed by athletic stardom in a rags-to-riches tale driven by narratives of the American dream and neoliberal capitalism.

The Elaborate Entrance of Chad Deity premiered at Chicago's Victory Gardens Theater in September 2009, just a few months after the city's own Barack Obama was sworn in as forty-fourth President of the United States. Shortly after the play's opening, *Deity* received productions in New York, Philadelphia, Boston, Minneapolis, Los Angeles, Dallas, Washington, DC, and many other cities across the country, peaking as a programming favorite during the Obama presidency. For playwright Kristoffer Diaz and President Obama alike, the narrative of the American dream, its meaning(s), and the strategies for attaining it are central. Obama constructed his 2008 run for the presidency around a message of success through meritocratic opportunity, as exemplified by his own biography as a black man positioned to run for the highest office in the United States: "I am the son of a black man from Kenya and a white woman from Kansas. I was raised with the help of a white grandfather who survived a Depression to serve in Patton's Army during World War II and a white grandmother who worked on a bomber assembly line at Fort Leavenworth while he was overseas. I've gone to some of the best schools in America and lived in one of the world's poorest nations. I am married to a black American who carries within her the blood of slaves and slave-owners—an inheritance we pass on to our two precious daughters. I have brothers, sisters, nieces, nephews, uncles and cousins, of every race and every hue, scattered across three continents, and for as long as I live, I will never forget that in no other country on Earth is my story even possible."[1]

In this campaign speech and other orations delivered on the campaign trail, Obama spoke about the need to reclaim the American dream through policies and legislation that would facilitate an individual's ability to accumulate the capital necessary to achieve financial sustainability and individual happiness regardless of racial/ethnic background or socioeconomic class.[2] While Obama uses the American dream narrative to make aspirational claims about American exceptionalism, these pronouncements come at the expense of what Cornell University law professor Aziz Rana refers to as a "broader left imagination" that might redress the fundamental structural problems of institutionalized racism and class disparity that continue to confront the nation in our present moment.[3] Contrarily, playwright Kristoffer Diaz draws upon the same myths of American meritocracy but uses his drama to critique the social and cultural conditions that lead the play's characters to imagine themselves within the American dream myth in order to envision an alternative model of personal fulfillment. In *The Elaborate Entrance of Chad Deity*, Mace consistently works to achieve his aspirations, THE Wrestling superstar Chad Deity uses the myth as a frame for his onstage persona, and CEO Everett K. Olson must determine how to best incorporate the narrative into his product in a way that will maximize profitability. Ostensibly all the play's central characters would claim that the myth is a narrative about seizing the reigns of economic opportunity, but Diaz uses the play to reveal the very concept of the American dream as a hollow tenet.

This essay explores the economic politics at the heart of *The Elaborate Entrance of Chad Deity* to unpack Diaz's assessment of neoliberalism during the Obama presidency, the falsehoods behind the American dream, and the ways in which race is bound up in the financial inequities of our nation's past and present. In undertaking this project, I hope to articulate the ways in which the playwright uses the character Vigneshwar Paduar to critique the economic and racial narratives that pervade American popular culture and to subvert what Adorno and Horkheimer call the culture industry. But first, a brief summation of plot for the uninitiated: Macedonia (Mace) Guerro is a journeyman wrestler employed by THE Wrestling and its CEO Everett K. Olson (EKO). Mace's career consists of playing a semi-anonymous heel falling to the likes of wrestling champion and American hero Chad Deity as part of THE Wrestling's storytelling apparatus. When Mace discovers a Brooklyn-born Indian-American named Vigneshwar Paduar (VP), he immediately sees the potential for superstardom and financial success through their partnership. To unearth that potential, however, both VP and Mace have to undergo some uncomfortable character transformations to attain their place at the center of THE Wrestling.

The Myth of Meritocracy, Neoliberalism, and the American Dream

Rhetoric scholars Robert C. Rowland and John M. Jones define the American dream as a romantic narrative that "depicts America as a place of unbridled opportunities where anyone with will and gumption can make a better economic life."[4] Its heroes are ordinary men made great by their pursuit and embrace of American values. This romantic narrative is embedded in the American cultural consciousness through what Adorno and Horkheimer call the culture industry—the interweaving structures that produce and reproduce dominant social values through film, television, music, literature, advertising, and so on.[5] Sociologist and African American studies professor Antwi Akom observes that American narratives in particular are filled with fictionalized stories that emphasize the meritocratic myth that individuals "do not inherit their social status, they attain it via their own ambition and ability."[6] Initially, *The Elaborate Entrance of Chad Deity* seems as though it is working within the literary and cultural traditions of American dream narratives. The play opens on Guerra standing in a wrestling ring and recounting his childhood in the Bronx during the 1980s in which he and his younger brother sat on "cold hardwood floors" eating "generic flakes of corn with generic scoops of sugar sprinkled on top" while play wrestling.[7] Guerra concludes by noting that, at present, he has achieved his childhood dreams and is employed by THE Wrestling, which is the largest wrestling organization in the world. While Mace's employer, CEO Everett K. Olson (EKO) reminds Guerra that he has "achieved the American Dream," the protagonist complicates that simplistic narrative by noting that his place in the organization is as a highly skilled, but anonymous laborer, whose significant talent is used to make other less-gifted but more televiseable commodities look good in scripted performances that inevitably end with his defeat.[8] Although Guerra ultimately admits that he has achieved his career ambitions by doing what he refers to as "the heavy lifting," the scene calls attention to the ways that sociocultural forces shape and define the possibilities of advancement for people of color.

However, Diaz's examination of racial exploitation and the limits of the American dream are complicated when he introduces THE Wrestling's World Champion, a "strong," "well-dressed" African American with a winning smile, charisma, and talented oratorical skills named Chad Deity. Deity's success in THE Wrestling is framed by the organization as the embodiment of the American dream, as demonstrated by his ringside entrance, which "makes soldiers remember what they fight for, makes fathers teach their sons to stand up and cheer on greatness . . . [serves] by proxy as America's elaborate entrance, giving proof through the night that the flag is still there, [and] defeats demons, so that we feel like our demons deserve that defeat, and we feel more importantly, that we can be the ones to achieve them."[9]

Intentionally or not, Deity's constructed narrative echoes the story of individual self-determination and natural talent as a means of collective improvement that is found in Obama's biography, as presented in campaign speeches and in his best-selling book *Dreams of My Father*. Latino Studies scholar J. David Cisneros's analysis of the president's policy speeches delineates how his discussion of exemplary people of color reinforces neoliberal values through their advocacy of Americanism through "entrepreneurialism, financial responsibility and an embrace of individual difference that simultaneously rejects racial identification and structural racism."[10]

Although it is important to note that Obama's biography and other narratives of people of color aspiring toward the American dream provide a reframing of the myth that includes black heroes, it is also significant to note that such stories are often "produced and reproduced without a discussion of the complex interplay of United States' racial hierarchies on social class formation in the Black community."[11] In other words, the culture industry produces and reproduces stories like Deity's to perpetuate the myth of meritocracy and to keep racial injustice invisible. When a black man like Chad Deity succeeds, he becomes the exception to the rule. In *The Elaborate Entrance of Chad Deity*, the titular character implies that he is the personal embodiment of the American dream. Deity's signature powerbomb move is framed as "one of the most profound expressions of the ideals of this damn nation."[12] It sounds like an empowering statement, but it actually serves to reinforce the myth of the American dream. If people of color like Mace don't follow in Chad Deity's footsteps, it is simply because they did not *apply* their skill sets adequately. Diaz's play constantly reminds us of Deity's individual success and in this way the work calls attention to the culture industry's myth of meritocracy, obscuring the fact that White America, as represented by EKO, ultimately scripts the narrative.

The pernicious effect of these stories becomes clear when we understand the systematic way in which legislators have encoded racial inequity into our laws and economies, what Akom refers to as "infraracial racism." This term is used to describe a private and state policy of racial injustice that "makes no mention of race yet reproduces a system of racially structured inequality."[13] Far more pernicious than a burning cross in the front yard, this racism operates like infrared rays: "It penetrates beneath the skin, to such an extent that it negatively impacts the health, wellbeing, and social mobility of Black people/people of color beyond the visible end of the spectrum."[14] How this infraracial racism affects people of color most heavily is made visible in *The Elaborate Entrance of Chad Deity*'s character arc for Vigneshwar Paduar, or VP, as he's referred to throughout the play. In *The Elaborate Entrance of Chad Deity*, Diaz uses the character VP to illustrate the limits of advancement, the cultural friction created by people of color in elite spaces, and ultimately the limits of the American dream.

Vigneshwar Paduar and Exceptions Unable to Be Reformed

Vigneshwar Paduar is introduced as the only character in the world of the play who regularly participates in a life outside of THE Wrestling. He is an Indian

American who spends most of his days playing pickup basketball in Brooklyn's Carroll Gardens, talking trash to competitors, and trying to pick up women in seven different languages. When Mace is first introduced to VP, he finds himself spellbound by the way "this kid works with words, switches codes, drops slang and makes me laugh."[15] Guerra sees in Paduar the potential to change the way that people look at the world. Moreover, while Mace encourages VP to use his charisma to develop a career as an entertainer in order to maximize his potential earning power, Vigneshwar instead articulates a desire to use his talents to create an alternative American dream grounded in resistance and community and in making the stories of people like him visible to white America. VP resists an ideology that would reform his construction of self according to what critical race scholar Lester Spence refers to as "market logic."[16] Nevertheless, Mace convinces Paduar to take a meeting with EKO in hopes of developing a wrestling tag team.

Yet as soon as VP agrees to join THE Wrestling, his identity is reconfigured to maximize EKO and THE Wrestling's profitability. Rather than imagine Paduar as a third-culture kid who might shift his audiences' understandings of American identity, Olson decides that his customers would more easily consume the idea of the Indian American as a "militant cave-dwelling fundamentalist" who wants to partner with the Mexican revolutionary Che Chavez Castro in order to bring America down from the inside by coming after Chad Deity, who embodies the "heart of America."[17] Initially, Vigneshwar agrees, hoping that he might work within the system to subvert the racial stereotypes that he and Mace have been forced to portray. However, the duo soon finds out that once ensnared within the culture industry, it is difficult to take ownership of one's own words and corporeality. Within a short time, VP finds himself consumed by The Fundamentalist persona, playing the stereotypical heel and drawing audience derision wherever he goes. Moreover, The Fundamentalist's popularity grows, to the delight of EKO's profit margins.

It becomes clear through VP's arc in *Chad Deity* that the market is not an objective space but rather reinscribes racial inequities. Paduar demonstrates that people of color are unable to be self-determinant within the market system because of systemic racism, which denies people of color control over the ways that their bodies are received and consumed. According to market logic, the neoliberal government must then punish these populations for the conditions it created. Spence argues, "The turn toward neoliberalism is not possible without the use of ideas about race—about racialized bodies and racialized spaces."[18] As failed subjects of the market system, these populations must be managed and, where possible, disappeared so that the story of an objective, virtuous market system rings true.

VP is on the verge of competing with Chad Deity for a match in which he will seize control of THE Wrestling's championship as part of a plan that will arouse the sport's fans to get further caught up in the series' nationalist story lines, but just before the seminal event, Vigneshwar decides to leave THE Wrestling. Throughout his run, VP has attempted to make known his displeasure with the culture industry and how it reinforces American consumerism and the myth of exceptionalism, but his critique only plays into what audiences expect of him. He also knows that winning the title will not change this perception. Capitalism always requires the consumers to consume and Paduar will be trapped in this role as long as he is at the mercy of EKO and The Wrestling. So, he quits, telling Mace: "You and me, we got stories to tell, and they're different, but they come from the same place, man—there's beauty in that. That's what I came here to do. But they want to turn us, they want to spin our story, fit us in to what they already got in mind. Chad Deity *is* Chad Deity. I don't want to be The Fundamentalist. You don't want to be Che Chavez Castro. And if we go along with it, no matter how we play it, if it's bad and fucked up, or if we sneak in some good and sneak in something to say, we gotta go back to Brooklyn, back to the Bronx, we gotta look little brown kids in the eye and defend our decision, we gotta explain why it ain't so bad to exist outside ourselves for the sake of twenty pounds of gold around our waist."[19] In that moment, VP bumps against the limits of his American dream trajectory, and rather than capitulating, he chooses to remove himself from the culture industry. The promising wrestler sees through the big lie of American capitalism and its dream of exceptionalism, choosing to return to Brooklyn where he can live in relative anonymity and create an alternative path for self-fulfillment.

Nevertheless, the neoliberal market demands to be sated and THE Wrestling desires to continue to uphold the American dream myth through Chad Deity. Mace is forced into competition as Che Chavez Castro in the championship match, but before the competition begins, Mace enters the wrestling ring, removes his costume, and begins to tell his story as a hungry young child growing up in the Bronx who wished for wrestling superstardom but ran up against the limits of THE Wrestling's economic superstructure. He notes EKO's consistent scripting of THE Wrestling's narratives to maximize profits and speaks to Chad Deity's complicity in all of this as a willing upholder of American values. In doing so, he seeks to remove the caricatured visions that the audience might have of him so that they see him as a real human being and to imagine an

American dream that is not reliant on blind belief in meritocracy and labor. But as we know, the culture industry must disappear failed subjects of the market system. Shortly thereafter, Mace is powerbombed by Chad Deity to the delight of THE Wrestling's audience. Nevertheless, the play's epilogue provides a glimmer of hope when it cuts to VP's apartment where he's watching Mace with his latest girlfriend and she turns to ask, "Why are they rooting for the bad guy?"[20] Mace gives voice to an understanding of how the American dream was built upon the exploitation of bodies of color, and while that narrative might not have been visible to most of THE Wrestling's audience, on one night in one apartment in Brooklyn, it helped a woman envision an alternative path for success that is less reliant on the pursuit of upward mobility and financial capital and contingent on creating resistance to racial and economic inequity.

Kristoffer Diaz has built a career investigating the fictions that Americans tell themselves about race, identity, and economic success. In *The Elaborate Entrance of Chad Deity* and his earlier play *Welcome to Arroyo's*, he has created artwork that disrupts these stories and works constantly to steal his words away from the cultural industry to which they belong. In sum, Diaz uses his satirical agency as a theatrical tool of political resistance. Mace and VP initially fall into the trap of the culture industry by allowing themselves to be framed as passive objects in EKO's fictionalized representation of the American dream, but as the play concludes, Diaz acknowledges the multiple powers who own wrestling, theatre, and popular culture. At a time when the myth of the American dream has become coopted by the son of a millionaire whose numerous failed business ventures and gutting of financial protection measures are masked by faux populism, politicians must challenge the hegemony of the American dream and advocate for alternative ways of modeling success and personal happiness. If our leaders are indeed interested in this task, they can look to Diaz's *Chad Deity*, which speaks to alternative strategies for envisioning success that are unreliant on the failed platitudes of meritocratic success through industrialism and labor.

Notes

1. Barack Obama, "A More Perfect Union" (speech, Philadelphia, March 18, 2008), http://www.npr.org/templates/story/story.php?storyId=88478467.
2. Barack Obama, "Reclaiming the American Dream" (speech, Bettendorf, Iowa, November 7, 2007), http://www.cnn.com/2007/POLITICS/12/21/obama.trans.american-dream/.
3. Aziz Rana, "Decolonizing Obama" *n+1* 27 (2017), https://nplusonemag.com/issue-27/politics/decolonizing-obama/.

4. Robert C. Rowland and John M. Jones, "Recasting the American Dream and American Politics: Barack Obama's Keynote Address to the 2004 Democratic National Convention," *Quarterly Journal of Speech* 93, no. 4 (2007): 427.
5. Theodor Adorno and Max Horkheimer, "The Culture Industry: Enlightenment as Mass Deception," in *Dialectic of Enlightenment*, ed. Gunzelin Schmid Noerr, trans. Edmund Jephcott (Palo Alto: Stanford University Press, 1994), 94–133.
6. A. A. Akom, "Ameritocracy and Infra-Racial Racism: Racializing Social and Cultural Reproduction Theory in the Twenty-first Century," *Race, Ethnicity, and Education* 11, no. 3 (2008): 207.
7. Kristoffer Diaz, *The Elaborate Entrance of Chad Deity* (New York: Samuel French, 2011), 7–9.
8. Ibid., 10–11.
9. Ibid., 25.
10. J. David Cisneros, "A Nation of Immigrants and a Nation of Laws: Race, Multiculturalism, and Neoliberal Exception in Barack Obama's Immigration Discourse," *Communication, Culture, and Critique* 8, no. 3 (2015): 358.
11. Akom, "Ameritocracy and Infra-Racial Racism," 209.
12. Diaz, *The Elaborate Entrance of Chad Deity*, 25.
13. Akom, "Ameritocracy and Infra-Racial Racism," 209.
14. Ibid., 210–211.
15. Diaz, *The Elaborate Entrance of Chad Deity*, 17–18.
16. Lester K. Spence, *Stare in the Darkness: The Limits of Racial Politics* (Minneapolis: University of Minnesota Press, 2011), 15.
17. Diaz, *The Elaborate Entrance of Chad Deity*, 26–28.
18. Spence, *Stare in the Darkness*, 15.
19. Diaz, *The Elaborate Entrance of Chad Deity*, 52.
20. Ibid., 62.

Part IV

BOOK REVIEWS

A History of Japanese Theatre. Edited by Jonah Salz. Cambridge: Cambridge University Press, 2016. xli + 550 pp. $155.00 hardcover.

As the first major text to cover the length and breadth of Japanese theatre since Benito Ortolani's *The Japanese Theater* in 1991, this ambitious work is successful in providing a comprehensive history of theatre in Japan while introducing various historiographical and performative methodologies that help the reader understand how the dozens of authors came to know what they know. It is also an engaging and enjoyable read, filled with strong prose and useful visual materials, including time lines and genealogies as well as depictions of costumes, masks, and performances.

Despite its many authors, the structure and tone is clear and contains an engaging survey of Japanese performances from the origins of Japanese civilization to contemporary plays and theories of performance. The structure is not strictly chronological: while the first two sections move in a linear fashion to discuss traditional theater in part 1 and modern theatres (Meiji and post-Meiji) in part 2, the last third of the book moves across time and space to discuss themes and patterns of Japanese theatre arts, the architecture of spaces, criticism from within and outside of Japan, and intercultural aspects of Japanese theatre.

However, even the linear history is interrupted with short sections that create opportunities for case studies and discussions of specific cultural traditions, performances, or biographies of significance. For example, during the forty-page chapter on Noh, brief one-to-two-page "Spotlights" focus on the Noh stage, Zeami's writings, and women in Noh; and "Focus" sections of similar length discuss Kurokawa Noh, Noh's first appearance in Europe, at the Venice Biennale in 1954, twentieth-century Noh actor Kanze Hisao, and the repertory of Noh plays. There are also more extended "interlude" sections that discuss larger issues. At the end of the Noh chapter, there is an interlude that discusses the history and function of Noh and Kyogen masks and costumes. This is effective in preventing the reader from falling into a singular narrative and helps fulfill the promise of such a collaborative work by creating a complicated, varied, and entertaining landscape of different types of Japanese theatre.

The most salient and unique part of the book is part 3, "Arcs and Patterns," which sets up helpful frameworks for discussing elements of Japanese theatre in ways that are directly useful for an undergraduate classroom. By having brief sections of different themes and issues that the study of Japanese theatre brings up, it allows for the reader, teacher, or student to see different approaches that can complement and even replace a strictly chronological course of study. This part also provides a bridge to those more accustomed to literary historical studies. Especially in J. Thomas Rimer's section, "Modern Plays as Literature," and Salz's, "Traditional Meta-patterns," we are encouraged to see the intertextuality of different kinds of performances across literature and other cultural traditions. While the text as a whole valorizes the study of performance and production, this part creates a linchpin that demonstrates how this focus on performance does not diminish the works as literature. Instead, by providing such fundamental materials about the larger cultural and performative contexts in which the texts were created, it allows us to better comprehend how the texts have worked in their historical or contemporary contexts.

Perhaps the smartest thing about this text is that it does not attempt to pretend that it is not created for an English-speaking audience. The egalitarian sensibility of the authorship allows for a clear diversity of voices, but at the same time it enables the reader to regularly recognize the perspectives that are offered by those voices. Salz makes sure that the kinds of issues and concerns that come from non-Japanese students and scholars are addressed in clear ways, including a very useful overview of English language scholarship provided near the end of the book by David Jortner and two excellent chapters (by Nakano Masaaki and Salz) discussing the use of Japanese training practices around the world, which has never been as widespread thanks to the influence of Tadashi Suzuki and the Saratoga International Theater Institute's use of his training regime. However, the structure of the text, with all its voices, interruptions, and variety, compels the reader to be aware of the complexity of Japanese theatre in its own contexts, not just as it is seen through Western eyes. The approach and execution of this book finds a sweet spot in the often fraught and contested realm of intercultural performance studies. It should find its way into many undergraduate and graduate-level courses and might even encourage others to start offering Japanese theatre courses, as they would have a strong text with which to work.

—**PETER A. CAMPBELL**
RAMAPO COLLEGE

Political Acts: Women in Northern Irish Theatre, 1921–2012. By Fiona Coleman Coffey. Syracuse: Syracuse University Press, 2016. 294 pp. $65 hardcover, $29.95 paper.

In this richly layered and detailed examination of the role of women in theatre in Northern Ireland, Fiona Coleman Coffey succeeds in her stated intention to "begin the process of painting a more comprehensive picture of women's theatrical contributions from the North" (18). Noting that geography and gender, as well as strict sectarian divisions within Northern Ireland, have marginalized and obscured the impacts of these theatre artists, the author employs "gendered, historical, and sociopolitical lenses as [a] contextual framework" (15) in this process.

Organized into three primarily chronological sections, Coffey creates a solid foundational understanding of important concepts in part 1, Theatre, Gender, and Politics, 1921–1979, exploring the notions of nation, feminism, sectarianism, and censorship in regard to Northern Ireland specifically and in contrast to the same ideas in the Republic of Ireland and Great Britain. The complex and intertwined histories of these three entities are deftly untangled, providing enough information so that the signal political events are clear and the impact of these events on the theatrical community is illuminated.

The discussion of Northern attitudes toward feminism is particularly strong, underscoring the role of both Protestantism and Catholicism as well as years of sectarian violence in the creation of these attitudes toward women. Coffey observes that maintaining strict gender roles was necessary in the light of sustained Nationalist/Unionist discourse and discord. Women occupy the domestic sphere, nurturing and grieving, while the men fight. Additionally, she points out that women's bodies have been "repressively policed for decades in the North" and that "women's sexuality has been synonymous with the community's integrity" (23). Awareness of these unique viewpoints becomes crucial in Coffey's examination and analysis of specific female playwrights and artists throughout the volume.

Throughout the balance of the book, Coffey lifts the multiple veils obscuring the indigenous theatre of Northern Ireland, introducing female theatre artists who, despite the challenges they faced, greatly impacted their communities and the development of theatre in Northern Ireland. Alice Milligan, Patricia O'Connor, and Mary O'Malley worked in the first half of the twentieth century, establishing, according to Coffey, a legacy of Northern Irish women using "theatre as a political tool to envision social and civic change" (53). Milligan, a Protestant, nationalist, and feminist, created tableaux vivant in response to the government censorship of spoken language in theatre. She toured extensively, cast Northern Irish actors, and included members of the community in her creations. Patricia O'Connor is one of the very few female playwrights to be produced multiple times in Northern Ireland in the 1940s and 1950s. The canon of her plays address issues such as education, marriage, land inheritance, religion, economic struggles, and the patriarchy of the Northern state. Mary O'Malley cofounded the Lyric Players Theatre in Belfast with her husband in 1951, while she was running for political office. Though she was a nationalist, the board and company of the theatre was inclusive. Under her direction, the theatre had a literary focus (Yeats was a much-produced playwright) and featured a symbolic and collaborative aesthetic. A tendency toward highly visual/theatrical production aesthetics, a grappling with current social and political problems, and a connection to community through touring, outreach, and inclusivity are traits that Coffey finds common among the many female theatre practitioners she examines in the rest of the volume.

The Troubles, the years of open, violent, sectarian warfare, which began in the 1960s and officially ended in 1998 with the signing of the Belfast Agreement, dominate the theatre and plays of the second half of the twentieth century. Part 2 is titled Troubles and the Stage, 1980–1997. The Charabanc Theatre Company, founded in 1983, included both Catholic and Protestant artists and worked "to create compassion and empathy for those identified as the adversary" (85). The company produced twenty-two productions, eighteen of which were new works, toured widely throughout the North and the Republic as well as internationally, and was the crucible for many female playwrights, directors, and actors, including Marie Jones.

Charabanc's practices and success laid the groundwork for numerous women-led theatre companies in the 1990s, including DubbelJoint and JustUs Community Theatre Company. DubbelJoint was founded in 1991 by Marie Jones and Pam Brighton and "defined by cross-border touring of politically engaged work, performing in areas without access to theatre, and support of community and women's theatre groups" (105). JustUs grew out of the desire of a group of amateur working-class women in Belfast to perform their personal experiences of the Troubles. Coffey skillfully traces the connections between, and impacts of, these three companies, illustrating that through their work they:

- shifted the focus of the story of the Troubles from the male perspective to the female
- performed theatre in working-class communities
- helped to train women for careers in theatre
- empowered and politicized women's voices
- "created a tradition of women's activism through the theatre that transformed the makeup of the Northern theatre scene" (148).

Part 3, The Post-Agreement North, 1998–2012, focuses on several female playwrights dealing with the legacy of the Troubles and the ensuing peace process. Through in-depth and insightful analysis of the plays of Abbie Spallen,

Stacey Gregg, and Rosemary Jenkins, Coffey exposes the ramifications of living through ever-present violence and the subsequent imposition of peace. Reflected in the stories, characters, and storytelling, Coffey contends, is the "cultural trauma" or fracturing of identities experienced by the citizens of the North during these decades of violence (176). The men, used to fighting for their communities, are now redundant, their violence turning inward. The women are often the victims of that inward, destructive violence, their traditional roles also corrupted in this new political landscape.

In the final chapter, Coffey examines the work of experimental, queer, expat theatremaker Shannon Yee. Yee's immersive, non-narrative, deeply personal work intersects with the Troubles, the peace process, the LGBT community, and performance in profound ways that Coffey argues "fosters compassion, empathy, and understanding for differences … promoting cultural pluralism and hybrid identities" (236).

Throughout this well-written and thoroughly researched book, Coffey effectively negotiates the complex political landscape, examines theatre artists and companies, and analyzes how both politics and theatre have influenced and impacted each other over the course of nearly a century of history in Northern Ireland. Consistently working across the borders of religion, politics, and gender, the enduring legacy of these innovative women is revealed. The work, struggles, and triumphs of these artists is inspiring, as is the scholarship that so skillfully acknowledges and celebrates their voices.

—**PENELOPE COLE**
Independent scholar

What Playwrights Talk About When They Talk About Writing. By Jeffrey Sweet. Yale University Press, 2017. 304 pp. $30 hardcover.

Playwright and historian Jeffrey Sweet anchors his collection of interviews *What Playwrights Talk About When They Talk About Writing* around the simple observation that "playwrights don't talk about writing with each other much" (xvii). Marking the tenth anniversary of the Yale Drama Series and the David Charles Horn Foundation Prize for emerging playwrights, the series of one-on-one interviews with past judges for the series offers insider insights to the playwriting process, as well as a broad oral history of the past three generations of British and American playwriting.

Sweet begins the collection with a reprint of a 2010 article he wrote for *Dramatics* about Edward Albee, who he frames as the father of contemporary playwriting. Sweet then presents the sixteen interviewees in a chronological fashion from Arthur Kopit to Nina Raine, bookending the Albee article with a previous interview with Lanford Wilson. While Sweet touches on many topics with every writer—What's your process? Who inspires you? Where do you get your material?—Sweet does an admirable job crafting uniquely individualized questions for each playwright. As with any such collection, as the interviews progress and are taken in totality, several themes emerge.

The most prevalent theme in the book is the difference between British and American theatre. Sweet posits to nearly every writer that British playwrights create large-scale "state-of-the-nation" plays, whereas American playwrights write smaller-scale plays seen "through the lens of the family." Kwame Kwei-Armah, a British playwright of émigré parents who is now artistic director of Baltimore's Center Stage, most eloquently sums up the contrast: "The British playwright has been schooled in the art of state-of-the-nation plays. We're trained by critique, by reaction, and production history that the role of the playwright is to be the person who says, 'This is our country right now—from a political as well as a social as well as a sociological perspective.'" On the flip side, he argues, American playwrights have been pushed into working "through the lens of metaphor, and using the family as metaphor" (187). Within this larger question, the differences in training as well as mediums weave their way through the interviews. Donald Margulies and others argue that in the theatre playwrights are "constrained" and that the big, epic, political type of writing is taking place within the world of television. Margulies continues: "The theater has its limitations economically. You can't tell big stories onstage, or you can't tell them in conventional or realistic ways. . . . I like getting my plays produced. And the reality is that plays with smaller casts or more manageable-sized casts get produced more readily than larger, fiscally unwieldy plays" (126–27).

While most playwrights agree with Sweet's appraisal, David Hare pushes back, providing one of the only contentious moments in an otherwise charmingly friendly book. Hare argues that the difference is artificial, after all: "Tony Kushner wrote *Angels in America* for a theatre that did not exist. That theatre came into being because he wrote this great play" (55). In an exchange about A. R. Gurney's negative reaction to *Stuff Happens* being produced in America (in short, why aren't American theatres putting resources behind American writers?), Hare says American dramatists "don't have the courage to write that play" (55). If anything, one wishes that Sweet pushed back more often with his subjects to create more moments of discord and resultant debate. Similarly, there is room for Sweet to push his subjects further in terms of the training of playwrights and its relationship to the type of work being created in the American theatre. While it is suggested that the American MFA model and the current economics of New York theatre are creating a generation of small-scale playwrights, there is room to dig deeper.

Sweet does delve into pedagogy with several of the playwrights, with Marsha Norman's and Lynn Nottage's interviews providing the most depth and insight. Sweet returns numerous times to Norman's concept of "writing your stuff," often asking the other playwrights what their stuff is and if/how they go about writing it. In discussing training and pedagogy, one major topic that is largely missing is the developmental process of the American theatre—the development to death phenomenon. The training and development of new plays can arguably be directly tied to the type of new plays being written and produced, but any deep discussion of those ties is overshadowed by more traditional exchanges about writing process, influences, and personal backstory.

As the book unfolds and we travel forward in time, the changes in the development and business side of the theatre are striking. From the emergence and almost reliance on MFAs to the monetary pressures of contemporary theatre, one can't help noticing that many of the older writers in the collection came to be in a far different theatrical world. As Nottage notes: "They're not allowing young playwrights to find their own voices. The minute they come out of these graduate programs they're given these big commissions and then those subsequent plays are produced before the playwrights have a sense of their own identity" (207). In part this is a result of the MFA system; many of the early writers in the collection spent their early years working in small theatres and performances spaces, whereas most of the more contemporary writers spent time in the MFA system. From a pedagogic standpoint, the reader can glean a sense of how playwright training has evolved, even if the book never explicitly goes there, and more importantly, how that training has impacted the current state of American playwriting. Sweet throughout laments the lack of epic playwriting and state-of-the-nation plays in America, and the book provides a launching pad for larger questions in that realm. What can we be doing differently in training our playwrights? How do the economics of theatre impact what is being written? How might we approach our MFA and development system differently? And if we want to achieve the state-of-the-nation plays that Sweet laments are absent from the American playwriting world, what economic models or initiatives are needed?

Any collection of interviews will inevitably lead to a criticism of who was not included. While Sweet is limited in his interview subjects by the parameters of the book (past judges for the Yale Drama Series), it is unfortunate that playwrights who have written very successful state-of-the-nation plays, such as Tony Kushner and Suzan-Lori Parks, are left out. Likewise, Paula Vogel's voice would have been a welcome addition to any discussion about the training and current state of American playwriting. While there are bones to pick, the collection does include a diverse slate of writers who represent a range of different eras, styles, and subject matter. Taken in totality, the interviews represent a broad cross-section of the past fifty years of British and American playwriting.

—MATT FOTIS
Albright College

Stanislavsky in the World: The System and Its Transformations across Continents. By Stefan Aquilina and Jonathan Pitches, eds. London: Bloomsbury Methuen Drama, 2017. xii + 480 pp. $33.95 paper.

This is an important volume for the scholarship on Russian theater innovator Konstantin Stanislavsky, actor training more generally, and theater itself in the twentieth and twenty-first centuries. Two opening essays offer a general context: first, an essay on the goals of the volume, which are to move beyond the "Moscow and New York" assumption of where Stanislavsky flourished; and second, a primer on Stanislavsky as a case study for transmission theory that shows how local circumstances influence and transform ideas on a wider basis. Then six sections, organized geographically, offer case studies covering the globe: Europe (Italy, France, Lithuania, Malta, Greece), China and Japan, Latin America (Brazil, Cuba, Argentina), Africa (Nigeria, Tunisia, South Africa), Australasia (Australia and Aotearoa), and India and Bangladesh. The sheer scope of this endeavor deserves appreciation.

There are too many fascinating insights to detail in a short review, but I will offer a few highlights. Marie-Christine Autant-Mathieu explains how Stanislavsky read Théodule Ribot, the father of French psychology, and how Ribot influenced Stanislavsky's ideas of *perezhivania*, experiencing. Yet the French theatre world did not, in general, accept Stanislavsky's system because they had their own well-established traditions. Arlete Cavaliere narrates a fascinating story of Stanislavsky's ideas on acting coming to Brazil through four Polish (and Polish Jewish) theater practitioners during and after World War II. This essay in particular highlights the "external factors" that Aquilina and Pitches set forth in their introductory essay: beyond publishing, people, and institutions, it is greater historical circumstances that shape how ideas travel. Were it not for World War II, in this case, Stanislavsky's ideas might not have come to Brazil or at least developed in Brazil in precisely the way they did. Lithuania is the only example offered from inside the Soviet Union. Ina Pukelyte argues that Stanislavsky was received differently in the interwar period, when Lithuania was a newly independent country, than in the postwar period, when Lithuania was a Soviet republic and Stanislavsky represented the canonized official and required method for acting. The reader then learns not only about the cultural transmission of a system of acting methodology but also about multiple theatrical traditions across the globe.

The greater argument of the entire volume, however, is that Stanislavsky and his system offer a fruitful case study for how ideas travel: the multiple case studies show the reader how local circumstances, historical context, and whether ideas travel by text, by individual, or via institutions all shape cultural transmission. Another volume could explore how Stanislavsky's system was interpreted variously throughout the Soviet Union itself. The case study on Lithuania raises the question of how the transmission of Stanislavsky's system was monitored and maintained in the state-supported drama schools and theaters throughout the Soviet empire, from Moscow to Vladivostok. Beyond "Moscow and New York" could include the many cultures in the Soviet Union and in the satellite states as well. Still, the volume certainly enriches our understanding of cultural transmission. For example, in Australia, as Ian Maxwell argues, there was no direct connection with Stanislavsky (that is, there was no theater artist who studied with the man himself). Rather, certain Australians trained in England with people who had themselves trained with Stanislavsky. That indirectness proved consequential for acting training in Australia. In China, as we learn in Pitches and Ruru Li's contribution, it was specific teachers sent from the Soviet Union to Communist China who trained young generations of students. In particular, it was one individual teacher, Boris Kulynov, whose students were able to combine this new imported methodology with traditional Chinese theatrical forms. Kaori Nakayama describes how in Japan the Stanislavsky system was associated with socialism, and therefore with the Soviet Union, while the "method" (that is, the Americanized version of the system) was viewed more favorably. Politics shaped reception. And yet Stanislavsky has not "stuck" in Japan because of different understandings of "what is an actor and what is a good play" (203).

In short, even the most expert scholar of Stanislavsky will find something new in this volume. My only critique would be that the reader would very much appreciate more on exactly what the system comprises. The opening essay briefly explains that Stanislavsky wanted to create a "transcendent language designed to surmount the individual problems experienced by actors and to achieve a cohesive approach, a system" (13). Throughout the essays, the reader catches that the system was about realism, how to experience a text authentically onstage, and ideas on physical action. Yet a more specific and detailed explanation of the system and how it differed from other methodologies would have been useful.

Such an explanation would be welcome because, ultimately, this collection of essays raises the question of how Stanislavsky's system interacted, or conflicted, or was conflated with other systems of theater practice, such as that of Vsevolod Meyerhold, for example. Indeed, what, in fact, was the innovation in Stanislavsky's system? Was the system itself innovative, or was Stanislavsky simply the first to articulate these ideas? Would theater artists have come to ask who their characters were, what they wanted, and how to experience life onstage regardless of connection with a Russian imperial textile magnate who happened to try his hand at acting? How Stanislavsky's ideas became so widespread may remain, in the end, a mystery, but Pitches and Aquilina's volume contributes to addressing that mystery and shows how scholars and students of theater history should continue to investigate and explore Stanislavsky.

—MAYHILL FOWLER
Stetson University

Chinatown Opera Theater in North America. By Nancy Yunhwa Rao. Music in American Life Series. Urbana: University of Illinois Press, 2017. xiv + 415 pp. + 63 illus. $95.00 cloth, $29.95 paper, $26.96 e-book.

Many of the available English-language sources on traditional Chinese performance, as informative as they are, suffer from a need to generalize in order to encapsulate a phenomenon that has been centuries in the making, can be traced through multiple regional genealogies, and is active throughout the globe. Nancy Yunhwa Rao's relatively focused contribution to the field, restricted to Cantonese opera in North America in the decade of the 1920s, is therefore refreshing in its detail. Although the author carefully charts transnational connections with China and other points on the Pacific Rim, her study is primarily concerned with the flows of theatrical people and ideas within the area bounded by the United States, Canada, and Mexico, as well as the liminal locations of Hawaii and Cuba. Rao justifies the narrowness of her focus with convincing arguments regarding the uniqueness of the North American scene in the 1920s, which was characterized by unprecedented artistic experimentation during an era of explosive globalization (a situation that displayed all the contradictory signs of our present age—unbridled creativity alongside intense regulation of labor flows). By confining herself to this temporal and geographic range, Rao produces a work of deep archival detail and also of encyclopedic broadness, covering a full spectrum of topics including performers, touring networks, theatres, spaces, repertoire, performance conventions, advertising, and musical recordings. The intensity of Rao's focus produces a richly detailed picture of a key moment in the performance history of traditional Chinese performance, one that is immensely useful as a reference for experts in the field but also tremendously satisfying for the more casual reader who may have been frustrated in the past by the elusiveness of more generalized studies.

The encyclopedic quality of Rao's work is signaled by its division into five parts and twelve chapters. Rao lays out her subject and approach in the introduction, highlighting her intentional use of Chinese sources—important because many studies on the same topic have unfortunately had to rely on accounts written by non-Chinese. In part 1, the author situates performance in the 1920s within key historical contexts. She then turns to the subject of immigration policy and its effect on Cantonese opera performance in North America, setting up a key framework that she returns to throughout the work. Part 2 offers the reader a primer on "Performance Practice of the 1920s," which covers repertoire, acting conventions, and a sophisticated treatment of playbills, concluding with a case study of a representative aria from the era, one that will satisfy those seeking sophisticated musical analysis. In part 3, Rao traces the historical vector, beginning in Canada, that brought Cantonese opera back to prominence in San Francisco following a long hiatus after the 1906 earthquake. That movement culminated in the rise of the famed Great China Theater, which became a world center of Cantonese opera performance in the mid-1920s, thanks in no small part to a major labor strike in southern China during that period. With part 4, Rao chronicles the story of the Great China Theater's major American rival, the Mandarin Theater, emphasizing the latter troupe's influential promotion of female stars. With the final section, part 5, the author collects the extant sources on Cantonese opera in New York (including the story of the troupes that were the last to occupy the historic Bowery Theatre), Boston, Cuba, and Hawaii. In an epilogue, Rao considers the effect of the Golden Era she has documented on subsequent American art, including its impact on Chinese American novelists, the Chinese American film industry, and modernist composers, making a case for Cantonese opera as "an interlocutor of American music history" (320).

Rao bookends her study with a short but highly useful opening essay on Chinese naming conventions and an appendix of Chinese names and terms (the latter appearing in both Romanized and Chinese characters). The book is also graced with extensive notes, as well as a full bibliography and index. All these elements strengthen the book's usefulness as a reference work.

Given its scope, this book has much to offer interested readers, though a few of Rao's discussions rate special attention. The author relies heavily upon immigration records as a guide to tracing the transnational flow of performers, a methodology she demonstrates to great effect, particularly in chapters 2 and 3. This approach resonates strongly in our present moment, when the effects of immigration policy on lives and ideas (artistic and otherwise) have gained newfound prominence in our discussions. Also of note is Rao's extensive treatment of female performers, both individually and as a phenomenon, a focus not only timely but also historically justified given the important role played by North American theatres in the shift of gender politics within worldwide Cantonese opera at the time. Finally, both Americanists and those interested in transnational studies will be intrigued by Rao's narrative, which situates North America at the center of Cantonese opera development during a period of great unrest in China itself.

The comparison with Rao's book that most readily comes to mind is the recent work of Daphne Pi-Wei Lei, particularly her *Operatic China: Staging Identity across the Pacific* (Palgrave Macmillan 2006). That book covers a much wider historical range than Rao's (stretching from the nineteenth century to the twenty-first), though it avoids the kind of generalization noted earlier because it focuses on specific examples chosen to highlight Lei's theoretical exploration of transnationalism and identity. Rao in fact makes use of Lei's theoretical constructs, but *Chinatown Opera Theater* is more centrally an archival project. Far from seeking to choose between the two, readers are encouraged to place the works side by side on their bookshelves or seminar reading lists.

—ANDREW GIBB
Texas Tech University

Tennessee Williams. By Paul Ibell. London: Reaktion, 2016. 192 pp. 32 illustrations. $17.06 paperback.

Paul Ibell's *Tennessee Williams* is a comprehensive survey of the American author as a playwright and novelist. Taking his cue from previously published biographies, Ibell documents close associations between Tennessee Williams's personal life and his written works. In each of the seven chapters, which are structured chronologically by decade, he offers a succinct analysis of Williams's writings and then juxtaposes his assessment with carefully selected biographical details. In chapter 1, "Early Life," he presents four examples from Williams's upbringing in St. Louis as sources of inspiration for the playwright's work: the instability of his parents' sexless marriage, his care for his sister and the guilt he felt for not being present to stop her lobotomy, the many people and experiences he encountered in school, and the environmental influence from various part-time jobs. Beyond the standard information about family and education often found in most biographies, the most compelling section of this chapter is Ibell's discussion of Williams's employment. He expertly demonstrates how Williams found inspiration while working as a movie house usher to create the settings for *The Mysteries of the Joy Rio* (1941), *Hard Candy* (1953), and the recently published *These Are the Stairs You Gotta Watch.*

Chapter 2, "The Later 1940s: A Streetcar to Success," includes a generic analysis of Williams's rise to fame with the professional triumph of *The Glass Menagerie* (1944) and the overwhelming reception of *A Streetcar Named Desire* (1947). For readers unfamiliar with Williams's formative works, this chapter provides an adequate introduction to his two most successful plays and concentrates on his commonly accepted familial influences; the characters of Laura, Amanda, and Tom Wingfield are typically recognized as embodiments of the playwright's sister (Rose), his mother (Edwina), and Williams himself, respectively. Ibell also introduces the reader to recurring themes that habitually consume Williams's plays, including variations on sexual desire, stultifying family ties, and the frustrating effects of fading beauty. Beginning with Blanche DuBois in *Streetcar,* these motifs haunt most of Williams's subsequent characters.

Ibell establishes a historical thread in the development of Williams's professional achievements by continuing his chronology in chapter 3, "The 1950s: A Cat on a Hot Tin Roof." He provides short summaries of Williams's critical successes, including *The Rose Tattoo* (1951), *Cat on a Hot Tin Roof* (1955), *Suddenly*

Last Summer (1958), and *Sweet Bird of Youth* (1959). The most engaging part of this chapter, however, is Ibell's overview of the lesser-known novel *The Roman Spring of Mrs. Stone* (1950). Closely based on Williams's intimate relationship with a young vagrant, Salvatore, who he met and cared for during his European travels, the novel reinforces his thematic preoccupation with sexual attraction and fading elegance through its depiction of an aging actress who falls in love with a younger man.

Chapter 4, "The 1960s: A Period of Adjustment," examines Williams's struggle with depression and the paralyzing effects of drug and alcohol abuse. Ibell suggests that Williams's last successful play was *The Night of the Iguana* (1961), which premiered two years before Frank Merlo, his life partner of more than fourteen years, died of lung cancer. Williams's grief over Merlo's death, combined with his growing addiction, resulted in multiple failed attempts to write another great play. Ibell analyzes two plays from this period as examples of Williams's struggle to find profitable connections between his life and his work. He discusses *The Milk Train Doesn't Stop Here Anymore* (1963) and its adaptation, along with other earlier plays, from stage to screen. He then examines the debate surrounding the inclusion of autobiographical details in *In the Bar of a Tokyo Hotel* (1969), which portrays an American artist who, similar to Williams, suffers from sexual problems, alcoholism, and potential madness.

The most exciting revelations of the book appear in both chapter 5, "The 1970s: Small Craft Warnings," and chapter 6, "The 1980s: Steps Must Be Gentle," where Ibell introduces the reader to some of Williams's often overlooked works. He begins by looking at the playwright's waning reputation and his persistent use of the same thematic ideas. The most prominent example of this appears in the moderately successful *Small Craft Warnings* (1972), which portrays a group of sexually charged characters desperately searching for companionship. The highlight of this chapter, however, is the analysis of two plays with definitive ties to Williams's personal life. These include the highly autobiographical *Vieux Carré* (1977), with its central character, a young writer, explicitly modeled after the playwright himself, and *A Lovely Sunday for Creve Coeur* (1979), a comedy with obvious connections to Williams's youth; the lead character, Bodey, is employed at the same shoe company in St. Louis where Williams worked as a young adult. In chapter 6, Ibell continues to effectively document connections between the playwright's work and his life. Of particular interest are his analyses of *Steps Must Be Gentle* (1980), a dramatic reading about a mother/son relationship that Williams wrote in the same year his mother passed away, and *Something Cloudy, Something Clear* (1981), which is based on the playwright's youthful affair with Kip Kiernan.

Chapter 7, "Afterlife: Into the Twenty-first Century," looks at Williams's legacy. Ibell examines the controversial self-appointment of Williams's longtime friend, Maria Britneva, as literary executor of the playwright's estate. He argues that the lack of attention to Williams's later works was, for many years, a result of Britneva's excessively strict control. After her death, in 1994, however, the lesser-known plays became more accessible to producers and scholars. Ibell highlights many of the theatre companies and artists who have championed these works.

Overall, this concise biography is an excellent resource for students and scholars seeking an informed introduction to the relationship between Williams's life and his work. Although Ibell often privileges autobiographical connections and chronology over detailed text analysis, his book is an engaging and sophisticated survey of Tennessee Williams as one of America's greatest playwrights.

—JEFF GRACE
Knox College

Experiments in Democracy: Interracial and Cross-Cultural Exchange in American Theatre, 1912–1945. Edited by Cheryl Black and Jonathan Shandell. Carbondale: Southern Illinois University Press, 2016. $40 paper.

In *Experiments in Democracy: Interracial and Cross-Cultural Exchange in American Theatre, 1912–1945*, coeditors Cheryl Black and Jonathan Shandell address a vital question: "At a time when racial segregation was de jure in the American southeast and de facto everywhere else … what role did theatrical performance play in testing and promoting more equitable models of democracy?" (1). Drawing inspiration from J. Ellen Gainor's *Performing America* and her argument that the early twentieth century was a particularly critical and lively moment in the debate over what being American meant, Black, Shandell, and their collaborators look at how theatre artists worked to create a vision of America that celebrated the diversity of the identities it contained, presenting America as a vibrant multicultural mosaic rather than a homogenizing melting pot. The theatrical ventures examined in these essays are all, in their ways, risky, novel, and seldom wholly successful, befitting the scientific terminology Black and Shandell conjure through the use of "Experiments" in their title. Their own editorial experiment is a rousing success; the essays are all individually insightful, and how they illuminate each other makes for a whole that is still greater than the sum of its parts.

At the core of the book's success is the broad range of American experiences that it examines. While scholarly engagement with minority theatrical traditions in America has blossomed in recent years, such histories are often somewhat insular and focused upon a single perspective; Shandell, drawing upon Horace M. Kallen, states that one of *Experiments in Democracy*'s goals is to explore the "'continuous, free and fruitful cross-fertilization' of cultures, traditions, aesthetics, and ideas" (3). Thus, against the background of the white, male, Christian, heterosexual, affluent, able-bodied hegemony (which, as Black reminds us in her afterword, was the select populace to whom the United States originally extended full democratic participation), Asian, black, Hispanic, indigenous, queer, immigrant, poor, disabled, female, and Jewish characters and artists all take focus in at least one essay within this volume. To better explore this cross-fertilization, Shandell and Black have arranged the book's thirteen essays chronologically, allowing the different histories to entwine and to speak to each other as much as they speak back to the hegemony.

At its best, the chronological arrangement creates echoes among the essays, helping the reader to draw parallels among the experiences examined. Chapters six through eight, for instance, examine Federal Theatre Project works from the 1930s that ranged widely in the cultural backgrounds of their key artists, united by the artists' mutual project of claiming a place for marginalized peoples as part of America. Elizabeth Coonrod Martínez asserts that Josefina Niggli's plays with the Carolina Playmakers implicitly argued for Mexicans as revolutionary and democratic kindred to Americans; Harry J. Elam Jr. examines Theodore Browne's play *Natural Man*, demonstrating how it attacked systems of white supremacy that prevent full black participation in American democracy; Margaret F. Savalonis offers a sensitive history of Myra Kinch's attempts to popularize modern dance as an American art form and her problematic attempts to transcend the races of her dancers' bodies to address the shortcomings of American democratic inclusiveness. The artists discussed in these essays differ widely in the tactics they used and the obstacles they encountered. Seeing their experiences side by side, however, throws into relief both the massiveness and the vulnerability of the systems of power and privilege that they called into question.

The volume is rich in larger echoes, too. Elam ties his exploration of *Natural Man* to contemporary movements such as Black Lives Matter, implicitly inviting the reader to seek connections between the other essays and the democratic turbulence of our own time. Stuart J. Hecht's argument that the Gershwins and

Oscar Hammerstein II helped make Broadway a showcase for urbane, Jewish identity and values in the 1920s enhances the resonance of Garrett Eisler's later discussion of "Fun to Be Free," an antifascist rally and performance in New York that predates US entry into World War II. Nearly half of the essays grapple with questions about the ethics of representation, especially when artists present characters whose backgrounds differ from their own.

The only essay that does not completely feel like it fits is Ju Yon Kim's "Trying on *The Yellow Jacket*: Performing Chinese Exclusion and Assimilation (1912–1928)." While it is a welcome inclusion on its own merits, it does feel somewhat tacked on in the context of the larger collection; it is one of two reprinted essays, and its contents predate the subjects of the other essays by a decade. While she does briefly trace *The Yellow Jacket*'s revivals into the 1920s, the bulk of Kim's essay is grounded in the 1910s, which is a very different sociohistorical milieu than appears in the rest of the book; by comparison, eleven of the other twelve essays fall between 1930 and 1945. An essay that examined the interplay between theatre and being Asian in America during the Great Depression or the run-up to World War II would have fit into the collection more cleanly.

Experiments in Democracy has something for anyone interested in performance and politics in the United States, especially during the Great Depression and World War II. Each essay is strong individually and brings fresh insights to its topic, and while most of the essays take an approach that uses, in varying degrees, close readings, contextual analysis, and archival research, some of the scholars also branch out beyond these methods, as in W. Douglas Powers's psychoanalytic exploration of Lynn Riggs and his use of the Cherokee in his plays and Andrea Nouryeh's examination of the social impact of the Stage Door Canteen. Where the collection shines, however, is in its intersectional approach, letting these topics stand together and inform each other. Its insights into theatre outside the canon during the 1930s and 1940s make it a worthwhile read for scholars who teach American theatre, and some of the essays could be used to enhance undergraduate or graduate courses on American theatre or race and performance.

—BECK HOLDEN
Tufts University

May Irwin: Singing, Shouting, and the Shadow of Minstrelsy. By Sharon Ammen. Urbana: University of Illinois Press, 2017. 252 pp. $24.37 paper.

In 1896, Thomas Edison made a fifteen-second film titled *The Kiss*. In the film, two fairly unattractive, middle-aged people press cheek to cheek, lips touching at only one corner while the kissers seem to be speaking to one another from "the other side" of their mouths. Then, the man pulls away, pulls his mustachios into perfect curls, and kisses the woman full on for just a few seconds. This little film has always struck me as being a bit salacious and unromantic, too broad and theatrical to be authentic. It turns out, *The Kiss* was indeed performed by John C. Rice and May Irwin, one of the most popular entertainers of the day. Those fifteen seconds were taken from a scene in Irwin's mega-hit farce *The Widow Jones*. If Irwin is remembered at all it is largely because of this little film.

Irwin may also be remembered and closely identified by the "coon songs" she wrote and recorded. The coon song was a type of ragtime rampant with racist images of African Americans. They were written in "negro dialect" and depicted racist caricatures of black life. Irwin was a "coon shouter," the name given to this style of performer, and her most popular song, *The Bully*, involved a cold-blooded murder. The titular character, a black man, is armed with a straight razor and looking for a fight. She is thus remembered for the racist and distasteful songs that made her a star. Presciently, Irwin wrote: "Sometimes I feel a certain regret that perhaps my name will go down in history, if it even trundles along that far, as 'the woman who sang coon songs,' more than the woman who made the public laugh. The latter would be the height of my ambition" (68).

In *May Irwin: Singing, Shouting, and the Shadow of Minstrelsy*, Sharon Ammen unapologetically examines the layered and complex meanings of Irwin's coon songs with their attendant negative images of black people, enacted through "comedy." "It is simply," Ammen writes, "not possible to write about May Irwin without delving into this subject, for if coon songs were indeed the 'nadir' of 'vulgarity in music,' then May Irwin was their most prominent purveyor throughout the period of their peak popularity—from the 1890s until World War I" (70). Nevertheless, Ammen's book and Irwin herself are indeed worthy of study beyond *The Kiss* and the coon songs that made her a star.

Sharon Ammen's exceedingly readable book introduces us to a complex, strong, savvy, and kind woman. Irwin's persona went far beyond her work on the stage. May was called by the critics the "personification of humor," and President

Wilson appointed her "Secretary of Laughter." Irwin was also a writer, homemaker, mother, landowner, dairy farmer, and a vigorous supporter of suffrage who also wrote a cookbook, and she was frequently a contributor to magazines such as *Green Book* and *Cosmopolitan*. Yet, despite her great wealth and power, "she was just a sweet, jolly, harmless, fat woman" (111).

Ammen examines a complicated life whose success lies in no small part to minstrel music that celebrates a form (the coon song) that today's reader will find shameful and deeply disturbing—no small feat, indeed. She handles the material with a gentle yet insistent hand that mediates the harsh nature of her subject's career. Ammen's writing reveals a sense of humor and irony, is impeccably researched, and very successfully contextualizes the culture of Irwin's time. The reader not only comes to know May and her personal and professional personas but also to understand how performers and audiences could call such racist, violent, exaggerated, and false portrayals of black people "entertainment."

Ammen has been studying May Irwin for more than twenty years, and this book is clearly the result of that labor of love. Ammen met with many challenges collecting material, as there are no major studies or archival collections of Irwin's work. She has painstakingly sorted through old newspaper articles, performance reviews, articles in Irwin's own hand, interviews, Irwin's cookbook of 1904, and private collections to uncover the details of Irwin's career and personal life. Ammen effectively puts forward the life of an immensely talented woman who rose to be one of the most popular performers of her day. Ammen tells not only Irwin's life but also the sometimes troubling and perplexing history of the time and culture in which she moved and rose to stardom. It was a time when the minstrelsy of white and black performers could portray with impunity black Americans in a most demeaning way. Her contextualizing of the coon songs in particular helps to make this history if not more palatable, then at least more easily understood.

Notably, Ammen, a professional actress, includes in her research descriptions of her public performances of excerpts from Irwin's farces and coon songs. She has performed the work in a variety of venues, and her audiences included black people, white people, students, and the general public. Through these performances, Ammen has been able to observe and analyze contemporary responses to this often disturbing material.

Ammen has organized her book more or less chronologically. Early chapters document Irwin's professional partnership with her sister Flo and May's apprenticeships with Tony Pastor and Augustine Daly, who nurtured her natural abilities while emphasizing the need to learn discipline and the craft of her profession. Ammen then examines her rise to stardom and May's mastering of timing, spontaneity, interaction with audiences, and the development of her woman/child stage persona.

Next, Ammen addresses the more problematic aspect of Irwin's career, specifically the coon songs that firmly established her popularity. Ammen divides the dozens of coon songs written and/or performed by Irwin into seven groups according to stereotypes and the narrative voices Irwin used most often, such as the "Female Victim," "Greedy Gal," and the male "Pathetic Coon." Irwin often employed her "child" persona with a high-pitched voice and exaggerated pronunciation to mitigate the violence and crude imagery in songs like "The Bully." Unlike other coon shouters, Irwin did not "cork up" and was unapologetic about her significant weight. Rather, she often performed these songs with a matronly air in elegant gowns, thereby disconnecting her personal style from the crude content of the songs.

Chapters 5 and 6 discuss Irwin's domestic persona with her articles and interviews on cooking, working her dairy farm, and raising her two sons. Though not overtly political, Irwin supported many causes including women's rights and animal rights. She considered herself a pacifist. The final chapter examines Irwin's strategies for success as a performer, wife, and mother. Irwin had hoped to be remembered for making people laugh, rather than for the coon songs that made her a star. "In the short run," Ammen laments, "she was remembered primarily as a coon shouter. In the longer run, she was probably ignored because of her association with a racist form of singing that is only recently beginning to be studied. And, sadly, her 'Bully Song' surely negatively affected the treatment of blacks in more ways than she could have possibly realized" (176). Fortunately for us, Ammen has brought our attention to this remarkable performer.

—RHONA JUSTICE-MALLOY
University of Mississippi

Women on Southern Stages, 1800–1865: Performance, Gender and Identity in a Golden Age of American Theater. By Robin O. Warren. Jefferson, NC: McFarland, 2016. vii + 267 pp. $35 paper.

Women on Southern Stages provides the field of theatre history with one of the few studies focused specifically on the contributions of women to southern theatres in nineteenth-century America. In fact, a few of the southern stock actresses Warren examines, such as Charlotte Wrighten Placide and Mary Maury Squires Ludlow, have received scant attention by historians as anything other than the actress-wives of their theatre-managing husbands. Additionally, Warren asserts that these regional actresses, managers, and playwrights "occupied influential public roles through which they complicated gendered identity," as well as race, and "made a significant contribution to the antebellum South" (7). *Women on Southern Stages* is a welcome addition to the publications about early US theatre and demonstrates that a wealth of material remains in this area for historians to uncover and contextualize.

Warren's eight chapters are organized by general topic, such as repertory and theatres, rather than by location or individual artist. Chapter 1, cleverly titled "The Cast," provides biographical summaries of about twenty women, most following the family business, who earned recognition during the antebellum period for their theatrical endeavors. One such example is Eliza Arnold Hopkins Poe, whose successful acting career in DC, Virginia, and Maryland began before her twentieth birthday. The future mother of Edgar Allen Poe impressed critics with her "sweetly melodious voice" (12) as Maria in Sheridan's *The School for Scandal* and, as was common for the period, in some twenty-five other roles. Other actresses helped establish theatres in frontier regions in the South. Julia Drake Fosdick Dean's British acting family made their way to Kentucky via Boston and Albany, New York, making them "the first professional actors to play west of Pittsburgh" (15). Warren argues that this public recognition and mobility enjoyed by Julia Dean and her sister-in-law, Frances Denny Drake, endowed them "with independence that other southern women lacked" (15). Not all the actresses included in *Women on Southern Stages* are as obscure, especially to scholars of feminist theatre and gender studies. Adah Isaacs Menken, aka "The Menken," is most often mentioned by historians in reference to her scandalous performances of *Mazeppa* in New York, but, as Warren demonstrates, Menken began her career in New Orleans and toured with a stock company in Los Angeles and Texas before rising to fame in the northern states. The inclusion of Menken is also notable because, unlike most of the women in this study, Menken created a successful career by thwarting convention on and off the stage, playing risqué roles and flouting nineteenth-century traditions of marriage.

The following two chapters, "The Theaters" and "The Repertory," offer detailed descriptions, visual evidence, and summaries of the important theatre buildings and plays, respectively, connected to the women examined in the first chapter. Much of the South remained rural and focused on agriculture throughout the antebellum period, but permanent theatres and acting troupes entertained audiences in the urban centers that did develop as places of commerce. Beginning with the Douglass-Hallam company's Douglass Theatre in Williamsburg, Virginia, Warren explores how the spread of repertory companies throughout the Southern states and territories resulted in the construction of permanent playhouses such as the twelve-hundred-seat Charleston Theatre, in Charleston, South Carolina, built by Thomas Wade West and Thomas Bignall in 1793. This theatre, Warren notes, "reflected the growth of theater in the early republic" (38). The plays that one would expect to see included in a study of antebellum theatre are present—Anna Cora Mowatt's *Fashion*, Aiken's *Uncle Tom's Cabin*, and *Guy Mannering*, one of the plays included in Charlotte Cushman's repertoire—but Warren leaves no doubt that Southern actresses of the time performed in a wide variety of heroic melodramas, sensational melodramas, Shakespearean plays and adaptations, and even Confederate-themed dramas during the Civil War. In particular, playwrights during the war began to incorporate female characters who aided the Confederacy either by providing sustenance to the troops or by struggling to preserve their family and land while the men fought on the battlefield. One of the most useful aspects of this book is the appendix of popular plays from the colonial, antebellum, and Civil War periods that provides bibliographic citations, as well as plot summaries and production information, for more than seventy plays.

Warren delves into a deeper analysis of gender and race in the four subsequent chapters, tackling the tension between the roles women theatre artists in the South played in public, as stage stars and melodramatic heroines, and in private, as mothers, wives, and businesswomen. Frances Denny Drake and Julia Dean Hayne, for example, portrayed "conservative personas" (91) onstage while cultivating "autonomous performative roles in their personal lives" (91). They "terminated unhappy marriages though they risked public censure [for doing so], and they subsequently juggled the demands of career and single motherhood with great success" (91). Warren also asserts that actresses in the South, as working women, occupied a place of liminality in the strict social hierarchy of the region, receiving praise for their professional success while simultaneously being deemed inferior and morally suspect by wealthy elites; women theatre artists of the time "straddled masculinity and femininity" (120) by the very nature of their work in the public (male) sphere and by playing roles that "supported the notion of separate spheres and biologically entrenched attributes" (120). During the Civil War, actresses whose actor-husbands joined the army found themselves in the position of running an acting troupe, managing play selection, and, in the case of Eliza Crisp, petitioning city councils to keep the theatres open. One corrective to scorn from polite society that an actress of the period could seek, according to Warren, came by way of employing servants or owning a slave, which could potentially raise their status by separating them "from other working women," who couldn't afford such a luxury, and aligning "them with women from wealthy families" (102).

In the penultimate chapter, Warren examines several antebellum melodramas in productions of which Southern audiences would have seen actresses enacting race: "whiteness, blackness, ... redness, ... [and] yellowness" (151). The popularity of Boucicault's *The Octoroon*, with the tragic mulatto heroine, and Stone's *Metamora*, with the equally tragic Nahmeokee who dies at the hands of her "noble savage" husband, helped to confirm antebellum audiences' "notions of white superiority" (133). Establishing the significance of nineteenth-century melodrama's capacity to assure white Southern antebellum audiences (as well as Northern white audiences) of their moral and racial superiority is not a new practice; several theatre historians of the past quarter century have published abundantly on this topic. Warren, though, also claims that Southern actresses who portrayed "Others" onstage "aligned femininity with the exotic" (154). "More specifically," she says, "they associated the exotic with the erotic ... [and] blurred racial boundaries and exposed the social construction of race" (154), though there is no evidence in *Women on Southern Stages* that antebellum audiences' beliefs about racial hierarchy were at all altered by these performances. In fact, in the next and final chapter Warren discusses how plays performed during the Civil War aided the Confederate cause by supplying audiences with propagandistic stories of brave soldiers and virtuous women, and actresses used benefit performances to help provide monetary support for the war effort. These productions affirmed the culture of the antebellum South and sought to protect its gender, class, and racial norms.

One small weakness of *Women on Southern Stages* is Warren's tendency to merely list biographical information about these important theatrical women, the effect being that the book reads rather like an encyclopedia at times. Yet that information, much of which is drawn from archival materials, is not insignificant and will prove useful to any scholar or student of nineteenth-century theatre. Warren's well-defined explanations of the repertory and star systems and the Southern women who navigated and negotiated theatrical careers in those systems, in particular, will prove especially useful to undergraduate and graduate students who are new to the study of nineteenth-century theatre history.

—KARIN MARESH
Washington & Jefferson College

Antitheatricality and the Body Public. By Lisa A. Freeman. Philadelphia: University of Pennsylvania Press, 2017. 361 pp. £36.00/$55.00 cloth.

In *Antitheatricality and the Body Public*, Lisa A. Freeman situates her study beyond the borders of Jonas Barish's suppositions of antitheatrical mistrust, presenting an innovative and valuable argument that antitheatricality is not a response to the public harm of theatre but rather a means to challenge and question, claim, reclaim, and shape power and authority. Her book demonstrates an integrated and complex conversation with historical and theoretical scholars ranging from Barish to Phelan. Contextualizing antitheatrical events as complex cultural performances, Freeman carefully and painstakingly traces the multiple threads of political power that pervade the antitheatrical debates that span from the seventeenth to the twentieth century. According to Freeman, theatre has "ever been located at the center of … broad cultural movements and conflicts and … antitheatrical incidents … provide us with occasions to trace major struggles over historical shifts" with regards to power and authority. It is through her careful examination of evidence—both original documents and the narratives that arose from the historical incidents—that she illuminates the broader cultural movements at play in these five case studies (2).

The five case studies, at first glance, hold only cursory connections in terms of religious fervor against playing, immoral behavior represented and lauded in plays, and attending the theatre: William Prynne's *Histrio-mastix*, Jeremy Collier's *A Short View of the Immorality and Profaneness of the English Stage*, John Home's *Douglas*, the Richmond Theatre fire, and the *National Endowment for the Arts v. Finley*. However, through her careful and thorough dissection of the evidence of each case study, Freeman reveals a long history of those using antitheatrical sentiment along with theatrical form, genre, and performance techniques to create a body public who, in turn, could become a body politic. Each chapter and case study establishes the foundation and framework for the one that follows, building from William Prynne's not-so-subtle attack on monarchic rule in the 1630s to the Christian conservative attack and Supreme Court ruling on the NEA Four in the 1990s. These case studies create an antitheatrical history that brings the readers to the present-day United States in which a conservative Christian body public is still working to marginalize other bodies public in the name of "American" values. Each chapter is useful on its own, but the real argument of the book is the history Freeman constructs between all five cases studies. The reach of her work goes beyond the field of theatre into journalism and political science, resonating with current media mistrust and culture wars. Freeman demonstrates how a body politic can silence the marginalized bodies public to maintain religious, cultural, and racial privilege and superiority.

Freeman's book demonstrates the craft of a meticulous and rigorous scholar, who is exhaustive in her examination of the evidence, no matter how seemingly tangential, that intersects with her argument. Even her chapter notes not only present a thorough and sensitive critique of other scholars' work but also invite readers to further research, if they are so inclined. A reader could easily lose themselves in the archives of her case studies, but she deftly guides her readers through labyrinthine controversies, meticulously working through each facet and returning the reader to the larger landscape of the case studies and the overall book itself. The author provides a rich and open-ended history of each incident, and the book is intended for an audience beyond theatre scholars. A small, but important critique on verbiage: the far-reaching scope of her study is quite evident; however, some language is too discipline-specific or obscure and, as such, may exclude or turn away a general readership from engaging in her study. In particular, the introduction is quite weighed down with complicated terminology that may not be welcoming to a layperson.

Freeman's writing style oscillates between rigorous exploration of her argument within the evidence and her experience of encountering the evidence of pamphlets, court documents, transcriptions, and playbills, placing the reader in the archives along with the author. She sets this up from her first case study, creating comparisons of the records of Prynne's trial and inviting her readers into her research process and her discoveries of contradictions, inconsistencies, and new evidence. According to Freeman, she set aside previous interpretations or assumptions regarding each incident and instead "followed the lead of the archive" and uncovered new documents and tangential elements that weave a more complete understanding of the events of each case study with her goal being "to let the histories … speak as much as possible for themselves" (10). In an era of alt-facts and optics rather than proof, Freeman's book takes on an eerie significance with regards to the creation and mistrust of narrative, a sort of nontheatrical antitheatricalism.

The fifth and final chapter brings the four previous case studies into the twentieth-century political climate, where a conservative religious body public found the tools to become a body politic. This is the era in which the US religious right secured its roots in politics and shifted the conversation on freedom of expression. The final chapter/case study on the NEA Four is dense, in part due to the language of the US legal system, and barring the inclusion of a primer in US law, Freeman is quite skillful in navigating the legalese for her readers. If there were a negative critique of *Antitheatricality and the Body Public*, it might be that readers could find themselves craving a conclusion after the final case study to draw together the threads from the *Histrio-Mastix* through to Sandra Day O'Connor's ruling, providing an overview of the blueprints and overlays of the case studies. However, the path she carves through the intricate evidence and histories of these significant instances of antitheatricality allows the reader to glean the larger sociopolitical picture and to understand the usefulness of Freeman's incredibly prescient argument with regards to current political arguments about power and authority.

—SHAWNA MEFFERD KELTY
SUNY Plattsburgh

When Movies Were Theater: Architecture, Exhibition, and the Evolution of American Film. By William Paul. New York: Columbia University Press, 2016. 426 pp. $40 paper.

With his new book, *When Movies Were Theater: Architecture, Exhibition, and the Evolution of American Film*, William Paul has provided readers with a revelatory way to think and critique the early years of film exhibition in the United States. Focusing primarily on the first thirty years of film exhibition, and with special attention paid to New York City, Paul challenges many of the mythologies surrounding the early years of American movie exhibition. Paul's book is meticulously researched and is a rewarding and provocative exploration of a history many people think they already know. Much of Paul's analysis concerns the study of how the architecture of the "movie house" affected both the reception and the evolution of the exhibition of movies. That is, despite the "infinite reproducibility" of the motion picture, Paul argues, "how the image is situated in architectural space" (5) greatly affects spectatorship. I am old enough, although just barely, to remember when movie houses had just one screen, when the interiors of movie houses where awash with outrageous architectural details (such as a proscenium stage) and gloriously campy decor, and when the auditorium fell silent as the giant curtains swept open to reveal the movie screen and the start of something "magical." It is this connection between the site of exhibition and the reception of the "performance," or, as Paul suggests, an "[o]ngoing reciprocal relationship between movies and theaters, between text and context, that has shaped both our expectations and our actual experiences of what a movie is" (19), that occupies the core of this book.

When Movies Were Theater is more than just a revisionist history of early American film history; it is part architectural history, part popular culture history, and part theater history. Of particular interest to theater scholars is Paul's contention that, until the late 1920s, film exhibition and reception (and to an extent production) were inextricably connected to the aesthetics and reception of "legitimate theater."[1] Paul challenges the notion that film and legitimate theater were immediate rivals and references many instances in the first thirty years of the twentieth century when film borrowed heavily from legitimate theater in order to legitimize the "moving images." For example, in chapter 2, "Store Theaters: A Radical Break," Paul draws upon several sources, including theater impresario/moving picture exhibitor S. L. Rothapfel to detail the importance of presenting a varied and deliberate program of moving shorts. This successful type of exhibition programing copied aspects of vaudeville: "The vaudeville inheritance, then, was not left behind when movies moved from the vaudeville theater to a different home [the storefront theater]: rather, it is key to the development of motion pictures" (65). Earlier, Paul suggests that reception of motion pictures and the acceptance of late nineteenth-century staging practices (i.e., realism) both benefited from a new architecture that rejected the horseshoe auditorium and replaced it with an auditorium in which all the seats faced the "picture frame" stage. This new architectural arrangement provided a solution that solved "issues around realism for both live theater and motion pictures" (41). "Realism on stage and realism in motion pictures were oddly connected for contemporary viewers" (41), but the shared experience of the "new" theatrical architecture, be it the storefront theater for motion pictures or a state of the art live theater, allowed spectators to internalize the commonalities of space and reception rather than the differences of the artistic form. One last example of how motion picture exhibition drew heavily from legitimate theater practices to normalize the motion picture experience is found in chapter 5, "Uncanny Theater." In this chapter, Paul discusses the increasingly common practice of motion pictures being exhibited in legitimate theaters and the ensuing problem of space, insofar as "screens at the time ranged from twelve to twenty feet, [and] an 'ordinary stage opening' is … 'forty or fifty feet across'" (195). The solution was the evolution of the "'picture set' or 'picture setting' … the motion picture screen placed upstage within a theatrical set of some sort" (195). The setting could be related to a particular movie or it could be connected to the overall decor of the theater, but regardless, having a "set surrounding the picture would make the space of the image continuous with that of the stage: there would be a setting across the entire stage as in any live performance" (195). This solution, Paul suggests, also addressed some of the unease that spectators experienced when viewing motion pictures.

Similarly, Paul argues, there were many times when legitimate theater borrowed from the new art form and there were times when legitimate theater suffered economically because of the success of the motion picture industry. Yet he successfully argues that the two art forms were much more entwined and reliant upon each other than has often been considered in the past: "The cinema might have presented a new kind of dramatic art, but as a dramatic art it could never be an island unto itself. Much as theatrical movies in the twenty-first century exist in an expanded media universe that has helped to redefine them, in their early history movies were effectively expanding the *theatrical* universe" (18). Paul's interrogation of movies and theaters also challenges some of the other "histories" that have become inextricably linked to the mythologies of the moviegoing experience in the early twenty-first century. Two secondary themes run through the monograph: an ongoing critique of "the understanding of motion pictures as the art form that democratized drama" (108) and a reexamination of the triumph of movies over the legitimate stage. Paul is suspicious of the claim that movies and, in particular, movie theaters were any more democratic than legitimate theater. He argues, questions, and successfully challenges this naive understanding of a democratized art form: "The familiar notion that movies democratized viewing because they presented the same view to every member of the audience was itself a myth" (108). That is, during the first thirty years of film exhibition every movie theatre had sightline issues.

Regarding the other major theme, Paul also challenges the notion that motion pictures became the dominant art form in America in relatively short order and with very little resistance from audiences. His well-researched narrative demonstrates repeatedly that up until the mid 1920s many people in the entertainment business were still unsure of the longevity of moving pictures. During this time, Paul repeatedly shows that in any fair-sized American city a great variety of entertainments and exhibitions were happening simultaneously. He further argues that well into the early 1920s many movie theater owners did not trust that the movies being shown would be considered enough entertainment and so padded the evening with live performances. Such entertainments could include "atmospheric prologues, vaudeville numbers, and expensive orchestras" (221), and Paul details examples such as *Romoma* (1915), in which "live performance sequences would intermingle with film sequences" (214), and *Fall of Babylon* (1919), which was "interspersed with ensemble numbers, including Kyra and a ballet of living dancers" (215). Paul spends some time detailing the extreme case of *In Old Kentucky* (1920) when "the movie was stopped, the screen raised and disclosed a corner of a typical Kentucky race course. Stable boys were lolling about ... off in one corner a crap game is in progress. The atmosphere of a hot summer day is conveyed.... The gong rings. All is activity.... As the excited crowd leans over the paddock fence cheering the riders on, the screen descends, the orchestra crashes into a lively air and the picture continues" (218). It was suggested by movie exhibitioners of the time that this standard practice was necessary to give spectators a break: "There is a need for something more—something that will show actual people as a contrast to the shadowy figures that flit across the silver screen" (218). Even as late as 1920 and even in New York City and Chicago, there was a reluctance to declare film triumphant. Until the mid-1920s, a night at the movies was a padded event, and "the use of vaudeville acts, some of which had appeared at Koster and Bial's, in fact, would seem to inscribe motion pictures as an extension of vaudeville in contrast to the initial demonstration of the Lumiére films in Paris" (30).

When Movies Were Theater is organized around thematic chapters: "Making Movies Fit," "Palatial Architecture, Democratized Audience," and "Elite Taste in a Mass Medium" are some of the chapter titles. The decision to organize the book thematically, instead of chronologically, means that it does not closely follow a traditional historical narrative. This might present a concern for some, but by challenging the "meta-narrative" that many canonical film history *and* theater history textbooks fall into, Paul is able to provide close readings of precise or particular (and often peculiar) historical moments of film exhibition history without having to fit them into a larger overarching historical structure. As already mentioned, this is a thoroughly researched monograph, and Paul's thesis and arguments are extremely nuanced. If there is a small concern, it is that the extraordinary detail of each chapter occasionally overwhelms, but Paul's relatively informal tone and writing style overcomes this attention to necessary minutia.

With *When Movies Were Theater: Architecture, Exhibition, and the Evolution of American Film*, William Paul has challenged the reader to rethink not only the history of American movie exhibition and the places (and palaces) that exhibited them but also how current movie viewing, often untethered from grandiose public architecture, is still influenced by the past. Further, he challenges the reader to rethink the powerful relationship that, until the early 1930s, movies and theater shared: "Early film theory often focused on defining the essence of cinema, certain that whatever it might be, it was not theater. On the other hand, American practitioners in the early days of the narrative feature film were convinced that's exactly what they were doing and doing so within spaces that came out of live theater" (293). This book will be of special significance to scholars of both film and theater history; it would make an excellent text for any number of interdisciplinary courses across a variety of subjects, as well as being a fascinating read for anyone interested in pop culture, American history, American urbanity, or media studies.

Note

1. "Legitimate theater" is Paul's term and is used to describe live dramatic/musical theater productions, which he differentiates from vaudeville and burlesque performances. As well, the term "legitimate theater" is used to differentiate between theaters that were built to present live theater and theaters that were built to exhibit motion pictures.

—WES D. PEARCE
University of Regina

Ira Aldridge: The Last Years, 1855–1867. By Bernth Lindfors. Rochester Studies in African History and the Diaspora. Rochester, NY: University of Rochester Press, 2015. xiv + 352 pp. $55.00 cloth, $24.99 e-book.

Bernth Lindfors's *Ira Aldridge: The Last Years, 1855–1867* is a fitting conclusion to the author's four-volume, in-depth biography of the African American expatriate actor Ira Aldridge, who spent most of his career in the British Isles and in Europe. Kate Roark, in her review of the first three volumes, called Lindfors's books "a gloriously deep history" (*THS* 35 [2016], 363). That assessment is certainly accurate, and Lindfors deservedly won the Theatre Library Association's 2016 Freedley Special Jury Prize for the work, which is the culmination of decades of research spanning multiple continents and myriad languages (this volume alone required Lindfors to utilize thirty-eight translators working in eleven foreign languages).

The book is essentially an archive in miniature, with scores of letters, published reviews, and personal accounts reproduced fully. These materials take up roughly a quarter of Lindfors's text, providing a wealth of primary source material for future generations of researchers, as well as thorough documentation as to the archives where materials can be found. At times, the examples significantly outweigh Lindfors's own analysis: chapter 2 consists of five pages of reproduced documents about Aldridge's trial for seducing a married young woman plus two pages of Lindfors's own writing. Furthermore, the book is gorgeously illustrated, featuring reproductions of playbills, newspaper illustrations, caricatures, photographs, lithographs, and even Aldridge's certificate of marriage to his second wife.

Ira Aldridge is certainly deserving of such an in-depth study. As Lindfors notes in his introduction, Aldridge was loved by audiences, a "popular performer in a wide range of tragedies, melodramas, and racial farces" (1), and on his first continental tour, the subject of Lindfors's third volume in the biography, he had earned from critics and noble patrons "more honors, awards, decorations, and medals than any actor of his day had ever received" (3). Furthermore, Aldridge was immensely well-paid for his skill as a performer and the audience that his celebrity could draw; in 1857, he earned what would be roughly $381,000 in today's currency for "eight nights' work spread over four weeks" in Stockholm (64).

Aldridge's exceptional success with popular audiences and many critics were not, as Lindfors repeatedly demonstrates, "color-blind assessments," since critics often commented, on the one hand, on "the irrelevance of race or skin color when assessing the ability of an actor" or, on the other, "attributed Aldridge's success to his race" (93). Several reviews quoted in the book utilize, quite casually and occasionally even seemingly in praise of Aldridge, racial slurs that are deeply offensive today.

Despite its immense value and testament to Lindfors's skill as an archival researcher, the book has significant flaws. At times, it verges on hagiography: Lindfors clearly admires Aldridge for his "perseverance and talent" (1) and can pejoratively dismiss critics who disliked Aldridge's performances. Moreover, the narrative can be quite repetitive; since Aldridge's repertoire was relatively stable, many chapters consist primarily of what he was performing, where, and the critical response. This repetitiveness can perhaps best be illustrated by the titles of chapters 7 through 17: "A Short Break," "The Third Continental Tour," "Home Again," "The Fourth Continental Tour," "The Fifth Continental Tour," "The Sixth Continental Tour," "Taking a Break," "The Seventh Continental Tour," "Another Break," "The Eight Continental Tour," and "The Ninth Continental Tour."

Such flaws are outweighed by moments that can make a reader gasp at encountering in theatre history moments and documents that illuminate the life of such a noteworthy performer, moments that remain clearly relevant in today's world. Frequently, these revelations come directly from the primary sources Lindfors quotes. For example, Aldridge, sounding not unlike twentieth- and twenty-first-century civil rights activists, was himself keenly aware of the conscious battle against racism that his race and celebrity allowed him to pursue. In a letter dated May 29, 1855, quoted in full by Lindfors, Aldridge writes: "My great ambition has been to prove that my fellow countrymen are not deficient in intellectual ability but that circumstances and prejudice have been almost insurmountable obstacles. Oh that the time may hasten on when all distinctions may cease, when man may be estimated by his individual worth, and not by consideration of Caste or Colour" (7). Throughout his career, Aldridge refused to perform in *Uncle Tom's Cabin*, despite repeatedly being asked to do so—perhaps because Stowe's novel and Aiken's theatrical adaptation infantilize African Americans, which was precisely the opposite of Aldridge's project. (Lindfors notes that Aldridge did perform, for a time, in an adaptation of Stowe's *Dred: A Tale of the Great Dismal Swamp* but ceased to do so after having little success with the play.)

It is a pity that Lindfors allows his thorough admiration for Aldridge to prevent him from digging into some of the actor's flaws. Lindfors does acknowledge Aldridge's affairs with younger women, his exorbitant fees for performances, and his legal and artistic conflicts with contemporaries. But the author often goes to extremes to euphemistically gloss over or excuse such behavior, such as when he describes him as a "womanizer" (31) or writes that "there is no evidence that Aldridge's wife, Margaret, had accompanied him on this tour, so it is possible that he sought out friendly female companionship along the way" (138). Some of these affairs read today as rather predatory seductions of quite young women by a major star. Firing his company during his first European tour and driving hard bargains with theatre owners are portrayed as savvy business. But Aldridge's flaws are part of what make him such a fascinating subject: he proved his humanity not just through his expert performances and celebrity but through his philandering and enthusiastic participation in the rampant capitalism of the nineteenth-century theatre business. This made him very much a man of his era. As Lindfors notes in the final chapter, "we can only speculate" (269) on what would have happened had Aldridge not died suddenly while on tour in Poland. He was planning a tour to the United States, "testing whether black people in the northern states of America were now freer after the Civil War" (276). It is in such moments, when Lindfors struggles to answer questions created by the gaps in the archive, instead of just providing a meticulously researched narrative of history, that his book most shines. This also demonstrates how the biography will remain not just a fascinating and masterfully researched book for those interested in Aldridge's career but useful for future generations of scholars looking to use this history to engage with crucial questions of race and nineteenth-century culture.

—DAN VENNING
UNION COLLEGE

DAH Theatre: A Sourcebook. Edited by Dennis Barnett. Foreword by Eugenio Barba. Lanham, MD: Lexington, 2016. xvi + 231 pp. $90.00 cloth.

In his foreword to this collection of mostly new essays, Eugenio Barba, a significant mentor to the DAH, declares that the group "doesn't fight uncertainty, it manages it" (ix). Considering DAH is a Serbian word for the process of breathing, I was struck how encountering uncertainties in life and art does indeed shift our breath, with a quickening or deepening, a catching of itself, or a laboring forward; fighting this need for breath is futile. The DAH, a group founded and maintained by a core group of women theatre artists, grew up surrounded by the uncertainties brought on by continued civil war, leaving them with a keen sense of social responsibility in their art. While the DAH's artistic lineage links them to Grotowski and Lecoq as well, it is Barba's Odin Teatret in Denmark that left the most indelible mark, so his words are a fitting introduction to this important trove. As editor Dennis Barnett points out in his introduction, the recent twenty-five-year anniversary of the group marks an ideal time to scrutinize and celebrate their achievements and longevity, especially amid the backdrop of war. Readers are afforded the opportunity to witness "what began as a street theatre … turn into an internationally recognized organization dedicated to using their performances to change the world, one audience, one student at a time" (xi).

The Sourcebook contains fifteen essays, thirteen new and two revised, authored by an impressive and varied list of contributors from all over the world: an eminent Yugoslavian dramaturg and playwright, one of Serbia's most esteemed critics, professors from Brown, Knox, and the University of Edinburgh, artistic directors from the United States and Germany, and an internationally recognized poet, playwright, and musician, to name a few. Much on the content employs an investigation of a specific DAH performance as a jumping-off point (there currently are twenty-six performances in total, from 1992 to 2015). The collection is organized into three sections, first exploring DAH Theatre's work in Serbia, next their reach worldwide, and, finally, multiple accounts from artists who have worked closely with them. In his introduction, Barnett shares not only a brief synopsis of each essay but also its leaning, be it theoretical, historical, practical, or personal. He is correct to point out that a healthy dose of sociopolitical context and cognizance is necessary to discuss or analyze the work of the DAH. Founded in the former Yugoslavia in 1991 by directors Dijana

Milošević and Jadranka Anđelić, then existing with a home base in Belgrade, their evolution weathered the chaos, destruction, and stigma brought on by the Balkan Wars, while their art constantly addressed and challenged the atrocities around them.

The running order of the contributions is orchestrated with care and intent by Barnett. The first two essays, the first by an early artistic associate of the DAH and the next through the lens of the political scientist, offer the reader the necessary history and background to fully engage with the content to follow. Beloit College associate professor Amy Sarno investigates the DAH's three site-specific "Angel" plays, reflecting on how the unearthing of personal and community-based memory can offer societal, healing mechanisms. Speaking to the audience experience, she shares that "socializing was expected. . . . [A] dialogic process evolved that helped people make sense of the world while strengthening communal bonds" (41). In the sixth essay, choreographer and Colorado College professor Shawn Womack tackles one of the DAH's most popular site-specific performances, *In/Visible City*. This performance was staged in the very cramped quarters of commuter buses, literally in motion, and sought to "build a momentary community of traveling citizens, to honor the different ethnicities that shaped the modern city" (84). Later, US director/scholar Elizabeth Carlin Metz shares a fascinating account of the DAH's contribution to a student production of Sam Shepard's *A Lie of the Mind* at Knox College in Galesburg, Illinois. Her interest in neuroscience provides an intriguing context: she states that "with regard to acting, contemporary neurobiological research on feeling, affect, and physical states . . . has provided insight into how human beings experience and recall feeling and make decisions about action to be taken" (117). Her evaluation of how the DAH approach acting will be of interest to anyone who trains young actors.

The tone of the essays noticeably shifts in the third section, which comprises personal accounts, a welcomed variation in my opinion. Admittedly, my response to this content was colored by my own time with the DAH in the summer of 2007, when I spent three challenging, profound weeks as a participant in their workshop "Inside the Laboratory." The former grade school we worked in was one of the structures left rattled but unscathed by the NATO bombs that fell in 1999 (many of the structures damaged still stand, potent reminders of the conflict). While too brief, those weeks left an indelible mark on my work as a teacher, performer, and devisor. What I appreciated most about these concluding essays was how they introduced the reader more personally to the DAH artists. These personal accounts provide readers with a window into how the DAH creates work, how they train for the work they create, and how they think and feel about all of it. After chapters of hearing others tell me about the DAH, it was refreshing to hear from DAH artists in their own words.

Overall, editor Dennis Barnett has compiled a coherent and well-coordinated collection of essays and personal accounts exploring the work of the DAH. The variety of access points into the group's genesis, their catalog of work, and their place in a tumultuous history provides readers with numerous opportunities to engage. No doubt, there is ample space left for further investigation into this vibrant company of women. For scholars and practitioners alike interested in street theatre, political theatre, Eastern European performance traditions, ensemble-based devising, or one of the Odin's most prolific lineal descendants, it will prove a fascinating and inspiring read.

—C. DREW VIDAL
Ball State University

BOOKS RECEIVED

Barnette, Jane. *Adapturgy: The Dramaturg's Art and Theatrical Adaptation*. Carbondale: Southern Illinois University Press, 2018.

Brauneck, Manfred and ITI Germany, eds. *Independent Theatre in Contemporary Europe: Structures, Aesthetics, Cultural Policy*. Bielefeld: Transcript Verlag, 2017.

Buckner, Jocelyn. *A Critical Companion to Lynn Nottage*. New York: Routledge, 2016.

Burden, Micahel, Wendy Heller, Jonathan Hicks, and Ellen Lockhart, eds. *Staging History: 1780–1840*. Oxford: Bodleian Library, 2016.

Cahill, Alex. *The Formation, Existence, and Deconstruction of the Catholic Stage Guild of Ireland*. Newcastle upon Tyne: Cambridge Scholars, 2017.

Chambers, Colin, and Richard Nelson, eds. *Granville Barker on Theatre: Selected Essays*. London: Bloomsbury, 2017. Crespy, David A. *Lanford Wilson: Early Stories, Sketches, and Poems*. Columbia: University of Missouri Press, 2017.

Damodaran, Sumangala. *The Radical Impulse: Music in the Tradition of the Indian People's Theatre Association*. New Delhi: Tulika, 2017.

Day, Stuart A. *Outside Theatre: Alliances that Shape Mexico*. Tucson: University of Arizona Press, 2017.

Ducomb, Christian. *Haunted City: Three Centuries of Racial Impersonation in Philadelphia*. Ann Arbor: University of Michigan Press, 2017.

Dugas, Don-Jon. *Shakespeare for Everyman: Ben Greet in Early Twentieth-Century America*. London: Society for Theatre Research, 2016.

Ellinghausen, Laurie, ed. *Approaches to Teaching Shakespeare's Plays: English History Plays*. New York: Modern Language Association of America, 2017.

Enders, Jody, ed. *Holy Deadlock and Further Ribaldries: Another Dozen Medieval*

French Plays in Modern English. Philadelphia: University of Pennsylvania Press, 2017.

Farfan, Penny. *Performing Queer Modernism*. New York: Oxford University Press, 2017.

Finke, Michael C., and Michael Holquist, eds. *Approaches to Teaching the Works of Anton Chekhov*. New York: Modern Language Association, 2016.

Goodman, Jessica. *Goldoni in Paris: La Gloire et le Malentendu*. Oxford: Oxford University Press, 2017.

Grene, Nicholas. *The Theatre of Tom Murphy: Playwright Adventurer*. New York: Bloomsbury, 2017.

Hess, Jonathan M. *Deborah and Her Sisters: How One Nineteenth-Century Melodrama and a Host of Celebrated Actresses Put Judaism on the World Stage*. Philadelphia: University of Pennsylvania Press, 2018.

Jackson-Schebetta, Lisa. *Traveler, There Is No Road: Theatre, the Spanish Civil War, and the Decolonial Imagination in the Americas*. Iowa City: University of Iowa Press, 2017.

Johnson, Odai. *London in a Box: Englishness and Theatre in Revolutionary America*. Iowa City: University of Iowa, 2017.

Jouve, Emeline. *Susan Glaspell's Poetics and Politics of Rebellion*. Iowa City: University of Iowa Press, 2017.

Kenrick, John. *Musical Theatre: A History*. London: Bloomsbury, 2017.

McAvinchey, Caoimbe, Lucy Richardson, and Fabio Santos, eds. *Phakma: Making Participatory Performance*. New York: Bloomsbury, 2018.

Montez, Noe. *Memory, Transitional Justice, and Theatre in Postdictatorship Argentina*. Carbondale: Southern Illinois University Press, 2018.

Morrison, Mathew. *The Soho Theatre, 1968–1981*. London: Society for Theatre Research, 2017.

Nathans, Heather S. *Hideous Characters & Beautiful Pagans: Performing Jewish Identity on the Antebellum American Stage*. Ann Arbor: University of Michigan Press, 2017.

Palmer, David, ed. *Visions of Tragedy in Modern American Drama*. New York: Bloomsbury, 2018.

Pangallo, Matteo A. *Playwriting Playgoers in Shakespeare's Theater*. Philadelphia: University of Pennsylvania Press, 2017.

Rodger, Gillian M. *Just One of the Boys: Female-to-Male Cross-Dressing on the American Variety Stage*. Urbana: University of Illinois Press, 2018.

Rodosthenous, George, ed. *The Disney Musical on Stage and Screen: Critical Approaches from Snow White to Frozen*. London: Bloomsbury, 2017.

Shannon, Sandra G., and Sandra L. Richards, eds. *Approaches to Teaching the*

Plays of August Wilson. New York: Modern Language Association of America, 2016.

Symonds, Dominic. *Broadway Rhythm: Imagining the City in Song*. Ann Arbor: University of Michigan Press, 2017.

Syssoyeva, Kathryn Mederos, and Scott Proudit, eds. *Women, Collective Creation, and Devised Performance*. New York: Palgrave, 2016.

Welch, Ellen R. *A Theatre of Diplomacy: International Relations and the Performing Arts in Early Modern France*. Philadelphia: University of Pennsylvania Press, 2017.

Wood, Michael. *Heiner Müller's Democratic Theater: The Politics of Making the Audience Work*. Rochester: Camden House, 2017.

Wright, Adrian. *Must Close Saturday: The Decline and Fall of the British Musical Flop*. Rochester, NY: Boydell, 2017.

CONTRIBUTORS

VIVIAN APPLER is an assistant professor of theatre at the College of Charleston. She is a 2010 Fulbright Fellow and a 2015 Huntington Library Dibner Research Fellow in the history of science. Her research interests include intersections of performance and science, feminist theatre and pedagogy, and physical theatre. Her scholarship has been published in *Comparative Drama*, *Journal of American Drama and Theatre*, and *The Routledge Companion to Jacques Lecoq*. She holds a PhD from the University of Pittsburgh, an MA from Queen Mary, University of London, and a certificate from the Dell'Arte International School of Physical Theatre.

STEFAN AQUILINA is the director of research of the School of Performing Arts and a theatre studies lecturer at the University of Malta. His main area of research is Russian and early Soviet theatre, particularly Stanislavsky, Meyerhold, and amateur theatre. His first book, coedited with Jonathan Pitches, is *Stanislavsky in the World: The System and Its Transformations across Continents.*

PETER A. CAMPBELL has published essays in *Contemporary Theatre Review*, *Journal of Dramatic Theory and Criticism*, *Modern Drama*, and *Theatre Topics*, among others. He is the founding editor of the journal *Theatre/Practice*. Professional productions include directing his pieces *medea & medea/for medea*, *iph.then*, and *Yellow Electras*. He is an associate professor of Theater History and Criticism at Ramapo College of New Jersey.

BRIAN E. G. COOK is an assistant professor of theatre at the University of Alaska Anchorage, where he teaches directing, theatre history, and dramaturgy and also directs productions. He is the chair of the Earth Matters on Stage New Play Festival and Symposium 2018. He has presented at conferences in the United States, the United Kingdom, and Canada and published articles and book reviews in *Theatre History Studies*, *Theatre Survey*, *Performing Arts Resources* and the *LMDA Sourcebook*. He has served as a contributing editor to *Theatre History Studies*, and in 2017, he was elected to serve as the new treasurer of the Mid-America Theatre Conference.

PATRICIA GABORIK, a fellow of the American Academy and an instructor at the American University of Rome, specializes in late nineteenth and early twentieth-century Italian theatre, with a focus on the fascist period. Her articles have appeared in several book collections and journals such as *Modern Drama* and *Teatro e Storia*, and she is the editor and translator of *Watching the Moon and Other Plays* by Massimo Bontempelli. She is editing the forthcoming *Pirandello in Context*.

KRISTI GOOD teaches script analysis and dramaturgy at Carnegie Mellon University's School of Drama. She earned her MA in dramaturgy from Villanova University and her PhD from the University of Pittsburgh. She has previously been published in *Theatre History Studies* and *Etudes*, and her research interests include the work of Irish writer Sebastian Barry, intersections of performance and cognitive science, and global theatre of trauma and human rights. She is a freelance dramaturg and has served as a cochair for the Mid-America Theatre Conference Playwriting Symposium.

JULIET GUZZETTA is an assistant professor of English and Romance and Classical Studies at Michigan State University, where she teaches courses on theatre, performance studies, and film, in addition to Italian language and culture. Her current book project, provisionally titled *The Theater of Narration: Performing Community-Based History in Italy*, explores a form of contemporary solo theatre in its historical, political, and performative dimensions. She has published on this practice in connection to modernism, feminist workerism, and the public sphere in several peer-reviewed journals and edited collections. Her research has been supported by a year-long Fulbright to Italy and Harvard's Mellon School for Theater and Performance Research.

SHULAMITH LEV-ALADGEM is an associate professor of theatre studies and the chair of the Theatre Arts Department at Tel Aviv University. She is a community-based theatre practitioner and researcher as well as a trained actress who uses her acting experience in both her research and her teaching. Her research has been published in numerous leading periodicals in the United States, Europe, and Israel. She has written two books: *Theatre in Co-Communities: Articulating Power* and *Standing Front Stage: Resistance, Celebration and Subversion in Community-Based Theatre.*

MEGAN LEWIS, an associate professor at the University of Massachusetts Amherst, is the author of *Performing Whitely in the Postcolony: Afrikaners in South African Theatrical and Public Life* and the coauthor of *Magnet Theatre: Three Decades of Making Space* (with Anton Krueger).

ASHLEY E. LUCAS is an associate professor of theatre and drama in the Residential College at the University of Michigan, where she also serves as director of the Prison Creative Arts Project. She is the coeditor of a volume *Razor Wire Women: Prisoners, Activists, Scholars, and Artists* and writes a blog with the same name: http://razorwirewomen.wordpress.com. Lucas is working on the book manuscript for the *Methuen Critical Companion on Prison Theatre.* She is also the author of an ethnographic play about the families of prisoners titled *Doin' Time: Through the Visiting Glass*, which she has performed as a one-woman show throughout the United States and in Ireland, Brazil, and Canada.

NOE MONTEZ is an associate professor and the director of graduate studies in drama and dance at Tufts University. He is the author of *Memory, Transitional Justice, and Theatre in Postdictatorship Argentina.* His essays have been published in *Theatre Topics, Latin American Theatre Review, Texas Theatre Journal, New England Theatre Journal*, the *Journal of Religion and Theatre, American Theatre Howlround*, and the edited collection *Public Theatres and Theatre Publics.*

LURANA DONNELS O'MALLEY is a professor of theatre at the University of Hawai'i at Mānoa, where she is both director of theatre and director of graduate studies in theatre. Her years of research on Russian theatre culminated in her book *The Dramatic Works of Catherine the Great: Theatre and Politics in Eighteenth-Century Russia.* Her research on early twentieth-century African American pageantry has been published in *Comparative Drama, Text & Presentation*, and *MELUS.* O'Malley is also a director and a dancer.

ANTHONY SORGE is a teacher, writer, and cartoonist based in New Haven, Connecticut. His work has appeared in anthologies published by the Dark Mountain Project and Ashland Creek Press, and he has been self-publishing small batches of zines and mini-comics since he was a teenager.

ILINCA TODORUȚ is a doctoral candidate at the Yale School of Drama. She is a contributor to *The Routledge Companion to Dramaturgy*, and her articles have appeared in publications such as *European Stages*, *Theater*, *Journal of Poverty*, *Scena.ro*, and *Images: Journal of Visual and Cultural Studies*.

CHRISTINE WOODWORTH is an associate professor of theatre at Hobart and William Smith Colleges. She is the coeditor of *Working in the Wings: New Perspectives on Theatre History and Labor*. Her scholarship has appeared in *Theatre Symposium*, *Theatre History Studies*, *Theatre Annual*, and *Text and Presentation* and in several edited collections. Woodworth is a member of SDC and the Lincoln Center Directors Lab and is a past participant in the SITI Summer Theater Workshop and the Mellon School of Theater and Performance Research at Harvard University. More information on her work can be found at www.thisworldofyes.com.